HISTORY OF THE FRENCH REVOLUTION

CLASSIC EUROPEAN HISTORIANS

A SERIES EDITED BY LEONARD KRIEGER

Jules Michelet

HISTORY OF THE FRENCH REVOLUTION

Translated by Charles Cocks

Edited and with an Introduction
by Gordon Wright

THE UNIVERSITY OF CHICAGO PRESS
CHICAGO & LONDON

THE UNIVERSITY OF CHICAGO PRESS
CHICAGO 60637
The University of Chicago Press, Ltd., London

© *1967 by The University of Chicago*
All rights reserved
Published 1967

First Phoenix Edition 1967

95 94 93 92 91 90 89   8 7 6

Printed in the United States of America

International Standard Book Number: 0–226–52332–2 (clothbound)

Library of Congress Catalog Card Number: 67–15315

Series Editor's Preface

THE aim of the University of Chicago Press's series, "The Classic European Historians," is the reproduction, in a form easy to purchase and to use, of works that have been milestones in the cumulative knowledge of the European past and in the development of our historical consciousness. Since the historical writing of a less scientific age usually belonged—and still belongs—to literature in its belletristic sense, it is hoped that the series will contribute to both of the fundamental functions ever served by history—to entertainment and to the provision of materials for the disciplined study of humanity. The criteria of the textual reprints and the purpose of the essays that introduce them therefore are directed primarily toward restoring the readability of historical classics.

The rules that guide the reproduction of each text are products of reverence for the original qualified by considerations of utility. Each reprint comprises a single substantial volume that cleaves to the original text and notes of the classic with a minimum of editorial intrusion. For histories written in a foreign language—generally the case for this series—English translations are provided, or, as for this volume, older translations are used if they have been adjudged generally satisfactory, with revisions by the volume editor where they have been adjudged particularly unsatisfactory. For extended histories—again a rule applicable to the present instance—selection is made of a continuous volume-length section, as representative of the work and as crucial for its subject as the editor may find, on the assumption that the integrity of the literary creation in each of its parts is more revealing of the whole than are the insulated samples of its scope.

The introductions, written by volume editors who are authorities in the special historical field of the work and adepts in general historiography, are designed to locate the classic along both of these axes and thereby to orient the modern reader in the setting of both the history and the historian. The editors follow two main lines in the attainment of this purpose. First, they analyze the distinctive contribution made by the work to the historical knowledge of its subject and estimate its current value in relation to subsequent studies and their claims to have superseded it. Secondly, each essay approaches the historian as himself a historical subject, drawing an intellectual portrait to show the circumstances and assumptions that conditioned his classic and to assess the particular contribution of man and work to the historical sensibilities of our culture.

Not surprisingly, considering the range of goals for the series, each classic satisfies these purposes in a different ratio. Jules Michelet's *History of the French Revolution,* partially reprinted in this volume, ranks especially high among the lasting monuments of historical writing for its entertainment value as history and its representative function as historiography. The two qualities, moreover, are connected, for the early- and mid-nineteenth-century school of history that spanned the North American and European continents and found in Michelet a prime exemplar retained the hallowed humanistic view of history as a branch of literature and of literary excellence as an essential ingredient of written history. Others of its characteristic traits Michelet reflected too—indeed, so intensely and so vividly as to become something close to what would later be called the "ideal type" of the school. Like such well-known contemporaries as Bancroft, Prescott, Parkman, Motley, Macaulay, and Guizot, but unconfined, larger than life, Michelet deemed freedom to be the thread of history, the nation to be its vehicle, events its moments, the people its life-force, and individuals their agents. Michelet may thus stand for that whole generation of historians between the Age of the Enlightenment and the scientific era who have been variously labeled "liberal," "nationalistic," "romantic," and "amateur."

But such labels, when applied to a group of historians or indeed to any group of writers, initiate rather than conclude the process of understanding. They raise problems that can be solved not in terms of the abstract relations among general tendencies but only in terms of the actual connections between specific traits in the work of the individual historian. Thus, in his illuminating sketch of Michelet and his work, Professor Gordon Wright reveals not only that re-creative historian's personal contribution to the understanding of the French Revolution but also the living conjunction in him of the qualities he shared with his contemporary historians. We learn from Professor Wright how those qualities, which in the large seem puzzling and ill-assorted to us, in the concrete did form compatible components of a comprehensible historical mentality. We learn how partisanship for the nation in history was part of a larger faith in the liberal destiny of humanity; how the passionate espousal of social and political values could fertilize the authentic reconstruction of the past; how the romantic impulse toward individuality in history extended rather than rejected the Enlightenment's historiographical achievement of secular universality; how the aesthetic impulse toward the communicable evocation of the historical drama bore with grace the weight of laborious archival research; how all the features that we tend, from American examples, to associate with amateur or popular—that is, non-professorial—history were ingrained in a French history professor and had in fact more to do with his approach than with his profession.

With Professor Wright as our guide, we become aware of a certain familiarity when we read Michelet—of a kinship beyond the mere acknowledgment of a past stage of historical consciousness that we can remember and have overcome. Behind the archaic sentimentality and floridity we recognize something of ourselves. In Michelet's combination of life, art, and scholarship historians today see a reflection not so much of their own achievements as of their own ambitions. When we revive Michelet we salute not what we are but what we should like again to become.

LEONARD KRIEGER

Editor's Introduction

Tastes in the writing of history, like those in the arts, political oratory, or women's dress, change with the times. Jules Michelet was viewed by many nineteenth-century Frenchmen as one of the greatest masters of his craft: an artist who sent life pulsing through his nation's history, who revived in his countrymen a vivid memory of their common past, who defined his goal as neither analysis nor synthesis but as "integral resurrection." In our day, when most historical writing has come to be soberly analytical and earthbound, Michelet's purple rhetoric, his flights of lyricism and his passionate prejudices seem shockingly out of style. The newer historians of France rarely cite him, save perhaps to list his works in their bibliographies. Who, in our prosaic age, would want to read Michelet? Yet the publishers' lists over the past few decades show a steady flow of books about Michelet's historical art; reports from Paris tell us that a definitive edition of Michelet's complete works is under way; and an advanced class in historiography at the Sorbonne, asked to name the greatest historian France ever produced, accords that supreme accolade to Michelet. We are even told that the most eminent of living Frenchmen, Charles de Gaulle, has found his own philosophy of history in Michelet's famous aphorism, "England is an empire, Germany a race, a country; France is a person."

Michelet belonged squarely in the romantic age and embodied many of the most representative traits of its protean spirit. The span of his life (1798–1874) closely coincided with that of Victor Hugo, whose impassioned prose and verse bore much resemblance to Michelet's historical poetry. Yet Michelet always looked to the eighteenth century for his inspiration; his intellectual heroes were Voltaire, Rousseau, and Giambattista Vico, that curiously anachronistic Neapolitan scholar whom Michelet always claimed as his real master. "Je suis né de Virgile et Vico," Michelet used to say. Vico sought what he called "a new science" that would be total in nature, uniting all of the human sciences in an organic whole. Michelet's *résurrection intégrale* sought the same goal. Vico stressed the use of legends as valid expressions of a historical tradition, conveying the collective wisdom of one's ancestors. Michelet, in his work on the Great Revolution, insisted on the use of "oral tradition," which he defined as "that which everybody says and repeats . . . , that which can be learned by an evening visit to any village tavern." Vico insisted that men make their own social world, create their own history; Michelet described man as "his own Prometheus." Vico played down the role of great men, and found the motive force of history in society as a whole. Michelet declared that the Revolutionary leaders "are usually but wrongfully considered as the sole actors. The fact is that they rather received than communicated the impulse. The chief actor is the people." Vico rejected the rigorous rationalism of Descartes, and emphasized the intuitive path to understanding. Michelet, in his inaugural lecture at the Sorbonne in 1834, warned his students against those cold analytical techniques that destroy rather than reveal life.

Michelet's heritage from Vico has been often stressed; the differences between them have been more neglected. Vico, after all, stood astride the Middle Ages and the modern era, whereas Michelet combined the Enlightenment and the nineteenth century. Vico's fervent Catholicism, his belief that men were safely cradled in the divine hand of Providence, could find no echo in Michelet. Nor did Vico's overarching concept of *corsi e ricorsi*—of a cyclical or spiral process by which history allegedly proceeded—attract Michelet's favor. Far closer to Michelet's temper was the eighteenth century's concept of history as linear progression: jerky, irregular, but in the end always bearing upward toward greater freedom and justice. If Michelet was Vico's disciple, his borrowing from the master was highly selective; he took only those ideas that reinforced his own intellectual and temperamental preferences. Perhaps Michelet's "je suis né de Vico" ought to be counterbalanced by another bit of self-analysis from his diary (1841): "Nobody has influenced me since my birth. I was born essentially solitary."

Until the age of thirty, Michelet remained somewhat uncertain as to choice of a career. Although he began as a secondary school teacher of history, he was more strongly inclined toward philosophy and the classics. The chair which he held at the Ecole Normale Supérieure during the late 1820's combined philosophy and history, but in 1829 his superiors divided the chair in two and insisted that Michelet take the historical half. His compliance was grudging rather than enthusiastic; historical writing in its currently orthodox form struck him as pedantic and narrow. Still, with the help of Vico he might yet free himself from the bonds of orthodoxy and soar off on his own imaginative wings.

Inspiration struck him suddenly during the glorious days of the 1830 revolution, and turned him to his life's work—the history of his native land. Forty years later, in a new preface to his seventeen-volume chef d'oeuvre, he was to recall that "lightning flash of July," when "a great light dawned, and I became aware of France." His glowing patriotism, his intense sense of Frenchness merged with and absorbed his passion for the brotherhood of all mankind. Modern France, he believed, was the brilliant culmination of universal history. As he recalled in later retrospect, "I arrived both through logic and through history at the same conclusion: that my glorious motherland is henceforth the pilot of the vessel of humanity." The first volume of the *History of France* came off the press in 1833, the seventeenth not until 1867. The literary brilliance of the work—especially such portions as the famous province-by-province portrait of the country and the chapters on Joan of Arc—dazzled his readers, and securely established Michelet as the quasi-official national historian. At the age of thirty-six he became Guizot's successor at the Sorbonne; four years later, he attained a chair at the most prestigious of French institutions, the Collège de France.

But already he was wearying of the seemingly endless task of resurrecting the whole long history of his country. As he plodded painfully through the Middle Ages, his attention was constantly drawn toward the culmination of this whole process, the high point of man's history—the Great Revolution. In 1841 he began to collect materials on the Revolution; in 1845 he gave his first course of lectures on the subject at the Collège de France; in 1846 he interrupted the *History of France* (which had reached Louis XI) and plunged ahead three centuries into his *History of the French Revolution*. It would, he thought, leap uninterrupted from his pen, "like a long cry of love and hate." The first two volumes did follow that jetlike course, and were published within a year; the remaining five, however, came more slowly, and the whole work was not completed until 1853. Problems both personal and political intervened: Michelet's second marriage, the unsettling upheaval of 1848, his dismissal from the Collège de France after Louis Napoleon's coup d'état, his self-exile to the provinces.

That the Revolution should have fascinated Michelet is scarcely surprising. His earliest memories and his formative years were suffused with recollections of the great upheaval. His birthplace, in the heart of old Paris, was a former church which had been secularized during the Revolution. His father, a printer and a fervent republican, was ruined by Napoleon's rigorous press censorship and even jailed for debt for a time, so that the boy grew up in poverty. The elder Michelet, along with other family acquaintances, provided young Jules with a rich storehouse of eyewitness tales. As a young man, nevertheless, Jules seemed indifferent to his father's fiercely anticlerical republican views. He chose to be baptized at age eighteen, and accepted posts as official tutor to princesses of first the Bourbon and then the Orleans house. As he neared middle age, however, his outlook underwent a drastic change.

By the time he embarked on his *History of the French Revolution,* his antagonism toward both the Church and the old monarchy matched that of his father. The Revolution, he believed, was destined to provide Frenchmen with a new and purer religion—a faith in justice and humanity, long since betrayed by decadent Catholicism.

Before Michelet's time, the Revolution had been a subject for polemics rather than for serious historical research. Only Mignet and Thiers had sought to examine the period in accordance with the canons of the historian's craft. Michelet was thus venturing into almost virgin territory. His predecessors, he declared, had all written "monarchical" histories that idealized either the autocrat Louis XVI or the autocrat Robespierre. "Mine," he asserted, "is the first republican history, the kind that has destroyed both idols and gods. From the first page to the last, it has had but one hero: the people." This intense populism, this almost childlike faith in the virtues and the perceptiveness of the common man, was revealed in his emphasis on what he called "national tradition" (that is, the ordinary Frenchman's view of the Revolution) as his most important source and inspiration. "Take careful note of the people's judgments," he wrote; "sometimes, on specific details, they are wrong, more often they don't know the facts. But about men they are not mistaken, they are rarely deceived." His populism was repeatedly reflected, too, in his treatment of the Revolutionary events themselves. During each of the great episodes when the crowd goes into action—the fall of the Bastille, the march of the women on Versailles, the Festival of the Federations in July, 1790—one gets a sense of direct participation, as though the historian had been there in the front ranks, fraternizing with the virtuous *peuple.* "Unforgettable days!" wrote Michelet in his preface to the 1868 edition. "Who am I to have recounted them? I still don't understand, I shall never understand how I was able to recapture them. The incredible joy of rediscovering them so alive, so ardent, after sixty years, swelled my heart with heroic joy, and my manuscript seemed intoxicated by my tears."

Although Michelet saw the great leaders of the time as mere agents of, and spokesmen for, the masses, he found himself attracted to many of them. In retrospect he recalled, "None of these great actors of the Revolution left me cold." His particular favorites were Sieyès and Danton; his most intense dislike was aimed at Robespierre. He prided himself, however, on seeing men not as didactic caricatures but as highly human mixtures of faults and virtues, whose conduct and even whose personalities changed as the Revolution moved on. In suggesting the development of character through a series of successive scenes, there is a kind of Shakespearian quality in Michelet's historical drama.

Michelet's history of the Revolution, rather surprisingly, was not an immediate critical or commercial success. It appeared almost simultaneously with Lamartine's immensely popular *History of the Girondins* and was closely followed by Louis Blanc's massive twelve-volume account of the Revolution, in which Blanc took perverse pleasure in listing all of the errors he claimed to find in Michelet's work. Students and left-wing republicans during the Second Empire were the first disciples; but it was not until the Third Republic that it won a wide circle of readers, thanks in part to the appearance of popular editions. The founders of the Third Republic, it has been said, cut their teeth on Michelet; his fervent patriotism, his passionate anticlericalism, his lyric flights fitted the temper of the radical republicans of the day. A few political leaders (Jules Simon, for example) had once been Michelet's students; more of them knew him through his glowing pages. Georges Clemenceau's father, a country doctor, inoculated his son with the pure essence of Michelet; Jean Jaurès, when he in turn undertook a Socialist history of the Revolution, chose as his inspirers Marx and Michelet.

The arrival of Marxian Socialism, however, dimmed Michelet's appeal to the left. Marxians found in Michelet's populism a petty-bourgeois affection for the small independent artisan or shopkeeper, a deep suspicion of state action for social reform. Indeed, Michelet's lack of interest in the economic aspects of the Revolutionary period and in social analysis of any precise kind, though quite understandable in a man of his time, undoubtedly flaws the permanent value of his work. Michelet's most direct heirs were certainly the bourgeois Radical Socialists of the Third Republic. Still, a Marxophile like Jean-Paul Sartre could continue to describe Michelet in 1947 as an "authentic genius" and a "prosateur de grande classe," and could charge the twentieth-century bourgeoisie with "leaving Michelet to vegetate in purgatory" because he had committed a cardinal sin—he had loved the people.

A second reason for Michelet's decline in stature toward the end of the nineteenth century was the dominant mode of positivism and scientism in historical writing. It fed a growing sentiment that Michelet was only a *vulgarisateur*, concerned to fascinate the lay reader with colorful anecdotes and literary fireworks. Even in Michelet's lifetime, some critics had complained of his unwillingness to cite his sources and had implied that the historian was drawing heavily on his fertile imagination. The charge irritated Michelet, who contended that any intelligent reader ought to be capable of recognizing his sources, and that batteries of footnotes would destroy the unity of his art. Viewers of modern television, who sit through great films interspersed with frequent commercials, may find Michelet's argument sympathetic. Michelet insisted, with considerable justice, that his work was "born from the womb of the archives." From 1831 to 1852 he held a high post in the National Archives, and spent several hours daily there; he could browse at will through that rich depository, and later he dipped extensively into the municipal records at the Hôtel de Ville as well. More than any predecessor, he wrote the history of the Great Revolution from its official records, supplemented by memoirs and eyewitness accounts. Still, it is undoubtedly true that he used his sources as though he were a lawyer pleading a case, seeking evidence to buttress his own deep predilections. Michelet could never be the impartial judge, weighing the evidence and letting it guide his decision. He was an *historien engagé*, the impassioned evangelizer of a new gospel.

The modern student of the French Revolution, or of the phenomenon of revolution in general, would not do well to begin with Michelet.[1] Several generations of scholarship since his time have broadened our understanding of that formidable episode, have given us a more sophisticated grasp of the social and psychological forces at work in that microcosm of humanity that was Paris in the late eighteenth century. Yet there is something here that can rarely be found in historical writing: a sense of the color and passion of a great social upheaval, conveyed to the reader as though he were one of the eyewitnesses along the sidewalks opposite the Hôtel de Ville or at the entrance to the palace courtyard at Versailles. Perhaps it is as well that European historiography has not produced many Michelets; we can nevertheless rejoice that one such

---

[1] The vast outpouring of Revolutionary scholarship and quasi-scholarship that has filled the century since Michelet cannot be readily distilled into a footnote. A few representative works may, however, be worth mentioning. On the heels of Michelet's final volume came Alexis de Tocqueville's *L'Ancien régime et la révolution* (Paris, 1856; trans. S. Gilbert, New York, 1955), which has proved to be a far more durable analysis of the forces at work in prerevolutionary France. Alphonse Aulard's *Histoire politique de la Révolution française* (Paris, 1901; trans. B. Miall, 4 vols., New York, 1910) eventually displaced Michelet as the bible of the Third Republic's bourgeois elite, more attracted now to prose than to poetry. Aulard's student Albert Mathiez, in his *La Révolution française* (3 vols.; Paris, 1922–27; trans. C. A. Phillips, New York, 1929), shifted the bias farther to the left, to a point just short of a Marxian stance. Then both were pushed into the discard by their successor at the Sorbonne, Georges Lefebvre, whose exhaustive monographic studies of rural France, colored by a quasi-Marxian bias, introduced a more precise kind of analysis of social groups and forces, solidly based on archival studies. Lefebvre's brief essay *Quatre-vingt-neuf* (Paris, 1939; trans. R. R. Palmer as *The Coming of the French Revolution* [Princeton, 1947]), and his general synthesis *La Révolution française* (2d ed.; Paris, 1957; trans. E. M. Evanson, 2 vols., New York, 1962–64) have come to represent the new orthodoxy of our generation—an orthodoxy that for the first time since 1789 represents near-consensus among students of the Revolution in France. Lefebvre's French and British disciples have continued to push along the path he marked out, notably in such works as Albert Soboul's *Les sans-culottes parisiens* (Paris, 1958; abridged trans. G. Lewis, Oxford, 1964); George F. Rudé's *The Crowd in the French Revolution* (Oxford, 1959); and Richard Cobb's *Les armées révolutionnaires* (2 vols., Paris, 1961–63).

Any orthodoxy, however, eventually inspires its own critics. The most

phenomenon exists. And in reading his *History of the French Revolution,* we may share the judgment of the historian Gérard Walter: "Prodigious, paradoxical book which . . . still remains a captivating enigma, an irritating miracle."

This edition of Michelet's most representative work is, I believe, the first to appear in English since 1902. It contains the introduction and the first three of the twenty-one "books" into which the original work was divided. This portion carries the story from the convocation of the Estates-General in 1789 to the Festival of the Federations on July 14, 1790. This latter episode, Michelet believed, was the zenith of French history, an apotheosis of brotherhood and unity toward which the nation had been aspiring for centuries. It provides, therefore, a

---

vigorous and persuasive voice has been that of Alfred Cobban, whose *The Social Interpretation of the French Revolution* (Cambridge, 1964) challenges some of the most basic tenets of the Lefebvrians. And Elizabeth L. Eisenstein, in a perceptive essay entitled "Who intervened in 1788? A Commentary on *The Coming of the French Revolution*" (*American Historical Review,* LXXI [1965]: 77–103), has suggested additional reasons for reexamining the new orthodoxy.

Recent scholarship, too, provides correctives for some of Michelet's more flagrant prejudices. His tendency to isolate events in France from those in the rest of Europe may be counterbalanced by such studies as R. R. Palmer's *The Age of the Democratic Revolution* (2 vols.; Princeton, 1959–64) and Jacques Godechot's *Les révolutions (1770–1779)* (Paris, 1963; trans. H. H. Rowen as *France and the Atlantic Revolution in the Eighteenth Century* [New York, 1965]). His rabid anticlericalism requires a look at André Latreille's *L'Eglise catholique et la Révolution française* (2 vols.; Paris, 1946–50). And his somewhat distorted Parisian view of provincial France ought to be set alongside such careful monographs as Henri Fréville's *L'Intendance de Bretagne 1689–1790* (3 vols.; Rennes, 1953); Robert Forster's *The Nobility of Toulouse in the Eighteenth Century* (Baltimore, 1960); and Charles Tilly's *The Vendée* (Cambridge, Mass., 1964).

Finally, it may be useful to compare Michelet's synthesis of the Revolutionary years with some of the best general accounts published in our own time: Crane Brinton's *A Decade of Revolution 1789–1799* (New York, 1934); J. M. Thompson's *The French Revolution* (New York, 1945); A. Goodwin's *The French Revolution 1789–1794* (London, 1956); Alfred Cobban's *A History of Modern France* (vol. I, London, 1957); and Norman Hampson's *A Social History of the French Revolution* (Toronto, 1963).

fitting culmination to his account of the Revolution's heroic period of constructive reform.

The translation was made in 1847 by Charles Cocks, professor of English in the *Collège Royale* in Paris. Cocks translated a great many of Michelet's books, and won additional distinction by publishing a widely read work on the wines of Bordeaux. His version retains some of the flavor of the mid-nineteenth century, and may therefore render Michelet's prose more faithfully than would a modern translation. I have corrected a number of errors, however, and have altered an even more considerable number of obscure or ambiguous passages, as well as a few anglicisms potentially misleading to American readers.

Stanford, California

GORDON WRIGHT

Contents

Contents

HISTORY OF THE FRENCH REVOLUTION

Preface

Every year, when I descend from my chair, at the close of my academic labours, when I see the crowd disperse,—another generation that I shall behold no more,—my mind is lost in inward contemplation.

Summer comes on; the town is less peopled, the streets are less noisy, the pavement grows more sonorous around my Pantheon. Its large black and white slabs resound beneath my feet.

I commune with my own mind. I interrogate myself as to my teaching, my history, and its all-powerful interpreter,—the spirit of the Revolution.

It possesses a knowledge of which others are ignorant. It contains the secret of all bygone times. In it alone France became conscious of herself. When, in a moment of weakness, we may appear forgetful of our own worth, it is to this point that we should recur in order to seek and recover ourselves again. Here, the inextinguishable spark, the profound mystery of life, is ever glowing within us.

The Revolution lives in ourselves,—in our souls; it has no outward monument. Living spirit of France, where shall I seize thee, but within myself?—The governments that have succeeded each other, hostile in all other respects, appear at least agreed in this, to resuscitate, to awaken remote and departed ages. But thee they would have wished to bury. Yet why? Thou, thou alone dost live.

Thou livest! I feel this truth perpetually impressed upon me at the present period of the year, when my teaching is sus-

3

pended,—when labour grows fatiguing, and the season becomes oppressive. Then I wander to the Champ de Mars, I sit me down on the parched grass, and inhale the strong breeze that is wafted across the arid plain.

The Champ de Mars! This is the only monument that the Revolution has left. The Empire has its Column, and engrosses almost exclusively the arch of Triumph; royalty has its Louvre, its Hospital of Invalids; the feudal church of the twelfth century is still enthroned at Notre Dame: nay, the very Romans have their Imperial Ruins, the Thermae of the Caesars!

And the Revolution has for her monument—empty space.

Her monument is this sandy plain, flat as Arabia. A tumulus on either hand, resembling those which Gaul was accustomed to erect,—obscure and equivocal testimonial to her heroes' fame.

The Hero! do you mean him who founded the bridge of Jena? No, there is one here greater even than he, more powerful and more immortal, who fills this immensity.

"What God? We know not. But here a God doth dwell."

Yes, though a forgetful generation dares to select this spot for the theatre of its vain amusements, borrowed from a foreign land,—though the English race-horse may gallop insolently over the plain, a mighty breath yet traverses it, such as you nowhere else perceive; a soul, and a spirit omnipotent.

And though that plain be arid, and the grass be withered, it will, one day, renew its verdure.

For in that soil is profoundly mingled the fruitful sweat of their brows who, on a sacred day, piled up those hills,—that day when, aroused by the cannon of the Bastille, France from the North and France from the South came forward and embraced; that day when three million heroes in arms rose with the unanimity of one man, and decreed eternal peace.

Alas! poor Revolution. How confidingly on thy first day didst thou invite the world to love and peace. "O my enemies," didst thou exclaim, "there are no longer any enemies!" Thou didst stretch forth thy hand to all, and offer them thy cup to drink to the peace of nations—but they would not.

And even when they advanced to inflict a treacherous

4

wound, the sword drawn by France was the sword of peace. It was to deliver the nations, and give them true peace—Liberty—that she struck the tyrants. Dante asserts Eternal Love to be the founder of the gates of hell. And thus the Revolution wrote *Peace* upon her flag of war.

Her heroes, her invincible warriors, were the most pacific of human beings. Hoche, Marceau, Desaix, and Kléber, are deplored by friends and foes, as the champions of peace; they are mourned by the Nile, and by the Rhine, nay, by war itself, —by the inflexible Vendée.

France had so completely identified herself with this thought, that she did her utmost to restrain herself from achieving conquests. Every nation needing the same blessing—liberty,—and pursuing the same right, whence could war possibly arise? Could the Revolution, which, in its principle, was but the triumph of right, the resurrection of justice, the tardy reaction of thought against brute force,—could it, without provocation, have recourse to violence?

This utterly pacific, benevolent, loving character of the Revolution seems to-day a paradox:—so unknown is its origin, so misunderstood its nature, and so obscured its tradition, in so short a time!

The violent, terrible efforts which it was obliged to make, in order not to perish in a struggle with the conspiring world, have been mistaken for the Revolution itself by a blind, forgetful generation.

And from this confusion has resulted a serious, deeply-rooted evil, very difficult to cure among this people; the adoration of force.

The force of resistance, the desperate effort to defend unity, 1793. They shudder, and fall on their knees.

The force of invasion and conquest, 1800; the Alps brought low, and the thunder of Austerlitz. They fall prostrate, and adore.

Shall I add, that, in 1815, with too much tendency to over-value force, and to mistake success for a judgment of God, they found at the bottom of their hearts, in their grief and their anger, a miserable argument for justifying their enemy. Many whispered to themselves, "they are strong, therefore they are just."

Thus, two evils, the greatest that can afflict a people, fell upon France at once. Her own tradition slipped away from her, she forgot herself. And, every day more uncertain, paler, and more fleeting, the doubtful image of Right flitted before her eyes.

Let us not take the trouble to inquire why this nation continues to sink gradually lower, and becomes more weak. Attribute not its decline to outward causes; let it not accuse either heaven or earth; the evil is in itself.

The reason why an insidious tyranny was able to render it a prey to corruption is, that it was itself corruptible. Weak and unarmed, and ready for temptation, it had lost sight of the idea by which alone it had been sustained; like a wretched man deprived of sight, it groped its way in a miry road; it no longer saw its star. What! the star of victory? No, the sun of Justice and of the Revolution.

That the powers of darkness should have laboured throughout the earth to extinguish the light of France, and to smother Right, was natural enough. But, in spite of all their endeavours, success was impossible. The wonder is, that the friends of light should help its enemies to veil and extinguish it.

The party who advocate liberty have evinced, of late, two sad and serious symptoms of an inward evil. Let them permit a friend, a solitary writer, to tell them his entire mind.

A perfidious, an odious hand,—the hand of death,—has been offered and stretched out to them, and they have not withdrawn their own. They believed the foes of religious liberty might become the friends of political freedom. Vain scholastic distinctions, which obscured their view! Liberty is liberty.

And to please their enemy, they have proved false to their friend—nay, to their own father, the great eighteenth century. They have forgotten that that century had founded liberty on the enfranchisement of the mind—till then bound down by the flesh, bound by the material principle of the double incarnation, theological and political, kingly and sacerdotal. That century, that of the spirit, abolished the gods of flesh in the state and in religion, so that there was no longer any idol, and there was no god but God.

Yet why have sincere friends of liberty formed a league with the party of religious tyranny? Because they had reduced themselves to a feeble minority. They were astonished at their own insignificance, and dared not refuse the advances of a great party which seemed to make overtures to them.

Our fathers did not act thus. They never counted their number. When Voltaire, a child, in the reign of Louis XIV. entered upon the perilous career of religious contention, he appeared to be alone. Rousseau stood alone, in the middle of the century, when, in the dispute between the Christians and the philosophers, he ventured to lay down the new dogma. He stood alone. On the morrow the whole world was with him.

If the friends of liberty see their numbers decreasing, they are themselves to blame. Not a few have invented a system of progressive refinement, of minute orthodoxy, which aims at making a party a sect,—a petty church. They reject first this, and then that; they abound in restrictions, distinctions, exclusions. Some new heresy is discovered every day.

For heaven's sake, let us dispute less about the light of Tabor, like besieged Byzantium—Mahomet II. is at our gates.

When the Christian sects became multiplied, we could find Jansenists, Molinists, &c., in abundance, but no longer any Christians; and so, the sects which are the offspring of the Revolution annul the Revolution itself; people became Constituants, Girondists, Montagnards; but the Revolutionists ceased to exist.

Voltaire is but little valued, Mirabeau is laid aside, Madame Roland is excluded, even Danton is not orthodox. What! must none remain but Robespierre and Saint-Just?

Without disavowing these two men, without wishing to judge them yet, let one word suffice here: if the Revolution excludes and condemns their predecessors, it excludes precisely those who gave it a hold upon mankind, those who for a moment made the whole world revolutionary. If it looks only to Robespierre and Saint-Just, if it places the images of these two apostles alone upon its altar, the conversion will be slow, French propaganda will be no threat, absolute governments may sleep in perfect security.

Fraternity! fraternity! It is not enough to re-echo the word to attract the world to our cause, as was the case at first. It must acknowledge in us a fraternal heart. It must be won over by the fraternity of love, and not by the guillotine.

Fraternity! Why who, since the creation, has not pronounced that word? Do you imagine it was first coined by Robespierre or Mably?

Every state of antiquity talked of fraternity; but the word was addressed only to citizens,—to men; the slave was but a thing. And in this case fraternity was exclusive and inhuman.

When slaves or freed-men govern the Empire,—when they are named Terence, Horace, Phedrus, Epictetus, it is difficult not to extend fraternity to the slave. "Let us be brethren," cries Christianity. But, to be a brother, one must first exist; man had no being; right and liberty alone constitute life. A theory from which these are excluded, is but a speculative fraternity between nought and nought.

"Fraternity, *or death,*" as the reign of Terror subsequently exclaimed. Once more a brotherhood of slaves. Why, by atrocious derision, impart to such an union the holy name of liberty?

Brethren who mutually fly from one another, who shudder when they meet, who extend, who withdraw a dead and icy hand. O odious and disgusting sight! Surely, if anything ought to be free it is the fraternal sentiment.

Liberty alone, as founded in the last century, has rendered fraternity possible. Philosophy found man without right, or rather a nonentity, entangled in a religious and political system, of which despotism was the base. And she said, "Let us create man, let him *be,* by liberty." No sooner was he created than he loved.

It is by liberty moreover, that our age, awakened and recalled to its true tradition, may likewise commence its work.

It will no longer inscribe amongst its laws, "Be my brother, *or die!*" But by a skilful culture of the best sentiments of the human soul, it will attain its ends in such a manner that all, without compulsion, shall wish to be brothers indeed. The state will realise its destiny, and be a fraternal initiation, an education, a constant exchange of the spontaneous ideas of inspiration and faith, which are common to us all, and of the reflected ideas of science and meditation, which are found among thinkers.[1]

Such is the task for our age to accomplish. May it at last set about the work in earnest!

It would indeed be a melancholy reflection, if, instead of achieving something great for itself, its time were wasted in censuring that age—so renowned for its labours, and to which it is so immensely indebted. Our fathers, we must repeat, did all that it was necessary then to do,—began precisely as it was incumbent on them to begin.

They found despotism in heaven and on earth, and they instituted law. They found individual man disarmed, bare, unprotected, confounded, lost in a system of apparent unity, which was no better than common death. And in order that he might have no appeal, even to the supreme tribunal, the

---

[1] Initiation, education, government, are three synonymous words. Rousseau had some notion of this, when, speaking of the states of antiquity, and of the crowd of great men produced by that little city of Athens, he says, "They were less governments than the most fruitful systems of education that have ever been." Unfortunately, the age of Rousseau invoking only deliberate *reason,* and but little analysing the faculties of instinct, of *inspiration,* could not well discern the mutual connexion which constitutes all the mystery of education, initiation, and government. The masters of the Revolution, the philosophers, famous antagonists, and very subtle, excellent logicians, were endowed with every gift, except that profound simplicity which alone enables one to comprehend the child and the people. Therefore, the Revolution could not organise the grand revolutionary machine: I mean that which, better than laws, ought to found fraternity—*education.* That will be the work of the nineteenth century; it has already entered upon it, in feeble attempts. In my little book, *The People,* I have, as far as in me lay, vindicated the rights of instinct—of inspiration—against her aristocratic sister, reflection, the reasoning science, that pretends to be the queen of the world.

religious dogma of the day held him bound for the penalty of a transgression which he had not committed; this eminently carnal dogma supposed that injustice is transmitted with our blood from father to son.

It was necessary, above all things, to vindicate the rights of man, which were thus so cruelly outraged, and to reëstablish this truth, which, though obscured, was yet undeniable: "Man has rights, he is something; he cannot be disowned or annulled, even in the name of God; he is a responsible creature but for his own actions alone, for whatever good or evil he himself commits."

Thus does this false liability for the actions of others disappear from the world. The *unjust transmission of good,* perpetuated by the rights of the nobility; *the unjust transmission of evil,* by original sin, or the civil brand of being descended from sinners, are effaced by the Revolution.

O men of the present age, is this the creed you tax with individualism—is this what you term an egotistical law? But, remember, that without these rights of the individual, by which alone man was constituted, he really had no existence, was incapable of action, and man, therefore, could not fraternize. It was actually necessary to abolish the fraternity of death to found that of life.

Speak not of egotism. History will answer here, quite as strongly as logic. It was at the first moment of the Revolution, at the moment she was proclaiming the rights of the individual, it was then that the soul of France, far from shrinking, extended, embraced the whole world in sympathetic thought: then did she offer peace to all, and wish to participate with all her treasure,—liberty.

The moment of birth, the entrance upon a still dubious life, seems to justify a feeling of egotism in every being. We may observe that the newly-born infant, above all things, wishes to live, to prolong its existence. Yet, in the case before us, it was far otherwise. When young French Liberty first opened her eyes to the light, and uttered that earliest cry which transports every new creature,—"I am!" even in that moment her thoughts were not confined to *self;* she did not indulge in a selfish joy, she extended to mankind her life and her hope; her first impulse, in her cradle, was to open her affectionate arms. "I am!" she exclaimed to all nations; "O my brethren, you shall be also!"

In this lay her glorious error, her touching and sublime weakness: the Revolution, it must be confessed, commenced by loving everything.

She loved even her enemy,—England.

She loved, and long she strove to save, royalty—the key-stone of the abuses which she had just demolished. She wanted to save the Church; she endeavoured to remain Christian, being wilfully blind to the contradiction of the old principle,—Arbitrary Grace, and of the new one,—Justice.

This universal sympathy which, at first, made her adopt, and indiscreetly mingle so many contradictory elements, led her to inconsistency,—to wish and not to wish, to do and undo, at the same time. Such is the strange result of our early assemblies.

The world has smiled at that work of hers: but let it not forget, that whatever was discordant in it, was partly owing to the too easy sympathy, to the indiscriminate benevolence which was the first feature in our Revolution.

Genius utterly humane! I love to follow and watch its progress, in those admirable fêtes wherein a whole people, at once the actors and spectators, gave and received the impulse of moral enthusiasm; wherein every heart expanded with all the sublimity of France,—of a country which, for its law, proclaimed the rights of humanity.

At the festival of the 14th of July, 1792, among the sacred images of Liberty and the Law,—in the civic procession,—in which figured, together with the magistrates, the representatives, the widows and orphans of those killed at the Bastille,—were seen divers emblems,—those of trades useful to men, instruments of agriculture, ploughs, sheaves, branches loaded with fruits; and the bearers were crowned with ears of corn and green vine-leaves. But others also were seen in mourning, crowned with cypress; they were carrying a table covered with crape, and, under the crape, a veiled sword,—that of the law!

A touching image! Justice, showing her sword in mourning, was no longer distinguished from Humanity herself.

A year after, the 10th of August, 1793, a very different festival was celebrated. This one was heroic and gloomy. But the law had been mutilated; the legislative power had been violated; the judiciary power, unguaranteed and annulled, was the slave of violence. They dared no longer show the sword; it was no longer that of Justice; the eye could have borne it no longer.

A thing to be told to everybody, and which it is but too easy to prove, is, that the humane and benevolent period of our Revolution had for its actors the very people, the whole people, —everybody. And the period of violence, the period of sanguinary deeds, into which danger afterwards thrust it, had for actors but an inconsiderable, an extremely small number of men.

That is what I have found established and verified, either by written testimony, or by such as I have gathered from the lips of old men.

The remarkable exclamation of a man who belonged to the Faubourg Saint-Antoine will never die: "We were all of us at the 10th of August, and not one at the 2nd of September."

Another thing which this history will render most conspicuous, and which is true of every party, is, that the people were generally much better than their leaders. The further I have searched, the more generally have I found that the more deserving class was ever underneath, buried among the utterly obscure. I have also found that those brilliant, powerful speakers, who expressed the thoughts of the masses, are usually but wrongfully considered as the sole actors. The fact is, that they rather received than communicated the impulse. The chief actor is the people. In order to find and restore the latter to its proper position, I have been obliged to reduce to their proportions those ambitious puppets whom they had set in motion, and in whom, till now, people fancied they saw, and have sought for, the secret transactions of history.

This sight, I must confess, struck me with astonishment. In

proportion as I entered more deeply into this study, I observed that the mere party leaders, those heroes of the prepared scene, neither foresaw nor prepared anything, that they were never the first proposers of any grand measure,—more particularly of those which were the unanimous work of the people at the outset of the Revolution.

Left to themselves, at those decisive moments, by their pretended leaders, they found out what was necessary to be done, and did it.

Great, astonishing results! But how much greater was the heart which conceived them! The deeds themselves are as nothing in comparison. So astonishing, indeed, was that greatness of heart, that the future may draw upon it for ever, without fearing to exhaust its resources. No one can approach its contemplation, without retiring a better man. Every soul dejected, or crushed with grief, every human or national heart has but to look there in order to find comfort: it is a mirror wherein humanity, in beholding itself, becomes once more heroic, magnanimous, disinterested; a singular purity, shrinking from the contamination of lucre as from filth, appears to be the characteristic glory of all.

I am endeavouring to describe to-day that epoch of unanimity, that holy period, when a whole nation, free from all party distinction, as yet a comparative stranger to the opposition of classes, marched together under a flag of brotherly love. Nobody can behold that marvellous unanimity, in which the self-same heart beat together in the breasts of twenty millions of men, without returning thanks to God. These are the sacred days of the world—thrice happy days for history. For my part, I have had my reward, in the mere narration of them. Never, since the composition of my Maid of Orleans, have I received such a ray from above, such a vivid inspiration from Heaven.

But as "our thread of life is of a mingled yarn," whilst I enjoyed so much happiness in reviving the annals of France, my own peace has been disturbed for ever. I have lost him who so often narrated the scenes of the Revolution to me, him whom I revered as the image and venerable witness of the Great Age, that is, of the eighteenth century. I have lost my father, with whom I had lived all my life,—forty-eight years.

When that blow fell upon me, I was lost in contemplation. I was elsewhere, hastily realizing this work, so long the object of my meditation. I was at the foot of the Bastille, taking that fortress, and planting our immortal banner upon its towers. That blow came upon me, unforeseen, like a shot from the Bastille.

Many of these important questions, which have obliged me to fathom deeply the foundations of my faith, have been investigated by me during the most awful circumstances that can attend human life, between death and the grave,—when the survivor, himself partly dead, has been sitting in judgment between two worlds. Then I resumed my course, even to the conclusion of this work, whilst death and life had equal claims upon my mind. I struggled to keep my heart in the closest communion with justice, strengthening myself in my faith by my very bereavements and my hopes; and, in proportion as my own household gods were shattered, I clung to the home of my native land.

INTRODUCTION

FIRST PART

On the Religion of the Middle Ages

IS THE REVOLUTION CHRISTIAN OR ANTI-CHRISTIAN?

I define the Revolution,—The advent of the Law, the resurrection of Right, and the reaction of Justice.

Is the Law, such as it appeared in the Revolution, conformable, or contrary, to the religious law which preceded it? In other words, is the Revolution Christian or Anti-Christian?

This question, historically, logically, precedes every other. It reaches and penetrates even those which might be believed to be exclusively political. All the institutions of the civil order which the Revolution met with, had either emanated from Christianity, or were traced upon its forms, and authorised by it. Religious or political, the two questions are deeply, inextricably intermingled. Confounded in the past, they will reappear to-morrow as they really are, one and identical.

Socialists' disputes, ideas which seem to-day new and paradoxical, were discussed in the bosom of Christianity and of the Revolution. There are few of those ideas into which the two systems have not deeply entered. The Revolution especially, in her rapid apparition, wherein she realised so little, saw, by the flashes of the lightning, unknown depths, abysses of the future.

17

Therefore, in spite of the developments which theories have been able to take, notwithstanding new forms and new words, I see upon the stage but two grand facts, two principles, two actors and two persons, Christianity and the Revolution.

He who would describe the crisis whence the new principle emerged and made room for itself, cannot dispense with inquiring what relation it bears to its predecessor, in *what respects* it continues or outsteps, sways or abolishes it:—a serious problem, which nobody has yet encountered face to face.

It is curious to see so many persons approaching, and yet nobody willing to look at this question seriously. Even those who believe, or pretend to believe, the question obsolete, show plainly enough, by their avoiding it, that it is extant, present, perilous, and formidable. If you are not afraid of the pit, why do you shrink back? Why do you turn aside your head? There is here, apparently, a power of dangerous attraction, at which the brain grows giddy.

Our great politicians have also, we must say, a mysterious reason for avoiding these questions. They believe that Christianity is still a great party, that it is better to treat it cautiously. Why fall out with it? They prefer to smile at it, keeping themselves at a distance, and to act politely towards it, without compromising themselves. They believe, moreover, that the religious world is generally very simple, and that to keep it in play, it is merely sufficient to praise the Gospel a little. That does not engage them very deeply. The Gospel, in its gentle morality, contains hardly any of the dogmas which make Christianity a religion so positive, so assuming, and so absorbing, so strong in its grasp upon man. All the philosophers, of every religion, of every philosophy, would subscribe, without difficulty, to the precepts of the Gospel. To say, with the Mahometans, that Jesus is a great prophet, is not being a Christian.

Does the other party expostulate? Does the zeal of God which devours them, fill their hearts with serious indignation against this trifling of politicians? Not so; they declaim much, but only about minor matters, being but too happy so long as they are not molested in what is fundamental. The conduct of politicians, often trifling and occasionally savouring of irony, does not grieve them much. They pretend not to understand the question. Ancient as that party is, it has still a strong hold upon the world. Whilst their opponents are occupied in their parliamentary displays, ever rolling their useless wheel and exhausting themselves without advancing, that old party still holds possession of all that constitutes the basis of life—the family and the domestic hearth, woman, and, through her instrumentality, the child. They who are the most hostile to this party, nevertheless abandon to its influence all they love, and all that makes them happy. They surrender to it every day the infant, man unarmed and feeble, whose mind, still dreaming, is incapable of defending itself. This gives the party many chances. Let it but keep and fortify this vast, mute, undisputed empire, its case is all the better; it may grumble and complain, but it will take good care never to drive politicians to a statement of their belief.

Politicians on either side! connivance against connivance! Where shall I turn to find the friends of truth?

The friends of the holy and the just? Does the world then contain no one who cares for God?

Children of Christianity, you who claim to be faithful, we here adjure you. Thus to pass by God in silence, to omit in every disputation what is truly the faith, as something too dangerous, offensive to the ear—is this religion?

One day, when I was conversing with one of our best bishops on the contradictions between Grace and Justice, which is the very basis of the Christian faith, he stopped me and said: "This question luckily no longer engages the attention of men. On that subject we enjoy repose and silence. Let us maintain it, and never go beyond. It is superfluous to return to that discussion."

Yet that discussion, my lord, is no less than the question, whether Grace and Salvation through Christ, the only basis of Christianity, is reconcilable with justice; it is to examine

19

whether such a dogma is founded on justice, whether it can subsist. Nothing lasts against justice. Does, then, the duration of Christianity appear to you an accessory question?

I well know, that after a debate of several centuries, after heaps of distinctions and scholastic subtleties had been piled together, without throwing light on the question, the pope silenced all parties, judging, like my bishop, that the question might be laid aside with no hope of settling the matter, and leaving justice and injustice in the arena to make up matters as they could.

This is much more than has ever been done by the greatest enemies of Christianity. To say the least, they have always been respectful enough to examine the question, and not put it out of court without deigning to grant it a hearing.

For how could we, who have no inimical feelings, reject examination and debate? Ecclesiastical prudence, the trifling of politicians, and their avoiding the question, do not suit us in the least. We owe it to Christianity to see how far it may be reconcilable with the Revolution, to know what regeneration the old principle may find in the bosom of the new one. We have desired fervently and heartily that it would transform itself and live again! In what sense can this transformation be achieved? What hope ought we to entertain that it is possible?

As the historian of the Revolution, I cannot, without this inquiry, advance one step. But even though I were not invincibly impelled towards it by the very nature of my subject, I should be urged to the investigation by my own heart. The miserable reluctance to grapple with the difficulty which either party evinces, is one of the overwhelming causes of our moral debasement,—a combat of condottieri, in which nobody fights; they advance, retire, menace, without touching one another,— contemptible sight! As long as fundamental questions remain thus eluded, there can be no progress, either religious or social. The world is waiting for a faith, to march forward again, to breathe and to live. But, never can faith have a beginning in deceit, cunning, or treaties of falsehood.

Single-handed and free from prejudices, I will attempt, in

my weakness, what the strong do not venture to perform. I will fathom the question from which they recoil, and I shall attain, perhaps, before I die, the prize of life; namely, to discover the truth, and to tell it according to one's heart.

Engaged as I am in the task of describing the heroic days of Liberty, I may venture to entertain a hope that she herself may deign to support me,—accomplish her own work through the medium of this my book, and lay the deep foundation upon which a better age may build the faith of the future.

SECTION II

IS THE REVOLUTION THE FULFILLING OF CHRISTIANITY?

SEVERAL eminent writers, with a laudable wish for peace and reconciliation, have lately affirmed that the Revolution was but the accomplishment of Christianity,—that it came to continue and to realize the latter, and to make good all it had promised.

If this assertion be well founded, the eighteenth century, the philosophers, the precursors, the masters of the Revolution, have grievously erred, and have acted very differently from their real intentions. Generally, they aimed at anything rather than the accomplishment of Christianity.

If the Revolution consisted in that, and nothing more, it would then not be distinct from Christianity, but the actual time of its existence, its virile age—its age of reason. It would be nothing in itself. In this case, there would not be two actors, but one,—Christianity. If there be but one actor, then no drama, no crisis; the struggle we believe we see, is a mere illusion; the world seems to be agitated, but, in reality, is motionless.

But no, it is not so. The struggle is but too real. There is no sham fight here between one and the same person. There are two distinct combatants.

Neither must it be said that the new principle is but a criticism on the old one,—a doubt, a mere negation. Who ever saw a negation? What is a living, an acting negation, one that vivifies like this? A world sprang forth from it yesterday. No: in order to produce, there must be existence.

Therefore, there are two things here, and not one,—it is impossible to deny it. There are two principles, two spirits—the old and the new.

In vain the former, confident of life, and for this reason so much the more pacific, would whisper to the latter: "I come to fulfil, and not to abolish." The old principle has no manner of wish to be *fulfilled*. The very word sounds ominous and sepulchral; it rejects that filial benediction, and desires neither tears nor prayers; it flings aside the branch that is shaken over it.

We must keep clear of misunderstandings, if we would know whither we are going.

The Revolution continues Christianity, and it contradicts it. It is, at the same time, its heir and its adversary.

In sentiment, and in all that is general and human between them, the two principles agree, but in all that constitutes very and special life,—in the operations of the mind, from which both derive their birth,—they are adverse and thwart each other.

They agree in the sentiment of human fraternity. This sentiment, born with man,—with the world, common to every society, has nevertheless been made more extensive and profound by Christianity. This is its glory, its eternal palm. It found fraternity confined to the banquets of ancient states; it extended its influence, and spread it throughout the vast Christian world. In her turn, the Revolution, the daughter of Christianity, has taught its lessons to the whole world, to every race, and to every religion under the sun.

This is the whole of the resemblance. Now for the difference.

The Revolution founds fraternity on the love of man for man, on mutual duty,—on Right and Justice. This base is fundamental, and no other is necessary.

It did not seek to add to this certain principle one derived from dubious history. It did not ground fraternity on a common relationship,—a filiation which transmits, with our blood, the participation of crime from father to son.

This carnal, material principle, which introduces justice and injustice into the blood, and transmits them, with the tide of life, from one generation to another, violently contradicts the spiritual notion of Justice which is implanted in the depths of the human soul. No; Justice is not a fluid, to be transmitted with generation. Will alone is just or unjust; the heart alone feels itself responsible. Justice is entirely in the soul; the body has nothing to do with it.

This barbarous material starting-point is astounding in a religion that has carried the subtlety of the dogma farther than any other. It impresses upon the whole system a profound character of arbitrariness, from which no subtlety will be able to extricate it. Arbitrariness reaches, penetrates the developments of the dogma, all the religious institutions which are derived from it; and, lastly, the civil order, which, in the middle ages, is itself derived from those institutions, imitates its forms and is swayed by its spirit.

Let us consider this grand sight:

I. The starting-point is this: Crime comes from one alone, salvation from one alone; Adam has lost, Christ has saved.

He has saved! Why? Because he wanted to save. No other motive. No virtue, no work of man, no human merit can deserve this prodigious sacrifice of God sacrificing himself. He gives himself, but for nothing: that is the miracle of love; he asks of man no work,—no anterior merit.

II. What does he require in return for this immense sacrifice? One single thing: people to believe in him, to believe themselves indeed saved by the blood of Jesus Christ. Faith is the condition of salvation, and not the works of justice.

No justice without faith. Whoever does not believe is unjust. Is justice without faith of any use? No.

Saint Paul, in laying down this principle of salvation by faith alone, has dismissed the case for justice. Henceforth she is, at most only an accessory, a sequel, one of the effects of faith.

III. Having once quitted justice, we must ever go on descending into the arbitrary.

Believe, or perish! The question being thus laid down, people discover with terror that they will perish, that salvation is attached to a condition independent of the will. We do not believe as we will.

Saint Paul had laid down that man can do nought by good works, but only by faith. Saint Augustine demonstrates man's helplessness with respect to faith as well. God alone gives it; he gives it even gratuitously, without requiring anything, neither faith nor justice. This *gratuitous* gift, this *grace*, is the only cause of salvation. God gives *grace* to whom he pleases. Saint Augustine has said: "I believe, because it is absurd." He might also say in this system: "I believe, because it is unjust."

Necessity goes no further. The system is consummated. God loves; no other explanation; he loves whom he pleases, the least of all, the sinner, the least deserving. Love is its own reason; it requires no merit.

What then would be *merit*, if we may still employ this word? To be loved, the elect of God, predestined to salvation.

And *demerit*, damnation! To be hated by God, condemned beforehand, created for damnation.

Alas! we believed just now that humanity was saved. The sacrifice of a God seemed to have blotted out the sins of the world. No more judgment, no more justice. Blind that we were! we were rejoicing, believing justice drowned in the blood of Jesus Christ. And lo! judgment re-appears more harsh,—a judgment without justice, or at least the justice of which will be hidden from us for ever. The elect of God, the favourite, receives from him, with the gift of faith, the gift of doing good works,—the gift of salvation. That justice should be a gift! For our part, we had thought it was active, the very act of the will. Yet here we have it passive, transmitted as a present, from God to the elect of his heart.

This doctrine, harshly formulated by the Protestants, is no less that of the Catholic world, such as it is acknowledged by the Council of Trent.

If *grace* (it says with the apostle) were not *gratuitous*, as its very name implies, if it ought to be merited by works of righteousness, it would be righteousness, and no longer grace. (*Conc. Trid.*, sess. vi. cap. viii.)

Such, says that council, has been the permanent belief of the church. And it could not be otherwise; it is the groundwork of Christianity; beyond that, there is philosophy, but no longer religion. The latter is the religion of grace,—of gratuitous, arbitrary salvation, and of the good pleasure of God.

Great was the embarrassment when Christianity, with this doctrine opposed to justice, was called to govern, to judge the world,—when Jurisprudence descended from her praetorium, and said to the new faith: "Judge in my place."

Then were people able to see at the bottom of this doctrine, which seemed to be sufficient for the world, an abyss of insufficiency, uncertainty, and discouragement.

If he remained faithful to the principle that salvation is a gift, and not the reward of Justice, man would have folded his arms, sat down, and waited; for well he knew that his works could have no influence on his lot. All moral activity ceased in this world. And how could civil life, order, human justice, be maintained? God loves, and no longer judges. How shall man judge? Every judgment, religious or political, is a flagrant contradiction in a religion founded solely on a dogma foreign to justice.

Without justice one cannot live. Therefore, the Christian world must put up with the contradiction. This introduces into many things something false and wrong; and this double position is only surmounted by means of hypocritical formulae. The church judges, yet judges not; kills, yet kills not. She has a horror of shedding blood; therefore she burns—What do I say? She does not burn. She hands over the culprit to another to burn, and adds moreover a little prayer, as if to intercede—a terrible comedy, wherein Justice, false and cruel justice, assumes the mask of grace!

A strange punishment of the excessive ambition which desired more than justice, and yet despised it! This church has remained without justice. When, in the middle ages, she sees the latter reviving again, she wants to draw nearer to her. She tries to speak like her, to assume her language; she avows that man can do something towards his salvation by works of righteousness. Vain efforts! Christianity can be reconciled with Papinian only by withdrawing from Saint Paul—quitting its proper base, and leaning aside at the risk of losing its equilibrium and being dashed to atoms.

Having the arbitrary for a starting-point, this system must remain in the arbitrary; it cannot step beyond it.[1] All the spurious attempts by which schoolmen, and others also since their time, have vainly attempted to institute a dogma founded upon reason, that is to say, a philosophical and jurist Christianity, must be discarded. They are devoid alike of virtue and strength. We can take no notice of them; they have passed into silence and oblivion. We must examine the system in itself, in its terrible purity, which constituted all its strength; we must follow it through its reign in the middle ages, and, above all things, mark its progress at the period when at length fixed, armed, and inflexible, it exercised a sway over the whole world.

---

[1] At the present day, people despair of reconciling these different views. They no longer attempt to make peace between the dogma and justice. They manage matters better. Now they show it, now they conceal it. To simple confiding persons, to women, to children, whom they keep docile and obedient, they teach the old doctrine which places a terrible arbitrariness in God and in the man of God, and gives up the trembling creature defenceless to the priest. This terror is ever the faith and the law of the latter; the sword ever remains keen-edged for those poor hearts.

If, on the contrary, they speak to the strong, to thinkers and politicians, they suddenly become indulgent: "Is Christianity, after all, anywhere but in the Gospel? Are faith and philosophy so at variance? The old dispute between Grace and Justice (that is, the question of knowing whether Christianity be just) is quite obsolete."

This double policy has two effects, and both fatal. It weighs heavily upon woman, upon the child, upon the family, in which it creates discord, maintaining in opposition two contrary authorities,—two fathers.

It weighs heavily upon the world by a negative power, which does little, but which impedes, especially by the facility of presenting either of two aspects,—to some the elastic morality of the Gospel, to others immutable fatality, adorned with the name of grace. Hence, many a misunderstanding. Hence, many are tempted to connect modern faith,—that of Justice and the Revolution,—with the dogma of ancient injustice.

A sombre doctrine this, which, at the destruction of the Roman empire, when civil order perished and human justice was, as it were, effaced, shut out all appeal to the supreme tribunal, and for a thousand years veiled the face of eternal justice.

The iniquity of conquest confirmed by decrees from God, becomes authorised and believes itself just. The conquerors are the elect, the conquered are the damned. Damnation without appeal. Ages may pass away and conquest be forgotten; but Heaven, devoid of justice, will not the less oppress the earth, though formed in its own image. Necessity, which constitutes the basis of this theology, will everywhere reappear with desperate fidelity in the political institutions, even in those wherein man had thought to build an asylum for justice. All monarchies, divine and human, govern for their elect.

Where then shall man take refuge? Grace reigns alone in heaven, and favour here below. That Justice, twice proscribed and banished, should venture to raise her head, requires indeed a difficult effort (so completely is the common sense of man extinguished beneath the weight of woes and the oppression of ages); it is necessary, in fact, that Justice should once more believe herself just, that she should arouse, remember herself, and resume the consciousness of right. This consciousness, slowly endeavouring to awake throughout a period of six centuries of religious efforts, burst forth in the year 1789 in the political and social world.

The Revolution is nothing but the tardy reaction of justice against the government of favour and the religion of grace.

SECTION III

LEGENDS OF THE MIDDLE AGES

If you have sometimes travelled among mountains, you may perhaps have observed the same spectacle which I once met with.

From among a confused heap of rocks piled together, amid a landscape diversified with trees and verdure, towered a gigantic peak. That object, black, bare, and solitary, was but too evidently thrown up from the deep bowels of the earth. Enlivened by no verdure, no season changed its aspect; the very birds would hardly venture to alight on it, as if they feared to singe their wings on touching the mass which was projected from earth's central fire. That gloomy evidence of the throes of the interior world seemed still to muse over the scene, regardless of surrounding objects, without ever rousing from its savage melancholy.

What were then the subterraneous revolutions of the earth, what incalculable powers combated in its bosom, for that mass, disturbing mountains, piercing through rocks, shattering beds of marble, to burst forth to the surface! What convulsions, what agony forced from the entrails of the globe that prodigious groan!

I sat down, and from my eyes tears of anguish, slow and painful, began to flow. Nature had but too well reminded me of history. That chaos of mountain heaps oppressed me with the same weight which had crushed the heart of man throughout the middle ages; and in that desolate peak, which from her inmost bowels the earth had hurled towards heaven, I saw pictured the despair and the cry of the human race.

That Justice should have borne for a thousand years that mountain of dogma upon her heart, and, crushed beneath its weight, have counted the hours, the days, the years, so many long years—is, for him who knows it, a source of eternal tears. He who through the medium of history has participated in that long torture, will never entirely recover from it; whatever may happen he will be sad; the sun, the joy of the world, will never more afford him comfort; he has lived too long in sorrow and in darkness; and my very heart bled in contemplating the long resignation, the meekness, the patience, and the efforts of humanity to love that world of hate and malediction under which it was crushed.

When man, resigning liberty and justice as something useless, entrusted himself blindly to the hands of Grace, and saw it becoming concentrated on an imperceptible point,—that is to say the privileged, the elect,—and saw all other beings, whether on earth or under the earth, lost for eternity, you would suppose there arose everywhere a howl of blasphemy! —No, only a groan.

And these affecting words: "If thou wilt that I be damned, thy will be done, O Lord!"

Then peaceful, submissive, and resigned, they folded themselves in the shroud of damnation!

This is, indeed, serious, worthy of remembrance; a thing which theology had never foreseen. It had taught that the damned could do nothing but hate. But these still loved. These damned souls trained themselves to love the elect, their masters. The priest, the lord, those chosen children of heaven, found, for ages, only meekness, docility, love, and confidence in that humble people. They served, they suffered, in silence; trod upon, they returned thanks; they did not sin even with their lips, as did the saintly Job.

What preserved them from death? One thing, we must say, which reanimated, refreshed the sufferer in his long torment. That astonishing meekness of soul which he preserved, gave him bliss; from that heart, so wounded, yet so good, sprang a living source of lovely and tender fancy, a flood of popular religion to counteract the dryness of the other. Watered by those fruitful streams, the legend flourished and grew; it shaded the unfortunate with its compassionate flowers—flowers of the native soil, blossoms of the fatherland, which somewhat refreshed and occasionally buried in oblivion Byzantine metaphysics and the theology of death.

Yet death was beneath those flowers. The patron, the good saint of the place, was not potent enough to defend his *protégé* against a dogma of dread. The Devil hardly waited till man expired in order to seize him. He beset him living. He was the lord of this world; man was his property, his fief. It appeared so but too plainly in the social order of the time.

What a constant temptation to despair and doubt! How

bondage here below was, with all its miseries, the beginning,—
the foretaste of eternal damnation! First, a life of suffering;
next, for consolation, hell!—Damned beforehand!—Then,
wherefore those comedies of Judgment represented in the
church-porches! Is it not barbarous to keep in uncertainty,
in dreadful anxiety, ever suspended over the abyss, him who,
before his birth, is adjudged to the bottomless pit, is due to it,
and belongs to it?

Before his birth!—The infant, the innocent, created expressly
for hell! Nay, did I say the innocent? This is the horror of the
system; innocence is no more. I know not, but I boldly and
unhesitatingly affirm this to be the insoluble knot at which the
human soul stopped short, and patience was staggered.

The infant damned! I have elsewhere pointed out that deep,
frightful wound of the maternal heart. I pointed it out, and
again drew the veil over it. In exploring its depths we should
find there much more than the terrors of death.

Thence it was, believe me, that the first sigh arose. Of protestation? No! And yet, unknown to the heart whence it escaped,
there was a terrible remonstrance in that humble, low, ago-
nising groan.

So low, but so heart-rending! The man who heard it at night,
slept no more—not for many a night after: and in the morning,
before day-light, he went to his furrow; and there found many
things were changed. He found the valley and the field of
labour lower—much lower,—deep, like a sepulchre; and the
two towers in the horizon more lofty—more gloomy and heavy;
gloomy the church-steeple, and dismal the feudal castle. Then
he began to comprehend the sounds of the two bells. The
church-bell murmured, *Ever;* that of the donjon, *Never.* But, at
the same time, a mighty voice spoke louder in his heart. That
voice cried, *One day!* And that was the voice of God! *One day*
justice shall return! Leave those idle bells; let them prate to
the wind. Be not alarmed with thy doubt. That doubt is already
faith. Believe, hope! Right, though postponed, shall have its
advent; it will come to sit in judgment, on the dogma and on
the world. And *that day* of Judgment will be called the Revolution.

SECTION IV

THE CLERGY AND THE PEOPLE

I have often asked myself, whilst pursuing the dismal study of the middle ages, through paths full of thorns "tristis usque ad mortem," how a religion, which is the mildest in its principle, and has its starting-point in love itself, could ever have covered the world with that vast sea of blood?

Pagan antiquity, entirely warlike, murderous, and destructive, had been lavish of human life, unconscious of its value. Youthful and merciless, beautiful and cold, like the virgin of Tauris, she killed and remained unmoved. You do not find in her grand immolations so much passion, inveteracy, or fury of hate, as characterise, in the middle ages, the combats and the vengeances of the religion of love.

The first reason which I have assigned for this, in my book *Du Prêtre*, is the prodigious intoxication of pride which this belief gives to its elect. What maddening dizziness! Every day, to make God descend upon the altar, to be obeyed by God!— Shall I say it? (I hesitated for fear of blaspheming) *to make God!* How shall he be called who does this miracle of miracles every day? A God? That would not be enough.

The more strange, unnatural, and monstrous this greatness, the more uneasy and full of misgiving is he who pretends to it: he seems to me as though he were sitting on the steeple of Strasburg, upon the point of the cross. Imagine his hatred and violence towards any man who dares to touch him, shake him, or try and make him descend!—Descend? There is no descending. He must fall from such a place,—he must fall; but so heavy is the fall, that it would bury him into the earth.

You may be sure that if, to maintain his position, he can destroy the world by a gesture; if he can exterminate with a word what God created with a word, the world will be exterminated.

This state of uneasiness, anger, and trembling hate explains

31

alone the incredible fury of the church in the middle ages, in proportion as she beheld her rival, Justice, arise against her.

The latter was scarcely perceptible at first. Nothing was so low, so minute, so humble. A paltry blade of grass, forgotten in the furrow; even stooping, you would hardly have perceived it.

Justice, thou who wast lately so feeble, how canst thou grow so fast! If I but turn aside a moment, I know thee no longer. I find thee every hour grown ten cubits higher. Theology quakes, reddens with anger, and turns pale.

Then begins a terrible, frightful struggle, beyond the power of language to express. Theology flinging aside the demure mask of grace, abdicating, denying herself, in order to annihilate Justice, striving to absorb—to destroy her within herself, to swallow her up. Behold them standing face to face; which of them, at the end of this mortal combat, is found to have absorbed, incorporated, assimilated the other?

Let the revolutionary reign of Terror beware of comparing herself with the Inquisition. Let her never boast of having, in her two or three years, paid back to the old system what it did to us for six hundred years! The Inquisition would have good cause to laugh! What are the twelve thousand men guillotined by the one, to the millions of men butchered, hanged, broken on the wheel,—to that pyramid of burning stakes,—to those masses of burnt flesh, which the other piled up to heaven. The Inquisition in one single province of Spain calculates, according to an authentic monument, that in sixteen years it burned twenty thousand men! But why speak of Spain, rather than of the Albigenses, of the Vaudois of the Alps, of the Beggars of Flanders, of the Protestants of France, or of the horrible crusade against the Hussites, and so many nations whom the pope abandoned to the sword?

History will inform us that in her most ferocious and implacable moments the Revolution trembled at the thought of aggravating death, that she shortened the sufferings of victims, removed the hand of man, and invented a machine to abridge the pangs of death.

And it will also inform us that the church of the middle ages exhausted herself in inventions to augment suffering, to render it poignant, intense; that she found out exquisite arts of torture, ingenious means to contrive that, without dying, one might long taste of death—and that, being stopped in the path by inflexible nature, who, at a certain degree of pain, mercifully grants death, she wept at not being able to make man suffer longer.

I cannot, I will not agitate that sea of blood. If God allow me one day to touch it, that blood shall boil again with life, flow in torrents to drown false history and the hired flatterers of murder, to fill their lying mouths.

Well do I know that the greater part of those grand butcheries can no longer be related. They have burnt the books, burnt the men, burnt the calcined bones over again, and flung away the ashes. When, for instance, shall I recover the history of the Vaudois, or of the Albigenses? The day when I shall have the history of the star that I saw falling to-night. A world, a whole world has sunk, perished, both men and things. A poem has been recovered, and bones have been found at the bottom of caverns; but no names, no signs. Is it with these sad remnants that I can form that history again? Let our enemies triumph that they have rendered us powerless, and at having been so barbarous that one cannot, with certainty, recount their barbarities! At least the desert speaks,—the desert of Languedoc, the solitudes of the Alps, the unpeopled mountains of Bohemia, and so many other places, where man has disappeared, where the earth has become sterile for ever, and where Nature, after man, seems itself exterminated.

But one thing cries louder than all their destructions (and this one thing is authentic), which is, that the system which killed in the name of a principle, in the name of a faith, made use indifferently of two opposite principles,—the tyranny of kings, and the blind anarchy of nations. In one single century, the sixteenth, Rome changed three times, throwing herself now to the right, now to the left, without either prudence or decency. First, she gives herself up to the kings; next, she throws herself into the arms of the people; then again, she returns to the kings. Three lines of policy, but one aim. How attained? No matter. What aim? To destroy the power of thought.

A writer has discovered that the pope's nuncio had no fore-knowledge of the Saint Bartholomew massacre. And I have discovered that the pope had prepared it,—worked at it, for ten years.

"A trifle," says another, "a mere local affair, a vengeance of Paris."

In spite of the utter disgust, the contempt, the sickness, which these theories occasion me, I have confronted them with the records of history, with unexceptionable documents. And I have found far and near, the blood-red traces of the massacre. I can prove that, from the day when Paris proposed (1561) the general sale of the goods of the clergy, from the day when the church beheld the king wavering, and tempted by the hopes of that booty, she turned hastily, violently towards the people, and employed every means in her power, by preaching, by alms, by different influences, and by her immense connection, her converts, trades-people, and mendicants, to organize the massacre.

"A popular affair," say you. True. But tell us also by what diabolical scheme, by what infernal perseverance, you worked during the space of ten years to pervert the understanding of the people, to excite and drive them mad.

O spirit of cunning and murder! I have lived too many centuries in face of thee, throughout the middle ages, for thee ever to deceive me. After having so long denied justice and liberty, thou didst assume their name for thy shout of war. In their name thou didst work a rich mine of hate,—that eternal melancholy which inequality implants in the heart of man, the envy of the poor for the rich. Thou tyrant, thou proprietor, and the most ravenous in the world, didst unhesitatingly embrace on a sudden, and exceed, with one bound, the most impracticable theories of the Levellers.

Before the Saint Bartholomew massacre, the clergy used to say to the people, in order to excite them, "The Protestants *are nobles,* provincial gentlemen." That was true; the clergy having already exterminated, stifled Protestantism in the towns. The castles alone being safe against attack, were still able to remain Protestant. But read of their earlier martyrs; they were the inhabitants of towns, petty tradesmen, and workmen. Those creeds which were pointed out to the hatred of people as those of the aristocracy, had sprung from the very people. Who does not know that Calvin was the son of a cooper?

It would be too easy for me to show how all this has been misrepresented in our time by writers subservient to the clergy, and then copied without consideration. I wanted only to show, by one example, the ferocious address with which the clergy urged the people, and made for themselves a deadly weapon of social jealousy. The detail would be curious; I regret to postpone it. I could tell you the plans resorted to, in order to work the ruin of an individual—or a set of men; calumny, skilfully directed by a special press, slowly manipulated in the schools and seminaries, especially in the parlours of convents, directly intrusted (in order to be more quickly diffused) to penitents, to the suborned trades-people of the curates and canons, was put in motion among the people. How it worked itself into fury in those establishments of gluttony, termed Brotherhoods, to which, among other things, they abandoned the immense wealth of the hospitals. Low, paltry, miserable details, but without which the wholesale murders perpetrated by a Catholic rabble would remain incomprehensible.

Occasionally, if it was sought to destroy a man of repute, superior art was added to these manoeuvres. By means of money or intimidation, some talented writer was found and let loose upon him. Thus, the king's confessor, to succeed in getting Vallée burnt, made Ronsard write against him. And so to ruin Théophile, the confessor instigated Balzac, who could not forgive Théophile for having drawn his sword for him, and saved him from personal chastisement.

In our own times, I have had an opportunity of noticing how the same set, in the name of the Church, arouse and foster hatred and disturbance in the breasts of the obscure and lower orders,—the very dregs of society. I once saw, in a city of the west, a young professor of philosophy, whom the ecclesiastics wanted to expel from his chair, followed, and pointed at in the street by a mob of women. What did they know about philosophical questions? Nothing, save what they were taught in the confessional. They were not less furious on that account, standing before their doors, pointing, and shouting: "There he is!"

In a large city in eastern France, I was witness to another, and, perhaps, still more odious spectacle. An old Protestant pastor, almost blind, who, every day, and often several times in the day, was followed and insulted by the children of a school, who pulled him behind, and strove to throw him down.

That is their usual way of beginning their game; by innocent agents, against whom you cannot defend yourself,—little children, women. On more favourable occasions, in unenlightened provinces, easy to be excited, men take a share in the game. The master, who holds to the church, as a member of some *confrérie*, as a tradesman or a lodger, grumbles, shouts, cabals, and collects a mob. The journeyman and the valet get drunk to do mischief; the apprentice follows—surpasses them—strikes, without knowing why,—the very children sometimes assassinate.

Next come false reasoners, foolish theorists, to baptize this pious assassination with the name of *justice of the people,* to canonize the crime perpetrated by tyrants in the name of liberty.

Thus it was, that, in the selfsame day, they found means to slaughter, with one blow, all that formed the honour of France, the first philosopher of the age, the first sculptor, and the first musician,—Ramus, Jean Goujon, and Goudimel. How much rather would they have butchered our great jurisconsult, the enemy of Rome and the Jesuits, the genius of the law, Dumoulin!

Happily, he was safe. He had spared them a crime; his noble life had taken refuge in God. But, before that time, he had seen riots organised four times by the clergy against him and his home. That holy temple of study four times violated and pillaged, his books profaned and dispersed, his manuscripts, irreparable patrimony of mankind, flung into the gutter and destroyed. They have not destroyed Justice; the living spirit contained in those books was emancipated by the flames; it expanded and pervaded everything, impregnating the very atmosphere, so that, thanks to the murderous fury of fanaticism, they could breathe no air but that of equity.

SECTION V

HOW FREE-THINKERS ESCAPED

AFTER a grand festival, a great carnage in the Coliseum of Rome, when the sand had been moistened with blood, and the lions were lying down, cloyed, surfeited with human flesh, then, in order to divert the people, to distract their attention a little, a farce was enacted. An egg was put into the hand of a miserable slave condemned to the wild beasts; and then he was cast into the arena. If he managed to reach the end, if, by good fortune, he succeeded in carrying his egg and laying it upon the altar, he was saved. The distance was not great, but how far it seemed to him! Those brutes, glutted, asleep, or just going to sleep, would nevertheless, at the sound of the light footstep, raise their heavy eyelids, and yawn fearfully, in doubt apparently whether they ought to interrupt their repose for such ridiculous prey. He, half dead with fear, stooping, shrinking, cringing, as if to sink into the earth, would have exclaimed, doubtless, could he have given utterance to his thought: "Alas! alas! noble lions, I am so meagre! Pray allow this living skeleton to pass; it is a meal unworthy of you." Never did any buffoon, any mimic, produce such an effect upon the people; the extraordinary comical contortions and agonies of fear convulsed all the spectators with laughter; they rolled on their benches in the excess of their mirth; it was a fearful tempest of merriment—a roar of joy.

I am obliged to say, in spite of every consideration, that this spectacle was revived towards the close of the middle ages, when the old principle, furious at the thought of dying, imagined it would still have time to annihilate human thought. Once more, as in the Coliseum, miserable slaves were seen carrying among wild beasts, uncloyed, unglutted, furious, atrocious and ravenous, the poor little deposit of proscribed truth,—the fragile egg which might save the world, if it reached the altar.

Others will laugh—and woe to them! But I can never laugh on beholding that spectacle—that farce, those contortions, those efforts to deceive, to dupe, the growling monsters, to amuse that unworthy multitude, wound me to the heart. Those slaves whom I see passing yonder across the bloody arena, are the sovereigns of the mind, the benefactors of the human race. O my fathers, O my brethren, Voltaire, Molière, Rabelais, beloved of my thoughts, it is you whom I behold trembling, suffering and ridiculous, under that sad disguise! Sublime geniuses, privileged to bear the sacred gift of God, have you then accepted, on our account, that degraded martyrdom to be the buffoons of fear?

Degraded!—Oh! no, never! From the centre of the amphitheatre they addressed me in a kind voice: "Friend, what matters if they laugh at us? What do we care at being devoured by wild beasts, at suffering the outrage of cruel men, if we but reach the goal, provided this dear treasure, laid safely upon the altar, be recovered by mankind, whom it will save sooner or later. Do you know what this treasure is?—Liberty, Justice, Truth, Reason."

When we reflect by what imperceptible degrees, through what difficulties and obstacles, every grand design is accomplished, we are less surprised on beholding the humiliation, the degradation, to which its originator is often subjected. Who would undertake the task of following, from unknown depths to the surface, the progress of a thought? Who can tell the confused forms, the modifications, the fatal delays it has to undergo for ages? With what slow steps does it emerge from instinct to musing, to reverie, and thence to the poetical chiaro-oscuro! How long is its progress confined to children and fools, to poets and madmen? And yet one day that madness proves to be the common sense of all! But this is not enough. All men think, but nobody dares speak.—Why? Is courage wanting?—Yes; and why is it wanting?—Because the discovered truth is not yet clear enough; it must first shine out in all its splendour for people to become its martyrs. At length it bursts forth luminous in some genius, and it renders him heroic; it inflames him with devotion, love, and sacrifice. He lays it to his heart and goes among the lions.

Hence that strange spectacle which I beheld just now, that sublime yet terrible farce. Look, see how he quakes as he passes, humble and trembling; how he clasps, conceals, presses something to his heart. Oh! he trembles not for himself.—Glorious trepidation! heroic fear! See you not that he is carrying the salvation of mankind?

Only one thing gives me uneasiness.—Where is the place of refuge in which that deposit is to be concealed? What altar is sacred enough to guard that holy treasure? And what god is sufficiently divine to protect what is no less than the conception of God himself? Great men, ye who are carrying that deposit of salvation with the tender care of a mother nursing her child, take heed, I beseech you; be wary in choosing the asylum to which you intrust it. Beware of human idols, shun the gods of flesh or of wood, who, far from protecting others, cannot protect themselves.

I behold you all, towards the close of the middle ages, from the thirteenth to the sixteenth century, emulating one another in building up and aggrandizing that sanctuary of refuge, the Altar of Royalty. In order to dethrone idols, you erect an idol—and you offer to her everything,—gold, incense, and myrrh. To her, gentle wisdom; to her, tolerance, liberty, philosophy; to her, the *ultima ratio* of society—the law.

How should this divinity not become colossal? The most powerful minds in the world, pursued and hunted to death by the old implacable principle, work hard to build up their asylum ever higher and higher; they would like to raise it to heaven. Hence, a series of legends, fables, adorned and amplified by every effort of genius: in the thirteenth century, it is the *saint*-king, more priest than the priest himself; the *chevalier*-king in the sixteenth; the *good*-king in Henri IV., and the God-king in Louis XIV.

SECOND PART

On the Old Monarchy

SECTION I

As early as the year 1300, I behold the great Ghibelin poet, who, in opposition to the pope, strengthens and exalts to heaven the Colossus of Caesar. *Unity* is salvation; *one* monarch, one for the whole earth. Then, blindly following up his austere, inflexible logic, he lays it down, that the greater this monarch, the more he becomes omnipotent,—the more he becomes a God, the less mankind must fear the abuse of his power. If he has all, he desires nought; still less can he envy or hate. He is perfect, and perfectly, sovereignly just; he governs infallibly, like the justice of God.

Such is the ground-work of all the theories which have since been heaped up in support of this principle: *Unity*, and the supposed result of unity, *peace*. And since then we have hardly ever had anything but wars.

We must dig lower than Dante, and discover and look into the earth for the deep popular foundation whereon the Colossus was built.

Man needs justice. A captive within the straight limits of a dogma reposing entirely on the arbitrary grace of God, he thought to save justice in a political religion, and made unto himself, of a man, a *God of Justice*, hoping that this visible God would preserve for him the light of equity which had been darkened in the other.

I hear this exclamation escape from the bosom of ancient

France,—a tender expression of intense love: "O my king!"

This is no flattery. Louis XIV., when young, was truly loved by two persons,—by the people and La Vallière.

At that time, it was the faith of all. Even the priest seems to remove his God from the altar, to make room for the new God. The Jesuits banish Jesus from the door of their establishment to substitute Louis-le-Grand; I read on the vaults of the chapel at Versailles: "Intrabit templum suum dominator." The words had not two meanings: the court knew but one God.

The Bishop of Meaux, is afraid lest Louis XIV. should not have enough faith in himself; he encourages him: "O kings, exercise your power boldly, for it is divine—Ye are gods!"

An astounding dogma, and yet the people were most willing to believe it. They suffered so many local tyrannies, that, from the most remote quarters, they invoked the distant God, the God of the monarchy. No evil is imputed to him: if his people suffer any, it is because he is too high or too distant.—"If the king did but know!"

We have here a singular feature of France; this nation for a long time comprehended politics only as devotion and love. A vigorous, obstinate, blind love, which attributes as a merit to their God all his imperfections; whatever human weakness they perceive in him is a cause of thanksgiving rather than of disgust. They believe he will be but so much the nearer to them, less haughty, less hardhearted, and more compassionate on that account. They feel obliged to Henri IV. for his love of Gabrielle.

This love for royalty during the earlier days of Louis XIV. and Colbert, was idolatry; the king's endeavours to do equal justice to all, to lessen the odious inequality of taxation, gained him the heart of the people. Colbert reduced forty thousand pretended nobles, and subjected them to taxation; he forced the leading burgesses to give an account at length of the finances of the towns, which they used to turn to their own advantage. The nobles of the provinces who, under favour of the confusion, made themselves feudal barons, received the formidable visits of the envoys of the parliament; royal justice was blessed for its severity. The king appeared as terrible, in his Judgment Days, as on the Last Day of Judgment, between the people and the nobility, the people being on his right, and huddling together by the side of their judge, full of love and confidence.

"Tremble, tyrants! Do you not see that we have God on our side?" This is exactly the language of a poor simple people, who believe they have the king in their favour. They imagine they already behold in him the Angel of the Revolution, and, with outstretched arms, they invoke him, full of tenderness and hope. Nothing is more affecting to read, among other facts of this kind, than the account of the *Grands jours d'Auvergne*, the ingenuous hope of the people, the quaking of the nobility. A peasant, whilst speaking to a lord, had not uncovered; the noble knocked his hat off: "If you do not pick it up," said the peasant, "the Judgment Days are approaching, and the king will cut your head off." The noble was afraid, and picked it up.[1]

Grand, sublime position of royalty! Would that she had never forsaken it; would that the judge of all had not become the judge of *a few*, and that his God of Justice had not, like the God of the theologians, wished also to have his *elect!*

---

[1] The *gens du roi*, or, *parlementaires*, who inspired the people with so much confidence (and who, it is true, have done important services) did not, however, represent Justice more seriously than the priests represented Grace. This regal justice was, after all, subject to the king's good pleasure. A great master of Machiavelism, Cardinal Dubois, explains, with much good sense and precision, in a memorial to the regent against the Estates-General (vol. i. of the *Moniteur*), the very simple mechanism of this parliamentary game, the steps of this minuet, the figures of this dance, up to the *lit de Justice* which ends the whole affair, by putting Justice under the feet of the king's good pleasure. As to the Estates-General, which were a subject of dread to Dubois, Saint Simon, his adversary, recommends them as an expedient at once innocent, agreeable and easy, for dispensing one from paying one's debts, for rendering bankruptcy honourable, *canonizing it*, to use his own expression; moreover, those Estates are never seriously effective, says he very properly: *verba, voces*, nothing more. I say that there was, both in the Estates and in the *parlements*, one thing most serious; which is, that those vain images of liberty occupied, employed, the little vigour and spirit of resistance that subsisted. The reason why France could not have a constitution, is, that she believed she had one.

Such confidence, and such love! and yet, all betrayed! That well-beloved king was hardhearted towards his people. Search everywhere, in books and pictures, contemplate him in his portraits: not a motion, not one look, reveals the least emotion of the heart. The love of a whole people—that grand rarity, that true miracle—has succeeded only in making of their idol a miracle of egotism.

He took Adoration at its word, and believed himself a God. But he comprehended nothing in that word *God*. To be a God is to live for all; but he becomes more and more the king of the court; the few he sees, that band of gilded beggars who beset him, are his people. A strange Divinity, he contracted and stifled a world in one man, instead of extending and aggrandizing that man to the measure of a world. His whole world now is Versailles; and even there, look narrowly; if you find some petty, obscure, dismal closet, a living tomb, that is all he wants; enough for one individual.[2]

SECTION II

FAMINE IN THE EIGHTEENTH CENTURY

I will presently investigate the idea on which France subsisted—the government of grace and paternal monarchy; that inquiry will be much promoted perhaps, if I first establish, by authentic proofs, the results in which this system had at length terminated. A tree is known by its fruits.

First, nobody will deny that it secured for this people the glory of a prodigious and incredible patience. Read the foreign travellers of the last two centuries; you behold them stupefied, when travelling through our plains, at their wretched appearance, at the sadness, the solitude, the miserable poverty, the

---

[2] I allude to the little dark apartment of Madame de Maintenon, where Louis XIV. expired. For his personal belief of his own divinity, see especially his surprising Memoirs written before his face and revised by himself.

dismal, naked, empty cottages, and the starving, ragged population. There they learn what man is able to endure without dying; what nobody, neither the English, the Dutch, nor the Germans, would have supported.

What astonishes them still more, is the resignation of this people, their respect for their masters, lay or ecclesiastical, and their idolatrous attachment for their kings. That they should preserve, amid such sufferings, so much patience and meekness, such goodness and docility, so little rancour for oppression, is indeed a strange mystery. It perhaps explains itself partly by the kind of careless philosophy, the too indifferent facility with which the Frenchman welcomes bad weather; it will be fine again sooner or later; rain to-day, sunshine to-morrow. He does not grumble at a rainy day.

French sobriety also, that eminently military quality, aided their resignation. Our soldiers, in this matter, as in every other, have shown the limits of human endurance. Their fasting, in painful marches and excessive toils, would have frightened the lazy hermits of the Thebais, such as Anthony and Pachomus.

We must learn from Marshal Villars how the armies of Louis XIV. used to live: "Several times we thought that bread would absolutely fail us; then, by great efforts, we got together enough for half a day: the next day is got over by fasting. When M. d'Artagnan marched, the brigades not marching were obliged to fast. Our sustenance is a miracle, and the virtue and firmness of our soldiers are marvellous. *Panem nostrum quotidianum da nobis hodiè*, say they to me as I pass through the ranks, after they have but the quarter and the half ration. I encourage them and give them promises; they merely shrug their shoulders, and gaze at me with a look of resignation that affects me. 'The Marshal is right,' say they; 'we must learn to suffer sometimes.'"

Patience! Virtue! Resignation! Can any one help being affected, on meeting with such traces of the goodness of our fathers?

Who will enable me to go through the history of their long sufferings, their gentleness and moderation? It was long the astonishment, sometimes the laughing-stock of Europe! Great merriment was it for the English to see those soldiers half-starved and almost naked, yet cheerful, amiable, and good towards their officers; performing, without a murmur, immense marches, and, if they found nothing in the evening, making their supper of songs.

If patience merits heaven, this people, in the two last centuries, truly surpassed all the merits of the saints; but how can one recount the story? The evidence is scanty. Misery is a general fact; the virtue to support it a virtue so common among us, that historians seldom deign to notice it. Moreover, history is defective in the eighteenth century; France, after the cruel fatigues of the wars of Louis XIV., suffers too much to relate her own story. No more memoirs; nobody has the courage to write his individual life; even vanity is mute, having but shame to tell. Till the philosophical movement, this country is silent, like the deserted palace of Louis XIV. who outlived his own family, like the bedroom of the dying man who still governs, the old Cardinal Fleury.

It is difficult to describe properly the history of those times, as they are unmarked by rebellions. No people ever had fewer. This nation loved her masters; she had no rebellion,—nothing but a Revolution.

It is from their very masters, their kings, princes, ministers, prelates, magistrates, and intendants, that we may learn to what extremities the people were reduced. It is they who are about to describe the restraints in which the people were held.

The mournful procession in which they all advance one after the other in order to recount the death of France, is led by Colbert in 1681: "One can go on no longer," says he, and he dies.—They do go on however, for they expel half a million industrious men about 1685, and kill still more, in a thirty years' war. But, good God! how many more die of misery!

As early as 1698, the result is visible. The intendants themselves, who create the evil, reveal and deplore it. In the memorials which they are asked to give for the young duke of Burgundy, they declare that such a province has lost a quarter of its inhabitants, another a third, and another a half. And the population is not renewed; the peasant is so miserable that his children are all weak, sickly, and unable to live.

Let us follow attentively the series of years. That deplorable period of 1698 becomes an object of regret. "Then," says Boisguillebert, a magistrate, "there was still oil in the lamp. To-day (1707) it goes out for want of nourishment."—A mournful expression; and he adds a threatening sentence; one would think it was the year 1789: "The trial will now be between those who pay, and those whose only function is to receive."

The preceptor to the grandson of Louis XIV., the Archbishop of Cambrai, is not less *révolutionnaire* than this petty Norman magistrate: "The people no longer live like men; it is no longer safe to rely upon their patience. The old machine will break up at the first shock. We dare not look upon the state of exhaustion which we have now attained; all we can do is to shut our eyes, open our hands, and go on taking."

Louis XIV. dies at last, and the people thank God. Happily we have the regent, that good duke of Orleans, who, if Fénelon still lived, would take him for his counsellor; he prints *Telemachus;* France shall be a Salentum. No more wars. We are now the friends of England; we give up to her our commerce, our honour, nay even our State secrets. Who would believe that, in the bosom of peace, this amiable prince, in only seven years, finds means to add to the two billions and a half of debts left by Louis XIV., *seven hundred and fifty millions*— all of it paid off—in paper.

"If I were a subject," he used to say, "I would most certainly revolt!" And when he was told that a disturbance was about to take place, "The people are right," said he; "they are good-natured fools to suffer so long!"

Fleury is as economical as the regent was lavish. Does France improve? I doubt it, when I see that the bread presented to Louis XV. as the bread that the people ate, is bread made of fern.

The Bishop of Chartres told him, that, in his diocese, the men browsed with the sheep. What is perhaps even more

47

outrageous is, that M. d'Argenson (a minister) speaking of the sufferings of those times, contrasts them with *the good time.* Guess which. That of the regent and the duke,—the time when France, exhausted by Louis XIV., and bleeding at every pore, sought a remedy in a bankruptcy of three billions!

Everybody sees the crisis approaching. Fénelon says, as early as 1709: "The old machine will break up at the first shock." It does not break up yet. Then Madame de Chateauroux, about 1742: "I see plainly that there will be a general overthrow, if no remedy be used."—Yes, Madam, everybody sees it,—the king and your successor, Madame de Pompadour, as well as the economists, the philosophers, foreigners, everybody. All admire the longsuffering nature of this people; it is Job sitting among the nations. O meekness! O patience!—Walpole laughs at it, but I mourn over it. That unfortunate people still loves; still believes; is obstinate in hoping. It is ever waiting for its saviour. Which? Its God-man, its king.

Ridiculous yet affecting idolatry—What will this God, this king, do? He possesses neither the firm will, nor the power, perhaps, to cure the deeply-rooted, inveterate, universal evil now consuming, parching, famishing the community, draining its life's blood from its veins,—from its very heart.

The evil consists in this, that the nation, from the highest to the lowest, is organised so as to go on producing less and less, and paying more and more. She will go on declining, wasting away, giving, after her blood, her marrow; and there will be no end to it, till having reached the last gasp, and just expiring, the convulsion of the death-struggle arouses her once more, and raises that pale feeble body on its legs—Feeble?—grown strong perhaps by fury!

Let us minutely examine, if you will, these words *producing less and less.* They are exact to the letter.

As early as under Louis XIV. the excise (*aides*) already weighed so heavily, that at Mantes, Etampes, and elsewhere, all the vines were uprooted.

The peasant having no goods to seize, the exchequer can lay hold of nothing but the cattle; it is gradually exterminated.

No more manure. The cultivation of wheat, though extended in the seventeenth century, by immense clearings of waste land, decreases in the eighteenth. The earth can no longer repair as the cattle may become extinct, so also the land now appears dead.

Not only does the land produce less, but it is less cultivated. In many places, it is not worth while to cultivate it. Large proprietors, tired of advancing to their peasants sums that never return, neglect the land which would require expensive improvements. The portion cultivated grows less, and the desert expands. People talk of agriculture, write books on it, make expensive experiments, paradoxical schemes of cultivation; —and agriculture, devoid of succour, of cattle, grows wild. Men, women, and children, yoke themselves to the plough. They would dig the ground with their nails, if our ancient laws did not, at least, defend the ploughshare,—the last poor implement that furrows the earth. How can we be surprised that the crops should fail with such half-starved husbandmen, or that the land should suffer and refuse to yield? The yearly produce no longer suffices for the year. As we approach 1789, Nature yields less and less. Like a beast over-fatigued, unwilling to move one step further, and preferring to lie down and die, she waits, and produces no more. Liberty is not only the life of man, but also that of nature.

SECTION III

DOES ANCIENT PATRONAGE SUBSIST IN THE EIGHTEENTH CENTURY?

NEVER accuse Nature of being a bad mother. Believe not that God has withdrawn the beneficent light of his countenance from the earth. The earth is always a good and bountiful mother, ever ready and willing to help mankind; though superficially she may appear sterile and ungrateful, yet she loves him tenderly in her innermost depths.

It is man who has ceased to love,—man who is the enemy

of mankind. The malediction which weighs him down is his own, the curse of egotism and injustice, the load of an unjust society. Whom must he blame? Neither nature, nor God, but himself, his work, his idols, his gods, whom he has created.

He has transferred his idolatry from one to another. To his wooden gods he has said, "Protect me, be my saviours!" He has said so to the priest, he has said so to the noble, he has said so to the king.—Alas! poor man, be thy own saviour,—save thyself.

He loved them,—that is his excuse; it explains his blindness. How he loved, how he believed! What artless faith in the *good Lord*, in the *dear, holy man of God!* How he would fall on his knees before them on the public road, and kiss the dust long after they had passed! How obstinately he put his trust and his hopes in them, even when spurned and trampled on! Remaining ever a minor,—an infant, he felt a sort of filial delight in concealing nothing from them, in intrusting to their hands the whole care of his future. "I have nothing: I am poor; but I am the baron's man, and belong to that fine *château* yonder!" Or else, "I have the honour to be the serf of that famous monastery. I can never want for anything."

Go now, go, good man, in the day of thy need; go and knock at their gate.

At the *château?* But the gate is shut; the large table, where so many once sat down, has long been empty; the hearth is cold; there is no fire, no smoke. The lord is at Versailles. He does not, however, forget thee. He has left his attorney behind, and his bailiff, to take care of thee.

"Well! I will go to the monastery. Is not that house of charity the poor man's home? The Church says to me every day: 'God so loved the world!—He was made man, and became food to nourish man!' Either the Church is nothing, or it must be charity divine realised upon earth."

Knock, knock, poor Lazarus! Thou wilt wait long enough. Dost thou not know that the Church has now withdrawn from the world, and that all these affairs of poor people and charity no longer concern her? There were two things in the middle ages,—wealth and functions, of which she was very jealous; more equitable, however, in modern times, she has made two divisions of them; the functions, such as schools, hospitals, alms, and the patronage of the poor,—all these things which mixed her up too much with worldly cares, she has generously handed over to the laity.

Her other duties absorb all her attention,—those principally which consist in defending till death the pious foundations of which she is the trustee, in allowing no diminution of them, and in transmitting them with increased wealth to future generations. In these respects she is truly heroic, ready for martyrdom, if necessary. In 1788, the State, weighed down with debt, and driven to its last extremity, at a loss to devise new schemes for draining a ruined people, applies as a suppliant to the clergy, and entreats them to pay their taxes. Their answer is admirable, and should never be forgotten: "No, the *people* of France is not taxable at pleasure."

What! invoke the name of the people as a ground to excuse themselves from succouring the people? That was the utmost, truly the sublimest pitch, which Phariseean wisdom could ever hope to attain. Come at length to the ever-memorable year of 1789. The clergy is after all but mortal. It must share the common lot. But it can *enjoy the thought,* so consoling in our last moments, to have been consistent till death.

The mystery of Christianity, a God giving himself to man— a God descending into man,—that doctrine, harsh to reason, could be imposed on the heart only by the visible continuation of the miracle,—alms ever flowing without a capability of exhaustion, and spiritual alms deriving a never-failing support from a similar doctrine; in this you might see some evidence of a God ever present in his Church. But the Church of the eighteenth century, sterile, and no longer giving anything, either material or intellectual, demonstrates precisely the very contrary of what religion teaches. (Oh, impiety!) I mean, "The absence of God in man."

SECTION IV

ROYAL POPULARITY

In the eighteenth century, the people no longer hoped for anything from that patronage which supported them at other times,—the clergy and the nobility. These will do nothing for them. But they still believe in the king; they transfer to the infant Louis XV. both their faith and their necessity of loving. He, the only remains of so great a family, saved like the infant Joas, is preserved apparently that he may himself save others. They weep on beholding that child! How many evil years have to run their course! But they wait with patience, and still hope; that minority, that long tuition of twenty or thirty years, must have an end.

It was night when the news reached Paris, that Louis XV., on his way to the army, had been seized with illness at Metz. "The people leaped from their beds, rushed out in a tumult, without knowing whither. The churches were thrown open in the middle of the night. Men assembled in the cross-roads, accosted, and asked questions, without knowing one another. In several churches, the priest who pronounced the prayer for recovery of the king, interrupted the chanting with his sobs, and the people responded by their cries and tears. The courier who brought the news of his recovery, was hugged, and almost stifled; they kissed his horse, and led him in triumph. Every street re-echoed the same joyful cry: '*Le Roi est guéri!*'"

This, in 1744. Louis XV. is named the *Well-beloved*. Ten years pass. The same people believe that the well-beloved takes baths of human blood; that, in order to renew his exhausted frame, he bathes himself in children's blood. One day, when the police, according to their atrocious custom, were carrying off men, children wandering in the streets, and little girls (especially such as were pretty), the mothers screamed, the people flocked together, and a riot broke out. From that moment, the king never resided in Paris. He seldom passed through it, except to go from Versailles to Compiègne. He had a road made in great haste, which avoided Paris, and enabled the king to escape the observation of his people. That road is still called *Le Chemin de la Révolte.*

These ten years (1744–1754) are the very crisis of the century. The king, that God, that idol, becomes an object of horror. The dogma of the regal incarnation perishes irrecoverably. And in its place arises the sovereignty of the mind. Montesquieu, Buffon, and Voltaire, in that short interval publish their great works; Rousseau was just beginning his.

Unity till then had reposed on the idea of an incarnation, either religious or political. A human God was an essential requisite—a God of flesh, for the purpose of uniting either the church or the state. Humanity, still feeble, placed its unity in a sign, a visible living sign, a man, an individual. Henceforth, unity, more pure, and free from this material condition, will consist in the union of hearts, the community of the mind, the profound union of sentiments and ideas arising from identity of opinions.

The great doctors of the new church, mentioned before, though dissenting in secondary matters, are admirably agreed on two essential points, which constitute the genius of the age in which they lived, as well as that of future times.

1st. Their mind is free from all forms of incarnation; disentangled from that corporeal vesture which had so long invested it.

2dly. The mind, in their opinion, is not only intelligence, it is warmth, love, an ardent love for mankind: love in itself, and not subject to certain dogmata, or conditions of religious policy. The *charity* of the middle ages, a slave to Theology, but too easily followed her imperious mistress; too docile, indeed, and so conciliating as to admit whatever could be tolerated by hate. What is the value of a charity which could enact the Massacre of Saint Bartholomew, fire the faggots at the stake, and organise the Inquisition?

Whilst endeavouring to divest religion of its carnal character, and to reject the doctrine of a religious incarnation, this century, at first timid in its audacity, remained for a long time carnal in its politics, and seemed anxious to respect the doctrine of a regal incarnation,—and through the king, that God-man, to achieve the happiness of mankind. It is the chimera of the philosophers and economists, of such men, I mean, as Voltaire and Turgot, to accomplish the revolution by the king.

Nothing is more curious than to behold this idol disputed as it were by both parties. The philosophers pull him to the right, the priests to the left. Who will carry him off? Women. This god is a god of flesh.

The woman who secures him for twenty years, Madame de Pompadour (whose maiden name was Poisson) would like, at first, to make an ally for herself of the public, against the court. The philosophers are summoned. Voltaire writes the king's history, and poems and dramas for the king; d'Argenson is made minister; and the comptroller-general, Machault, demands a statement of ecclesiastical property. That blow awakens the clergy. The Jesuits do not waste time in arguing the point with a woman; they bring another woman to oppose her, and they triumph. But what woman? The king's own daughter. Here we need Suetonius. Such things had never been since the days of the twelve Caesars.

Voltaire was dismissed; and so was d'Argenson, and Machault later. Madame de Pompadour humbled herself, took the Communion, and put herself at the feet of the queen. Meanwhile, she was preparing an infamous and pitiful machine, whereby she regained and kept possession of the king till his death: a seraglio, composed of children whom they bought.

And there slowly expired Louis XV. The god of flesh abdicated every vestige of mind.

Avoiding Paris, shunning his people, ever shut up at Versailles, he finds even there too many people, too much daylight. He wants a shadowy retreat, the wood, the chace, the secret lodge of Trianon, or his convent of the Parc-aux-cerfs.

How strange and inexplicable that those *amours*, at least those shadows, those images of love, cannot soften his heart.

54

He purchases the daughters of the people; by them he lives with the people; he receives their childish caresses, and assumes their language. Yet he remains the enemy of the people; hard-hearted, selfish, and unfeeling; he transforms the king into a dealer in grain, a speculator in famine.

In that soul, so dead to sentiment, one thing still remained alive: the fear of dying. He was ever speaking of death, of funerals, and of the grave. He would often forebode the death of the monarchy; but provided it lasted his time, he desired no more.

In a year of scarcity (they were not uncommon then), he was hunting, as usual, in the forest of Sénart. He met a peasant carrying a bier, and inquired "whither he was conveying it?— To such a place.—For a man or woman?—A man.—What did he die of?—Hunger."

SECTION V

NO HOPE BUT JUSTICE

THAT dead man is Old France, and that bier, the coffin of the Old Monarchy. Therein let us bury, and for ever, the dreams in which we once fondly trusted,—paternal royalty, the government of grace, the clemency of the monarch, and the charity of the priest; filial confidence, implicit belief in the gods here below.

That fiction of the old world,—that deceitful legend, which was ever on its tongue,—was to substitute *love in the place of law*.

If that world, almost annihilated under the title of love, wounded by charity, and heart-broken by grace, can revive, it will revive by means of law, justice, and equity.

O blasphemy! They had opposed grace to law, love to justice. As if unjust grace could still be grace; as if those things which our weakness divides, were not two aspects of the same truth,—the right and the left-hand of God.

They have made justice a negative thing, which forbids, prohibits, excludes,—an obstacle to impede, and a knife to slaughter. They do not know that justice is the eye of Providence. Love, blind among us, clear-sighted in God, sees by justice—a vital-absorbing glance. A prolific power is in the justice of God; whenever it touches the earth, the latter is blest, and brings forth. The sun and the dew are not enough, it must have Justice. Let her but appear, and the harvests come. Harvests of men and nations will spring up, put forth, and flourish in the sunshine of equity.

A day of justice, one single day, which is called the Revolution, produced ten millions of men.

But how far off? Did it appear, in the middle of the eighteenth century, remote and impossible? Of what materials shall I compose it? all is perishing around me. To build, I should need stones, lime, and cement; and I am empty-handed. The two saviours of this people—the priest and the king—have destroyed them, beyond the possibility of restoration. Feudal life and municipal life are no more,—both swallowed up in royalty. Religious life became extinct with the clergy. Alas! not even a local legend or national tradition remains:—no more of those happy prejudices which constitute the life of an infant people. They have destroyed everything, even popular delusions. Behold them now stripped and empty,—*tabula rasa;* the future must write as best it may.

O, pure spirit, last inhabitant of that destroyed world; universal heir of all those extinct powers, how wilt thou guide us to the only bestower of life? How wilt thou restore to us Justice and the idea of Right?

Here, thou beholdest nothing but stumbling-blocks, old ruins, that one must pull down, crumble to powder, and neglect. Nothing is standing, nothing living. Do what thou wilt, thou wilt have at least the consolation of having destroyed only that which was already dead.

The working of the pure spirit is even that of God—the art of God is its art. Its construction is too profoundly harmonious within, to appear so without. Seek not here the straight lines and the angles, the stiff regularity of your buildings of stone and marble. In a living organisation, harmony of a far superior strength is ever deeply seated within.

First, let this new world have material life; let us give it for a beginning, for a first foundation,—the colossal *Histoire Naturelle:* [3] let us put order in Nature; for her order is justice.

But order is as yet impossible. From the bosom of Nature, —glowing, boiling, as when Etna awakes,—flames forth an immense volcano.[4] Every science and every art bursts forth. The eruption over, a mass remains,—an enormous mass mingled with dross and gold: the *Encyclopédie.*

Behold two ages of the young world,—two days of the creation. Order is lacking and so is unity. Let us create man, the unity of the world, and with him let order come, along with that long-desired light of divine Justice for which we have been waiting.

Man appears in three forms: Montesquieu, Voltaire, and Rousseau. Three interpreters of the Just.

Let us take note of the Law, let us seek after the Law; perhaps we may find it hidden in some corner of the globe. There may perhaps be some clime favourable for justice,— some better land which naturally yields the fruit of equity. The traveller, the inquirer, who pursues it through the earth, is the calm, majestic Montesquieu. But justice flies before him; it remains relative and moveable; law, in his estimation, is a relation,—merely abstract, and inanimate; it is not endowed with vitality.[5]

Montesquieu may be resigned to this result; but not so

---

[3] Buffon; the first volume, 1748. See the edition of MM. Geoffroy-Saint-Hilaire.

[4] Diderot, who published the two first volumes of the *Encyclopédie* in 1751. M. Génin has just written an article on him, which everybody will find witty, brilliant, full of amusement, charming. I find it penetrating; it goes to the very marrow of the subject.

[5] Montesquieu's *Esprit des Lois* appeared in 1748. I shall frequently have occasion to explain how very little that great genius possessed the perception of Right. He is unwittingly, the founder of our absurd English school.

Voltaire. Voltaire is the one who suffers, who has taken upon him all the agony of mankind, who feels and hunts out every iniquity. All the ills that fanaticism and tyranny have ever inflicted upon the world, have been inflicted upon Voltaire. It was he, the martyr, the universal victim, whom they slaughtered in their Saint Bartholomew, whom they buried in the mines of the new world, whom they burned at Seville, whom the parlement of Toulouse broke on the wheel with Calas.—He weeps, he laughs, in his agony,—a terrible laugh, at which the bastilles of tyrants and the temples of the Pharisees fall to the ground.[6]

And down fell at the same time all those petty barriers within which every church intrenched itself, calling itself universal, and wishing to destroy all others. They fall before Voltaire, to make room for the *human* church, for that catholic church which will receive and contain them all in justice and in peace.

Voltaire is the witness of Right,—its apostle and its martyr. He has settled the old question put from the origin of the world: Is there religion without justice, without humanity?

SECTION VI

THE THREE MASTER MINDS

MONTESQUIEU is the writer, the interpreter of Right; Voltaire weeps and clamours for it; and Rousseau founds it.

It was a grand moment, which found Voltaire overwhelmed by a new calamity, the disaster of Lisbon; when, blinded by tears, and doubting Heaven, Rousseau comforted him, restored God to him, and upon the ruins of the world proclaimed the existence of Providence.

---

[6] Read, on Voltaire, four pages, stamped with the seal of genius, which no man of mere talent could ever have written.—Quinet, Ultramontanism.

Far more than Lisbon, it is the world which is tumbling to pieces. Religion and the State, morals and laws, everything is perishing.—And where is the family? Where is love?—even the child—the future? Oh! what must we think of a world wherein even maternal love is perishing?

And is it thou, poor, ignorant, lonely, abandoned workman, hated by the philosophers and detested by the clergy, sick in the depth of winter, dying upon the snow, in thy unprotected pavilion of Montmorenci, who art willing to resist alone, and to write (though the ink freezes in thy pen) to protest against death!

Is it indeed with thy spinet and thy "Village Curate," poor musician, that thou art going to re-construct a world? Thou hadst a slender voice, some energy and warmth of language on thy arrival at Paris, rich in thy Pergolèse, in music, and in hope. It is long since then; soon thou wilt have lived half a century; thou art old; all is over. Why dost thou speak of regeneration to that dying society, when thou thyself art no more?

Yes, it was truly difficult, even for a man less cruelly treated by fate, to extricate his feet from the quicksand, from that deep mire where everything was swallowed up.

Where did he find his foothold, that strong man who, digging in his feet, stopped and held fast—and all stood fast with him?

Where did he find it, O feeble world, O weak and sickly men who called for it, forgetful sons of Rousseau and of the Revolution?

He found it in what has grown too faint among you—in his heart. In the depths of his suffering he read, and read distinctly, what the middle ages were never able to read: *A Just God.* And what was said by a glorious child of Rousseau? *"Right is the sovereign of the world."*

That splendid motto was uttered only at the end of the century; it is its revelation,—its profound and sublime formula.

Rousseau spoke by the mouth of another, by Mirabeau; yet it is no less the soul of Rousseau's genius. When once he severed himself from the false science of the time, and from a no less

59

false society, you behold in his writings the dawn of a celestial effulgence,—Duty, Right!

Its sweet and prolific power shines forth in all its brilliancy in the profession of faith of the Vicar of Savoy. God himself subject to Justice, subject to Right!—Let us say rather that God and Right are identical.

If Rousseau had spoken in the terms of Mirabeau, his language would not have taken effect. Necessities change with the times.—To a world ready to act, on the very day of action, Mirabeau said: "Right is the sovereign of the world," you are the subjects of Right.—To a world still slumbering, inert, feeble, and devoid of energy, Rousseau said, and said well: "The general will is right and reason." Your will is Right. Then arouse yourselves, ye slaves!

"Your collective will is Reason herself." In other words, Ye are Gods!

And who, indeed, without believing himself God, could ever do anything great? Then it is that you may fearlessly cross the bridge of Arcola; then it is, that, in the name of duty, you sever yourself from your dearest affections, your heart.

Let us be God! The impossible becomes possible and easy. Then, to overthrow a world is a mere trifle; why, one creates a world.

This it is which explains how a feeble breath from a manly breast, a simple melody arising from the heart of the poor musician, raised the dead.

France is moved in her innermost soul. All Europe is changed by it. The vast massy German empire rocks on her old foundations. They criticise, but obey. "Mere sentimentality," say they, with an attempt to smile. And yet these dreamers follow it. The very philosophers, the abstractors of quint-essence, take, in spite of themselves, the simple path of the poor Vicar of Savoy.

What, then, has happened? What divine light has shone, to produce so great a change? Is it the power of an idea, of a new inspiration, of a revelation from above? Yes, there has been a revelation. But the novelty of the doctrine is not what affects us most. We have here a more strange, a more mysterious phenomenon,—an influence felt even by those who do not read, and could never comprehend. Nobody knows why, but since that glowing language impregnated the air, the temperature has changed; it seems as though a breath of life had been wafted over the world; the earth begins to bear fruits that she would never else have borne.

What is it? Shall I tell you? It is what vivifies and melts the heart; it is the breath of youth; and that is why we all yield to its influence. In vain would you prove to us that this language is weak, or overstrained, or of vulgar sentiment. Such is youth and such is passion. Such have we been, and, if we occasionally recognise therein the foibles of our early youth, we do but feel more vividly the sweet yet bitter charms of the time that will return no more.

Warmth and thrilling melody, such is the magic of Rousseau. His power, as it is in his "Emile" and the "Social Contract," may be discussed and combated. But, by his "Confessions" and his "Reveries," by his weakness, he has vanquished us, and drawn tears from every eye.

Foreign, hostile geniuses were able to reject the light, but they have all felt the influence of the warmth. They did not listen to the words; but the music subdued them. The gods of profound harmony, the rivals of the storm, which thundered from the Rhine to the Alps, themselves felt the all-powerful incantation of that sweet melody, that soft human voice,—the little morning ditty, sung for the first time beneath the vine at Charmettes.

That youthful affecting voice, that melody of the heart, is heard long after that tender heart has been buried in the earth. The "Confessions," which appeared after the death of Rousseau, seem a sigh from the tomb. He returns—rises from the dead, more potent, more admired, more adored than ever.

That miracle he shares in common with his rival, Voltaire. His rival?—No. Enemy?—No. Let them be forever upon the same pedestal, those two Apostles of Humanity.[7]

---

[7] A noble and tender idea of Madame Sand, which shows how genius rises superior to those vain oppositions which the *esprit de système* creates

Voltaire, nearly octogenarian, buried among the snows of the Alps, broken down by age and labour, nevertheless rises also from the dead. The grand thought of the century, inaugurated by him, is also to be closed by him; he who was the first to open, is also to resume and finish the chorus. Glorious century! Well does it deserve to be called forever the heroic age of the mind. An old man on the verge of the grave; he has seen the others, Montesquieu, Diderot, and Buffon pass away; he has witnessed the extraordinary success of Rousseau,—three books in three years. "And the earth was silent." Voltaire is not discouraged; behold him entering, lively and young, upon a new career. Where, then, is the old Voltaire? He was dead. But a voice has roused him all alive from the tomb, that voice which had ever given him life,—the voice of Humanity.

Ancient champion, to thee the crown! Here thou art again, conqueror of conquerors. Throughout a century, in every kind of warfare, with every weapon and doctrine, opposite, contrary, no matter what, thou hast pursued, without ever deviating, one interest, one cause—holy Humanity. And yet they have called thee a sceptic! And they have termed thee changeable! They thought to surprise thee in the seeming contradictions of a flexible language ever serving the selfsame thought!

Thy faith shall be crowned by the very work of faith. Others have spoken of Justice, but thou shalt perform it; thy words are acts, realities. Thou defendest Calas and La Barre, thou savest Sirven, and dost annihilate the scaffold of the Protestants. Thou has conquered for religious liberty, and moreover, for civil freedom, as advocate of the last serfs, for the reform of our barbarous legislation and criminal laws, which themselves were crimes.

Behold in all this the dawn of the Revolution. Thou dost make it, and see it. Look for thy reward, look, behold it yonder!

---

for itself between those great witnesses, of truth not opposed, but harmonising. When it was lately proposed to raise statues to Voltaire and Rousseau, Madame Sand, in an admirable letter, requested that the two reconciled geniuses might be placed upon the same pedestal. Noble thoughts come from the heart.

Now thou mayest die; thy firm faith deserved that thou shouldst not take thy flight before thou hadst seen the holy land.

SECTION VII

THE REVOLUTION COMMENCES

WHEN those two men have passed, the Revolution is accomplished in the intellectual world.

Now it becomes the duty of their sons, legitimate and illegitimate, to expound and diffuse it in a hundred ways: some in eloquence and fiery satire, others will strike bronze medals to transmit it from hand to hand; Mirabeau, Beaumarchais, Raynal, Mably, and Sieyès, are now to do their work.

The Revolution is on her march, with Rousseau and Voltaire still in front. Kings themselves are in her train; Frederick, Catherine, Joseph, Leopold—that is the court of the two chieftains of the age. Reign, great men, ye true sovereigns of the world; reign, O my kings!

All appear converted, all wish for the Revolution; though every one, it is true, wishes it, not for himself, but for others. The nobility would willingly carry it out against the clergy, and the clergy against the nobility.

Turgot is the touchstone for all: he summons them to say whether they wish truly to reform; they all unanimously answer: No, let what ought to be done, be done!

Meanwhile, I see the Revolution everywhere, even in Versailles. All admit it to a certain limit, where it will not hurt them: Louis XVI. as far as the plans of Fénelon and the Duke of Burgundy, and the Count d'Artois as far as Figaro; he forces the king to allow the trying drama to be played. The queen wishes for the Revolution, at least in her palace, for the *parvenus;* that queen, devoid of prejudices, turns all her grand ladies out of doors, in order to keep her beautiful friend Madame de Polignac.

Necker, the *borrower*, himself discredits his loans by publishing the misery of the monarchy. A *révolutionnaire* by publicity, he believes he is so by his little provincial assemblies, wherein the privileged are to say what must be taken from the privileged.

The witty Calonne comes next, and being unable to glut the privileged even by breaking into the public treasury, he takes his course, accuses them, and hands them over to the hatred of the people.

He has accomplished the Revolution against the notables; Loménie, a philosophical priest, accomplishes it against the *parlements*.[8]

Calonne said admirably, when he avowed the *deficit*, and pointed to the yawning gulf: "What remains to fill it with? *The abuses.*"

That seemed clear to everybody; the only thing obscure was whether Calonne did not speak in the name of *the very Prince of abuses*, of him who sustained all others, and was the keystone of the whole wretched edifice? In two words, was Royalty the support or the remedy of those abuses denounced by the King's own creature.

That the clergy was an abuse, and the nobility an abuse, seemed but too evident.

The privilege of the clergy, founded on teaching, and the example they formerly set the people, had become nonsense; nobody possessed the faith less. In their last assembly, they strive hard to get the philosophers punished, and, to make the demand, they are represented by an atheist and a sceptic: Loménie and Talleyrand.

The privilege of the nobility had likewise become nonsense: formerly they paid nothing because they paid with their sword; they furnished the regulars and the reserves; a vast undisciplined multitude, called together for the last time in 1674. They continued to furnish the army with officers, by shutting out all others from the career, and rendering the formation of a real

---

*The highest law courts in the old regime (Ed. note).

army impossible. The civil army, the administration, the bureaucracy, was invaded by the nobility; the ecclesiastical army, in its higher ranks, was also filled with nobles. Those who made it their profession to live in grand style, that is to say, to do nothing, had undertaken to do all; and everything remained undone.

Once more, the clergy and the nobility were a burden to the land, the malediction of the country, a gangrene which it was necessary to cut away; that was as clear as daylight to everybody.

The only obscure question was that of Royalty; a question, not of mere form, as people have so often repeated, but a fundamental, intimate question, more vital than any other in France; a question not only of politics, but of love and religion. No people ever loved their kings so dearly.

The eyes of men, open under Louis XV., shut again under Louis XVI., and the question remained once more in the dark. The hope of the people still clung to royalty; Turgot hoped, Voltaire hoped, that poor young king, so ill born and bred, would have desired to do good. He struggled, and was dragged away. The prejudices of his birth and education, even his hereditary virtues, hurried him to his ruin—a sad historical problem! Honest men have excused him, and honest men have condemned him. Duplicity, mental reservations, (but little surprising, no doubt, in a pupil of the Jesuit party,) such were his faults; and lastly his crime, which led him to death, his appeal to foreigners. With all that, let us not forget that he had been sincerely anti-Austrian and anti-English; that he had truly, fervently desired to improve our navy; that he had founded Cherbourg at eighteen leagues from Portsmouth; that he helped to cut England in two, and set one part of England against the other. That tear which Carnot shed on signing his death-warrant, remains for him in history; History, and even Justice, in judging him, will weep.

Every day brings on his punishment. This is not the time for me to relate these things. Let it suffice to say here that the best was the last—great lesson of Providence!—so that it might appear plain to all that the evil was less in the man than in the institution itself; that it might be more than the condemnation of the king—the condemnation of ancient royalty. That religion is at an end. Louis XV. or Louis XVI., infamous or honest, the god is nevertheless still a man; if he be not so by vice, he is by virtue, by easy good nature. Human and feeble, incapable of refusing, of resisting, every day sacrificing the people to the courtiers, and like the God of the priests, damning the many, and saving his *elect*.

As we have already said: The *religion of grace*, partial for the elect, and the *government of grace*, in the hands of favourites, are perfectly analogous. Privileged mendicity, whether it be filthy and monastic, or gilded, as at Versailles, is ever mendicity. Two paternal powers: ecclesiastical paternity, characterised by the Inquisition; and monarchical paternity, by the Red Book and the Bastille.

SECTION VIII

THE RED BOOK

WHEN Queen Anne of Austria was regent, "there remained," says Cardinal Retz, "but two little words in the language: 'The queen is so good!'"

From that day France declines in energy; the elevation of the lower classes, which notwithstanding the harsh administration of Richelieu had been so remarkable, subsides and disappears. Wherefore? Because the "queen is good," she loads with presents the brilliant crowd besetting her palace; all the provincial nobility who fled under Richelieu return, demand, obtain, take, and pillage; the least they expect is to be exempted from taxation. The peasant who has managed to purchase a few acres has the sole duty of payment; he must bear all—he is obliged to sell again, and once more becomes a tenant, steward, or a poor domestic.

Louis XIV. is severe at first; no exemption from taxes; Colbert suppresses 40,000 such exemptions. The country thrives. But Louis XIV. grows good-natured; he is more and more affected by the fate of the poor nobility; everything is for them,— ranks, places, pensions, even benefices, and Saint-Cyr for noble young ladies. The nobility flourishes, and France is at her last extremity.

Louis XVI. is also severe at first, grumbles, and even refuses; the courtiers jest bitterly about his incivility and rough answers (*coups de boutoir*). The reason is, he has a bad minister—that inflexible Turgot: and, alas! the queen has no power yet. In 1778, the king at last yields; the reaction of nature acts powerfully in favour of the queen; he can no longer refuse anything, neither to her nor to her brother. The most amiable man in France becomes comptroller-general; M. de Calonne uses as much wit and grace to give, as his predecessors had used skill to elude and refuse. "Madam," he would say to the queen, "if it be possible, it is done; if impossible, it shall be done." The queen purchases Saint Cloud; the king, so parsimonious till then, allows himself to be seduced, and buys Rambouillet. Vaudreuil, the disinterested friend of the Count d'Artois, will receive nothing; he sells to the crown, for a million, his estates in America, receives them back and keeps them. Who can say how many estates and what sums *Diane de Polignac*, by cleverly directing Jules de Polignac, managed to secure? The crowned Rosina, having become in course of time Countess Almaviva, could refuse nothing to Suzanne,—to the versatile charms of her who was Suzanne or Chérubino.

The Revolution spoiled all. It roughly tore aside the graceful veil that masked the public ruin. The veil, being removed, revealed the vessel of the Danaides. The monstrous affair of the Puy Paulin and Fenestrange, those millions squandered (between a famine and a bankruptcy), flung away by a silly woman into a woman's lap, far surpassed anything that satire had exposed. People laughed,—with horror.

The inflexible reporter of the Finance Committee apprised the Assembly of a mystery of which no one knew: "In expenditures, the king is the *sole authority*."

The only standard of expenditure was the king's good nature. Too tender-hearted to refuse—to grieve those whom he saw about him—he found himself in reality dependent on them. At the slightest inclination towards economy, they were moody and sullen. He was obliged to yield. Several of them were still bolder; they spoke out, loud and resolutely, and took the king to task. M. de Coigny (the queen's first or second lover, according to dates), refused to submit to a retrenchment which they had proposed in one of his enormous pensions; a scene ensued, and he got into a passion with Louis XVI. The king shrugged his shoulders, and made no answer. In the evening, he said: "Indeed, had he beaten me, I should have submitted to it."

No noble family in difficulties, no illustrious mother marrying her daughter and son, but draws money from the king. "Those great families contribute to the splendour of the monarchy and the glory of the throne," &c. &c. The king signs with a heavy heart, and copies into his Red Book: To Madam—, 500,000 francs. The lady carries the order to the minister: "I have no money, Madam." She insists, threatens; she may be troublesome, being in high favour with the queen. The minister ultimately finds the money. He will rather postpone, like Loménie, the payment of the small pensioners; let them starve, if they will; or else, as he did, he will take the charitable funds intended to repair the disasters of storms and fire; nay, even plunder the funds of the hospitals.

France is in good hands. Everything is going on well. So good-natured a king, such an amiable queen. The only difficulty is, that, independently of the privileged paupers at Versailles, there is another class, no less noble, and far more numerous, the provincial privileged paupers, who have nothing, receive nothing, say they; they rend the air with their exclamations. Those men, long before the people, will begin the Revolution.

By-the-by, there is a people. Between these paupers and those paupers, who are all persons of fortune, we had forgotten the people.

The people! Oh! that is the business of the farmers of the revenue. Things are altered. Formerly, financiers were hard-hearted men. Now they are all philanthropists, kind, amiable, and magnificent; with one hand they starve, it is true; but often they nourish with the other. They reduce thousands to beggary, and give alms. They build hospitals, and fill them.

"Persepolis," says Voltaire, in one of his stories, "has thirty kings of finance, who draw millions from the people and give a little to the king." Out of the *gabelle*, for instance, which brought in one hundred and twenty millions, the *Ferme générale* kept back sixty, and deigned to leave some fifty or sixty for the king.

Tax-gathering was nothing but an organised warfare; it caused an army of two hundred thousand drones to oppress the soil. Those locusts devoured,—wasted everything. To drain substance out of a people, thus devoured, it was necessary to have cruel laws, terrible penalties, the galleys, gibbets, racks. The farming agents were authorised to employ arms; they murdered, and were afterwards judged by the special tribunals of the *Ferme générale*.

The most shocking part of the system was the easy good nature of the king and the farmers of the revenue. On one hand the king, on the other the thirty kings of the exchequer, gave away (or sold cheap) exemptions from taxation; the king created nobles; the farmers created for themselves fictitious *employés*, who, under that title, were exempt. Thus, the exchequer was working against itself; whilst it was augmenting the sum to be paid, it diminished the number of the payers; the load weighing upon fewer shoulders, became more and more oppressive.

The two privileged orders paid whatever they pleased,—the clergy a gratuitous non-collectible tax; the nobles contributed for certain imposts, but according to whatever they thought proper to declare, which the treasury-agents registered with a bow, without either examination or verification. The neighbours had to pay so much the more.

O, heaven! O, earth! O, justice! If it were through conquest, or by a master's tyranny, that the people were perishing, they could endure it. But they perish through good nature! They would perhaps endure the hard-heartedness of a Richelieu; but how can they endure the good nature of Loménie and Calonne, the tender-heartedness of the financiers, and the philanthropy of the farmers of the revenue!

To suffer and die, so be it! But to suffer *by choice*, so that a kindness for one should be the death and ruin of another! That is too much, oh, too much by half!

Kind-hearted men, you who weep over the evils of the Revolution (doubtless with too much reason), shed also a few tears for the evils which occasioned it.

Come and see, I beseech you, this people lying in the dust, like poor Job, amid their false friends, their patrons, their influential protectors—the clergy and royalty. Behold the look of anguish that they turn upon their king, without speaking. What language is in that look!

"O king, whom I made my god, to whom I erected an altar, and to whom I prayed even before God himself, from whom, in the jaws of death, I implored salvation; you, my only hope, you, whom I have adored. What! have you then felt nothing?"

SECTION IX

THE BASTILLE

The illustrious Quesnay, physician to Louis XV. and to Madame de Pompadour, who lived in the house of the latter at Versailles, saw the king one day rush in suddenly, and felt alarmed. Madame du Hausset, the witty *femme de chambre*, who has left such curious memoirs, inquired of him why he seemed so uneasy. "Madam," returned he, "whenever I see the king, I say to myself: 'There is a man who can cut my head off.'" "Oh!" said she "the king is *too good!*"

The lady's maid thus summed up, in one word, the guarantees of the monarchy.

The king was too good to cut a man's head off; that was no longer agreeable to custom. But he could, with one word, send him to the Bastille, and there *forget* him.

It remains to be decided which is best,—to perish by one blow, or to suffer a lingering death for thirty or forty years.

There were some twenty Bastilles in France, of which six only (in 1775) contained three hundred prisoners. At Paris, in 1779, there were about thirty prisons where people might be incarcerated without any sentence. An infinite number of convents were subsidiary to these Bastilles.

All these state-prisons, towards the close of the reign of Louis XIV., were, like everything else, controlled by the Jesuits. They were, in their hands, instruments of torture for the Protestants and the Jansenists—dens for conversion. A secrecy more profound than that of the *leads* and the *wells* of Venice, the oblivion of the tomb, enshrouded everything. The Jesuits were the confessors of the Bastille, and of many other prisons; the prisoners who died were buried under false names in the church of the Jesuits. Every means of terror was in their hands, especially those dungeons whence the prisoners occasionally came out with their ears or noses gnawed away by the rats. Not only of terror, but of flattery also—both so potent with female prisoners. The almoner, to render grace more efficacious, employed even *culinary* arguments, starving, feeding, pampering the fair captive according as she yielded or resisted. More than one state-prison is mentioned in which the gaolers and the Jesuits paid alternate visits to the female prisoners, and had children by them. One preferred to strangle herself.

The lieutenant of police went, from time to time, to breakfast at the Bastille. That was reckoned as a visit,—a magisterial supervision. That magistrate was ignorant of everything; and yet it was he alone who gave an account to the minister. One family, one dynasty, Châteauneuf, his son La Vrillière, and his grandson Saint-Florentin (who died in 1777) possessed, for a century, the department of the state-prisons and the *lettres-de-cachet*. For this dynasty to subsist, it was necessary to have prisoners; when the Protestants were liberated, their places were filled up with the Jansenists; next, they took men of letters, philosophers, the Voltaires, Frèrets, Diderots. The minister used to give generously blank *lettres-de-cachet* to the intendants, the bishops, and people in the administration. Saint-Florentin, alone, gave away as many as 50,000. Never had man's dearest treasure, liberty, been more lavishly squandered. These letters were the object of a profitable traffic; they were sold to fathers who wanted to get rid of their sons, and given to pretty women, who were inconvenienced by their husbands. This last cause of imprisonment was one of the most common.

And all through good-nature. The king was too good to refuse a *lettre-de-cachet* to a great lord. The intendant was too good-natured not to grant one at a lady's request. The government-clerks, the mistresses of the clerks, and the friends of these mistresses, through good-nature, civility, or mere politeness, obtained, gave, or lent, those terrible orders by which a man was buried alive. Buried;—for such was the carelessness and levity of those amiable clerks,—almost all nobles, fashionable men, all occupied with their pleasures,—that they never had the time, when once the poor fellow was shut up, to think of his position.

Thus, the *government of grace,* with all its advantages,—descending from the king to the lowest clerk in the administration,—disposed, according to caprice or fancy, of liberty, of life.

Let us understand this system well. Why does such a one succeed? What does he possess, that everything should thrive with him? He has the grace of God, and the king's good grace. Let him who is in disgrace, in this world of grace, go out of the world,—banished, sentenced, and damned.

The Bastille, the *lettre-de-cachet,* is the king's excommunication.

Are the excommunicated to die? No. It would require a decision of the king, a resolution painful to take, which would grieve the king himself. It would be a judgment between him and his conscience. Let us save him the task of judging, of killing. There is a middle term between life and death; a lifeless, buried life. Let us organize a world expressly for oblivion. Let us set falsehood at the gates within and without, in order that life and death be ever uncertain. The living corpse no longer knew anything about his family. "But my wife?" Thy wife is dead—I make a mistake—re-married. "Are any of my friends alive? Do they ever remember me?" "Thy friends, poor fool, why, they were the persons who betrayed thee." Thus the soul of the miserable prisoner, a prey to their ferocious merriment, is fed on derision, calumny, and lies.

Forgotten! O terrible word! That a soul should perish among souls! Had not he whom God created for life the right to live at least in the mind? What mortal shall dare inflict, even on the most guilty, this worst of deaths,—to be eternally forgotten?

No, do not believe it. Nothing is forgotten,—neither man nor thing. What once has been, cannot be thus annihilated. The very walls will not forget, the pavement will become accomplice, and convey sounds and noises; the air will not forget; from that small skylight, where a poor girl is sewing, at the Porte Saint-Antoine, they have seen and understood. Nay, the very Bastille itself will be affected. That surly turnkey is still a man. I see inscribed upon the walls the hymn of a prisoner to the glory of a gaoler, his benefactor.—Poor benefit! A shirt that he gave to that Lazarus, barbarously abandoned, devoured by vermin in his tomb!

Whilst I have been writing these lines, a mountain, a Bastille has been crushing my breast. Alas! why stay so long talking of dilapidated prisons, and wretches whom death has delivered? The world is covered with prisons, from Spielberg to Siberia, from Spandau to Mont-St.-Michel. The world is a prison!

Vast silence of the globe, stifled groans and sobs from the ever-silent earth, I hear you but too plainly. The captive mind, dumb among inferior animals, and musing in the barbarous world of Africa and Asia, thinks, and suffers in our Europe!

Where does it speak, if not in France, in spite of chains? It is ever here that the mute genius of the earth finds a voice,— an organ. The world thinks, France speaks.

And it is precisely on that account that the Bastille of France,

the Bastille of Paris (I would rather say the prison of thought),
was, of all other Bastilles, execrable, infamous, and accursed.
From the last century, Paris was already the voice of the globe.
The earth spoke by the voice of three men—Voltaire, Jean-
Jacques, and Montesquieu. That the interpreters of the world
should behold unworthy threats perpetually suspended over
them, that the narrow issue through which the agony of mankind
could breathe its sighs, should ever be shut up, was beyond
human endurance.

Our fathers shivered that Bastille to pieces, tore away its
stones with their bleeding hands, and flung them afar. Afterwards, they seized them again; and, having hewn them into a
different form, in order that they might be trampled under
foot by the people for ever, built with them the Bridge of
Revolution!

All other prisons had become more merciful; but this one
had become more cruel. From reign to reign, they diminished
what the gaolers would laughingly term,—the liberties of the
Bastille. The windows were walled up one after another, and
other bars were added. During the reign of Louis XVI., the
use of the garden and the walk on the towers were prohibited.

About this period two circumstances occurred which added
to the general indignation,—Linguet's memoirs, which made
people acquainted with the ignoble and ferocious interior; and,
what was more decisive, the unwritten, unprinted case of Latude: whispered mysteriously, and transmitted from mouth to
mouth, its effect was only rendered more terrible.

For my part, I must acknowledge the extremely agonizing
effect which the prisoner's letters produced on me. Though a
sworn enemy to barbarous fictions about everlasting punishments, I found myself praying to God to construct a hell for
tyrants.

Ah! M. de Sartines, Ah! Madame de Pompadour, how heavy
is your burden! How plainly do we perceive, by that history,
how, having once embraced injustice, we go on from bad
to worse; how terror, descending from the tyrant to the slave,
returns again more forcibly to torment the tyrant. Having once

kept this man a prisoner without judgment, for some trifling fault, Madame de Pompadour and M. de Sartines are obliged to hold him captive for ever, and seal over him with an eternal stone the hell of silence.

But that cannot be. That stone is ever restless; and a low, terrible voice—a sulphurous blast—is ever arising. In 1781, Sartines feels its dread effect,—in 1784, the king himself is hurt by it,—in 1789, the people know all, see all, even the ladder by which the prisoner escaped. In 1793, they guillotine the family of Sartines.

For the confusion of tyrants, it so happened that they had in that prisoner confined a daring, terrible man, whom nothing could subdue, whose voice shook the very walls, whose spirit and audacity were invincible. A body of iron, indestructible, which was to wear out all their prisons, the Bastille, Vincennes, Charenton, and lastly the horrors of Bicêtre, wherein any other would have perished.

What makes the accusation heavy, overwhelming, and without appeal, is, that this man, good or bad, after escaping twice, twice surrendered himself by his own acts. Once, from his hiding-place, he wrote to Madame de Pompadour, and she caused him to be seized again! The second time, he goes to Versailles, wishes to speak to the king, reaches his antechamber, and she orders him again to be seized. What! Not even in the king's apartment a sacred asylum?

I am unfortunately obliged to say that in the feeble, effeminate, declining society of that period, there were a great many philanthopists,—ministers, magistrates, and great lords, to mourn over the adventure; but not one stirred. Malesherbes wept, and so did Gourgues, and Lamoignon, and Rohan,—they all wept bitterly.

He was lying upon his dunghill at Bicêtre, *literally* devoured by vermin, lodged under ground, and often howling with hunger. He had addressed one more memorial to some philanthropist or other, by means of a drunken turnkey. The latter luckily lost it, and a woman picked it up. She read it, and shuddered; *she* did not weep, but acted instantly.

Madame Legros was a poor mercer who lived by her work,—
by sewing in her shop; her husband was a private teacher of
Latin. She did not fear to embark in that terrible undertaking.
She saw with her firm good sense what others did not, or
would not, see: that the wretched man was not mad, but the
victim of a frightful necessity, by which the government was
obliged to conceal and perpetuate the infamy of its old transgressions. She saw it, and was neither discouraged nor afraid.
No heroism was ever more complete: she had the courage to
undertake; the energy to persevere; and the obstinacy to sacrifice every day and every hour; the courage to despise the
threats, the sagacity, and saintly plots of every kind in order
to elude and foil the calumny of the tyrants.

For three consecutive years, she persevered in her endeavours
with an unheard-of obstinacy; employing in the pursuit of justice
and equity that singular eagerness peculiar to the huntsman
or the gamester, and to which we seldom resort but for the
gratification of our evil passions.

All kinds of misfortunes beset her; but she will not give up
the cause. Her father dies; then her mother; she loses her little
business, is blamed by her relations, nay, subjected to villainous
suspicion. They tax her with being the mistress of that prisoner
in whom she is so much interested. The mistress of that spectre,
that corpse, devoured with filth and vermin!

The temptation of temptations, the summit, the highest point
of the Calvary are the complaints, the injustices, the distrust
of that very man for whom she is wearing herself out, sacrificing
herself!

Oh! It is a grand sight to see that poor woman, so ill-
dressed, begging from door to door, courting the valets to gain
admittance into the mansions, pleading her cause before
grandees, and demanding their assistance.

The police are furious and indignant. Madame Legros may
be kidnapped, shut up, lost for ever; everybody gives her warning. The lieutenant of police sends for her, and threatens her;
he finds her firm and unalterable; it is she who makes him
tremble.

Happily, they manage to get her the protection of Madame

Duchesne, a *femme de chambre* to the princesses. She sets
out for Versailles, on foot, in the depth of winter; she was
in the seventh month of her pregnancy. The protectress was
absent; she runs after her, sprains her foot, but still runs on.
Madame Duchesne sheds many tears, but alas! what can she
do? One *femme de chambre* against two or three ministers;—
it is a difficult game! She was holding the petition, when an
abbé of the court, who happened to be present, tore it out of
her hands, telling her that it was all about a miserable mad-
man, and that she must not interfere.

A word of this sort was enough to freeze the heart of Marie
Antoinette, who had been told about the matter. She had tears
in her eyes; someone spoke in jest; all was over.

There was hardly a better man in France than the king.
At length they applied to him. Cardinal de Rohan (a debauchee,
but charitable after all) spoke three times to Louis XVI., who
thrice refused to interfere. Louis XVI. was too good not to
believe M. de Sartines. He was no longer in power, but that
was no reason for dishonouring him, and handing him over to
his enemies. Setting Sartines out of the question, we must say
that Louis XVI. was fond of the Bastille, and would not wrong
it, or injure its reputation.

The king was very humane. He had suppressed the deep
dungeons of the Châtelet, done away with Vincennes and created La Force to receive prisoners for debt, to separate them
from criminals.

But the Bastille! the Bastille! That was an old servant not
to be lightly ill-treated by the ancient monarchy. It was a
mystery of terror, what Tacitus calls, "Instrumentum regni."

When the count d'Artois and the Queen, wishing to have
Figaro played, read it to him, he merely observed, as an un-
answerable objection, "Then must the Bastille be suppressed?"

When the Revolution of Paris took place, in July 1789, the
king, indifferent enough, seemed to be reconciled to the matter.
But when he was informed that the Parisian municipality had
ordered the demolition of the Bastille, he seemed as if he had
been shot to the heart; "Oh!" said he, "this is awful!"

He was unable, in 1781, to listen to a request that compromised the Bastille. He rejected also the one which Rohan presented to him in favour of Latude. But noble ladies insisted. He then made a conscientious study of the business, read all the papers; they were few, save those of the police and people interested in keeping the victim in prison until death. At length he decided that he was a dangerous man, and that he could *never* restore him to liberty.

Never! Any other person would have stopped there. Well then, what is not done by the king shall be done in spite of him. Madame Legros persists. She is well received by the Condé family, ever discontented and grumbling; welcomed by the young duke of Orleans and his kind-hearted spouse, the daughter of the good Penthièvre; and hailed by the philosophers, by the Marquis de Condorcet, perpetual secretary of the Academy of Sciences, by Dupaty, by Villette, Voltaire's quasi son-in-law, &c. &c.

The public voice murmurs louder and louder, like a flood, or the waves of the rising tide. Necker had dismissed Sartines; his friend and successor, Lenoir, had also fallen in his turn. Perseverance will presently be crowned. Latude is obstinately bent on living, and Madame Legros as obstinately bent on delivering Latude.

The queen's man, Breteuil, succeeds in 1783; he wants to win admirers for her. He allows the Academy to award the prize for virtue to Madame Legros, to crown her—on the singular condition that no reasons for the award be given.

At length, in 1784, they force from Louis XVI, the deliverance of Latude.[9] And a few weeks after, comes a strange and whimsical ordinance enjoining the intendants never more to incarcerate anybody, at the request of families, without a *well-grounded reason*, and to indicate the *duration of confinement,* &c. That is to say, they unveiled the depth of the monstrous abyss of arbitrariness into which France had been plunged. She already knew much; but the government confessed still more.

---

[9] Latude's admirable letters are still unpublished, save the few quoted by Delort. They refute but too well the vain polemics of 1787.

From the priest to the king, from the Inquisition to the Bastille, the road is straight, but long. Holy, holy Revolution, how slowly dost thou come!—I, who have been waiting for thee for a thousand years in the furrows of the middle ages,—what! must I wait still longer?—Oh! how slowly time passes! Oh! how I have counted the hours!—Wilt thou never arrive?

Men believed no longer in its near approach. All had foreseen the Revolution in the middle of the century. Nobody, at the end, believed in it. Far from Mont-Blanc, you see it; when at its foot, you see it no more.

"Alas! it is all over," said Mably, in 1784; "we have fallen too low; morals have become too depraved. Never, oh! never now will the Revolution appear!"

O ye of little faith, do you not see that as long as it remained among you, philosophers, orators, sophists, it could do nothing? God be praised, now it is everywhere, among the people and in women.—Here is one who, by her persevering, unconquerable will, bursts open the prisons of State; she has taken the Bastille beforehand.—The day when liberty—reason, emerges from arguments, and descends into nature, into the heart (and the heart of hearts is woman), all is over. Everything artificial is destroyed.—O Rousseau, now we understand thee; thou wast truly right in saying, "Return to nature!"

A woman is fighting at the Bastille. Women accomplish the 5th of October. As early as February 1789, I read with emotion the courageous letter of the women and girls of Angers: "Having read the decrees of the male portion of our youthful community (*messieurs de la jeunesse*), we declare that *we will join the nation,* reserving to ourselves the care of the baggage and provisions, and such consolations and services as may depend on us; we will perish rather than abandon our husbands, lovers, sons, and brothers."

O France, you are saved! O world, you are saved!—Again do I behold in the heavens my youthful star in which I so long placed my hope,—the star of Joan of Arc. What matters, if the maid, changing her sex, has become a youth, Hoche, Marceau, Joubert, or Kléber!

Grand period, sublime moment, when the most warlike of men are nevertheless the harbingers of peace! When Right, so long wept for, is found at the end of ages; when Grace, in whose name Tyranny had crushed us, is found to be consonant, identical with Justice.

What is the old regime, the king and the priest in the old monarchy? Tyranny, in the name of Grace.

What is the Revolution? The re-action of equity, the tardy advent of Eternal Justice.

O Justice, my mother! Right, my father! ye who are but one with God!

Whom else should I invoke, I, one of the crowd, one of those ten millions of men, who would never have existed but for our Revolution.

O Justice, pardon me! I believed you were austere and hardhearted, and I did not perceive that you were identical with Love and Grace. And that is why I have been no enthusiast of the middle ages, which have ever repeated the word Love without performing the offices of Love.

But now, absorbed in deep reflection, and with all the ardour of my heart, I humbly crave forgiveness, O heavenly Justice of God.

For thou art truly Love, and identical with Grace.

And as thou art Justice, thou wilt support me in this book, where my path has been marked out by the emotions of my heart and not by private interest, nor by any thought of this sublunar world. Thou wilt be just towards me, and I will be so towards all. For whom then have I written this, but for thee, Eternal Justice?

JANUARY 31st, 1847

BOOK I

APRIL TO JULY, 1789

I

Elections of 1789

THE convocation of the Estates-General, in 1789, is the true era of the birth of the people. It called the whole nation to the exercise of their rights.

They could at least write their complaints, their wishes, and choose the electors.

Small republican states had already admitted all their members to a participation of political rights; but never had a great kingdom,—an empire like France. The thing was new, not only in French annals, but even in those of the world.

Accordingly, when, for the first time, in the course of ages, these words were heard: *All* shall assemble to elect,[1] *all* shall send in their complaints, there was an immense, profound commotion, like an earthquake; the mass felt the shock even in obscure and mute regions, where movement would have been least expected.

All the towns elected, and not the *good* towns only, as in the ancient Estates-General; country districts also elected, and not the towns alone.

It is affirmed that five million men took part in the election.

Grand, strange, surprising scene! To see a whole people

---

[1] See the *Actes* in the first vol. of the *Moniteur*. The *tax-payers of more than twenty-five years of age* were to choose the electors, who were to name the deputies, and concur in the drawing-up of the *returns*. As taxation affected everybody, at least by poll-tax, the whole of the population, excepting servants, was thus called upon.

emerging, at once, from nonentity to existence, who, till then silent, suddenly found a voice.

The same appeal of equality was addressed to populations, prodigiously unequal, not only in status, but in culture, in their moral state and ideas. How would that people answer? That was a great question. The exchequer on one side, feudality on the other,[2] seemed striving to brutalise them under the weight of miseries. Royalty had deprived them of their municipal rights,—of that education which they derived from business connected with the commune. The clergy, the teachers thrust upon them, had not taught them for a long time past. They seemed to have done everything to render them dull, dumb, speechless, and senseless, and then they said to them, "Arise now, walk, and speak!"

They had relied, too much relied, upon that incapacity; otherwise they would never have ventured to make this great move. The first who pronounced the name of the Estates-General,—the *parlements* which demanded them,—the ministers who promised them,—Necker who convoked them,—all, believed the people incapable of taking any serious part therein. They only thought, by this solemn convocation of a great lifeless mass, to frighten the privileged classes. The court, which was itself the privilege of privileges, the abuse of abuses, had no desire to make war on them. It merely hoped, by the forced contributions of the clergy and nobility, to fill the public coffers, from which they filled their own.

And what did the queen desire? Given up to *parvenus,* lampooned by the nobility, gradually despised, and alone, she wanted to have a slight revenge on those revilers, to intimidate them, and oblige them to rally round the king. She saw her brother Joseph attempting, in the Netherlands, to oppose the smaller towns to the larger, to the prelates and grandees.[3] That

---

[2] This expression is not ill-employed. Feudality was very oppressive in 1789, more fiscal than ever, being entirely in the hands of intendants, attorneys, &c. Names and forms had changed,—nothing more.

[3] See, for the revolution in Brabant, so different from ours, the documents collected by Gachard (1834), Gerard (1842), and the histories by Gross-

example, doubtless, rendered her less adverse to Necker's ideas; she consented to give to the *Tiers* (or Third Estate) as many deputies as the nobility and clergy had together.

And what did Necker desire? Two things at once,—to pretend much and do little.

For ostentation, for glory,—to be celebrated and extolled by the salons and the immense body of the public, it was necessary to double generously the number of the deputies of the Third Estate.

In reality, they wanted to be generous at a cheap price.[4] The Third Estate, more or less numerous, would never be anything but one of three orders,—would have but one vote against two; Necker reckoned surely on maintaining the voting by orders, which had so often before paralysed the ancient Estates-General. The Third Estate, moreover, had at all times been very modest, very respectful, too well-bred to wish to be represented by men of its own class. It had often named nobles for deputies, mostly newly-created nobles, *parlement* people and others, who prided themselves on voting with the nobility, against the interests of the Third Estate which had named them.

A strange circumstance, but a proof that they had no real intention,—that they merely wanted by this grand phantasma-

---

Hoffinger (1837), Borgnet (1844), and Ramshorn (1845). That revolution of *abbés*, of which the Capuchin-friars were the terrorists, deceived everybody here (in France), both the court and our Jacobins. Dumouriez alone comprehended, and said, that it was primitively the work of the powerful *abbés* of the Netherlands. M. Mercy d'Argenteau, the Austrian ambassador, believed at first, and doubtless made Marie-Antoinette believe, that in France, as in Belgium, the peril was on the side of the aristocracy. Hence, many false steps.

[4] For all this, one must see Necker's curious confessions, his pleading for the Third Estate. (*Oeuvres,* vi., 419, 443, &c.) Therein, as in all his works, one always perceives the foreigner anything but esteemed in France, a clerk ever clerk-like, who stands bowing before the nobility,—a Protestant who wants to find grace with the clergy. To reassure the privileged classes about the poor Third Estate, he presents it to them feeble, timid, and subservient; he seems to be secretly signaling to them. He, moreover, gives them to understand that his client is an easy sort of person,—easily duped.

goria, to overcome the selfishness of the privileged classes, and open their purses, is, that in these Estates, called against them, they managed nevertheless to secure them a predominant influence.[5] The popular assemblies were to elect by acclamation (*à haute voix*). They did not suppose that inferior people, in such a mode of election, in presence of the nobles and notables, would possess sufficient firmness to oppose them,—enough assurance to pronounce other names than those which were dictated to them.

In calling the people of the country, of the villages, to the election, Necker, no doubt, expected to do something very political; in proportion as the democratic spirit was aroused in the towns, in such proportion the country-places were influenced by the nobles and the clergy,—the possessors of two thirds of the lands. Millions of men arrived thus at election, who were dependent on the privileged classes, as tenants, cultivators, &c., or who indirectly would be influenced, or intimidated, by their agents, stewards, attorneys, and men of business. Necker knew, from the experience of Switzerland and the history of the petty cantons, that universal suffrage may be, in certain conditions, the stay of the aristocracy. The notables whom he consulted, so completely adopted this idea, that they wanted to make even their servants electors. Necker would not consent to it, as then the election would have fallen entirely into the hands of the large proprietors.

The result deceived all their calculations.[6] This people, though wholly unprepared, showed a very sure instinct. When they were called to election and informed of their rights, it was

---

[5] The privileged orders were doubly favoured: 1st. They were not subjected to the two degrees of election; they elected their deputies in a direct manner. 2dly. The nobles were *all* electors, and not *the nobles who had fiefs* exclusively, as in the ancient states; the privilege was the more odious still, as being extended to a whole generation of nobles; the pretensions were the more ridiculous.

[6] Very uncertain calculations. The king confesses, in the convocation of Paris, that he does not know the number of the inhabitants of the best-known town in the kingdom, that he cannot guess the number of the electors, &c.

found that little remained to be taught them. In that prodigious movement of five or six millions of men, there was some sort of hesitation, through their ignorance of forms, and especially, because the majority knew not how to read. But they knew how to speak; they knew how, in presence of their lords, without infringing upon their respectful habits, or laying aside their humble demeanour, to select worthy electors, who all nominated safe and certain deputies.

The admission of the country districts to election had the unexpected result of placing even among the deputies of the privileged orders a numerous democracy, of whom they had never thought, two hundred *curés* and more, very hostile to their bishops. In Brittany, and in the South, the peasant willingly nominated his *curé*, who, moreover, alone knowing how to write, received the votes, and directed all the election.[7]

The people of the towns, rather better prepared, having been somewhat enlightened by the philosophy of the age, evinced an admirable eagerness, a lively consciousness of their rights. This appeared plain at the elections, by the rapidity, the certainty with which crowds of inexperienced men took this their first political step. It appeared evident in the uniformity of the memorials (*cahiers*) in which they recorded their complaints,—an unexpected, powerful combination, which imparted irresistible strength to the will of the people. How long had those complaints existed in every heart! It was but too easy to write them. Many a memorial of our districts, containing almost a code, was begun at midnight, and finished at three in the morning.[8]

A movement so vast, so varied, so wholly unprepared, and yet so unanimous, is most wonderful! All took part in it, and (except an insignificant number) they all desired the same thing.[9]

---

[7] However, in several *communes*, sworn scriveners were appointed to write down the votes.—Duchatellier, *La Révolution en Bretagne,* i., 281.

[8] *Mémoires de Bailly,* i., 12.

[9] The same thing in every essential point. To which every corporation and every town added something special.

Unanimous! There was a complete and unreserved concord, a perfectly simple state of things,—the nation on one side and privilege on the other. Yet, there was no possible distinction then in the nation between the people and the citizens; [10] only one distinction appeared,—the instructed and the ignorant; the educated alone spoke and wrote; but they wrote the thoughts of all. They drew up into a formula the general demands; and they were the demands of the mute masses as much as, and more than their own.

Oh! who would not be touched by the remembrance of that unrivalled moment, when we started into life? It was short-lived; but it remains for us the ideal whereunto we shall ever tend, the hope of the future! O sublime Concord, in which the rising liberties of classes, subsequently in opposition, embraced so tenderly, like brothers in the cradle,—shall we never more see thee return upon our earth?

This union of the different classes, this grand appearance of the people in their formidable unity, struck terror to the court which used every effort with the king to prevail on him to break his word. The Polignac faction had contrived, in order to place him in an uncomfortable position, to get the princes to write and sign an audacious letter in which they menaced the king, assumed to be the chiefs of the privileged classes, spoke of refusing taxes, of divisions, almost of civil war.

And yet, how could the king elude the Estates? Recommended by the Court of Aids, demanded by the *parlements* and by the Notables, promised by Brienne, and again by Necker, they were at length to open on the 27th of April. They were further prorogued till the 4th of May. A perilous delay! To so many voices then arising another was added, alas! one often heard in the eighteenth century,—*the voice of the earth—*

---

[10] It was a vital error of the authors of the *Histoire Parlementaire*, to mark this distinction at that important moment when nobody saw it. It will come but too soon; we must wait. Thus to be blind to the real consequence of facts, and to drag them forcibly forward before their time by a sort of systematic pre-arrangement, is precisely contrary to history.

the desolate, sterile earth refusing food to man! The winter had been terrible; the summer was dry and gave nothing: and famine began. The bakers being uneasy, and always in peril before the starving riotous crowd, themselves denounced companies who were monopolising the wheat. Only one thing restrained the people, and made them fast patiently and wait,—their hope in the Estates-General. A vague hope; but it supported them; the forthcoming assembly was a Messiah; it had only to speak, and the stones were to change into bread.

The elections, so long delayed, were still longer postponed at Paris. They were not convoked till the eve of the assembling of the Estates. It was hoped that the deputies would not be present at the first sittings, and that before their arrival, they would secure the separation of the three orders, which gave a majority to the privileged.

There was another cause for discontent, and one most serious for Paris. In that city, the most enlightened in the kingdom, election was subjected to more severe conditions. A special regulation, made after the convocation, called, as primary electors, not all who were taxed, but those only who paid a rate of six francs.

Paris was filled with troops, every street with patrols, and every place of election surrounded with soldiers. Arms were loaded in the street, in face of the crowd.

In presence of these vain demonstrations, the electors were very firm. Scarcely had they met, when they rejected the presidents given to them by the king. Out of sixty districts, three only re-appointed the president named by the monarch, making him declare that he presided by election. A serious measure,—the first act of the national sovereignty. And it was indeed that which it was necessary to acquire,—it was Right that it was necessary to found. Questions of finance and reform would come afterwards. Without Right, what guarantee was there, or what serious reform?

The electors, created by these district assemblies, acted in precisely the same manner. They elected as president the advocate Target; Camus, the advocate of the clergy, as vice-president, and the academician Bailly and Doctor Guillotin, a philanthropical physician, as secretaries.[11]

The court was astonished at the decision, firmness, and regularity, with which twenty-five thousand primary electors, so new to political life, then proceeded. There was no disturbance. Assembled in the churches, they transferred thither the emotion of the great and holy task they were accomplishing. The boldest measure, the destitution of the presidents named by the king, was effected without any noise or exclamation, with the forcible simplicity imparted by a consciousness of right.

The electors, under a president of their choice, were sitting at the Archbishop's Palace, and about to make a total of the district polls, and to draw up one common resolution; they were already agreed on one point, which Sieyès had recommended,—the utility of prefacing with a declaration of the rights of man. In the middle of this delicate and difficult metaphysical task, they were interrupted by a terrible uproar. A ragged multitude had come to demand the head of one of their colleagues, of Réveillon, an elector,—a paper-manufacturer in the Faubourg Saint-Antoine. Réveillon was concealed; but the riot was not less dangerous on that account. It was now the 28th of April; the Estates-General, promised for the 27th, and then postponed again till the 4th of May, ran a great risk, if the riots lasted, of being adjourned once more.

The riot broke out precisely on the 27th, and it was but too easy to spread, entertain, and increase it, among a starving population. A report had been spread in the Faubourg Saint-Antoine, that Réveillon, the paper-manufacturer,—a workman grown rich,—had said unfeelingly that it was necessary to lower wages to fifteen sous a day; and, it was added, that he was to

---

[11] This assembly, so firm in its first proceedings, was nevertheless composed of notables, functionaries, merchants, or advocates. The latter led the assembly; they were Camus, Target, Treilhard, the advocate of the *Ferme Générale*, Lacretelle Senior, and Desèze. In the second rank came the academicians,—Bailly, Thouin, and Cadet, Gaillard, Suard, Marmontel. Next, the bankers, such as Lecouteulx, and the printers, librarians, and stationers, Pankoucke, Baudouin, Réveillon, &c.

receive the decoration of the *cordon-noir*. That report was followed by a great commotion. First, a band, in front of Réveillon's door, take his effigy, decorated with the *cordon*, carry it in
procession to La Grève, and burn it with much ceremony beneath the windows of the Hôtel-de-Ville, before the eyes of the
municipal authority, who remain perfectly unmoved. This authority and the others, so vigilant just before, seemed fast
asleep. The lieutenant of police, the prevost Flesselles, and
Berthier the intendant,—all those court-agents, who lately surrounded the elections with soldiers, had lost their activity.

The band exclaimed aloud that it would go, on the morrow,
to do justice at Réveillon's. It kept its word. The police, though
so well warned, used no precaution. The colonel of the French
Guards sends, of his own accord, some thirty men,—a ridiculous
force; in a compact crowd of a thousand or two thousand
pillagers and a hundred thousand idle spectators, the soldiers
will not, cannot, act. The house is broken open, and everything
demolished, shattered to pieces, and burnt. Nothing was carried away, except five hundred *louis d'or*.[12] Many took up their
quarters in the cellars, drank the wine, and the colours of the
manufactory, mistaking them for wine.

What seems incredible is, that this shameful scene lasted all
day. It took place too at the very entrance of the faubourg,

---

[12] According to the statement of Réveillon himself: *Exposé justificatif*, p.
422, (printed at the end of Ferrieres). The *Histoire Parlementaire* is again
inexact here. It makes of all this, without the least proof, a war of the
people against the citizens. It exaggerates the extent of the riot, the
number of the dead, &c. Bailly, on the contrary, and no less wrongfully, in
p. 28 of his Memoirs, reduces it to nothing: "Nobody perished, as far as I
know." A very important testimony, on the Réveillon riot, is that of the
illustrious surgeon Desault, who received several of the wounded at the
Hôtel-Dieu: "*Ils n'avaient l'air que du crime foudroyé; au contraire, les
blessés de la Bastille*," &c.: See *l'Oeuvre des sept Jours*, p. 411. What
showed plainly that the people did not consider the pillage of Réveillon's
house as a patriotic act is, that they were near hanging, on the 16th of
July, a man whom they mistook for the *abbé* Roy, *accused of having
excited this riot* (Bailly, ii., p. 51), and of having subsequently offered to
the court a means of slaughtering Paris.—(*Procès-verbal des Électeurs*, ii,
p. 46.)

under the cannon of the Bastille, at the gate of the fort. Réveillon, who was concealed there, saw all from the towers.

A few companies of the French Guards were sent from time to time, who fired, first with powder, and next with ball. The pillagers paid no attention to them, though they had only stones to throw in return. Late, very late, the commandant, Besenval, sent some Swiss; the pillagers still resisted, and killed a few men; the soldiers replied by some destructive discharges, which left a number of dead and wounded on the pavement. Many of these bodies in rags had money about them.

If, during those two long days, when the magistrates were asleep and Besenval abstained from sending troops, the faubourg Saint-Antoine had allowed itself to be seduced to follow the band that was sacking Réveillon's house,—if fifty thousand workmen, without either work or bread, had, on that example, set about pillaging the rich mansions, everything would have changed its aspect; the court would then have had an excellent motive to concentrate an army on Paris and Versailles, and a specious pretext for adjourning the Estates. But the great mass of the faubourg remained honest, and abstained; it looked on, without moving. The riot, thus confined to a few hundred people, drunkards and thieves, became a disgrace to the authority that permitted it. Besenval at length found his part too ridiculous; he acted, and ended the whole affair abruptly. The court did not thank him for it; it durst not blame him, but it did not say one word to him.[13]

The *parlement* could not, for its honour, dispense with opening an inquiry; but the inquiry stopped short. It has been said,

---

[13] *Mémoires de Besenval,* ii., p. 347. Madame de Genlis and other friends of the *ancien régime,* will have it, that these memoirs, so overwhelming against them, were drawn up by the Vicomte de Ségur. Let it be so: he must then have written from the notes and memory of Besenval. The memoirs do not the less belong to the latter. Besenval was, I know, but little able to write; but without his *confidence,* the amiable lampooner would never have made this book so strong, so historical under an aspect of levity; the truth bursts forth and shines there, often with a terrible light; nothing remains but to cast down our eyes.

without sufficient proof, that it was forbidden in the king's name to proceed.

Who were the instigators? Perhaps nobody. Fire, on those stormy occasions, may burst forth of its own accord. People did not fail to accuse "the revolutionary party." What was that party? As yet, there was no active association.

It was said that the Duke of Orleans had given money. Why? What did he then gain by it? The great movement then beginning offered to his ambition too many legal chances, for him, at that period, to need to have recourse to riots. True, he was led on by intriguing persons, ready for anything; but their plan at this period was entirely directed towards the Estates-General; they felt sure, from their duke being the only popular one among the princes, that he was about to take the lead. Every event that might delay the Estates, appeared to them a misfortune.

Who desired to delay them? Who found an advantage in terrifying the electors? Who derived a profit from riot?

The court alone, we must confess. The affair happened so exactly at the right time for it, that it might be believed to be the author. It is nevertheless more probable that it did not begin it, but saw it with pleasure, did nothing to prevent it, and regretted it was so soon over. The faubourg Saint-Antoine had not then its terrible reputation; a riot under the very cannon of the Bastille did not seem dangerous.

The nobles of Brittany had given an example of troubling the legal operations of the provincial Estates, by exciting the peasants, and pitting against the people a populace mingled with lackeys. Even at Paris, a newspaper, the *Ami du Roi*, a few days before the Réveillon affair, seemed to be attempting the same manoeuvre:—"What matter these elections?" said this journal, in a hypocritical tone, "the poor will ever be poor; the lot of the most interesting portion of the kingdom is forgotten," &c. As if the first results of the Revolution which these elections were beginning,—the suppression of tithes and that of the *octroi* duties, and the *aides*, and the sale, at a low price, of half the lands in the kingdom, had not produced the most sudden amelioration in the condition of the poor that any people had ever witnessed!

On the morning of the 29th, all had become quiet again. The assembly of the electors was able peaceably to resume its labours. They lasted till the 20th of May; and the court obtained the advantage that it had proposed to itself by this tardy convocation,—the preventing the deputation of Paris from being present at the first sittings of the Estates-General. The last person elected by Paris, and by France, was he who, in public opinion, was the first of all, he who had traced beforehand for the Revolution so straight and simple a path, and had marked its first steps, one by one. Everything was marching forward, according to the plan given by Sieyès with a motion majestic, pacific, and firm, like the Law. Law alone was about to reign; after so many ages of despotism and caprice, the time was arriving when nobody would be right against Right.

Let, then, those dreaded Estates-General at length assemble and open. They who convoked them, and now would wish they had never spoken of them, cannot alter the matter. It is a rising ocean: causes infinite and profound, acting from the depths of ages, agitate the boiling mass. Bring against it, I pray you, all the armies in the world, or an infant's finger; it makes no difference. God is urging it forward: tardy justice, the expiation of the past, the salvation of the future!

II

Opening of the Estates-General

On the eve of the opening of the Estates-General, the Mass of the Holy Ghost was solemnly said at Versailles. It was certainly that day or never, that they might sing the prophetic hymn:—"Thou wilt create peoples, and the face of the earth shall be renewed."

That great day was the 4th of May. The twelve hundred deputies, the king, the queen, the whole court, heard the *Veni Creator* at the Church of Notre-Dame. Next, the immense procession, passing through the whole town, repaired to Saint-Louis. The broad streets of Versailles, lined with French guards and Swiss, and hung with the crown tapestry, could not contain the crowd. All Paris was there. The windows, the very roofs, were loaded with people. The balconies were adorned with precious stuffs, and ornamented with brilliant women, in the coquettish and whimsical costume of that period, diversified with feathers and flowers. All that mass of beings was moved, affected, full of anxiety and hope.[14] Something grand was beginning. What would be its progress, issue, and results? who could tell? The splendour of such a sight, so varied and majestic, and the music which was heard at different intervals, silenced every other thought.

A great day,—the last of peace, yet the first of an immense future!

---

[14] See the eye-witnesses, Ferrières, Staël, &c.

95

The passions were doubtless strong, diverse, and opposite, but not embittered, as they soon became. Even they who had the least desired this new era, could not help sharing the common emotion. A deputy of the nobility confesses that he wept for joy: "I saw France, my native land, reclining on Religion, saying to us: 'Stifle your quarrels.' Tears flowed from my eyes. My God, my country, my fellow-citizens, had become myself."

At the head of the procession appeared first a mass of men clothed in black,—the strong, deep battalion of the five hundred and fifty deputies of the Third Estate; in that number, more than three hundred jurists, advocates, or magistrates, represented forcibly the advent of the law. Modest in their dress, firm in their look and deportment, they marched forward still united, without any distinction of party, all happy on that grand day, which they had made and which was their victory.

The brilliant little troop of the deputies of the nobility came next with their plumed hats, their laces, and gold ornaments. The applause that had welcomed the Third Estate suddenly ceased. Among those nobles, however, about forty seemed as warm friends of the people as the men of the Third-Estate.

The same silence for the clergy. In this order, two orders were distinctly perceptible: a Nobility and a Third Estate: some thirty prelates in lawn sleeves and violet robes; and apart, and separated from them by a choir of musicians, the humble troop of the two hundred *curés*, in their black, priestly robes.

On beholding that imposing mass of twelve hundred men animated with noble passion, an attentive spectator would have been struck with one thing in particular. They presented very few strongly-delineated individualities; doubtless many men both honourable and of highly prized talents, but none of those who, by the united authority of genius and character, have the right to transport the multitude,—no great inventor,—no hero. The powerful innovators who had opened the way for that century, then existed no more. Their thought alone remained to guide nations. Great orators arose to express and apply that thought; but they did not add to it. The glory of the Revolution in her earlier moments,—but her peril also,—which might render her less certain in her progress, was to go without men, to go alone, by the transport of ideas, on the faith of pure reason, without idols and false gods.

The body of the nobility, which presented itself as the depositary and guardian of our military glory, showed not one celebrated general. "Obscure men of illustrious origin were all those grand lords of France." One alone perhaps excited some interest, he who, in spite of the court, had been the first to take a part in the American war,—the young and fair Lafayette. Nobody then suspected the prominent part which fortune was about to thrust upon him. The Third Estate, in its obscure mass, already contained the Convention. But who could have seen it? Who recognised, among that crowd of advocates, the stiff form and pale face of a certain lawyer of Arras?

Two things were noticed: the absence of Sieyès, and the presence of Mirabeau.

Sieyès had not yet come: in that grand movement, people looked for him whose singular sagacity had seen, regulated, calculated, and directed it beforehand.

Mirabeau was present, and attracted everybody's attention. His immense mass of hair, his lion-like head, stamped with extreme ugliness, were astounding, almost frightful; nobody could take his eyes off him. He indeed was visibly a man, and the others were but shadows,—a man, unfortunately, of his time and class, vicious, like the higher society of the day, moreover scandalous, noisy, and courageous in vice: that is what ruined him. The world was full of the romance of his adventures, amours, and passions. For he had had passions, violent, furious ones. Who then had such passions? And the tyranny of those passions, so exacting and absorbing, had often led him very low. Poor by the harsh treatment of his family, he suffered moral misery, the vices of the poor besides those of the rich. Family tyranny, state tyranny, moral, internal tyranny,—that of passion. Ah! nobody could hail more fervently that aurora of liberty. He did not despair of there finding liberty, the regeneration of the soul; he used to say so to his friends.[15] He was about to grow

---

[15] Et. Dumont, *Souvenirs*, p. 27.

young with France, and throw aside his old stained cloak. Only, it was necessary to live longer; on the threshold of this new life opening before him, though strong, ardent, and impassioned, he had nevertheless seriously injured his constitution; his complexion was altered, and his cheeks had fallen. No matter! He still bore his enormous head erect, and his looks were full of audacity. Everybody sensed that his would be the resounding voice of France.

The Third Estate was in general applauded; next, among the nobility, the Duke of Orleans alone; and lastly the King, whom they thanked for having convoked the Estates. Such was the justice of the people.

On the passage of the Queen, there were a few murmurs; a few women shouted: *"Vive le duc d'Orléans!"* thinking to pique her the more by naming her enemy. This made a great impression upon her; she was nearly fainting, and they had to support her; [16] but she recovered very soon, carrying erect her haughty and still handsome countenance. She attempted from that moment to meet the public hatred with a steadfast, disdainful stare. A sad effort, which did not heighten her beauty. In her solemn portrait which was left us in 1788, by her painter, Madame Lebrun, who loved her, and must have let her affection influence the work, we perceive nevertheless something already repulsive, disdainful, and hardened.[17]

Thus this grand festival of peace and union, showed symptoms of war. It pointed out a day for France to unite and embrace in one common thought, and at the same time went the very way to divide it. On merely beholding that diversity of costumes imposed on the deputies, one found the harsh but

---

[16] Campan, ii., p. 37.

[17] Compare the three portraits at Versailles. In the first (in white satin) she is a coquette, still pleasing; she feels she is loved. In the second (in red velvet and furs) surrounded by her children; her daughter is leaning gently upon her; but all in vain; the want of feeling is incurable; her look is fixed, dull, and singularly harsh (1787). In the third (in blue velvet, 1788), alone, with a book in her hand, quite a queen, but melancholy and unfeeling.

true expression of Sieyès at once realised: "Three orders? no: three nations!"

The court had hunted into old books, to find out the odious details of a gothic ceremonial, those oppositions of classes, those signs of social distinctions and hatred which it should rather have buried in oblivion. Blazonry, figures, and symbols, after Voltaire, after Figaro! It was late. To tell the truth, it was not so much the mania for old costumes that had guided the court, as the secret pleasure of mortifying and lowering those petty people who, at the elections, had been acting the part of kings, and to remind them of their low origin. Weakness was playing at the dangerous game of humiliating the strong for the last time.

As early as the 3rd of May, on the eve of the Mass of the Holy Ghost, the deputies being presented at Versailles, the king, at that moment of cordiality and easy emotion, chilled the deputies, who had almost all arrived favourably disposed towards him. Instead of receiving them mingled together by provinces, he made them enter by orders: the clergy, the nobility first—then, after a pause, the Third Estate.

They would willingly have imputed such petty insolence to the officers and valets; but Louis XVI. showed but too plainly that he himself was tenacious of the old ceremonial. At the sitting on the 5th, the king having covered himself, and the nobility after him, the Third Estate wished to do the same; but the king, to prevent it from thus assuming an equality with the nobility, preferred to uncover himself.

Who would believe that this mad court remembered and regretted the absurd custom of making the Third Estate harangue on their knees. They were unwilling to dispense with this ceremony expressly, and preferred deciding that the president of the Third should make no speech whatever. That is to say, that, at the end of two hundred years of separation and silence, the king dismissed his people and forbade them to speak.

On the 5th of May, the Assembly opened, not in the king's palace, but in the Paris avenue, in the *Salle des Menus*. That hall, which unfortunately no longer exists, was immense; it was able to contain, besides the twelve hundred deputies, four thousand auditors.

An eye-witness, Madame de Staël, Necker's daughter, who had gone thither to behold her father applauded, tells us accordingly that he was so, and that on Mirabeau taking his place, a few murmurs were heard. Murmurs against the immoral man? That brilliant society, dying of its vices, and present at its last festival, had no right to be severe.[18]

The Assembly had to endure three speeches,—the king's, that of the keeper of the seals, and Necker's, all on the same text, and all unworthy of the occasion. The king at length found himself in presence of the nation, and he had no paternal speech to utter, not one word from his heart for their hearts. The exordium was an awkward, timid, sullen grumbling about the spirit of innovation. He expressed his sensibility for the two superior orders, "who showed themselves disposed to renounce their pecuniary privileges." A preoccupation with money prevailed throughout the three discourses; little or nothing on the question of right, that which filled and exalted every soul, the right of equality. The king and his two ministers, in awkward phrase, in which bombastic style contends alternately with baseness, seem convinced that the matter in question is merely one of taxation, of money, subsistence,—a question of feeding. They believe that if the privileged classes grant, as alms, to the Third Estate an equality of taxation, everything will be amicably settled at once.[19] Hence, three eulogies, in the three

---

[18] "When the king went and placed himself upon the throne, in the middle of that assembly, I experienced, for the first time, a feeling of dread. First, I noticed that the queen was much moved; she arrived later than the hour appointed, and the colour of her complexion was altered."— Staël, *Considérations*, i., ch. xvi.

[19] First, to speak only of money, what was called the *impôt* was but a very small portion of the total impost, of what was paid under different names to the clergy and nobility, as tithes or feudal tributes. And then again, money was not all. For the people, the question was not to pick up a few sous flung to them, but indeed to assume their rights: nothing more and nothing less.

speeches, on the sacrifice of the superior orders, who are so kind as to forego their exemption. These eulogies go on even *crescendo* up to Necker, who sees no heroism in history comparable to it.

These eulogies, which look rather like an invitation, announce too clearly that this admirable and extolled sacrifice is not yet made. Let it be made then, and quickly! This is the whole question for the king and the ministers, who have called the Third Estate there as a bugbear, and would willingly send it away. They have as yet but partial, dubious assurances of that great sacrifice: a few lords have offered it, but they have been laughed at by the others. Several members of the clergy, contrary to the known opinion of the Assembly of the clergy, have given the same hope, The two orders are in no great haste to explain themselves in this matter; the decisive word cannot leave their lips; it sticks in their throat. It requires two months, and the most serious and terrible circumstances,—the victory of the Third Estate,—for the clergy, on the 26th of June, at length subdued, to renounce, and even then the nobility to *promise* only to do the same.

Necker spoke for three hours on finance and morality: "There is nothing," said he, "without public morality and private morality." His speech was not the less on that account an immoral enumeration of the means possessed by the king to do without the Estates-General, and continue despotism. The Estates, from that moment, were a pure gift, a granted and revocable favour.

He avowed imprudently that the king was *uneasy*. He expressed the desire that the two superior orders, remaining alone and free, should accomplish their sacrifices, with the exception that they might unite with the Third Estate in order subsequently to discuss questions of common interest. A dangerous insinuation! The minister being once free to derive the taxes from those rich sources of large property, would not have insisted much on obtaining the union of the orders. The privileged classes would have preserved their false majority; and two orders leagued against one would have prevented every reform. What matter! Bankruptcy being avoided, scarcity having ceased, and public opinion slumbering again, the question of right of security was adjourned, and inequality and despotism strengthened; Necker reigned, or rather the court, who, once safe from the danger, would have sent the sentimental banker back to Geneva.

On the 6th of May, the deputies of the Third Estate took possession of the large hall, and the impatient crowd, that had been besieging the doors, rushed in after them.

The nobility apart, and the clergy apart, take up their quarters in their chambers, and, without losing time, decide that the powers ought to be verified by each order and in its own circle. The majority was great among the nobility, and small among the clergy; a great many curates wanted to join the Third Estate. The Third, strong in its great number, and master of the large hall, declares that *it is waiting for the two other orders*. The emptiness of that immense hall seemed to accuse their absence: the very hall spoke.

The question of the union of the orders contained every other. That of the Third, already double in number, was likely to gain the votes of some fifty nobles and a hundred curates, thereby commanding the two orders with an immense majority, and becoming their judges in everything. Privilege judged by those against whom it was established! It was easy to foresee the sentence.

So, the Third waited for the clergy and the nobility: it awaited in its strength, and patiently, like everything immortal. The privileged were agitated; they turned round, when too late, towards the source of privilege, the king, their natural centre, which they themselves had disturbed. Thus, in that time of expectation, which lasted a month or more, things became classed according to their affinity: the privileged with the king,—the Assembly with the people.

It lived with them, spoke with them, all the doors being wide open; and as yet no barriers. Paris was sitting at Versailles, pell-mell with the deputies. A continual communication existed all along the road. The assembly of the electors of Paris, and the irregular tumultuous assembly held by the crowd in the Palais-Royal, were asking every moment for news of the deputies; they questioned with avidity whoever came from Versailles. The Third, that saw the court becoming more and more irritated, and surrounding itself with soldiers, felt it had but one defence, the crowd that was listening to it, and the press, which caused it to be listened to by the whole kingdom. The very day of the opening of the Estates, the court endeavoured to stifle the press; a decree of the Council suppressed and condemned the journal of the Estates-General, published by Mirabeau; another decree forbade the publication of any periodical without permission. Thus was censorship, which for several months had remained inactive and as if suspended, re-established in face of the assembled nation,— re-established for the necessary and indispensable communications of the deputies and those who had deputed them. Mirabeau paid but little attention to this, and went on publishing under this title: *Letters to my Constituents.* The assembly of the electors of Paris, still working at their written resolutions (*cahiers*) left off (on the 7th of May), to protest unanimously against the decree of the Council.[20] This was the first time Paris interfered in general affairs. The great and capital question of the liberty of the press was thus carried in a trice. The court might now bring together its cannon and its armies; a more powerful artillery, that of the press, was henceforth thundering in the ears of the people; and all the kingdom heard it.

On the 7th of May, the Third, on the proposal of Malouet and Mounier, permitted some of its members to invite the clergy and the nobility to come and take their seats. The nobility went on and formed themselves into an assembly. The clergy, more divided and more timorous, wanted to see what course things would take; the prelates, moreover, believing that, in time, they should gain votes among the curates.

Six days lost. On the 12th of May, Rabaud de Saint-Etienne,

---

[20] *Procès-verbal des électeurs, rédigé par Bailly et Duveyrier,* i., 34.

a Protestant deputy from Nimes, and the son of the old Martyr of Cévennes, proposed a conference to bring about the union. To which the Breton Chapelier wished to have substituted "a *notification* of the astonishment of the Third-Estate at the absence of the other orders, of the impossibility of conferring elsewhere than in a common union, and of the interest and right that every deputy had to judge of the validity of the title of all; the Estates being once opened, there is no longer any deputy of order or province, but representatives of the nation; the deputies of privilege gain by it, their functions being aggrandized."

Rabaut's motion was carried, as being the more moderate. Conferences took place; but they only served to embitter things. On the 27th of May, Mirabeau reproduced a motion that he had already brought forward, to attempt to detach the clergy from the nobility, and invite them to the union "in the name of the God of peace." The motion was a very shrewd one; a number of *curés* were waiting impatiently for an opportunity to unite. This new invitation nearly carried away the whole order. With great difficulty, the prelates obtained a delay. In the evening, they ran to the castle, to the Polignac party. By means of the queen,[21] they got from the king a letter in which he declared "that he desired that the conferences might be resumed in presence of the keeper of the seals and a royal commission." The king thus impeded the union of the clergy with the Third, and made himself visibly the agent of the privileged classes.

This letter was a snare unworthy of royalty. If the Third Estate accepted, the king, arbiter of the conferences, could quash the question by a decree of the council, and the orders remained divided. If the Third alone refused and the other orders accepted, it bore alone the odium of the common inaction; it alone, at that moment of misery and famine, would

---

[21] Droz, ii., 189.—The testimony of M. Droz has often the weight of a contemporary authority; he frequently transmits to us the verbal information and revelation of Malouet and other important actors of the Revolution.

not take one step to succour the nation. Mirabeau, in pointing out the snare, advised the assembly to appear duped, to accept the conferences, whilst protesting by an address.

Another snare. In these conferences, Necker made an appeal to sentiment, generosity, and confidence. He advised that each order should intrust the validity of its elective returns to the others; and, in case of difference of opinion, *the king should judge.* The clergy accepted without hesitation. If the nobility had accepted, the Third would have remained alone against two. Who drew it out of this danger? The nobility themselves, mad, and running headlong to their ruin. The Polignac committee would not accept an expedient proposed by their enemy, Necker. Even before reading the king's letter, the nobility had decided in order to bar every chance of conciliation, that deliberation by orders and the *veto* of each order on the decisions of the others, were constituent principles of the monarchy. Necker's plan tempted many moderate nobles; two new nobles of great talent, only violent and weak-headed, Cazalès and d'Eprémesnil, embroiled the question and contrived to elude this last means of salvation,—to reject the plank which the king presented to them in their shipwreck (June 6th).

A month lost, after the delay of the three adjournments which the convocation had suffered! One month, in open famine! Observe, that in this long expectation, the rich kept themselves motionless, and postponed every kind of expenditure. Work had ceased. He who had but his hands, his daily labour to supply the day, went to look for work, found none, begged, got nothing, robbed. Starving gangs overran the country; wherever they found any resistance, they became furious, killed, and burned. Horror spread far and near; communications ceased, and famine went on increasing. A thousand absurd stories were in circulation. They were said to be brigands paid by the court. And the court flung back the accusation on the Duke of Orleans.

The position of the Assembly was difficult. It was obliged to sit inactive, when every remedy that could be hoped for was in action. It was obliged to shut its ears, in a manner, to the painful cry of France, in order to save France herself, and found her liberty!

The clergy aggravated that cruel position, and contrived a truly Phariseean invention against the Third Estate. A prelate came into the Assembly, to weep over the poor people and the misery of the rural districts. Before the four thousand persons present at that meeting, he drew from his pocket a hideous lump of black bread: "Such," said he, "is the bread of the peasant." The clergy proposed to act, to form a commission to confer together on the question of food and the misery of the poor. A dangerous snare. Either the Assembly yielded, became active, and thus consecrated the separation of the orders, or else it declared itself insensible to public misfortunes. The responsibility of the disorder which was everywhere beginning, fell on it at once. The usual orators however remained silent on this compromising question. But some obscure deputies, MM. Populus and Robespierre,[22] expressed forcibly and with talent the general sentiment. They invited the clergy to come into the *common hall* to deliberate on these public calamities by which the Assembly was no less touched than they.

This answer did not lessen the danger. How easy would it have been for the court, the nobles, and the priests, to turn the people! What a fine text was a proud, ambitious assembly of lawyers, that had promised to save France, and let her die of misery, rather than give up any of their unjust pretensions!

The court seized this weapon with avidity, and expected to destroy the Assembly. The king said to the president of the clergy, who came to submit to him the charitable proposal of his order on the question of food: "That he should see with pleasure a commission formed of the Estates-General that could assist him with its counsels."

Thus, the clergy were thinking of the people, and so was

---

[22] Robespierre retorted felicitously. He said very cleverly: "The old canons authorise, for the relief of the poor, to sell even the sacred vases." The *Moniteur*, incomplete and inexact, as it so often is, needs to be completed here by Etienne Dumont.—*Souvenirs*, p. 60.

the king; nothing prevented the nobility from uttering the same words. And then, the Third would be quite alone. It would be said that everybody desired the welfare of the people except the Third Estate.

III

National Assembly

On the 10th of June, Sieyès said, on entering the Assembly: "Let us cut the cable; it is time." From that day, the vessel of the Revolution, in spite of storms and calms, delayed, but never stopped, sails onwards to the future.

That great theoretician, who had beforehand calculated so exactly, showed himself here truly a statesman; he had said what ought to be done, and he did it at the right moment.

Everything has its right moment. Here, it was the 10th of June, neither sooner nor later. Sooner, the nation was not sufficiently convinced of the hard-heartedness of the privileged classes; it required a month for them to display clearly all their ill-will. Subsequently, two things were to be feared, either that the people, driven to extremity, might abandon their freedom for a bit of bread, and the privileged finish all, by renouncing their exemption from taxes; or else, that the nobility, uniting with the clergy, might form (as they were advised) an upper chamber. Such a chamber, which, in our own days, has no part to play but that of being a machine convenient to royalty, would, in '89, have been a power by itself: it would have assembled together those who then possessed half or two-thirds of the lands in the kingdom, those who, by their agents, tenants, and innumerable servants, had so many means of influencing the rural districts. The Netherlands had just given an example of the concord of those two orders, which had won over the people, driven out the Austrians, and dispossessed the emperor.

On Wednesday, the 10th of June, 1789, Sieyès proposed to summon the clergy and nobility for the last time, to warn them that the call would be made *in an hour,* and that *default would be the sentence* for non-appearance.

This summons in judiciary form, was an unexpected blow. The deputies of the commons were taking, towards those who contested equality with them, a superior position, somewhat like that of judges.

This was wise; for there was too much risk in waiting; but it was also bold. It has often been said, that they who had a whole people behind them, and a city like Paris, had nothing to fear; that they were the stronger party, and advanced without any danger. After the event, and everything having succeeded, the thesis may be supported. Doubtless, they who took that step felt themselves very strong; but this strength was by no means organised; the people were not military as they became at a later period. An army surrounded Versailles, partly of Germans and Swiss (nine regiments at least out of fifteen); a battery of cannon was before the Assembly. The glory of the great logician who reduced the national mind to a formula, and the glory of the Assembly that accepted the formula, was to see nothing of that, but to believe in logic, and to advance in their faith.

The court, very irresolute, could do nothing but assume a disdainful silence. Twice the king avoided receiving the president of the commons; he was out hunting, so they said, or else, he was too much afflicted at the recent death of the Dauphin. But it was known that he received every day the prelates, nobles, and *parlementaires.* They were beginning to be alarmed, and now came to offer themselves to the king. The court listened to them and then bargained and speculated on their fears. However, it was evident that the king being besieged by them, and their prisoner to a certain degree, would belong to them entirely, and show himself more and more what he was, a partisan of privilege at the head of the privileged classes. The situation of parties became clear and easy to be defined,—privilege on one side and right on the other.

The Assembly had spoken out. It expected its proceeding would cause it to be joined by a part of the clergy. The *curés* felt they were the people, and wished to go and take their true place by the side of the people. But habits of ecclesiastical subordination, the intrigues of the prelates, their authority and menaces, with the court and the queen on the other hand, kept them still immovable on their benches. Only three ventured, then seven,—ten in all. Great was the merriment at court about this fine conquest made by the Third Estate.

The Assembly must either perish or go on and take a second step. It was necessary for it to look boldly on the plain but terrible situation to which we alluded just now,—right opposed to privilege—the right of the nation concentrated in the Assembly. Neither was it sufficient to see that; it was necessary to show it, cause it to be promulgated, and to give to the Assembly its true name: *The National Assembly*.

In his famous pamphlet, which everybody knew by heart, Sieyès had said these remarkable words, which were not uttered in vain: "The Third alone, they will say, cannot form the Estates-General.—Well! so much the better; it shall compose a *National Assembly*."

To assume this title,—thus to entitle itself the nation, and realize the revolutionary dogma laid down by Sieyès—*The Third is everything*, was too bold a step to be taken all at once. It was necessary to prepare minds for it, and march towards that goal gradually and step by step.

At first the words *National Assembly* were not uttered in the Assembly itself but at Paris, among the electors who had elected Sieyès, and were not afraid to speak his language.

On the 15th of May, M. Boissy d'Anglas, then obscure and without influence, pronounced the words, but only to set them aside and adjourn them, warning the Chamber that it ought to be on its guard against every kind of precipitation, and remain free from the least reproach of *levity*. Before the movement began, he wanted already to efface the appellation.

The Assembly finally adopted the name of *Communes*, which, in its humble and ill-defined significance, divested it however of the petty, inappropriate, and special name of *Third Estate*. The nobility strongly protested.

On the 15th of June, Sieyès, with boldness and prudence, demanded that the Commons should assume the title of *Assembly of the known and acknowledged representatives of the French nation*. It seemed to express only a fact impossible to be contested; the deputies of the Commons had subjected their powers to a public verification, made solemnly in the great open hall and before the crowd. The two other orders had verified among themselves with closed doors. The simple word, *acknowledged* deputies, reduced the others to the name of *presumed* deputies. Could the latter prevent the others from acting? Could the absent paralyse the *present?* Sieyès reminded them that the latter *represented already the ninety-six hundredths* (at least) *of the nation*.

They knew Sieyès too well not to suspect that this proposal was a step to lead to another, bolder and more decisive. Mirabeau reproached him from the very first, "with starting the Assembly on its course without showing it the goal which he intended."

And indeed, on the second day of the battle, the light burst forth. Two deputies served as precursors to Sieyès. M. Legrand proposed that the Assembly should constitute itself a *General* Assembly, and allow itself to be stopped by nothing that might be separate from the *indivisibility of a National Assembly*. M. Galand demanded that, as the clergy and nobility were simply two corporations, and the nation one and indivisible, the Assembly should constitute itself the legitimate and active Assembly *of the representatives of the French nation*. Sieyès then laid aside every obscurity and circumlocution, and proposed the title of *National Assembly*.

Since the sitting of the 10th, Mirabeau had seen Sieyès advancing under ground, and was frightened. That march led straight to a point, where it found itself face to face with royalty and the aristocracy. Would it halt out of respect for that worm-eaten idol? It did not appear likely. Now, in spite of the cruel discipline by which tyranny formed Mirabeau for liberty, we must say that the famous tribune was an aristocrat by taste and manners, and a royalist in heart; he was so in fact by birth and blood. Two motives, one grand, and the other base, likewise impelled him. Surrounded by greedy women, he wanted money; and monarchy appeared to him with open lavish hands, squandering gold and favours. That royalty had been cruel and hard-hearted to him; but even that now interested him the more: he would have considered it noble to save a king who had so often signed the order for his imprisonment. Such was this poor great man, so magnanimous and generous, that one would wish to be able to attribute his vices to his deplorable acquaintances, and the paternal barbarity which excluded him from his family. His father persecuted him throughout his life, and yet he requested, with his dying breath, to be buried by his side.[23]

On the 10th, when Sieyès proposed to pronounce *default* for non-appearance, Mirabeau seconded that severe proposition, and spoke with firmness and energy. But, in the evening seeing the peril, he took upon himself to go and see his enemy, Necker; [24] he wished to enlighten him on the situation of things, and offer royalty the succour of his powerful oratory. Although ill-received and offended, he did not the less undertake to block the road against Sieyès, and he, the tribune, raised but yesterday by the Revolution, and who had no power but in her, even he wanted to throw himself before her, and imagined he could stop her.

Any other would have perished at once, without ever being able to extricate himself. That he should have fallen more than once into unpopularity, and yet been able to regain his footing, is what gives a very grand idea of the power of eloquence upon this nation, sensitive beyond all others, to the genius of oratory.

What could be more difficult than Mirabeau's thesis? In presence of that excited and transported multitude, before a

---

[23] *Mémoires de Mirabeau*, édité par M. Lucas de Montigny, t. viii., liv. x.
[24] Compare the different, but reconcilable, versions of E. Dumont and Droz, (who follow the oral testimony of Malouet).

people exalted above themselves by the greatness of the crisis, he endeavoured to establish "that the people were not interested in such discussions; that all they asked for was to pay only what they could, and to bear their misery peaceably."

After these base, afflicting, discouraging words, false moreover in terms, he ventured to put the question of principle: "Who convoked you? The king. Do your mandates and written resolutions authorize you to declare yourselves the Assembly only of the known and acknowledged representatives? and if the king refuses you his sanction? The consequence is evident. You will have pillage and butcheries: you will not have even the execrable honour of a civil war."

What title then was it necessary to take?

Mounier and the imitators of the English government proposed: Representatives of the *Major part* of the Nation, in the absence of the Minor part. That divided the nation into two parts, and led to the establishment of two Chambers.

Mirabeau preferred the formula: Representatives of the French *People*. That word, said he, was elastic,—might mean little or much.

This was precisely the reproach brought against him by two eminent legists, Target (of Paris), and Thouret (of Rouen). They asked him whether *people* meant *plebs* or *populus*. The equivocation was laid bare. The king, the clergy, and the nobility would doubtless have interpreted *people* in the sense of *plebs,* or inferior people,—a simple *part* of the nation.

Many had not perceived the equivocation, nor how much ground it would have caused the Assembly to lose. But they all understood it, when Malouet, Necker's friend, accepted the word *people*.

The fear which Mirabeau attempted to inspire by his reference to the royal veto, excited only indignation. Camus, the Jansenist, one of the firmest characters in the Assembly, replied in these strong terms: "We are what we are. Can the *veto* prevent truth from being one and immutable? Can the royal sanction change the order of things and alter their nature?"

Mirabeau, irritated by the contradiction, and losing all prudence, became so angry as to say: "I believe the king's *veto* so necessary, that I would rather live at Constantinople than in France if he had it not. Yes, I declare I know nothing more terrible than the sovereign aristocracy of six hundred persons, who might tomorrow render themselves irrevocable, hereditary the day after, and end, like the aristocracies of every country in the world, by invading everything."

Thus, of two evils, one possible, the other present, Mirabeau preferred the one present and certain. In the hypothesis that this Assembly might one day wish to perpetuate itself and become an hereditary tyrant, he armed, with the tyrannical power of preventing every reform, that incorrigible court which it was expedient to reform. *The king! the king!* Why should they always misuse that old religion? Who did not know that since Louis XIV. there had been no king? The war was between two republics: one, sitting in the Assembly, composed of the master minds of the age, the best citizens, was France herself; the other, the republic of abuses, held its council with the old cabinets of such as Dubois, Pompadour, and Du Barry, in the house of Diana de Polignac.

Mirabeau's speech was received with thunders of indignation and a torrent of imprecations and abuse. The eloquent rhetoric with which he refuted what nobody had said (that the word *people* is vile) was unable to dupe his auditory.

It was nine in the evening. The discussion was closed in order to take the votes. The singular precision with which the question had been brought to bear on royalty itself, caused some apprehension that the court might do the only thing that it had to do to prevent the people from being king on the morrow; it possessed brute force,—an army round Versailles, which it might employ to carry off the principal deputies, dissolve the Estates, and, if Paris stirred, famish Paris. This bold crime was its last cast, and people believed that it was going to be played. They wished to prevent it by constituting the Assembly that very night. This was the opinion of more than four hundred deputies; a hundred, at most, were against it. That small minority precluded, all night, by shouts and violence, every possibility of calling over the names. But this shameful sight of a majority being tyrannized over, and the Assembly endangered by a delay, together with the idea that, one moment or other, the work of liberty, the salvation of the future, might be annihilated,—all contributed to transport with fury the crowd that filled the tribunes; a man rushed forward and seized Malouet, the principal leader of the obstinate shouters, by the collar.[25]

The man escaped. The shouts continued. In presence of that tumult, says Bailly, who presided, the assembly remained firm and worthy; as patient as strong, it waited in silence till that turbulent band had exhausted itself with shouting. An hour after midnight, the deputies being less numerous, voting was formally postponed till the morrow.

On the following morning, at the moment of voting, the president was informed that he was summoned to the *chancellerie* to receive a letter from the king. This letter, in which he reminded them that they could do nothing without the concurrence of the three orders, would have arrived just at the right moment to furnish a text for the hundred opponents, to give rise to long speeches, and unsettle and disaffect many weak minds. The Assembly, with royal gravity, adjourned the king's letter, and forbade its president to leave the hall before the end of the meeting. It wanted to vote and voted.

The different motions might be reduced to three, or rather to two:—

1st. That of Sieyès—*National* Assembly.

2ndly. That of Mounier—Assembly of the Representatives of the *Major* part of the Nation, in the absence of the *Minor* part. The equivocal formula of Mirabeau was equivalent to Mounier's, as the word *people* could be taken in a limited sense, and as the *major part of the nation.*

Mounier had the apparent advantage of a judaic literalness, an arithmetical exactness, but was fundamentally contrary

---

[25] The principal witness, Bailly, does not give this circumstance, which M. Droz alone relates, doubtless on the authority of Malouet.

to justice. It brought into symmetrical opposition, and compared, as on a level, two things of an enormously different value. The Assembly represented the nation, minus the privileged; that is to say, 96 or 98 hundredths to 4 hundredths (according to Sieyès), or 2 hundredths (according to Necker). Why should such an enormous importance be given to these 2 or 4 hundredths? Certainly not for the moral power they contained; they no longer had any. It was, in reality, because all the large properties of the kingdom, two-thirds of the lands, were in their possession. Mounier was the advocate of the landed property against the population,—of the land against man:—a feudal, English, and materialist point of view. Sieyès had given the true French formula.

With Mounier's arithmetic and unjust justness, and with Mirabeau's equivocation, the nation remained *a class*, and the fixed property—the land—constituted also *a class* in face of the nation. We remained in the injustice of antiquity; the Middle Ages was perpetuated—the barbarous system by which the ground was reckoned more precious than man; and the land, manure, and ashes, were the liege lords of the mind.

Sieyès, being put to the vote at once, had near five hundred votes for him, and not one hundred against him.[26] Therefore the Assembly was proclaimed *National Assembly*. Many cried, *Vive le Roi!*

Two interruptions again intervened, as if to stop the Assembly,—one from the nobility, who sent for a mere pretext; the other from certain deputies, who wanted to have a president and a regular *bureau* created before everything else. The Assembly proceeded immediately to the solemnity of the oath. In presence of a multitude of four thousand deeply affected spectators, the six hundred deputies, standing in profound silence, with upraised hands and contemplating the calm, honest countenance of their president, listened to him whilst reading the formula, and exclaimed: "We swear." A universal sentiment of respect and religion filled every heart.

---

[26] Four hundred and ninety-one votes against ninety. Mirabeau dared not vote either for or against, and remained at home.

The Assembly was founded; it existed; it lacked but strength, the certainty of living. It secured this by asserting the right of taxation. It declared that the impost, *till then illegal,* should be collected *provisionally* "till the day of the separation of the present Assembly." This was, with one blow, condemning all the past and seizing upon the future.

It adopted openly the question of honour, the public debt, and guaranteed it.

And all these royal acts were in royal language, in the very formulae which the king alone had hitherto taken: "The Assembly *intends and decrees.*"

Finally, it evinced much concern about public subsistences. The administrative power having declined as much as the others, the legislature, the only authority then respected, was forced to interfere. It demanded, moreover, for its committee of subsistence, what the king himself had offered to the deputation of the clergy,—a communication of the information that would throw a light upon this matter. But what he had then offered, he was no longer willing to grant.

The most surprised of all was Necker; he had, in his simplicity, believed he could lead the world; and the world was going on without him. He had ever regarded the young Assembly as his daughter—his pupil; he warranted the king that it would be docile and well-behaved; yet, behold, all of a sudden, without consulting its tutor, it went alone, advanced and climbed over the old barriers without deigning even to look at them. When thus motionless with astonishment, Necker received two counsels, one from a royalist, the other from a republican, and both came to the same thing. The royalist was the intendant Bertrand de Molleville,—an impassioned and narrow-minded intendant of the *ancien régime;* the republican was Durovray, one of those democrats whom the king had driven from Geneva in 1782.

It is necessary to know who this foreigner was, who, in so serious a crisis, took so great an interest in France, and ventured to give advice. Durovray, settled in England, pensioned by the English, and grown English in heart and maxims, was, a little later, a leader of the emigrants. Meanwhile, he formed a part of a little Genevese *coterie* which, unfortunately for us, was circumventing Mirabeau. England seemed to be surrounding the principal voice of French liberty.[27] Unfavourable towards the English till then, the great man had allowed himself to be taken by those ex-republicans,—the self-termed martyrs of liberty. The Durovrays, the Dumonts, and other indefatigable writers of mediocrity, were ever ready to assist his idleness. He was already an invalid, and going the very way to render himself worse and worse. His nights destroyed his days. In the morning he remembered the Assembly and business, and collected his thoughts; he had there, ready at hand, the English policy, sketched by the Genevese; he received it with his eyes shut, and embellished it with his talent. Such was his readiness and his lack of preparation, that, at the tribune, even his admirable language was occasionally only a translation of the notes which these Genevese handed to him from time to time.

Durovray, who was not in communication with Necker, made himself his semi-official counsellor in this serious crisis.

Like Bertrand de Molleville, his opinion was that the king should *annul the decree* of the Assembly, deprive it of its name of *National Assembly*, command the union of the three orders, declare himself the *Provisional Legislator of France*, and do, *by royal authority*, what the Commons had done without it. Bertrand believed justly, that, after this *coup d'état*, the Assembly could but dissolve. Durovray maintained that the Assembly, crushed and humiliated under the royal pre-

---

[27] These Genevese were not precisely agents of England. But the pensions they received from her,—the monstrous present of more than a million (of francs) that she made them to found an Irish Geneva (which remained on paper),—all that imposed on them the obligation to serve the English. Moreover, they became two parties. Yvernois became English and our most cruel enemy; Clavière alone was French. What shall we say of Etienne Dumont, who pretends that those people, with their leaden pens, wrote all Mirabeau's orations? His *Souvenirs* bear witness to a base ingratitude towards the man of genius who honoured him with his friendship.

rogative, would accept its petty part, as a machine to make laws.[28]

On the evening of the 17th, the heads of the clergy, Cardinal de Larochefoucauld, and the Archbishop of Paris, had hastened to Marly, and implored the king and the queen. On the 19th, vain disputes in the Chamber of the nobility; Orleans proposed to join the Third, and Montesquiou to unite with the clergy. But there was no longer any order of the clergy. The very same day, the *curés* had transferred the majority of their order to form a union with the Third, and thus divided the order into two. The cardinal and the archbishop return the same evening to Marly, and fall at the feet of the king: "Religion is ruined!" Next, come the *parlement* people: "The monarchy is lost, unless the Estates be dissolved."

Dangerous advice, and already impossible to follow. The flood was rising higher every hour. Versailles and Paris were in commotion. Necker had persuaded two or three of the ministers, and even the king, that his project was the only means of salvation. That project had been read over again in a last and definitive council on Friday evening, the 19th; everything was finished and agreed: "The portfolios were already being shut up," says Necker, "when one of the royal servants suddenly entered; he whispered to the king; and His Majesty immediately arose, commanding his ministers to remain in their places. M. de Montmorin, sitting by my side, said to me: 'We have effected nothing; the queen alone could have ventured to interrupt the Council of State; the princes, apparently, have circumvented her.'"

Everything was stopped: this might have been foreseen; it was, doubtless, for this that the king had been brought to Marly, away from Versailles and the people; and, alone with the queen, more affectionate and liable to be influenced by her,

---

[28] Compare the two plans in Bertrand's *Mémoires* and Dumont's *Souvenirs*. The latter confesses that the Genevese had taken good care not to confide their fine project to Mirabeau; he was not informed of it till after the event, and then said with much good sense: "This is the way kings are led to the scaffold."

in their common affliction for the death of their child. A fine opportunity, an excellent chance for the suggestions of the priests! Was not the Dauphin's death a severe judgment of Providence, when the king was yielding to the dangerous innovations of a Protestant minister?

The king, still undecided, but already almost overcome, was content to command (in order to prevent the clergy from uniting with the Third Estate) that the hall should be shut on the morrow, (Saturday June 20th); the pretext was the preparations necessary for a royal meeting to be held on Monday.

All this was settled in the night, and placarded in Versailles at six in the morning. The president of the National Assembly learned, by mere chance, that it could not be held. It was past seven when he received a letter, not from the king (as was natural, the king being accustomed to write with his own hand to the president of the *Parlement*), but simply a notice from young Brézé, the master of ceremonies. It was not to the president, to M. Bailly, at his lodging, that such a notice ought to have been given, but to the Assembly itself. Bailly had no power to act of himself. At eight o'clock, the hour appointed the night before, he repaired to the door of the hall with a great number of deputies. Being stopped by the sentinels, he protested against the hindrance, and declared the meeting convened. Several young members made a show of breaking open the door; the officer commanded his soldiers to take up arms, thus announcing that his orders contained no reservation for inviolability.

Behold our new kings, put out, kept out of doors, like unruly scholars. Behold them wandering about in the rain, among the people, on Paris avenue. All agree about the necessity of holding the meeting and of assembling. Some shout, Let us go to the Place d'Armes! Others, to Marly! Another, to Paris! This last was an extreme measure; it was firing the powder-magazine.

The deputy Guillotin made a less hazardous motion, to repair to Old Versailles, and take up their quarters in the

Tennis-court (*Jeu-de-Paume*),—a miserable, ugly, poor, and un-furnished building, but the better on that account. The Assembly also was poor, and represented the people, on that day, so much the better. They remained standing all day long, having scarcely a wooden bench. It was like the manger of the new religion,—its stable of Bethlehem!

One of those intrepid *curés* who had decided the union of the clergy—the illustrious Grégoire—long after, when the Empire had so cruelly effaced every trace of the Revolution, its parent, used often to go near Versailles to visit the ruins of Port-Royal; one day (doubtless on his return), he entered the *Jeu-de-Paume* [29]—the one in ruins, the other abandoned—tears flowed from the eyes of that firm man, who had never shown any weakness. Two religions to weep for! this was too much for the heart of man.

We too revisited, in 1846, that cradle of Liberty, that place whose echo repeated her first words, that received, and still preserves her memorable oath. But what could we say to it? What news could we give it of the world that it brought forth? Oh! time has not flown quickly; generations have succeeded one another; but the work has not progressed. When we stepped upon its venerable pavement, we felt ashamed in our heart of what we are,—of the little we have done. We felt we were unworthy, and quitted that sacred place.

---

[29] *Mémoires de Grégoire*, i., p. 380.

IV

Oath at the Tennis Court

BEHOLD them now in the Tennis-court, assembled in spite of the king. But what are they going to do?

Let us not forget that at that period the whole Assembly was royalist, without excepting a single member.[30]

Let us not forget that on the 17th, when it assumed the title of National Assembly, it shouted *Vive le Roi!* And when it attributed to itself the right of voting the impost, declaring illegal the impost collected till then, the opposition members had left the Assembly, unwilling to consecrate, by their presence, this infringement of the royal authority.[31]

The king, that shadow of the past, that ancient superstition, so powerful in the hall of the Estates-General, grew pale in the Tennis-court. The miserable building, entirely modern, bare, and unfurnished, has not a single corner where the dreams of the past can yet find shelter. Let, therefore, the pure spirit of Reason and Justice, that king of the future, reign here!

That day there was no longer any opponent; [32] the Assembly was one, in thought and heart. It was one of the moderate party, Mounier of Grenoble, who proposed to the Assembly the

---

[30] See further, the 22nd of July, a note relating to Robespierre.

[31] As appears to me by comparing the numbers of the votes. The illegality of the impost not consented to, &c., was voted *unanimously* by the four hundred and twenty-six deputies alone remaining in the hall.— *Archives du Royaume, Procès-verbaux MSS. de l'Assemblée Nationale.*

[32] There was only one member who refused to take the oath. The ninety opponents of the 17th of June joined the majority.

celebrated declaration: That wherever it might be forced to unite, there was ever the National Assembly; that *nothing could prevent it* from continuing its deliberations. And, till the completion and establishment of the constitution, it took *an oath never to separate.*

Bailly was the first who took the oath; and he pronounced it so loud and distinctly that the whole multitude of people crowding without could hear, and applauded in the excess of their enthusiasm. Shouts of *Vive le Roi!* arose from the Assembly and from the people. It was the shout of ancient France, in her extreme transports, and it was now added to the oath of resistance.[33]

In 1792, Mounier, then an emigrant, alone in a foreign land, questions and asks himself whether his motion of the 20th of June was founded on right; whether his loyalty as a royalist was consistent with his duty as a citizen. And even there, in emigration, and among all the prejudices of hatred and exile, he replies, Yes!

"Yes," says he, "the oath was just; they wanted dissolution, and it would have taken place without the oath; the court, freed from the Estates, would never have convoked them; it would have been necessary to renounce the founding of that constitution claimed unanimously in the old writings of France." That is what a royalist, the most moderate of the moderate, a jurist accustomed to find moral decisions in positive texts, pronounces on the primordial act of our Revolution.

What were they doing all this time at Marly? On Saturday and Sunday, Necker was contending with the *parlement* people, to whom the king had abandoned him, and who, with the coolness sometimes possessed by madmen, were overthrowing his project, abridging it of what might have caused it to pass, and

---

[33] The Assembly went no further. It rejected the strong, but true motion of Chapelier, who was bold enough to speak out plainly what was in the minds of all. He proposed an address: "To inform His Majesty that the enemies of the country were besieging the throne, and that their counsels tended *to place the monarch at the head of a* PARTY."

took from it its bastard character, in order to convert it into a simple but brutal *coup d'état,* in the manner of Louis XV., a simple *lit de justice,* as the *parlement* had suffered so many times. The discussion lasted till the evening. It was not till midnight that the president, then in bed, was informed that the royal meeting could not take place in the morning,—that it was postponed till Tuesday.

The nobility had come to Marly on Sunday in great numbers and with much turbulence. They had again showed the king, in an address, that the question now concerned him much more than the nobility. The court was animated with a chivalrous daring; these swordsmen seemed to wait only for a signal to resist the champions of the pen. The Count D'Artois, amid these bravadoes, became so intoxicated with insolence, as to send word to the Tennis-court that he would play on the morrow.

On Monday morning, therefore, the Assembly found itself once more in the open streets of Versailles, wandering about, without house or home. Fine amusement for the court! The master of the hall was afraid; he feared the princes. The Assembly does not succeed better at the door of the Récollets where it next knocks; the monks dare not compromise themselves. Who then are these vagrants, this dangerous band, before whom every door is shut? Nothing less than the Nation itself.

But why not deliberate in the open air? What more noble canopy than the sky? But on that day the majority of the clergy wish to come and sit with the commons. Where are they to receive them? Luckily, the hundred and thirty-four *curés,* with a few prelates at their head, had already taken up their quarters, in the morning, in the church of Saint-Louis. The Assembly was introduced there into the nave; and the ecclesiastics, at first assembled in the choir, then came forth, and took their places among its members. A grand moment, and one of sincere joy! "The temple of religion," says an orator, with emotion, "became the temple of the native land!"

On that very day, Monday the 22nd, Necker was still con-

124

tending, but in vain. His project, fatal to liberty because he preserved in it a shadow of moderation, had to give way to another more liberal and better calculated to place things in their proper light. Necker was now nothing more than a guilty mediator between good and evil, preserving a semblance of equilibrium between the just and the unjust,—a courtier, at the same time, of the people and the enemies of the people. At the last council held on Monday at Versailles, the princes, who were invited to it, did liberty the essential service of removing this equivocal mediator, who prevented reason and unreasonableness from seeing each other plainly face to face.

Before the sitting begins, I wish to examine both projects,— Necker's and the court's. In what concerns the former, I will believe none but Necker himself.

NECKER'S PROJECT

In his book of 1796, written at a time of decided reaction, Necker avows to us confidentially what his project was; he shows that that project was, *bold, very bold*—in favour of the privileged. This confession is rather painful for him, and he makes it with an effort. "The defect of my project was its being too bold; I risked all that it was possible for me to risk. Explain yourself. I will, and I ought. Deign to listen to me." [34]

He is speaking to the emigrants, to whom this apology is addressed. A vain undertaking! How will they ever forgive him for having called the people to political life, and made five millions of electors?

1st. Those necessary, inevitable reforms, which the court had so long refused, and which they accepted only by force, he promulgated by the king. He, who knew, to his cost, that the king was the puppet of the queen and the court, a mere cipher, nothing more,—even he became a party for the continuing of that sad comedy.

Liberty, that sacred right which exists of itself, he made a present from the king, *a granted charter*, as was the charter of

---

[34] *Oeuvres de Necker*, vi., p. 191.

the invasion in 1814. But it required thirty years of war, and all Europe at Paris, for France to accept that constitution of false-hood.

2ndly. No legislative unity,—*two Chambers,* at least. This was like a timid advice to France to become English; in which there were two advantages: to strengthen the privileged, priests and nobles, henceforth concentrated in one upper Chamber; next, to make it easier for the king to delude the people, to refuse by the upper Chamber, instead of refusing by himself, and of having (as we see to-day) two vetos for one.

3rdly. The king was to permit the three orders to deliberate in common on *general* affairs; but as to *privileges* of personal distinction, of honour, and as to *rights attached to fiefs,* no discussion in common. Now this was precisely what France considered as the superlatively *general* business. Who then dared to see a special business in the question of honour?

4thly. These crippled Estates-General, now united, now separated into three orders, at one time active, at another supine, through their triple movement, Necker balances, shackles, and neutralises still more, by *provincial Estates,* thus augmenting division, when France is thirsting for unity.

5thly. That is what he gives, and as soon as given, he takes away again. This fine legislative machine is never to be seen at work by anybody; he grudges us the sight of it; it is to work with closed doors: *no publicity of its sittings.* The law is thus to be made, far from daylight, in the dark, as one would make a plot against the law.

6thly.—The law? What does this word mean, without personal liberty? Who can act, elect, or vote freely, when nobody is sure of sleeping at home? This first condition of social life, anterior to, and indispensable for political action, is not yet secured by Necker. The king is to invite the Assembly *to seek the means that might permit* the abolition of the *lettres-de-cachet.* Meanwhile, he keeps them together with the arbitrary power of kidnapping, the state-prisons, and the Bastille.

Such is the extreme concession which ancient royalty makes, in its most favourable moment, and urged on by a popular minister. Moreover, it cannot go even thus far. The nominal king promises; the real king, the court—laughs at the promise. Let them die in their sin!

THE KING'S DECLARATION (JUNE 23, 1789)

The plan of the court is worth more than the bastard plan of Necker; at least it is plainer to understand. Whatever is bad in Necker is preciously preserved, nay richly augmented.

This act, which may be called the testament of despotism, is divided into two parts: 1st. The prohibition of guarantees: under this head, Declaration concerning the *present* session of the Estates. 2ndly. The reforms and benefits as they say,[35] Declaration of the king's *intentions*, of his wishes and desires for future contingencies. The evil is sure, and the good possible. Let us see the detail.

I. The king annihilates the will of five millions of electors, declaring that their demands merely provide information.

The king annihilates the decisions of the deputies of the Third Estate, declaring them "null, illegal, unconstitutional."

The king will have the three orders remain distinct, that one may be able to shackle the others (that two hundredths of the nation may weigh as much as the whole nation).

If they wish to meet, he permits it, but *only for this time,* and also only for *general* business; in this general business is included neither the rights of the three orders, the constitution of the future Estates, the feudal and seigneurial properties, nor the privileges of money or of honour. All the *ancien régime* is thus found to be an exception.

All this was the work of the court. Here is, by all appearances, the king's manifesto, the one he fondly cherished, and wrote himself. The order of the clergy shall have a special *veto*

---

[35] The style on a par with the matter; now bombastic, now flat, and strongly savouring of false valour: "Never did a king do so much!" Towards the end is a phrase of admirable impudence and awkwardness (Necker claims it accordingly, tome ix., p. 196): "Reflect, gentlemen, that none of your projects can have the force of law without my special approbation."

(against the nobility and the Third Estate) for everything relating to religion, the discipline and government of the secular *and regular* orders. Thus, not one monk less; no reform to be made. And all those convents, every day more odious and useless, for which recruits could no longer be found, the clergy wanted to maintain. The nobility was furious. It lost its dearest hope. It had reckoned that, one day or other, that prey would fall into its hands; at the very least, it hoped that, if the king and the people pressed it too much to make some sacrifice, it would generously sacrifice the clergy.

Veto on veto. For what purpose? Here we have a refinement of precautions, far more sure to render every result impossible. In the common deliberations of the three orders, it is sufficient that the *two-thirds of one order* protest against the deliberation, for the decision to be referred to the king. Nay more, the thing being decided, it is *sufficient that a hundred members* protest for the decision to be referred to the king. That is to say, that the words assembly, deliberation, and decision, are only a mystification, a farce. And who could play it without laughing?

II. Now come the BENEFITS: publicity for finance, voting of taxes, regulation of the expenditure for which *the Estates will indicate the means,* and his Majesty "will adopt them, *if they be compatible with the kingly dignity,* and the despatch of the public service."

Second benefit: The king will sanction the equality of taxation, *when the clergy and the nobility shall be willing to renounce their pecuniary privileges.*

Third benefit: Properties shall be respected, *especially tithes, feudal rights, and duties.*

Fourth benefit: Individual liberty? No. The king invites the Estates to *seek* for and to *propose* to him means for *reconciling* the abolition of the *lettres-de-cachet,* with the precautions *necessary* either for protecting the honour of families, or for repressing the commencement of sedition, &c.

Fifth: Liberty of the press? No. The Estates shall seek the means of *reconciling* the liberty of the press with *the respect due to religion,* the morals, and the honour of the citizens.

Sixth: Admission to every employment? No. Refused *expressly for the army*. The king declares, *in the most decided manner*, that he will preserve entire, and without the slightest alteration, *the institution of the army*. That is to say, that the plebeian shall never attain any grade, &c. Thus does the idiotic legislator subject everything to violence, force, and the sword: and this is the very moment he chooses to break his own. Let him now call soldiers, surround the assembly with them, and urge them towards Paris; they are so many defenders that he gives to the Revolution.

On the eve of the great day, three deputies of the nobility, MM. d'Aiguillon, de Menou, and de Montmorency, came at midnight to inform the president of the results of the last council, held the same evening at Versailles: "M. Necker will not countenance, by his presence, a project contrary to his own; he will not come to the meeting; and will doubtless depart." The meeting opened at ten o'clock; and Bailly was able to tell the deputies, and the latter many others, the great secret of the day. Opinions might have been divided and duped, had the popular minister been seen sitting beside the king; he being absent, the king remained discovered, and forsaken by public opinion. The court had hoped to play their game at Necker's expense, and to be sheltered by him; they have never forgiven him for not having allowed himself to be abused and dishonoured by them.

What proves that everything was known is, that on his very exit from the castle, the king found the crowd sullenly silent.[36] The affair had got abroad, and the grand scene, so highly wrought, had not the least effect.

The miserable petty spirit of insolence which swayed the court, had suggested the idea of causing the two superior orders to enter in front, by the grand entrance, and the commons behind, and to keep them under a shed, half in the rain. The Third Estate, thus humbled, wet and dirty, was to have entered crest-fallen, to receive its lesson.

---

[36] Dumont (an eye-witness), p. 91.

Nobody to admit them; the door shut; and the guard within. Mirabeau to the president: "Sir, conduct the nation into the presence of the king!" The president knocks at the door. The body-guards from within: "Presently." The president: "Gentlemen, where is then the master of ceremonies?" The body-guards: "We know nothing about it." The deputies: "Well then, let us go; come away!" At last the president succeeds in bringing forth the captain of the guards, who goes in quest of Brézé.

The deputies, filing in one by one, find, in the hall, the clergy and the nobility, who, already in their places, and holding the meeting, seem to be awaiting them, like judges. In other respects, the hall was empty. Nothing could be more desolate than that hall, from which the people were excluded.

The king read, with his usual plainness of manner, the speech composed for him,—that despotic language so strange from his lips. He perceived but little its provoking violence, for he appeared surprised at the aspect of the Assembly. The nobles having applauded the article consecrating feudal rights, loud distinct voices were heard to utter: "Silence there!"

The king, after a moment's pause and astonishment, concluded with a grave, intolerable sentence, which flung down the gauntlet to the Assembly, and began the war: "If you abandon me in so excellent an enterprise, I will, alone, effect the welfare of my people; *alone, I shall consider myself as their true representative!*"

And at the end: "*I order you, gentlemen, to disperse immediately,* and to repair to-morrow morning to the chambers appropriated to your order, there to resume your sitting."

The king departed, followed by the nobility and the clergy. The commons remained seated, calm, and silent.[37] The master

---

[37] There was neither hesitation, nor consternation, notwithstanding what Dumont says, who was not there. The ardent, like Grégoire (Mém., i., 381), and the moderate, like Malouet, were perfectly agreed. The latter says, on this head, these fine and simple words: "We had no other course to take. We owed France a constitution."—Malouet, *Compte-rendu à mes Commettants.*

of ceremonies then entered, and said to the president in a low tone: "Sir, you heard the king's order!" He replied: "The Assembly adjourned after the royal meeting; I cannot dismiss it till it has deliberated." Then turning towards his colleagues near him: "It seems to me that the assembled nation cannot receive any orders."

That sentence was admirably taken up by Mirabeau, who addressed it to the master of ceremonies. With his powerful and imposing voice, and with terrible dignity, he hurled back these words: "We have heard the intentions suggested to the king; and you, sir who can never be his spokesman to the National Assembly, you, who have here neither place, voice, nor right to speak, you are not a man to remind us of his discourse. Go and tell those who send you, that we are here by the will of the people, and are to be driven hence only by the power of bayonets." [38]

Brézé was disconcerted, thunderstruck; he felt the power of that new royalty, and, rendering to the one what etiquette commanded for the other, he retired walking backwards, as was the custom before the king.[39]

The court had imagined another way to disperse the commons,—a brutal means formerly employed with success in the Estates-General,—merely to have the hall dismantled, to demolish the amphitheatre and the king's estrade. Workmen accordingly enter! but, at one word from the president, they stop, lay down their tools, contemplate with admiration the calm majesty of the Assembly, and become attentive and respectful auditors.

A deputy proposed to discuss the king's resolutions on the morrow. He was not listened to. Camus laid down forcibly, and it was declared: "That the sitting was but a ministerial

---

[38] This version is the only one likely. Mirabeau was a royalist; he would never have said: *"Go and tell your master,"* nor the other words that have been added.

[39] Related by M. Frochot, an eye-witness, to the son of Mirabeau. (Mém., vi., p. 39). That family has thought proper to contest a few details of this well-known scene, forty-four years after the event.

act, and that the Assembly persisted in its decrees." Barnave, the young member for Dauphiny: "You have declared what you are; you need no sanction." Glezen, the Breton: "How now! does the sovereign speak as a master, when he ought to consult!" Pétion, Buzot, Garat, Grégoire, spoke with equal energy; and Sieyès, with simplicity: "Gentlemen, you are today what you were yesterday."

The Assembly next declared, on Mirabeau's proposal, that its members were inviolable; that whoever laid hands on a deputy was a traitor, infamous, and worthy of death.

This decree was not useless. The body-guards had formed in a line in front of the hall. It was expected that sixty deputies would be kidnapped in the night.

The nobility, headed by their president, went straightway to thank their protector, the Count d'Artois, and afterwards to Monsieur, who was prudent and took care not to be at home. Many of them went to see the queen, who, triumphant and smiling, leading her daughter and carrying the dauphin, said to them: "I intrust him to the nobility."

The king was far from sharing their joy. The silence of the people, so new to him, had overwhelmed him. When Brézé, who came and informed him that the deputies of the Third Estate remained sitting, asked for orders, he walked about for a few minutes, and said at last, in the tone of one tired to death: "Very well; leave them alone."

The king spoke wisely. The moment was fraught with danger. One step more and Paris would have marched against Versailles. Versailles was already in commotion. Behold five or six thousand men advancing towards the castle. The queen sees with terror that strange and novel court, which, in a moment, fills the gardens, the terraces, and even the apartments. She begs, she entreats the king to undo what she has done, to recall Necker. His return did not take long; he was there, near at hand, convinced, as usual, that nothing could ever go on without him. Louis XVI. said to him good-naturedly: "For my part I am not at all tenacious of that declaration."

Necker required no more, and made no condition. His

vanity once satisfied, his delight in hearing everybody shout
Necker! deprived him of every other thought. He went out,
overjoyed, into the great court of the castle, and to comfort
the multitude, passed in the midst of them. There a few silly
persons fell on their knees and kissed his hands. He, much
affected, said: "Yes, my children,—yes, my children,—I remain;
be comforted." He burst into tears, and then shut himself up in
his office.

The poor tool of the court remained without exacting anything; he remained to shield the cabal with his name, to serve
them as an advertisement, and reassure them against the
people; he restored courage to those worthies, and gave them
the time to summon more troops.

V

Movement of Paris

THE situation of things was strange,—evidently temporary.

The Assembly had not obeyed. But the king had not revoked anything.

The king had recalled Necker; but he kept the Assembly like a prisoner among his troops; he had excluded the public from the sitting; the grand entrance remained shut; the Assembly entered by the small one, and debated with closed doors.

The Assembly protested feebly and but slightly. The resistance, on the 23rd, seemed to have exhausted its strength.

Paris did not imitate its weakness.

It was not content to see its deputies making laws in prison.

On the 24th the ferment was terrible.

On the 25th it burst out in three different ways at once; by the electors, by the crowd, and by the soldiery.

The seat of the Revolution fixes itself at Paris.

The electors had agreed to meet again after the elections, in order to complete their instructions to the deputies whom they had elected. Though the ministry refused its permission,[40] the *coup d'état*, on the 23rd, urged them on; they had likewise their *coup d'état*, and assembled, of their own accord, on the 25th, in the Rue Dauphine. A wretched assembly-room,

---

[40] Compare the *Mémoires de Bailly* with the *Procès-verbal des Electeurs,* drawn up by *Bailly et Duveyrier.*

occupied at that moment by a wedding-party, which made room for them, received, at first, the Assembly of the electors of Paris. This was *their* Tennis-court. There Paris, through their medium, made an engagement to support the National Assembly. One of them, Thuriot, advised them to go to the Hôtel-de-Ville, into the great hall of Saint-Jean, which nobody dared refuse them.

These electors were mostly rich men, citizens of note; the aristocracy was numerous in this body; but among them were, also, men of over-excited minds. First, two men, fervent *révolutionnaires*, with a singular tendency to mysticism; one was the *abbé* Fauchet, eloquent and intrepid; the other, his friend Bonneville, (the translator of Shakespeare). Both, in the thirteenth century, would have caused themselves, most certainly, to be burnt as heretics. In the eighteenth they were as forward as any, or rather the first, to propose resistance; which was scarcely to be expected from the burgess assembly of the electors.[41] On the 6th of June, Bonneville proposed that Paris should be armed, and was the first to cry, "To arms." [42]

Fauchet, Bonneville, Bertolio, and Carra, a violent journalist, made these bold motions, which ought to have been made from the first in the National Assembly:—firstly, the Citizen Guard; secondly, the early organization of a true, elective, and annual *Commune;* thirdly, an address to the King, for the removal of the troops and the liberty of the Assembly, and for the revocation of the *coup d'état* of the 23rd.

On the very day of the first assembly of the electors, as if the cry *to arms* had resounded in the barracks, the soldiers of the French Guards, confined for several days past, overpowered their guard, walked about in Paris, and went to frat-

---

[41] Yet, nowhere had more reliance been placed on the weakness of the people. The well-known gentleness of Parisian manners, the multitude of government people, and financiers, who could but lose in a rebellion, the crowds of those who lived on abuses, had altogether created a belief, before the elections that Paris would prove very citizen-like, easy, and timid. See Bailly, pp. 16, 150.

[42] Dussaulx, *Oeuvre des Sept Jours,* p. 271, (ed. 1822).

ernise with the people in the Palais Royal. For some time past, secret societies had been forming among them; they swore they would obey no orders that might be contrary to those of the Assembly. The Act of the 23rd, in which the king declared, in the strongest manner, that *he would never change the institution of the army;* that is to say, that the nobility should for ever monopolize every grade, and that the plebeian could never rise, but that the common soldier would die in the ranks:— that unjustifiable declaration necessarily finished what the revolutionary contagion had begun.

The French Guards, residents in Paris, and mostly married men, had seen the school in which the children of the soldiers were educated, free of expense, shortly before suppressed by M. Du Châtelet, their hard-hearted colonel. The only change made in the *military institutions,* was made against them.

In order to appreciate properly the words *institution of the army,* we should know, that in the budget of that time, the officers were reckoned at forty-six millions (of francs), and the soldiers at forty-four.[43] We should know, that Jourdan, Joubert, and Kléber, who had served at first, quit the military profession, as a hopeless career,—a sort of no thoroughfare. Augereau was an under-officer in the infantry, Hoche a sergeant in the French Guards, and Marceau a common soldier; those noble-hearted and aspiring youths were fixed in this low condition for ever. Hoche, who was twenty-one years of age, nevertheless completed his own education, as if about to be a General-in-Chief; he devoured everything, literature, politics, and even philosophy; must we add, that this great man, in order to purchase a few books, used to embroider officers' waistcoats, and sell them in a coffee-house.[44] The trifling pay of a soldier was, under one pretence or other, absorbed by deductions, which the officers squandered away among themselves.[45]

---

[43] Necker, *Administration,* ii., 422, 435. (1784).

[44] Rousselin, *Vie de Hoche,* i., 20.

[45] The single regiment of Beauce believed it was cheated of the sum of 240,727 francs.

The insurrection of the French Guards was not a pretorian mutiny, a brutal riot of the soldiery,—it came in support of the declarations of the electors and the people. That truly French troop, Parisian in a great measure, followed the lead of Paris, followed the law, the living law,—the National Assembly.

They arrived in the Palais Royal, saluted, pressed, embraced, and almost stifled by the crowd. The soldier, that true pariah of the ancient monarchy, so ill-treated by the nobles, is welcomed by the people. And what is he, under his uniform, but the very people? Two brothers have met each other, the soldier and the citizen, two children of the same mother; they fall into each other's arms, and burst into tears.

Hatred and party-spirit have vilified all that, disfigured those grand scenes, and soiled the page of history, at pleasure. A vast importance has been attached to this or that ridiculous anecdote; a worthy amusement for petty minds! All these immense commotions they have attributed to some miserable, insignificant causes. Paltry fools! try to explain by a straw, washed away by the waves, the agitation of the ocean.

No: those movements were those of a whole people, true, sincere, immense, and unanimous; France had her share in them, and so had Paris; all men, (each in his own degree,) acted, some with their hands and voices, others with their minds, with their fervent wishes, from the depths of their hearts.

But why do I say France? It would be more true to say the world. An envious enemy, a Genevese, imbued with every English prejudice, cannot help avowing, that at that decisive moment, the whole world was looking on, observing with uneasy sympathy the march of our Revolution, and feeling that France was doing, at her own risk and peril, the business of mankind.[46]

Arthur Young, an English agriculturist, a positive, special man, who had, whimsically enough, come to France, to study its modes of agriculture, at such a moment, is astonished at the deep silence reigning about Paris; no coach, hardly a man. The

---

[46] E. Dumont, *Souvenirs,* p. 135.

terrible agitation concentrating everything within, made a desert of all beyond. He enters; the tumult frightens him; he traverses, in astonishment, that noisy capital. He is taken to the Palais Royal, the centre of the conflagration, the burning focus of the furnace. Ten thousand men were speaking at once; ten thousand lights in the windows; it was a day of victory for the people; fire-works were let off, and bonfires made. Dazzled and confounded by that moving Babel, he hastily retires. Yet the lively and excessive emotion of that people, united in one common thought, soon gains upon the traveller; he gradually becomes associated, without even being aware of his change of sentiments, with the hopes of liberty; the Englishman prays for France.[47]

All men forgot themselves. The place, that strange place where the scene was passing, seemed, at such moments, to forget itself. The Palais Royal was no longer the Palais Royal. Vice, in the grandeur of so sincere a passion, in the heat of enthusiasm, became pure for an instant. The most degraded raised their heads, and gazed at the sky; their past life, like a bad dream, was gone, at least for a day; they could not be virtuous, but they felt themselves heroic, in the name of the liberties of the world! Friends of the people, brothers to one another, having no longer any selfish feeling, and quite ready to share everything.

That there were interested agitators in that multitude, cannot be doubted. The minority of the nobility, ambitious men, fond of noise, such as Lameth and Duport, worked upon the people by their pamphlets and agents. Others, still worse, joined them. All that took place, we must say, beneath the windows of the Duke of Orleans, before the eyes of that intriguing, greedy, polluted court. Alas! who would not pity our Revolution? That ingenuous, disinterested, sublime movement, spied and overlooked by those who hoped one day or other to turn it to their advantage!

Let us look at those windows. There I see distinctly a pure

---

[47] Of course with many exceptions, and on condition that France adopts the constitution of England. Arthur Young's Travels, vol. i., *passim.*

woman and a wicked man. These are Virtue and Vice, the king's counsellors, Madame de Genlis and Choderlos de Laclos. The parts are distinctly separated. In that house, where everything is false, Virtue is represented by Madame de Genlis,— hard-heartedness and mock sensibility, a torrent of tears and ink, the quackery of a model education, and the constant exhibition of the pretty Pamela.[48] On this side of the palace is the philanthropic *bureau*, where charity is organised with much ostentation on the eve of elections.[49]

The time has gone by when the jockey-prince used to lay a wager after supper to run stark naked from Paris to Bagatelle. He is now the statesman before everything else, the head of a party; his mistresses will have it so. They have fondly wished for two things,—a good law for divorces, and a change of dynasty. The political confidant of the prince is that gloomy taciturn man, who seems to say: "I conspire, we conspire." That mysterious Laclos who, by his little book, *Liaisons dangereuses*, flatters himself that he has caused the romantic to pass from vice to crime, and insinuates therein that crafty gallantry is a useful prelude to political villainy. That is the name he covets of all others, and that part he acts to perfection. Many, in order to flatter the prince, say: "Laclos is a villain."

It was not easy, however, to make a leader of this Duke of Orleans; he was broken down at that period, wasted in body and heart, and of very weak mind. Swindlers made him fabricate gold in the garrets of the Palais Royal, and they had made him acquainted with the devil.[50]

---

[48] Even so far as to send her, on horseback, into the middle of the riot, followed by a domestic in the Orleans livery.—Read the *Souvenirs* (i., p. 189,) of Madame Lebrun, who was a witness of this scene.

[49] Brissot worked there some time.—*Mémoires*, ii., p. 430.

[50] The prince made gold, as it is ever made, with gold. However, among other ingredients, it was necessary to have a human skeleton that had been buried so many years and days. They sought among such dead bodies as were known, and it so happened that Pascal exactly fulfilled the conditions required. They bribed the keepers of Saint Etienne-du-Mont, and poor Pascal was handed over to the crucibles of the Palais Royal. Such, at least, is the account of a person, who, having long lived with Madame de Genlis, received from her this strange anecdote.

Another difficulty was, that this prince, besides all his acquired vices, possessed a natural one, both fundamental and durable, which does not cease with exhaustion, like the others, but remains faithful to its master: I mean avarice. "I would give," he would say, "public opinion for a six-franc piece." This was not an idle word. He had put it well in practice, when, in spite of public clamour, he built the Palais Royal.

His political advisers were not skilful enough to raise him from such abasement. They caused him to commit more than one false and imprudent step.

In 1788, Madame de Genlis' brother, a youth without any other title than that of officer in the house of Orleans, writes to the king, to ask nothing less than to be prime minister,—to get the place of Necker or Turgot; he will undertake to reestablish in a moment the finances of the monarchy. The Duke of Orleans allows himself to be the bearer of the incredible missive, hands it to the king, recommends it, and becomes the laughing-stock of the court.

The sage counsellors of the prince had hoped thus to bring the government quietly into his hands. Deceived in their hopes, they acted more openly, endeavoured to make a Guise a Cromwell, and courted the people. There, also, they met with great difficulties. All were not dupes; the city of Orleans did not elect the prince; and, by way of retaliation, he unceremoniously withdrew from it the benefits by which he had expected to purchase his election.

And yet nothing had been spared, neither money nor intrigue. Those who had the management of the business had had the precaution to attach a whole pamphlet of Sieyès to the electoral instructions which the duke sent into his domains, and thus to place their master under the name and patronage of that great thinker, then so popular, who however had no kind of connection with the Duke of Orleans.

When the Commons took the decisive step of assuming the title of *National Assembly*, the Duke of Orleans was informed that the time was come to show himself, to speak and act, and that a leader of a party could not remain mute. They prevailed upon him at least to read a speech of some four lines to engage the nobility to unite with the Third Estate. He did so; but whilst reading, his heart failed him, and he fainted. On opening his vest, they saw that, in the dread of being assassinated by the court, this over-prudent prince used to wear, by way of armor, five or six waistcoats.[51]

The day the *coup d'état* failed (June 23), the duke believed the king lost, and himself king on the morrow, or next day; he could not conceal his joy.[52] The terrible fermentation in Paris on that evening and the next morning, sufficiently announced that a vast insurrection would burst forth. On the 25th, the minority of the nobility, perceiving that they must decline in importance if Paris should be the first to begin, went, with the Duke of Orleans at their head, to join the Commons. The prince's man, Sillery, the convenient husband of Madame de Genlis, pronounced, in the name of all, an ill-concocted discourse, such as might have been made by a mediator, an accepted arbiter between the king and the people: "Let us never lose sight of the respect that we owe to the best of kings. He offers us peace; can we refuse to accept it?" &c. In the evening, great was the rejoicing in Paris for this union of the noble friends of the people. An address to the assembly was lying at the Café de Foy; everybody signed it, as many as three thousand persons, in haste, and most of them without reading it. That article, drawn by an able hand, contained one strange word respecting the Duke of Orleans: "This Prince, the object of public *veneration*." Such a word, for such a man, seemed cruelly derisive; an enemy would not have been more bitter. The duke's awkward agents believed apparently that the boldest eulogium would also be the best paid.

Thank God! the grandeur, the immensity of the movement, spared the Revolution that unworthy mediator. Ever since the 25th, the excitement was so unanimous, and the concord so

---

[51] Ferrières, i., p. 52.

[52] Arthur Young, who was dining with him and other deputies, was shocked at seeing him laughing in his sleeve.

powerful, that the agitators themselves, hurried along by it, were obliged to abandon every pretension of directing it. Paris led the leaders. The Catalines of the salons and *cafés* had only to follow in its train. An authority was suddenly found to be in Paris, which had been supposed to be without any chief or guide, the assembly of the electors. On the other hand, as the French Guards began to declare themselves, it was easy to foresee that the new authority would not be wanting in force. To sum up all in one word, these anxious mediators might remain quiet; if the assembly was a prisoner at Versailles, it had its asylum here, in the very heart of France, and, if necessary, Paris for an army.

The court, trembling with anger and indignation, and still more with fear, decided, on the evening of the 26th, to grant the re-union of the orders. The king invited the nobility to it, and in order to reserve to himself a means of protesting against all that was being done, the Count d'Artois was made to write those imprudent words (then untrue): "The king's life is in danger."

On the 27th, therefore, the long-expected union at length took place. The rejoicing at Versailles was excessive, foolish, and ungovernable. The people made bonfires, and shouted "*Vive la Reine!*" The queen was obliged to appear in the balcony. The crowd then asked her to show them the dauphin, as a token of complete reconciliation and oblivion. She consented again, and re-appeared with her child. She did but so much the more despise that credulous crowd; and she sent for troops.

She had taken no part in the union of the orders. And could it truly be called a union? They were still enemies, though now assembled in the selfsame hall, brought into contact, and looking at one another. The clergy had made their express restrictions. The protests of the nobles were brought forward one by one, like so many challenges, and engrossed the whole time of the Assembly; such as came, did not condescend to sit, but wandered about, or stood gazing like simple spectators. They did sit, but elsewhere,—in a meeting of their own. Many had said that they were leaving, but still remained at Versailles; evidently, they were waiting.

The Assembly was wasting time. The lawyers, who composed the majority, spoke frequently and at great length, trusting too much to language. According to them, if the constitution were but made, everything was saved. As if a constitution can be anything with a government continually conspiring! A paper liberty, written or verbal, whilst despotism possesses the power and the sword! This is nonsense,—absurdity!

But neither the court nor Paris desired any compromise. Everything was inclining towards open violence. The military gentlemen of the court were impatient to act. M. Du Châtelet, the colonel of the French Guards, had already sent to the Abbaye eleven of those soldiers who had sworn to obey no orders contrary to those of the Assembly. Neither did he stop there. He wanted to remove them from the military prison, and send them to the one for thieves, to that horrible sink, gaol and hospital at once, which subjected to the same lash the galley-slaves and the *vénériens*.[53] The terrible case of Latude, cast there to die, had revealed Bicêtre,—thrown the first light upon it; and a recent book, by Mirabeau, had filled every heart with disgust and every mind with terror.[54] And it was there they were going to imprison men whose greatest offence was to wish to be only the soldiers of the law.

The very day they were to be transferred to Bicêtre, the news reached the Palais Royal. A young man standing upon a chair, called out, "To the Abbaye! and let us deliver those who would not fire upon the people!" Soldiers offer themselves; but the citizens thank them, and go alone. The crowd increases on the road, and is joined by workmen with strong iron bars. At the Abbaye, they were four thousand in number. They burst

---

[53] Will it be believed that in 1790, they still executed at Bicêtre the old barbarous ordinances which prescribed that the medical treatment of such patients should begin by a flagellation? The celebrated doctor Cullorier stated the fact to one of my friends.

[54] *Observations d'un Anglais sur Bicêtre, trad. et commentées par Mirabeau*, 1788.

open the wicket, and break down the large inside doors with their mallets, axes, and crow-bars. The victims are liberated. As they were going out, they met a body of hussars and dragoons, who were arriving full gallop with their swords drawn. The people rush at their bridles; an explanation ensues; the soldiers will not massacre the soldiers' deliverers; they sheathe their swords, and take off their helmets; wine is brought; and they all drink together to the king and the nation.

Everybody in the prison was set at liberty at the same time. The crowd conduct their conquest home,—to the Palais Royal. Among the prisoners delivered, they carried off an old soldier who had been rotting many years in the Abbaye, and was no longer able to walk. The poor fellow, who had so long been accustomed to receive nothing but ill-treatment, was overpowered by his emotion: "I shall die, gentlemen," said he, "so much kindness will kill me!"

There was only one great criminal among them, and he was taken back to prison. All the others, citizens, soldiers, and prisoners, forming an immense procession, arrive at the Palais Royal. There they place a table in the garden, and make them all sit down. The difficulty was to lodge them. They house them for the night in the *Théatre des Variétés*, and mount guard at the door. The next morning, they were located in a hotel, under the arcades, and paid for and fed by the people. All night, either side of Paris had been illuminated, the neighbourhood of the Abbaye and the Palais Royal. Citizens, workmen, rich and poor, dragoons, hussars, and French Guards, all walked about together, and no other noise was heard but the shouts of *"Vive la nation!"* They all gave themselves up to the transports of that fraternal union, to their dawning confidence in the birth of liberty.

Early in the morning, the young men were at Versailles, at the doors of the Assembly. There, everything wore a freezing aspect. A military insurrection and a prison broken open, appeared, at Versailles, most ill-omened. Mirabeau, avoiding the chief question, proposed an address to the Parisians, to advise them to be orderly. They at length came to the conclusion (not very comfortable for those who claimed the interference of the Assembly) of declaring that the affair belonged to nobody but the king, and all they could do was to implore his clemency.

This was on the 1st of July. On the 2nd, the king wrote,— not to the Assembly, but to the Archbishop of Paris,—that if the culprits returned to prison, he might pardon them. The crowd considered this promise so unsatisfactory, that they repaired to the Hôtel-de-Ville and demanded of the electors what they were to believe. The latter hesitated a long time; but the crowd insisted; and was increasing every instant. An hour after midnight, the electors promise to go on the morrow to Versailles, and *not to return without the pardon.* Trusting to their word, the liberated again returned to prison, and were soon released.

This was not a state of peace. Paris was surrounded by war: all the foreign troops had arrived. The old Marshal De Broglie, that Hercules and Achilles of the old monarchy, had been called to command them. The queen had sent for Breteuil, her confidential man, the ex-ambassador at Vienna, a valiant penman, but who, for noise and bravado, was equal to any swordsman. "His big manly voice sounded like energy; he used to step heavily and stamp with his foot, as if he would conjure an army out of the earth."

All this warlike preparation at length aroused the Assembly. Mirabeau, who had read on the 27th an address for peace, without being listened to, now proposed a new one for the removal of the troops; that sonorous and harmonious speech, extremely flattering for the king, was very much relished by the Assembly. The best thing it contained, a demand for a citizen guard, was the only part they suppressed.[55]

The Paris electors, who had been the first to make this request now rejected by the Assembly, resumed it energetically on the 10th of July. Carra, in a very abstract dissertation, in

---

[55] It is not unlikely that the Duke of Orleans, seeing that his mediation was by no means solicited, urged Mirabeau to speak, in order to perplex the court, before it had completed its preparations for war. M. Droz assigns to this period the first connexion of Mirabeau with Laclos, and the money he received from him.

the manner of Sieyès, set forth the right of the Commune,—an imprescriptible right, and, said he, *even anterior to that of the monarchy,* which right specially comprehends that of self-protection. Bonneville demanded, in his own name, and in that of his friend Fauchet, that they should pass on from theory to practice, and think of constituting themselves as a commune, temporarily preserving the self-styled *corps municipal.* Charton wished moreover the sixty districts to be assembled again, their decisions to be transmitted to the National Assembly, and *an understanding to be reached with the chief cities* of the kingdom. All these bold motions were made in the great hall of Saint-Jean, in the Hôtel de Ville, in presence of an immense multitude. Paris seemed to crowd fondly about this authority which it had created, and to trust to no other; it wanted to obtain from it the permission to organize and arm itself, and thus to work out its own salvation.

The weakness of the National Assembly was not calculated to give it comfort. On the 11th of July it had received the king's answer to the address, and remained satisfied with it. Yet, what was the answer? That the troops were there to secure the liberty of the Assembly; but that, if they gave umbrage, the king would transfer it to Noyon or Soissons; that is, would place it between two or three divisions of the army. Mirabeau could not prevail on them to insist on the troops being removed. It was evident that the junction of the five hundred deputies of the clergy and nobility had enervated the Assembly. It set the important business aside, and gave its attention to a declaration of the rights of man presented by Lafayette.

One of the moderate, most moderate members, the philanthropic Guillotin, went to Paris on purpose to communicate this state of tranquillity to the assembly of the electors. That honest man, doubtless deceived, assured them that everything was going well, and that M. Necker was stronger than ever. That excellent news was hailed with loud applause, and the electors, no less duped than the Assembly, amused themselves in like manner with admiring the declaration of rights which, by good fortune, was also just brought from Versailles. That very day,

146

whilst honest Guillotin was speaking, M. Necker, dismissed, was already very far on his road to Brussels.

When Necker received the order to depart immediately, it was three o'clock, and he was sitting down to table. The poor man, who always so tenderly embraced the ministry, and never left it without weeping, contrived however to restrain his emotion before his guests, and to keep his countenance. After dinner he departed with his wife, without even giving notice to his daughter, and took the nearest way out of the country,— the road to the Netherlands. The queen's party, shameful to relate, were anxious to have him arrested; they were so little acquainted with Necker, that they were afraid he might disobey the king, and throw himself into Paris.

MM. de Broglie and de Breteuil, the first day they were summoned, had themselves been frightened to see the dangers into which they were running. Broglie was unwilling that Necker should be sent away. Breteuil is said to have exclaimed: "Give us then a hundred thousand men and a hundred millions." "You shall have them," said the queen. And they set about secretly fabricating paper-money.[56]

M. de Broglie, taken unawares, stooping beneath his burden of seventy-one years, bustled about but did nothing. Orders and counter-orders flew to and fro. His mansion was the headquarters, full of scribes, ordinances, and aides-de-camp, ready to mount on horse-back. "They made out a list of general officers and drew up an order of battle." [57]

The military authorities were not too well agreed among themselves. There were no less than three commanders. Broglie, who was about to be minister, Puységur, who was one still, and lastly Besenval, who had had for eight years the command of the provinces of the interior, and to whom they intimated unceremoniously that he would have to obey the old marshal. Besenval explained to him the dangerous position of things, and that they were not *en campagne*, but before a city of

---

[56] "Several of my colleagues told me they had seen printed ones."—Bailly, i., pp. 395, 331.
[57] Besenval, ii., 359.

eight hundred thousand souls in a state of feverish excitement. Broglie would not listen to him. Strong in his conceit of his Seven Years' War, being acquainted with nothing but soldiers and physical force, full of contempt for citizens, he felt perfectly convinced that at the mere sight of a uniform the people would run away. He did not consider it necessary to send troops to Paris; he merely surrounded it with foreign regiments, being quite unconcerned about thus increasing the popular excitement. All those German soldiers presented the appearance of a Swiss or an Austrian invasion. The outlandish names of the regiments sounded harsh to the ear: Royal-Cravate was at Charenton, Reinach and Diesbach at Sèvres, Nassau at Versailles, Salis-Samade at Issy, the hussars of Bercheny at the Military School; at other stations were Châteauvieux, Esterazy, Roemer, &c.

The Bastille, sufficiently defended by its thick walls, had just received a reinforcement of Swiss soldiers. It had ammunition and a monstrous quantity of gunpowder, enough to blow up the town. The cannon, mounted *en batterie* upon the towers ever since the 30th of June, frowned upon Paris, and ready loaded, thrust their menacing jaws between the battlements.

VI

Insurrection of Paris

FROM the 23rd of June to the 12th of July, from the king's menace to the outbreak of the people, there was a strange pause. It was, says an observer of those days, a stormy, heavy, gloomy time, like a feverish, painful dream, full of illusions and anxiety. There were false alarms, false news, and all sorts of fables and inventions. People knew, but nothing for certain. They wished to account for and guess at everything. Profound causes were discovered even in indifferent things. Partial risings began, without any author or project, of their own accord, from a general fund of distrust and sullen anger. The ground was burning, and as if undermined; and, underneath, you might hear already the grumbling of the volcano.

We have seen that, at the very first assembly of the electors, Bonneville had cried: "To arms!"—a strange cry in that assembly of the notables of Paris, and which expired of itself. Many were indignant, others smiled, and one of them said prophetically: "Young man, postpone your motion for a fortnight."

To arms? What, against a ready organised army at the gates? To arms? when that army could so easily famish the city, when famine was already beginning to be felt, and when the crowd was hourly growing larger at the doors of the bakers. The poor of the neighbouring country were flocking to town by every road, wan and ragged, leaning on their long walking-staffs. A mass of twenty thousand beggars, employed at Montmartre, was suspended over the town; and if Paris made a movement, this other army might come down. A few had already attempted to burn and pillage the barrier-houses.

It was almost certain that the court would strike the first blow. It was necessary for it to compel the king to lay aside his scruples, his hankering for peace, and do away at once with every compromise. To effect this it was necessary to conquer.

Young officers in the hussars, such as Sombreuil and Polignac, went even into the Palais Royal to defy the crowd, and left it sword in hand. Evidently, the court fancied itself too strong; it wished for violence.[58]

On Sunday morning, July 12th, nobody at Paris, up to 10 o'clock, had yet heard of Necker's dismissal. The first who spoke of it in the Palais Royal was called an aristocrat, and insulted. But the news is confirmed; it spreads; and so does the fury of the people. It was then noon, and the cannon of the Palais Royal was fired. "It is impossible," says the *Ami du Roi*, "to express the gloomy feeling of terror which pervaded every soul on hearing that report." A young man, Camille Desmoulins, rushed from the Café de Foy, leaped upon a table, drew a sword, and showed a pistol:—"To arms!" cried he; "the Germans in the Champ de Mars will enter Paris to-night, to butcher the inhabitants! Let us hoist a cockade!" He tore down a leaf from a tree, and stuck it in his hat: everybody followed his example; and the trees were stripped of their leaves.

"No theatres! no dancing! This is a day of mourning!" They go and fetch, from a collection of wax-figures, a bust of Necker; others, ever at hand to seize the opportunity, add one of the Duke of Orleans. They cover them with crape, and carry them through Paris: the procession, armed with staves, swords, pistols, and hatchets, proceeds first up the Rue Richelieu, then

---

[58] "Take care," said Doctor Marat, a philanthropic physician, in one of the innumerable pamphlets of the day, "take care, consider what would be the fatal consequences of a seditious movement. If you are so unfortunate as to engage in it, you are treated as rebels; blood flows," &c. This prudence was conspicuous in many people.

turning the *boulevard*, and the streets St. Martin, Saint-Denis, and Saint-Honoré, arrives at the Place Vendôme. There, in front of the town houses of the farmers of the revenue, a detachment of dragoons was waiting for the people; it charged them, put them to flight, and destroyed their Necker; one of the French guards, unarmed, stood his ground, and was killed.

The barriers, which were scarcely finished,—those oppressive little bastilles of the farmers of the revenue,—were attacked everywhere on that same Sunday, by the people, and but ill-defended by the troops, who however killed a few persons. They were burnt during the night.

The court, so near Paris, could not be ignorant of what was passing. It remained motionless, and sent neither orders nor troops. Apparently, it was waiting till the disturbance, increasing to rebellion and war, should give it what the Réveillon riot (too soon appeased) had not been able to give—a specious pretext for dissolving the Assembly. Therefore, it allowed Paris to go on doing mischief at pleasure. It guarded well Versailles, the bridges of Sèvres and Saint-Cloud, cut off all communication, and believed itself sure of being able, if things came to the worst, to starve out the city of Paris. As for itself, surrounded by troops, of which two-thirds were German, what had it to fear? Nothing, but to lose France.

The minister of Paris (there was one still) remained at Versailles. The other authorities, the lieutenant of police, Flesselles the provost, and Berthier the intendant, appeared equally inactive. Flesselles, summoned to court, was unable to go there; but it is likely he received instructions.[59]

Besenval, the commander, without any responsibility, since he could act only by the orders of Broglie, remained idly at the Military School. He dared not make use of the French guards, and kept them confined. But he had several detachments of different corps, and three disposable regiments, one of Swiss, and two of German cavalry. Towards the afternoon,

---

[59] As we learn from the king himself. See his first reply (July 14th) to the National Assembly.

seeing the riot increasing, he posted his Swiss in the *Champs-Elysées* with four pieces of cannon, and drew up his cavalry on the Place Louis XV.

Before evening, before the hour at which people return home on Sunday, the crowd was coming back by the Champs-Elysées, and filling the gardens of the Tuileries; they were, for the most part, quiet people taking their walk, families who wanted to return home early "because there had been disturbances." However, the sight of those German soldiers, drawn up in order of battle on the spot, necessarily excited some indignation. Some of the men abused them, and children threw stones.[60] Then Besenval, fearing at length lest he should be reproached at Versailles with having done nothing, gave the insensate, barbarous order, so like his thoughtlessness, to drive the people forward with the dragoons. They could not move in that dense crowd without trampling on some of them. Their colonel, prince of Lambesc, entered the Tuileries, at first at a slow pace. He was stopped by a barricade of chairs; and being assailed by a shower of bottles and stones, he fired upon the crowd. The women shrieked, and the men tried to shut the gates behind the prince. He had the presence of mind to retire. One man was thrown down and trampled upon; and an old man whilst trying to escape was grievously wounded.

The crowd, rushing out of the Tuileries, with exclamations of horror and indignation, filled Paris with the account of this brutality, of those Germans driving their horses against women and children, and even the old man wounded, so they said, by the hand of the prince himself. Then they run to the gunsmiths and take whatever they find. They hasten also to the Hôtel de Ville to demand arms and ring the alarm-bell. No municipal

---

[60] If there had been any pistols fired by the people, or any dragoons wounded, as Besenval has stated, Desèze, his very clever defender, would not have failed to make the most of it in his *Observations sur le rapport d'accusation*. See this report in the *Histoire Parlementaire*, iv., p. 69; and Desèze, at the end of Besenval, ii., p. 369. Who is to be believed, Desèze, who pretends that Besenval gave no orders, or Besenval, who confesses before his judges that *he had a strong desire* to drive away that crowd, and that he gave orders to charge?—*Hist. Parl.*, ii., p. 89.

magistrate was at his post. A few electors, of their own good-will, repaired thither about six in the evening, occupied their reserved seats in the great hall, and tried to calm the multitude. But behind that crowd, already entered, there was another in the square, shouting "Arms!" who believed the town possessed a secret arsenal, and were threatening to burn everything. They overpowered the guard, invaded the hall, pushed down the barriers, and pressed the electors as far as their office. Then they related to them a thousand accounts at once of what has just happened. The electors could not refuse the arms of the city guards; but the crowd had sought, found, and taken them; and already a man in his shirt, without either shoes or stockings, had taken the place of the sentinel, and with his gun on his shoulder was resolutely mounting guard at the door of the hall.[61]

The electors declined the responsibility of authorising the insurrection. They only granted the convocation of the districts, and sent a few of their friends "to the posts of the armed citizens, to entreat them, in the name of their native land, to suspend riotous meetings and acts of violence." They had begun that evening in a very serious manner. Some French guards having escaped from their barracks, formed in the Palais Royal, marched against the Germans, and avenged their comrade. They killed three of the cavalry on the *boulevard,* and then marched to the Place Louis XV., which they found evacuated.

On Monday, July 13th, Guillotin the deputy, with two electors, went to Versailles, and entreated the Assembly to "concur in establishing a citizen guard." They gave a terrible description of the crisis of Paris. The Assembly voted two deputations, one to the king, the other to the city. That to the king obtained from him only a cold unsatisfactory answer, and a very strange one when blood was flowing: That he could make no alterations in the measures he had taken, that he was the only judge of their necessities, and that the presence of the deputies at

---

[61] *Procès-Verbal des Électeurs,* i., p. 180. Compare Dussaulx, *Oeuvre des Sept Jours.* Dussaulx, who wrote some time after, often inverts the order of the facts.

Paris could do no good. The indignant Assembly decreed:—1st, that M. Necker bore with him the regret of the nation; 2ndly, that it insisted on the removal of the troops; 3rdly, that not only the ministers, but the king's counsellors, of *whatever rank* they might be, were personally responsible for the present misfortunes; 4thly, that no power had the right to pronounce the infamous word "bankruptcy." The third article sufficiently designated the queen and the princes, and the last branded them with reproach. The Assembly thus resumed its noble attitude; unarmed in the middle of the troops, without any other support than the law, threatened that very evening to be dispersed or made away with, it yet bravely branded its enemies on their brow with their true name: *bankrupts.*[62]

After that vote, the Assembly had but one asylum—the Assembly itself, the room it occupied; beyond that, it had not an inch of ground in the world; not one of its members dared any longer sleep at home. It feared also lest the court should seize upon its archives. On the preceding evening, Sunday, Grégoire, one of the secretaries, had folded up, sealed, and hidden all the papers in a house at Versailles.[63]

On Monday he presided, *per interim,* and sustained by his courage the weak-hearted, by reminding them of the Tennis-Court, and the words of the Roman: "Fearless amid the crush of worlds." (Impavidum ferient ruinae.)

The sitting was declared permanent, and it continued for seventy-two hours. M. Lafayette, who had contributed not a little to the vigorous decree, was named vice-president.

Meanwhile Paris was in the utmost anxiety. The Faubourg Saint-Honoré expected every moment to see the troops enter. In spite of the efforts of the electors, who ran about all night to make the people lay down their arms, everybody was arming; nobody was disposed to receive the Croats and the Hungarian hussars peaceably, and to carry the keys to the queen. As early

---

[62] They were going to make payments with paper-money, without any other guarantee than the signature of an insolvent king. See *ante,* p. 131.

[63] *Mémoires de Grégoire,* i., p. 382.

as six o'clock on Monday morning, all the bells in every Church sounding alarm, a few electors repaired to the Hôtel-de-Ville, found the crowd already assembled, and sent it off to the different districts. At eight o'clock, seeing the people were in earnest, they affirmed that the citizen guard was authorised, which was not yet the case. The people were perpetually shouting for arms. To which the electors reply: If the town has any, they can only be obtained through the mayor. "Well then," cried they, "send for him!"

The mayor, or provost, Flesselles, was on that day summoned to Versailles by the king, and to the Hôtel-de-Ville by the people. Whether he dared not refuse the summons of the crowd, or thought he could better serve the King at Paris, he went to the Hôtel-de-Ville, was applauded in La Grève, and said in a fatherly tone: "You shall be satisfied, my friends, I am your father." He declared in the hall that he would preside only by election of the people. Thereupon, a fresh burst of enthusiasm.

Though there was as yet no Parisian army, they were already discussing who should be its general. The American Moreau de Saint-Mèry, the president of the electors, pointed to a bust of Lafayette, and that name was received with applause. Others proposed and obtained that the command should be offered to the Duke d'Aumont, who demanded twenty-four hours for reflection, and then refused. The second in command was the Marquis de la Salle, a well-tried soldier, a patriotic writer, full of devotion and probity.

All this was wasting time, and the crowd was in a fever of impatience; it was in a hurry to be armed, and not without reason. The beggars of Montmartre, throwing away their pick-axes, came down upon the town; crowds of unknown vagrants were prowling about. The frightful misery of the rural districts had poured, from all sides, their starving populations towards Paris: it was peopled by famine.

That same morning, on a report that there was some grain at Saint-Lazare, the crowd ran thither, and found indeed an enormous quantity of flour, amassed by the good friars, enough to load more than fifty carts which were driven to market. They broke open everything, and ate and drank what was in the house; however, they carried nothing away; the first who attempted to do so, was hanged by the people themselves.

The prisoners of Saint-Lazare had escaped. Those of La Force who had been imprisoned for debt were set at liberty. The criminals of Le Châtelet wanted to take advantage of the opportunity, and were already breaking down the doors. The gaoler called in a band of the people who were passing; it entered, fired upon the rebels, and forced them to become orderly again.

The arms of the store-room were carried off, but subsequently all restored.

The electors, being unable to defer the arming any longer, attempted to keep it within limits. They voted, and the provost pronounced: That each of the sixty districts should elect and arm two hundred men, and that all the rest should be disarmed. It was an army of *twelve thousand* respectable persons, wonderfully good for police, but very bad for defence. Paris would have been given up. In the afternoon of the same day, it was decided: That the Parisian police should consist of *forty-eight thousand* men. The cockade was to be of the colours of the city, blue and red.[64] This decree was confirmed on the same day by all the districts.

A permanent committee is named to watch night and day over public order. It is formed of electors. "Why electors alone?" said a man, stepping forward. "Why, whom would you have named?" "Myself," said he. He was appointed by acclamation.

The provost then ventured to put a very serious question: "To whom shall the oath be taken?" "To the Assembly of the Citizens," exclaimed an elector with energy.

The question of subsistence was as urgent as that of arms. The lieutenant of police, on being summoned by the electors,

---

[64] But as they were also those of the house of Orleans, white, the old colour of France, was added, on the proposal of M. de Lafayette.—See his *Mémoires*, ii., p. 266. "I give you," said he, "a cockade which will go round the world."

said that the supplies of grain were entirely beyond his jurisdiction. The town was necessarily obliged to think about obtaining provisions as it could. The roads in every direction were
occupied with troops; it was necessary for the farmers and
traders who brought their merchandise to run the risk of
passing through military posts and camps of foreigners, who
spoke nothing but German. And even supposing they did arrive, they met with a thousand difficulties in re-passing the
barriers.

Paris was evidently to die of hunger, or conquer, and to
conquer in one day. How was this miracle to be expected?
It had the enemy in the very town, in the Bastille, and at the
Military School, and every barrier besieged; the French guards,
except a small number, remained in their barracks, and had
not yet made up their minds. That the miracle should be
wrought by the Parisians quite alone, was almost ridiculous to
suppose. They had the reputation of being a gentle, quiet,
good-natured sort of population. That such people should become, all of a sudden, an army, and a warlike army, was most
unlikely.

This was certainly the opinion of the cool-headed notables
and citizens who composed the committee of the town. They
wanted to gain time, and not to increase the immense responsibility which weighed already upon them. They had governed
Paris ever since the 12th; was it as electors? did the electoral
power extend so far? They expected every moment to see the
old Marshal de Broglie arrive with all his troops to call them
to account. Hence their hesitation, and their conduct so long
equivocal; hence, also, the distrust of the people, who found
in them their principal obstacle, and did business without them.

About the middle of the day, the electors who had been sent
to Versailles, returned with the king's threatening answer, and
the decree of the Assembly.

There was nothing left but war. The envoys had met on the
road the green cockade, the colour of the Count d'Artois. They
had passed through the cavalry and all the German troops
stationed along the road in their white Austrian cloaks.

The situation was terrible, almost hopeless, so far as equipment was concerned. But the courage of the people was immense; everybody felt his heart waxing hourly stronger within his bosom. They all marched to the Hôtel-de-Ville, to offer themselves for the fight; there were whole corporations, whole quarters of the town forming legions of volunteers. The company of arquebusiers offered its services. The school of surgery came forward with Boyer at its head; the Basoche [65] wanted to take the lead and fight in the vanguard: all those young men swore they would die to the last man.

Fight? But with what? Without arms, guns, and powder?

The arsenal was said to be empty. The people however were not so easily satisfied. An invalid and a peruke-maker kept watch in the neighbourhood; and soon they saw a large quantity of powder brought out, which was going to be embarked for Rouen. They ran to the Hôtel-de-Ville, and obliged the electors to command the powder to be brought. A brave *abbé* undertook the dangerous mission of guarding it and distributing it among the people.[66]

Nothing was now wanting but guns. It was well known that there was a large magazine of them in Paris. Berthier, the intendant, had caused thirty thousand to be imported, and had commanded two hundred thousand cartridges to be made. The provost could not possibly be ignorant of these active measures at the intendant's office. Urged to point out the depot, he said the manufactory at Charleville had promised him thirty thousand guns, and moreover, twelve thousand were momentarily expected. To support this falsehood, waggons inscribed with the word *Artillerie* are seen passing through La Grève. These must evidently be the guns. The provost orders the cases to be stowed in the magazines. But he must have French

---

[65] Body of clerks attached to the law courts (Ed. note).

[66] This heroic man was the *abbé* Lefebvre d'Ormesson. Nobody rendered a greater service to the Revolution and the city of Paris. He remained forty-eight hours upon that volcano, among madmen fighting for the powder; they fired at him several times; a drunken man went and smoked upon the open casks, &c.

guards to distribute them. The people run to the barracks; but, as they might have expected, the officers will not give a single soldier. So the electors must distribute the guns themselves. They open the cases! Judge what they find. Rags! The fury of the people knows no bounds; they shout out "Treason!" Flesselles, not knowing what to say, thinks it best to send them to the Célestin and the Chartreux friars, saying:—"The monks have arms concealed." Another disappointment: the Chartreux friars open and show everything; and not a gun is found after the closest search.

The electors authorised the districts to manufacture fifty thousand pikes; they were forged in thirty-six hours; yet even that dispatch seemed too slow for such a crisis. Everything might be decided in the night. The people, who always knew things when their leaders did not, heard, in the evening, of the great depot of guns at the Invalides. The deputies of one district went, the same evening, to Besenval, the commandant, and Sombreuil, the governor of the Hôtel. "I will write to Versailles about it," said Besenval, coldly. Accordingly, he gave notice to the Marshal de Broglie. Most strange to say, he received no answer!

This inconceivable silence was doubtless owing, as it has been alleged, to the complete anarchy that reigned in the council: all differing on every point, excepting a very decided one, the dissolution of the National Assembly. It was likewise owing, in my opinion, to the misconception of the court, who, over cunning and subtle, looked upon that great insurrection as the effect of a petty intrigue, believed that the Palais Royal was doing everything, and that Orleans was paying for all. A puerile explanation. Is it possible to bribe millions of men? Had the duke financed also the insurrections at Lyons and in Dauphiné, which, at that very moment, had loudly refused to pay the taxes? Had he bribed the cities of Brittany, which were rising up in arms, or the soldiers, who, at Rennes, refused to fire upon the citizens?

The prince's effigy had, it is true, been carried in triumph. But the prince himself had come to Versailles to surrender to his enemies, and to protest that he was as much afraid of the riot as anybody, or even more so. He was requested to have the goodness to sleep at the castle. The court, having him under its hand, thought it held fast the fabricator of the whole machination, and felt more at its ease. The old marshal, to whom all the military forces were intrusted at that moment, surrounded himself well with troops, held the king in safety, put Versailles, which nobody thought of, in a state of defence, and looking upon the insurrection of Paris as so much smoke, left it to subside of itself.

VII

The Taking of the Bastille, July 14, 1789

VERSAILLES, with an organised government, a king, ministers, a general, and an army, was all hesitation, doubt, uncertainty, and in a state of the most complete moral anarchy.

Paris, all commotion, destitute of every legal authority, and in the utmost confusion, attained, on the 14th of July, what is morally the highest degree of order,—unanimity of feeling.

On the 13th, Paris thought only of defending itself; on the 14th, it attacked.

On the evening of the 13th, some doubt still existed, but none remained in the morning. The evening had been stormy, agitated by a whirlwind of ungovernable frenzy. The morning was still and serene,—an awful calm.

With daylight, one idea dawned upon Paris, and all were illumined with the same ray of hope. A light broke upon every mind, and the same voice thrilled through every heart: "Go! and thou shalt take the Bastille!" That was impossible, unreasonable, preposterous. And yet everybody believed it. And the thing was done.

The Bastille, though an old fortress, was nevertheless impregnable, unless besieged for several days and with an abundance of artillery. The people had, in that crisis, neither the time nor the means to make a regular siege. Had they done so, the Bastille had no cause for fear, having enough provisions to wait for succour so near at hand, and an immense supply of ammunition. Its walls, ten feet thick at the top of the towers, and thirty or forty at the base, might long laugh at cannon-balls; and its batteries firing down upon Paris, could, in the meantime, demolish the whole of the Marais and the Faubourg Saint-Antoine. Its towers, pierced with windows and loop-holes, protected by double and triple gratings, enabled the garrison, in full security, to make a dreadful carnage of its assailants.

The attack on the Bastille was by no means reasonable. It was an act of faith.

Nobody proposed; but all believed, and all acted. Along the streets, the quays, the bridges, and the boulevards, the crowd shouted to the crowd: "To the Bastille! The Bastille!" And the tolling of the tocsin thundered in every ear: "*à la Bastille!*"

Nobody, I repeat, gave the impulse. The orators of the Palais Royal passed the time in drawing up a list of proscription, in condemning the queen to death, as well as Madame de Polignac, Artois, Flesselles the provost, and others. The names of the conquerors of the Bastille do not include one of these makers of motions. The Palais Royal was not the starting-point, neither was it to the Palais Royal that the conquerors brought back the spoils and prisoners.

Still less had the electors, assembled in the Hôtel-de-Ville, the idea of the attack. On the contrary, in order to prevent it, as well as the carnage which the Bastille could so easily make, they went so far as to promise the governor, that if he withdrew his cannon he should not be attacked. The electors did not behave treacherously, though they were accused of having done so; but they had no faith.

Who had? They who had also the devotion and the strength to accomplish their faith. Who? Why, the people,—everybody.

Old men who have had the happiness and the misery to see all that has happened in this unprecedented half century, in which ages seem to be crowded together, declare, that the grand and national achievements of the Republic and the Empire, had nevertheless a partial non-unanimous character, but that the 14th of July alone was the day of the whole people. Then let that great day remain ever one of the eternal *fêtes* of the human race, not only as having been the first of deliverance, but as having been superlatively the day of concord!

What had happened during that short night, on which nobody slept, for every uncertainty and difference of opinion to disappear with the shades of darkness, and all to have the same thoughts in the morning?

What took place at the Palais Royal and the Hôtel-de-Ville is well known; but what would be far more important to know, is, what took place on the domestic hearth of the people.

For there indeed, as we may sufficiently divine by what followed, there every heart summoned the past to its day of judgment, and every one, before a blow was struck, pronounced its irrevocable condemnation. History returned that night a long history of sufferings to the avenging instinct of the people. The souls of fathers who, for so many ages, had suffered and died in silence, descended into their sons, and spoke.

O brave men, you who till then had been so patient, so pacific, who, on that day, were to inflict the heavy blow of Providence, did not the sight of your families, whose only resource is in you, daunt your hearts? Far from it: gazing once more at your slumbering children, those children for whom that day was to create a destiny, your expanding minds embraced the free generations arising from their cradle, and felt at that moment the whole battle of the future!

The future and the past both gave the same reply; both cried Advance! And what is beyond all time,—beyond the future and the past,—immutable right said the same. The immortal sentiment of the Just imparted a temper of adamant to the fluttering heart of man; it said to him: "Go in peace; what matters? Whatever may happen, I am with thee, in death or victory!"

And yet what was the Bastille to them? The lower orders seldom or never entered it. Justice spoke to them, and, a voice that speaks still louder to the heart, the voice of humanity and mercy; that still small voice which seems so weak but that overthrows towers, had, for ten years, been shaking the very foundations of the doomed Bastille.

Let the truth be told; if any one had the glory of causing its downfall, it was that intrepid woman who wrought so long for the deliverance of Latude against all the powers in the world. Royalty refused, and the nation forced it to pardon; that woman, or that hero, was crowned in a public solemnity. To crown her who had, so to speak, forced open the state-prisons, was already branding them with infamy, devoting them to public execration, and demolishing them in the hearts and desires of men. That woman had shaken the Bastille to its foundations.

From that day, the people of the town and the faubourg, who, in that much-frequented quarter, were ever passing and re-passing in its shadow, never failed to curse it.[67] And well did it deserve their hatred. There were many other prisons, but this one was the abode of capricious arbitrariness, wanton despotism, and ecclesiastical and bureaucratic inquisition. The court, so devoid of religion in that age, had made the Bastille a dungeon for free minds,—the prison of thought. Less crowded during the reign of Louis XVI., it had become more cruel; the prisoners were deprived of their walk: more rigorous, and no less unjust: we blush for France, to be obliged to say that the crime of one of the prisoners was to have given a useful secret to our navy! They were afraid lest he should tell it elsewhere.

The Bastille was known and detested by the whole world. Bastille and tyranny were, in every language, synonymous terms. Every nation, at the news of its destruction, believed it had recovered its liberty.

In Russia, that empire of mystery and silence,—that monstrous Bastille between Europe and Asia, scarcely had the news arrived when you might have seen men of every nation shouting and weeping for joy in the open streets; they rushed

---

[67] *Elle écrasait la rue Saint-Antoine,* is Linguet's energetical expression, p. 147. The best known conquerors of the Bastille were, either men of the Faubourg, or of the quarter Saint-Paul, of the Culture-Sainte-Catherine.

into each other's arms to tell the news: "Who can help weeping for joy? *The Bastille is taken.*" [68]

On the very morning of that great day, the people had as yet no arms.

The powder they had taken from the arsenal the night before, and put in the Hôtel-de-Ville, was slowly distributed to them, during the night, by only three men. The distribution having ceased for a moment, about two o'clock, the desperate crowd hammered down the doors of the magazine, every blow striking fire on the nails.

No guns!—It was necessary to go and take them, to carry them off from the Invalides; that was very hazardous. The *Hôtel des Invalides* is, it is true, an open mansion; but Sombreuil, the governor, a brave old soldier, had received a strong detachment of artillery and some cannon, without counting those he had already. Should those cannon be brought to act, the crowd might be taken in the flank, and easily dispersed by the regiments that Besenval had at the military school.

Would those foreign regiments have refused to act? In spite of what Besenval says to the contrary, there is reason to doubt it. What is much plainer, is, that being left without orders, he was himself full of hesitation, and appeared paralysed in mind. At five o'clock that same morning, he had received a strange visit;—a man rushed in; his countenance was livid, his eyes flashed fire, his language was impetuous and brief, and his manner audacious. The old coxcomb, who was the most frivolous officer of the *ancien régime*, but brave and collected, gazed at the man, and was struck with admiration. "Baron," said the man, "I come to advise you to make no resistance; the barriers will be burnt to-day; [69] I am sure of it, but cannot prevent it; neither can you—do not try."

---

[68] This fact is related by a witness above suspicion, Count de Ségur, ambassador at the court of Russia, who was far from sharing that enthusiasm: "This madness which I can hardly believe whilst relating it," &c. Ségur, *Mémoires* iii., p. 508.

[69] By these words we perceive that at five o'clock, no plan had been formed. The man in question, who was not one of the people, repeated, apparently, the rumours of the Palais Royal.—The Utopians had long been

Besenval was not afraid; but he had, nevertheless, felt the shock, and suffered its moral effect. "There was something eloquent in that man," says he, "that struck me; I ought to have had him arrested, and yet I did not." It was the *ancien régime* and the Revolution meeting face to face, and the latter left the former lost in astonishment.

Before nine o'clock thirty thousand men were in front of the Invalides; the Attorney General of the City was at their head: the committee of the electors had not dared to refuse him. Among them were seen a few companies of the French Guards, who had escaped from their barracks, the Clerks of the Basoche, in their old red dresses, and the Curate of Saint-Etienne-du-Mont, who, being named president of the Assembly formed in his church, did not decline the perilous office of heading this armed multitude.

Old Sombreuil acted very adroitly. He showed himself at the gate, said it was true he had guns, but that they had been intrusted to him as a deposit, and that his honour, as a soldier and a gentleman, did not allow him to be a traitor.

This unexpected argument stopped the crowd at once; a proof of the admirable candour of the people in that early age of the Revolution. Sombreuil added, that he had sent a courier to Versailles, and was expecting the answer; backing all this with numerous protestations of attachment and friendship for the Hôtel-de-Ville and the city in general.

The majority was willing to wait. Luckily, there was one man present who was less scrupulous, and prevented the crowd from being so easily mystified.[70]

"There is no time to be lost," said he, "and whose arms are these but the nation's?" Then they leaped into the trenches, and the Hôtel was invaded; twenty-eight thousand muskets were found in the cellars, and carried off, together with twenty pieces of cannon.

---

talking of the utility of destroying the Bastille, forming plans, &c.; but the heroic, wild idea of taking it in one day, could be conceived only by the people.

[70] One of the assembled citizens. *Procès-verbal des électeurs,* i., p. 300.

All this between nine and eleven o'clock; but, let us hasten to the Bastille.

The governor, De Launey, had been under arms ever since two o'clock in the morning of the 13th; no precaution had been neglected; besides his cannon on the towers, he had others from the arsenal, which he placed in the court, and loaded with grape-shot. He caused six cart-loads of paving-stones, cannon-balls, and old iron, to be carried to the tops of the towers, in order to crush his assailants.[71] In the bottom loop-holes he had placed twelve large rampart guns, each of which carried a pound and a half of bullets. He kept below his trustiest soldiers, thirty-two Swiss, who had no scruple in firing upon Frenchmen. His eighty-two *Invalides* [72] were mostly distributed in different posts, far from the gates, upon the towers. He had evacuated the outer buildings which covered the foot of the fortress.

On the 13th, nothing save curses bestowed on the Bastille by passersby.

On the 14th, about midnight, seven shots were fired at the sentinels upon the towers.—Alarm!—The governor ascends with staff, remains half-an-hour, listening to the distant murmuring of the town; finding all quiet he descends.

The next morning many people were about, and, from time to time, young men (from the Palais Royal, or others) were calling out that they must give them arms. They pay no attention to them. They hear and introduce the pacific deputation of the Hôtel-de-Ville, which, about ten o'clock, intreats the governor to withdraw his cannon, promising that if he does not fire, he shall not be attacked. He, willingly, accepts, having no orders to fire, and highly delighted, obliges the envoys to breakfast with him.

As they were leaving, a man arrives who speaks in a very different tone.

---

[71] *Biographie* Michaud,—article *De Launey,* written from information furnished by his family.

[72] Pensioned soldiers (Ed. note).

A violent, bold man, unacquainted with human respect, fearless and pitiless, knowing neither obstacle nor delay, and bearing in his breast the passionate genius of the Revolution—he came to summon the Bastille.

Terror accompanied him. The Bastille was afraid; the governor, without knowing why, was troubled and stammered.

That man was Thuriot, a monster of ferocity, one of the race of Danton. We meet with him twice, in the beginning and at the end. And twice his words are deadly; he destroys the Bastille,[73] and he kills Robespierre.

He was not to pass the bridge; the governor would not allow it; and yet he passed. From the first court, he marches to a second; another refusal; but he passes on, and crosses the second ditch by the draw-bridge. Behold him now in front of the enormous iron gate by which the third court was shut. This seemed a monstrous well rather than a court, its eight towers united together, forming its inside walls. Those frightful gigantic towers did not look towards the court, nor had they a single window. At their feet, in their shadow, was the prisoners' only walk. Lost at the bottom of the pit, and overwhelmed by those enormous masses, he could contemplate only the stern nudity of the walls. On one side only, had been placed a clock, between two figures of captives in chains, as if to fetter time itself, and make the slow succession of hours still more burdensome.

There were the loaded cannon, the garrison, and the staff. Thuriot was daunted by nothing. "Sir," said he to the governor, "I summon you, in the name of the people, in the name of honour, and of our native land, to withdraw your cannon, and surrender the Bastille."—Then, turning towards the garrison, he repeated the same words.

If M. De Launey had been a true soldier, he would not thus have introduced the envoy into the heart of the citadel; still

---

[73] He destroyed it in two ways. He introduced division and demoralization, and when it was taken, it was he who proposed to have it demolished. He killed Robespierre, by refusing to let him speak, on the 9th thermidor. Thuriot was then president of the Convention.

less would he have let him address the garrison. But, it is very necessary to remark, that the officers of the Bastille were mostly officers by favour of the lieutenant of police; even those who had never seen service, wore the cross of Saint Louis. All of them, from the governor down to the scullions, had bought their places, and turned them to the best advantage. The governor found means to add every year to his salary of sixty thousand francs, a sum quite as large by his rapine. He supplied his establishment at the prisoners' expense; he had reduced their supply of firewood, and made a profit on their wine,[74] and their miserable furniture. What was most infamous and barbarous, was, that he let out to a gardener the little garden of the Bastille, over a bastion; and, for that miserable profit, he had deprived the prisoners of that walk, as well as of that on the towers; that is to say, of air and light.

That greedy, sordid soul had moreover good reason to be dispirited; he felt he was known; Linguet's terrible memoirs had rendered De Launey infamous throughout Europe. The Bastille was hated; but the governor was personally detested. The furious imprecations of the people, which he heard, he appropriated to himself; and he was full of anxiety and fear.

Thuriot's words acted differently on the Swiss and the French. The Swiss did not understand them; their captain, M. de Flue, was resolved to hold out. But the Staff and the *Invalides* were much shaken; those old soldiers, in habitual communication with the people of the faubourg, had no desire to fire upon them. Thus the garrison was divided; what will these two parties do? If they cannot agree, will they fire upon each other?

The dispirited governor said, in an apologetic tone, what had just been agreed with the town. He swore, and made the garrison swear, that if they were not attacked they would not begin.

---

[74] The governor had the privilege of ordering in a hundred casks of wine free of duty. He sold that right to a tavern, and received from it vinegar to give to the prisoners; Linguet, p. 86. See in *La Bastille Dévoilée*, the history of a rich prisoner, whom De Launey used to conduct, at night, to a female, whom he, De Launey, had kept, but would no longer pay.

Thuriot did not stop there. He desired to ascend to the top of the towers, to see whether the cannon were really withdrawn. De Launey, who had been all this time repenting of having allowed him already to penetrate so far, refused; but, being pressed by his officers, he ascended with Thuriot.

The cannon were drawn back and masked, but still pointed. The view from that height of a hundred and forty feet was immense and startling; the streets and openings full of people, and all the garden of the arsenal crowded with armed men. But, on the other side, a black mass was advancing. It was the faubourg Saint Antoine.

The governor turned pale. He grasped Thuriot by the arm: "What have you done? You abuse your privilege as an envoy! You have betrayed me!"

They were both standing on the brink, and De Launey had a sentinel on the tower. Everybody in the Bastille was bound by oath to the governor; in his fortress, he was king and the law. He was still able to avenge himself.

But, on the contrary, it was Thuriot who made him afraid: "Sir," said he, "one word more, and I swear to you that one of us two shall be hurled headlong into the moat!" [75]

At the same moment, the sentinel approached, as frightened as the governor, and, addressing Thuriot: "Pray, Sir," said he, "show yourself; there is no time to lose; they are marching forward. Not seeing you, they will attack us." He leaned over through the battlements; and the people seeing him alive, and standing boldly upon the tower, uttered deafening shouts of joy and approbation.

Thuriot descended with the governor, again crossed through the court, and addressing the garrison once more: "I am going to give my report," said he; "I hope the people will not refuse to furnish a citizen guard [76] to keep the Bastille with you."

---

[75] Account of M. Thuriot's conduct, at the end of Dussaulx, *Oeuvre des sept jours*, p. 408.—Compare the *Procès-verbal des électeurs*, i., p. 310.

[76] This bold dignified language is related by the besieged. See their declaration at the end of Dussaulx, p. 449.

The people expected to enter the Bastille as soon as Thuriot came forth. When they saw him depart, to make his report to the Hôtel-de-Ville, they took him for a traitor, and threatened him. Their impatience was growing into fury. The crowd seized on three *Invalides*, and wanted to tear them to pieces. They also seized on a young lady whom they believed to be the governor's daughter, and some wanted to burn her, if he refused to surrender. Others dragged her from them.

What will become of us, said they, if the Bastille be not taken before night? The burly Santerre, a brewer, whom the faubourg had elected its commander, proposed to burn the place by throwing into it poppyseed and spikenard oil [77] that they had seized the night before, and which they could fire with phosphorus. He sent off for the fire-engines.

A blacksmith, an old soldier, without wasting time in idle talk, sets bravely to work. He marches forward, hatchet in hand, leaps upon the roof of a small guard-house, near the first drawbridge, and, under a shower of bullets, coolly plies his hatchet, cuts away, and loosens the chains; down falls the bridge. The crowd rush over it, and enter the court.

The firing began at once from the towers and from the loop-holes below. The assailants fell in crowds, and did no harm to the garrison. Of all the shots they fired that day, two took effect: only one of the besieged was killed.

The committee of electors, who saw the wounded already arriving at the Hôtel-de-Ville, and deplored the shedding of blood, would have wished to stop it. There was now but one way of doing so, which was to summon the Bastille, in the name of the city, to surrender, and to allow the citizen-guard to enter. The provost hesitated for a long time; Fauchet insisted; [78] and other electors entreated him. They went as deputies; but in the fire and smoke, they were not even seen; neither the Bastille nor the people ceased firing. The deputies were in the

---

[77] He himself boasts of this folly. *Procès-verbal des électeurs*, i., p. 385.

[78] If we may believe him, he had the honour of being the first to propose it. Fauchet, *Discours sur la liberté prononcé le 6 Août 89 à Saint Jacques*, p. 11.

greatest danger. A second deputation, headed by the city proctor, with a drum and a flag of truce, was perceived from the
fortress. The soldiers who were upon the towers hoisted a
white flag, and reversed their arms. The people ceased firing,
followed the deputation, and entered the court. There, they
were welcomed by a furious discharge, which brought down
several men by the side of the deputies. Very probably the
Swiss who were below with De Launey, paid no attention
to the signs made by the *Invalides*.[79]

The rage of the people was inexpressible. Ever since the
morning, it had been said that the governor had enticed the
crowd into the court to fire upon them; they believed themselves twice deceived, and resolved to perish, or to be revenged
on the traitors. To those who were calling them back, they
exclaimed in a transport of frenzy: "Our bodies at least shall
serve to fill the moats!" And on they rushed obstinately and
nothing daunted, amid a shower of bullets and against those
murderous towers, as if, by dying in heaps, they could at length
overthrow them.

But then, numbers of generous men, who had hitherto taken
no part in the action, beheld, with increased indignation, such
an unequal struggle, which was actual assassination. They
wanted to lend their assistance. It was no longer possible to
hold back the French Guards; they all sided with the people.
They repaired to the commandants nominated by the town, and
obliged them to surrender their five cannons. Two columns were
formed, one of workmen and citizens, the other of French
Guards. The former took for its chief a young man, of heroic
stature and strength, named Hullin, a clockmaker of Geneva,
but now a servant, being gamekeeper to the Marquis de Con-
flans; his Hungarian costume as a *chasseur* was doubtless taken
for a uniform; and thus did the livery of servitude guide
the people to the combat of liberty. The leader of the other
column was Élie, an officer of fortune belonging to the Queen's

---

[79] This is the most satisfactory way of reconciling the apparently
contradictory declarations of the besieged and of the deputation.

regiment, who, changing his private dress for his brilliant uniform, showed himself bravely a conspicuous object to both friends and foes.

Among his soldiers, was one admirable for his valour, youth, and candour, Marceau, one of the glories of France, who remained satisfied with fighting, and claimed no share in the honour of the victory.

Things were not very far advanced when they arrived. Three cart-loads of straw had been pushed forward and set on fire, and the barracks and kitchens had been burnt down. They knew not what else to do. The despair of the people was vented upon the Hôtel-de-Ville. They blamed the provost and the electors, and urged them, in threatening language, to issue formal orders for the siege of the Bastille. But they could never induce them to give those orders.

Several strange and singular means were proposed to the electors for taking the fortress. A carpenter advised the erection of a Roman catapult, in wood-work, to hurl stones against the walls. The commanders of the town said it was necessary to attack in a regular way, and open a trench. During this long and useless debate, a letter at that moment intercepted, was brought in and read; it was from Besenval to de Launey, commanding him to hold out to the last extremity.

To appreciate the value of time at that momentous crisis, and understand the dread felt at any delay, we must know that there were false alarms every instant. It was supposed that the court, informed at two o'clock of the attack on the Bastille, which had begun at noon, would take that opportunity of pouring down its Swiss and German troops upon Paris. Again, would those at the Military School pass the day in inaction? That was unlikely. What Besenval says about the little reliance he could place on his troops seems like an excuse. The Swiss showed themselves very firm at the Bastille, as appeared from the carnage; the German dragoons had, on the 12th, fired several times, and killed some of the French Guards; the latter had killed several dragoons; a spirit of mutual hatred ensured fidelity.

In the faubourg Saint Honoré, the paving-stones were dug up, the attack being expected every moment; La Villette was in the same state, and a regiment really came and occupied it, but too late.

Every appearance of dilatoriness appeared treason. The provost's shuffling conduct caused him to be suspected, as well as the electors. The exasperated crowd perceived that it was wasting time with them. An old man exclaimed: "Friends, why do we remain with these traitors? Let us rather hasten to the Bastille!" They all vanished. The electors, thunderstruck, found themselves alone. One of them goes out, but returns with a livid, spectral countenance: "You have not two minutes to live," says he, "if you remain here. La Grève is filled by a furious crowd. Here they are coming." They did not, however, attempt to fly; and that saved their lives.

All the fury of the people was now concentrated on the provost. The envoys of the different districts came successively to accuse him of treachery to his face. A part of the electors, finding themselves compromised with the people, by his imprudence and falsehood, turned round and accused him. Others, the good old Dussaulx (the translator of Juvenal), and the intrepid Fauchet endeavoured to defend him, innocent or guilty, and to save him from death. Being forced by the people to move from their office into the great hall of Saint Jean, they surrounded him, and Fauchet sat down by his side. The terrors of death were impressed on his countenance. "I saw him," says Dussaulx, "chewing his last mouthful of bread; it stuck in his teeth, and he kept it in his mouth two hours before he could swallow it." Surrounded with papers, letters, and people who came to speak to him on business, and amid shouts of death, he strove hard to reply with affability. The crowds of the Palais Royal and from the district of Saint Roch, being the most inveterate, Fauchet hastened to them to pray for pardon. The district body was assembled in the church of Saint Roch; twice did Fauchet ascend the pulpit, praying, weeping, and uttering the fervent language which his noble heart dictated in that hour of need; his robe, torn to tatters by the bullets of the Bastille,[80] was eloquent also; it prayed for the people, for the honour of that great day, and that the cradle of liberty might be left pure and undefiled.

The provost and the electors remained in the hall of Saint Jean, between life and death, guns being levelled at them several times. All those who were present, says Dussaulx, were like savages; sometimes they would listen and look on in silence; sometimes a terrible murmur, like distant thunder, arose from the crowd. Many spoke and shouted; but the greater number seemed astounded by the novelty of the sight. The uproar, the exclamations, the news, the alarms, the intercepted letters, the discoveries, true or false, so many secrets revealed, so many men brought before the tribunal, perplexed the mind and reason. One of the electors exclaimed: "Is not doomsday come?" So dizzy, so confounded was the crowd, that they had forgotten everything, even the provost and the Bastille.[81]

It was half-past five when a shout arose from La Grève. An immense noise, like the growling of distant thunder, resounds nearer and nearer, rushing on with the rapidity and roaring of a tempest. The Bastille is taken.

That hall already so full is at once invaded by a thousand men, and ten thousand pushing behind. The wood-work cracks, the benches are thrown down, and the barrier driven upon the bureau, the bureau upon the president.

All were armed in a fantastical manner; some almost naked, others dressed in every colour. One man was borne aloft upon their shoulders and crowned with laurel; it was Élie, with all the spoils and prisoners around him. At the head, amid all that din, which would have drowned a clap of thunder, advanced a young man full of meditation and religion; he carried suspended and pierced with his bayonet a vile, a thrice-accursed object,—the regulations of the Bastille.

---

[80] Fauchet, *Bouche de fer*, No. XVI., No. 90, t. iii., p. 244.

[81] The *Procès verbal* shows, however, that a new deputation was being prepared, and that De la Salle, the commandant, meant at length to take a part in the action.

The keys too were carried,—those monstrous, vile, ignoble keys, worn out by centuries and the sufferings of men. Chance or Providence directed that they should be intrusted to a man who knew them but too well,—a former prisoner. The National Assembly placed them in its Archives; the old machine of tyrants thus lying beside the laws that had destroyed them. We still keep possession of those keys, in the iron safe of the Archives of France. Oh! would that the same iron-chest might contain the keys of all the Bastilles in the world!

Correctly speaking, the Bastille was not taken; it surrendered. Troubled by a bad conscience it went mad, and lost all presence of mind.

Some wanted to surrender; others went on firing, especially the Swiss, who, for five hours, pointed out, aimed at, and brought down whomsoever they pleased, without any danger or even the chance of being hurt in return. They killed eighty-three men and wounded eighty-eight. Twenty of the slain were poor fathers of families, who left wives and children to die of hunger.

Shame for such cowardly warfare, and the horror of shedding French blood, which but little affected the Swiss, at length caused the *Invalides* to drop their arms. At four o'clock the subaltern officers begged and prayed De Launey to put an end to this massacre. He knew what he deserved; obliged to die one way or other, he had, for a moment, the horribly ferocious idea of blowing up the citadel: he would have destroyed one-third of Paris. His hundred and thirty-five barrels of gunpowder would have blown the Bastille into the air, and shattered or buried the whole faubourg, all the Marais, and the whole of the quartier of the Arsenal. He seized a match from a cannon. Two subaltern officers prevented the crime; they crossed their bayonets and barred his passage to the magazines. He then made a show of killing himself, and seized a knife, which they snatched from him.

He had lost his senses and could give no orders.[82] When

---

[82] Even in the morning, according to Thuriot's testimony. See the *Procès-verbal des électeurs*.

the French Guards had ranged their cannon and fired (according to some), the captain of the Swiss saw plainly that it was necessary to come to terms; he wrote and passed a note,[83] in which he asked to be allowed to go forth with the honours of war. Refused. Next, that his life should be spared. Hullin and Élie promised it. The difficulty was to fulfil their promise. To prevent a revenge accumulating for ages, and now incensed by so many murders perpetrated by the Bastille, was beyond the power of man. An authority of an hour's existence, that had but just come from La Grève, and was known only to the two small bands of the vanguard, was not adequate to keep in order the hundred thousand men behind.

The crowd was enraged, blind, drunk with the very sense of their danger. And yet they killed but one man in the fortress. They spared their enemies the Swiss, whom their smock-frocks caused to pass for servants or prisoners; but they ill-treated and wounded their friends the *Invalides*. They wished to have annihilated the Bastille; they pelted and broke to pieces the two slaves of the clock-dial; they ran up to the top of the towers to spurn the cannon; several attacked the stones, and tore their hands in dragging them away. They hastened to the dungeons to deliver the prisoners: two had become mad. One, frightened by the noise, wanted to defend himself, and was quite astonished when those who had battered down his door threw themselves into his arms and bathed him with their tears. Another, whose beard reached to his waist, inquired about the health of Louis XV., believing him to be still reigning. To those who asked him his name, he replied that he was called the Major of Immensity.

The conquerors were not yet at the end of their labours: in the Rue Saint Antoine they had to fight a battle of a different kind. On approaching La Grève, they came on successive crowds of men, who, having been unable to take any part in the fight, wanted at all events to do something, were it merely

---

[83] To fetch it, a plank was placed on the moat. The first who ventured, fell; the second (Arné?—or Maillard?) was more lucky and brought back the note.

to massacre the prisoners. One was killed at the Rue des Tournelles, and another on the quay. Women, with dishevelled hair, came rushing forward, and recognizing their husbands among the slain, left them to fly upon their assassins; one of them, foaming at the mouth, ran about asking everybody for a knife.

De Launey was conducted and supported in that extreme danger by two men of extraordinary courage and strength, Hullin, and another. The latter went with him as far as the Petit Antoine, but was there torn from his side by the rush of the crowd. Hullin held fast. To lead his man from that spot to La Grève, which is so near, was more than the twelve labours of Hercules. No longer knowing how to act, and perceiving that they knew De Launey only by his being alone without a hat, he conceived the heroic idea of putting his own upon his head; and, from that moment, he received the blows intended for the governor.[84] At length, he passed the Arcade Saint Jean; if he could but get him on the flight of steps, and push him toward the stairs, all was over. The crowd saw that very plainly, and accordingly made a desperate onset. The Herculean strength hitherto displayed by Hullin no longer served him here. Stifled by the pressure of the crowd around him, as in the crushing fold of an enormous boa, he lost his footing, was hurled to and fro, and thrown upon the pavement. Twice he regained his feet. The second time he beheld aloft the head of De Launey at the end of a pike.

---

[84] The royalist tradition which aspires to the difficult task of inspiring interest for the least interesting of men, has pretended that De Launey, still more heroic than Hullin, gave him his hat back again, wishing rather to die than expose him. The same tradition attributes the honour of a similar deed to Berthier, the intendant of Paris. Lastly, they relate that the major of the Bastille, on being recognized and defended at La Grève, by one of his former prisoners, whom he had treated with kindness, dismissed him, saying: "You will ruin yourself without saving me." This last story, being authentic, very probably gave rise to the two others. As for De Launey and Berthier, there is nothing in their previous conduct to incline us to believe in the heroism of their last moments. The silence of Michaud, the biographer, in the article *De Launey*, drawn up from information furnished by that family, sufficiently shows that they did not believe in that tradition.

Another scene was unfolding in the hall of Saint Jean. The prisoners were there, in great danger of death. The crowd was particularly bent on punishing three *Invalides,* whom they supposed to have been the cannoneers of the Bastille. One was wounded; De la Salle, the commandant, by incredible efforts, and proclaiming loudly his title of commandant, at last managed to save him; whilst he was leading him out, the two others were dragged out and hung up to the lamp at the corner of the Vannerie, facing the Hôtel-de-Ville.

All this great commotion, which seemed to have caused Flesselles to be forgotten, was nevertheless what caused his destruction. His implacable accusers of the Palais Royal, few in number, but discontented to see the crowd occupied with any other business, kept close to the bureau, menacing him, and summoning him to follow them. At length he yielded: whether the long expectation of death appeared to him worse than death itself, or that he hoped to escape in the universal pre-occupation about the great event of the day. "Well! gentlemen," said he, "let us go to the Palais Royal." He had not reached the quay before a young man shot him through the head with a pistol bullet.

The dense multitude crowding the hall did not wish for bloodshed; according to an eye-witness, they were stupefied on beholding it. They stared gaping at that strange, prodigious, grotesque, and maddening spectacle. Arms of the middle ages and of every age were mingled together; centuries had come back again. Élie, standing on a table, with a helmet on his brow, and a sword hacked in three places, in his hand, seemed a Roman warrior. He was entirely surrounded by prisoners, and pleading for them. The French Guards demanded the pardon of the prisoners as their reward.

At that moment, a man, followed by his wife, is brought or rather carried in; it was the Prince de Montbarrey, a former minister, arrested at the barrier. The lady fainted; her husband was thrown upon the bureau, held down by the arms of twelve men, and bent double. The poor man, in that strange posture, explained that he had not been minister for a long time, and that his son has taken a prominent part in the revolution of his province. De la Salle, the commandant, spoke for him, and exposed himself to great danger. Meanwhile, the people relented a little, and for a moment let go their hold. De la Salle, a very powerful man, caught him up, and carried him off. This trial of strength pleased the people, and was received with applause.

At the same moment, the brave and excellent Élie found means to put an end at once to every intention of trial or condemnation. He perceived the children of the Bastille, and began to shout: "Pardon! for the children, pardon!"

Then you might have seen sunburnt faces and hands blackened with gunpowder, washed with big tears, falling like heavy drops of rain after a shower. Justice and vengeance were thought of no longer. The tribunal was broken up; for Élie had conquered the conquerors of the Bastille. They made the prisoners swear fidelity to the nation, and led them away; the *Invalides* marched off in peace to their Hôtel; the French Guards took charge of the Swiss, placed them in safety within their ranks, conducting them to their own barracks, and gave them lodging and food.

What was most admirable, the widows showed themselves equally magnanimous. Though needy, and burdened with children, they were unwilling to receive alone a small sum allotted to them; they shared it with the widow of a poor *Invalide* who had prevented the Bastille from being blown up, but was killed by mistake. The wife of the besieged was thus adopted, as it were, by those of the besiegers.

BOOK II

JULY 14 TO OCTOBER 6, 1789

I

The Hollow Truce

THE Assembly passed the whole of the 14th of July in a state of two-fold trepidation, between the violent measures of the Court, the fury of Paris, and the chances of an insurrection, which, if unsuccessful, would stifle liberty. They listened to every rumour, and with their ears anxiously open imagined they heard the faint thunder of a distant cannonade. That moment might be their last; several members wished the bases of the constitution to be hastily established, that the Assembly, if it was to be dispersed and destroyed, should leave that testamentary evidence behind, as a beacon for the opponents of tyranny.

The Court was preparing the attack, and little was wanting for its execution. At two o'clock, Berthier, the intendant, was still at the military school, giving orders for the details of the attack. Foulon, his father-in-law, the under-minister of war, was at Versailles, completing the preparations. Paris was to be attacked, that night, at seven points simultaneously.[1] The council was discussing the list of the deputies who were to be carried off that evening; one was proscribed, another excepted; M. de Breteuil defended the innocence of Bailly. Meanwhile the queen and Madame de Polignac went into the *Orangerie* to encourage the troops and to order wine to be given to the soldiers, who were dancing about and singing roundelays. To complete the general intoxication, this lovely

---

[1] Bailly, i., pp. 391, 392.

creature conducted the officers to her apartments, excited them with liqueurs, with sweet words and glances. Those madmen, once let loose, would have made a fearful night. Letters were intercepted, wherein they had written: "We are marching against the enemy." What enemy? The law and France.

But see! a cloud of dust is rising in the *Avenue de Paris*, it is a body of cavalry, with Prince de Lambesc and all his officers flying before the people of Paris. But he meets with those of Versailles: if they had not been afraid of wounding the others, they would have fired upon him.

De Noailles arrives, saying: "The Bastille is taken." De Wimpfen arrives: "The governor is killed; he saw the deed, and was nearly treated in the same way." At last, two envoys of the electors come and acquaint the Assembly with the frightful state of Paris. The Assembly is furious, and invokes against the Court and the ministers the vengeance of God and men. "Heads!" cried Mirabeau; "We must have De Broglie's head!" [2]

A deputation of the Assembly waits upon the king, but it can get from him only two equivocal expressions: he sends officers to take the command of the local militia, and orders the troops in the Champ-de-Mars to fall back. A movement very well devised for the general attack.

The Assembly is furious and clamorous; it sends a second deputation. "The king is heart-broken, but he can do no more."

Louis XVI., whose weakness has been so often deplored, here made a show of deplorable firmness. Berthier had come to stay with him; he was in his closet and comforted him,[3] telling him there was no great harm done. In the present troubled state of Paris, there was still every chance of the great attack in the evening. However, they soon discovered that the town was on its guard. It had already placed cannon on Montmartre, which covered La Villette, and kept Saint-Denis in check.

---

[2] Ferrières, i., p. 132.

[3] *Rapport d'Accusation, Hist. Parl.*, iv., p. 83.

Amid the contradictory reports, the king gave no orders; and, faithful to his usual habits, retired to rest at an early hour. The Duke de Liancourt, whose duties gave him the privilege of entering at any hour, even in the night, could not see him perish thus in his apathy and ignorance. He entered, and awoke him. He loved the king, and wanted to save him. He told him the extent of his danger, the importance of the movement, its irresistible force; that he ought to meet it, get the start of the Duke of Orleans, and secure the friendship of the Assembly. Louis XVI., half asleep (and who was never entirely awake): "What then," said he, "is it a revolt?" "Sire, it is a Revolution."

The king concealed nothing from the queen; so everything was known in the apartment of the Count d'Artois. His followers were much alarmed; royalty might save itself at their expense. One of them, who knew the prince, and that fear was the weak point in his character, secured him by saying that he was proscribed at the Palais Royal, like Flesselles and De Launey, and that he might tranquillise every mind by uniting with the king in the popular measure dictated by necessity. The same man, who was a deputy, ran to the Assembly (it was then midnight); he there found the worthy Bailly, who dared not retire to rest, and asked him, in the name of the prince, for a speech that the king might read on the morrow.

There was one man at Versailles who grieved as much as any. I mean the Duke of Orleans. On the 12th of July, his effigy had been carried in triumph, and then brutally broken to pieces. There the matter rested; nobody had cared about it. On the 13th, a few had spoken of the election of a lieutenant-general, but the crowd seemed deaf, and either did not, or would not, hear. On the morning of the 14th, Madame de Genlis took the daring and incredible step of sending her Pamela with a lackey in red livery into the middle of the riot.[4] Somebody exclaimed: "If it were only the queen!" And the

---

[4] Madame Lebrun, *Souvenirs*, i., p. 189.

phrase was repeated . . . All their petty intrigues were swamped in that immense commotion, every paltry interest was smothered in the excitement of that sacred day.

The poor Duke of Orleans went on the morning of the 15th to the council at the castle. But he had to stay at the door. He waited; then wrote; not to demand the lieutenancy-general, not to offer his mediation (as had been agreed between him, Mirabeau, and a few others), but to assure the king, as a good and loyal subject, that if matters grew worse, he would go over to England.

He did not stir all day from the Assembly, or from Versailles, and went to the castle in the evening; [5] he thus made good an *alibi* against every accusation of being an accomplice, and washed his hands of the taking of the Bastille. Mirabeau was furious, and left him from that moment. He said (I soften the expression): "He is a eunuch for crime; he would, but cannot!"

Whilst the duke was being kept waiting like a petitioner at the council door, Sillery-Genlis, his warm partisan, was striving to avenge him; he read, and caused to be adopted, an insidious project of address, calculated to diminish the effect of the king's visit, deprive it of the merit of being spontaneous, and chill, beforehand, every heart: "Come, sire, your majesty will see the consternation of the Assembly, but you will be perhaps astonished at its calmness," &c. And, at the same time, he announced that loads of flour going to Paris had been stopped at Sèvres. "What if this news reached the capital!"

To which, Mirabeau, addressing the deputies whom they were sending to the king, added these alarming words: "Go, and tell the king that the foreign hordes by which we are invested, were visited yesterday by the princes and princesses, by his male and female favourites, who lavished on them their caresses, presents, and exhortations. Tell him that all night long, those foreign satellites, gorged with wine and gold, have predicted, in their impious songs, the servitude of France, and

---

[5] Ferrières, i., p. 135. Droz, ii., p. 342.

that their brutal vows have invoked the destruction of the National Assembly. Tell him that in his very palace, his courtiers danced to the sounds of that barbarous music, and that such was the prelude to the massacre of Saint Bartholomew. Tell him that king Henry, whose memory is adored by the universe, that ancestor of his whom he affected to wish to take as his model, ordered provisions to be sent into revolted Paris, which he was besieging in person; whilst his ferocious counsellors have driven back the grain which commerce was bringing to his starving but faithful Paris."

As the deputation was departing, the king arrives. He enters without his guards, accompanied only by his brothers. He advances a few paces into the hall, and, standing in front of the Assembly, announces that he has given orders to the troops to depart *from Paris and Versailles*, and he engages the Assembly to give this information to Paris. A sad confession that his own word will obtain little credit unless the Assembly affirmed that the king has not told a lie! He added, however, more nobly and adroitly: "People have dared to spread a report that your persons are not in safety. Can it be necessary to reassure you against such wicked rumours, already belied by my well-known character? Well then, I, who am but one with the nation, I come to intrust myself to you!"

To remove the troops from Paris and Versailles, without stating any distance, was yet but an equivocal, uncertain promise, that gave but little comfort. But the Assembly were generally so alarmed at the obscure immensity opening before them, so stupefied by the victory of Paris, and had so much need of order, that they showed themselves credulous, enthusiastic for the king, even so far as to forget what they owed to themselves.

They all rushed round him and followed him. He returned on foot. The Assembly and the people crowded about him to suffocation; the king, who was very corpulent, was quite exhausted in crossing the Place d'Armes in such scorching weather; deputies, among whom was the Duke of Orleans, formed a circle around him. On his arrival, the Swiss band played the air: *"Où peut on être mieux qu'au sein de sa famille?"* A family too limited in number: the people formed no part of it; the gates being shut against them. The king gave orders to open them again. However, he declined to receive the deputies who wished to see him once more; he was going to his chapel to return thanks to God.[6] The queen appeared in the balcony with her children, and those of the Count d'Artois, with all the appearance of great delight, and hardly knowing what to think of an enthusiasm so ill deserved.

Versailles was overcome with joy. Paris, in spite of its victory, was still in alarm and affliction. It was burying its dead; many of them had left families without resource. Such as had no family were paid their last respects by their companions. They had placed a hat beside one of the dead, and said to passengers: "Sir, something for this poor fellow who was killed for the nation! Madam, it is for this poor fellow who was killed for the nation!"[7] An humble and simple funeral oration for men whose death gave life to France.

Everybody was guarding Paris; nobody was working. There was no work; food was scarce and dear. The Hôtel-de-Ville maintained that Paris had provision enough for a fortnight; but it had not enough for three days. It was necessary to order a tax for the subsistence of the poor. The supplies of flour had been stopped at Sèvres and Saint-Denis. Two fresh regiments arrived while they were promising to send back the troops. The hussars came and reconnoitered the barriers; and a report was spread that they had attempted to surprise the Bastille. At length the alarm was so great, that, at two o'clock, the electors could not refuse the people an order to dig up the paving-stones of Paris.

At two o'clock precisely, a man arrives breathless and almost fainting.[8] He had run all the way from Sèvres, where the

---

[6] *Point du Jour*, No. 35, t. i., p. 207.

[7] *Lettres écrites de France à un Ami*, p. 29, quoted in Dussaulx's Notes, p. 333.

[8] *Procès-verbal des Électeurs, rédigé par Duveyrier*, i, p. 431.

troops wanted to stop him. "It is all over; the Revolution is finished; the king came into the Assembly, and said: 'I trust myself to you.' A hundred deputies are now on their road from Versailles, sent by the Assembly to the city of Paris."

Those deputies had immediately set forth; Bailly would not dine. The electors had barely the time to run to meet them, just as they were, in disorder, not having been to bed for several nights. They wanted to fire the cannon; but they were still ranged *en batterie,* and could not be got ready. There was no need of them to solemnise the *fête.* Paris was grand enough with its sun of July, its commotion, and all that population in arms. The hundred deputies, preceded by the French Guards, the Swiss, the officers of the city militia, and by the deputies of the electors, marched up the Rue Saint Honoré to the sound of trumpets. Every arm was stretched towards them, and every heart leaped with joy. From every window were showered flowers, blessings, and tears.

The National Assembly and the people of Paris, the oath of the Jeu-de-Paume and the taking of the Bastille; victory and victory, kissed each other.

Several deputies kissed and wept over the flags of the French Guards: "Flags of our native land!" cried they, "flags of liberty!"

On their arrival at the Hôtel-de-Ville, Lafayette, Bailly, the archbishop of Paris, Sieyès, and Clermont-Tonnerre were made to sit at the bureau. Lafayette spoke coolly and prudently; next, Lally Tollendal with his Irish impetuosity and easy tears. It was at that same Grève that Lally's father, thirty years before, had been gagged and beheaded by the *ancien régime;* his speech, full of emotion, was nothing but a sort of amnesty for the *ancien régime,* an amnesty certainly too premature, whilst it still kept Paris surrounded by troops.

Emotion nevertheless took effect also in the citizen assembly of the Hôtel-de-Ville. "The fattest of tender-hearted men," as Lally was called, was crowned with flowers, and led, or rather carried, to the window, and shown to the crowd. Resisting as much as he could, he put his crown on the head of Bailly, the first president the National Assembly had. Bailly likewise refused; but it was held and fastened on his head by the hand of the archbishop of Paris. A strange and whimsical spectacle, which showed, in a strong light, the false position of the parties. Here was the president of the Jeu-de-Paume, crowned by the prelate, who advised the *coup d'état,* and forced Paris to conquer. The contradiction was so little perceived, that the archbishop did not fear to propose a *Te Deum,* and everybody followed him to Notre Dame. It was rather a *De Profundis* that he first owed to those whose deaths he had occasioned.

Notwithstanding the general emotion, the people kept their senses. They did not tamely allow their victory to be meddled with; that, we must say, was neither fair nor useful; that victory was not yet sufficiently complete to sacrifice and forget it so soon. Its moral effect was immense, but its material result still feeble and uncertain. Even in the Rue Saint Honoré, the citizen guard (then it was all the people) brought before the deputies, with military music, that French Guardsman who had been the first to arrest the governor of the Bastille; he was led in triumph in De Launey's chariot, crowned with laurel, and wearing the cross of Saint Louis, which the people had snatched from the gaoler to put upon his conqueror. He was unwilling to keep it; however, before he gave it back, in presence of the deputies, he adorned himself with it, proudly showing it upon his breast.[9] The crowd applauded, and so did the deputies, thus sanctioning with their approbation what had been done the day before.

Another incident was still clearer. Among the speeches made at the Hôtel-de-Ville, M. De Liancourt, a good-natured, but

---

[9] Camille Desmoulins, so amusing here and everywhere else, triumphed also in his manner: "I marched with my sword drawn," &c., (*Correspondance,* p. 28, 1836). He took a fine gun with a bayonet and a pair of pistols from the *Invalides;* if he did not make use of them, it is because unfortunately the Bastille was taken so quickly! He ran there, but it was too late. Several go so far as to say, that it was he who caused the Revolution (p. 33); for his part, he is too modest to believe it.

inconsiderate man, said that the king willingly *pardoned* the French Guards. Several of them, then present, stepped forward, and one of them exclaimed: "We need no pardon. In serving the nation, we serve the king; the intentions which he displays to-day prove sufficiently to France that we alone have been faithful to the king and the country."

Bailly is proclaimed mayor, and Lafayette commandant of the citizen militia. They depart for the Te Deum. The archbishop gave his arm to that brave *abbé* Lefebvre who had guarded and distributed the gunpowder, who left that den for the first time, and was still quite black. Bailly was, in like manner, conducted by Hullin, applauded by the crowd, pressed, and almost stifled. Four fusileers followed him; but, notwithstanding the rejoicings of that day and the unexpected honour of his new position, he could not help thinking "that he looked like a man being led to prison." Had he been able to foresee better, he would have said: to death!

What was that Te Deum, but a falsehood? Who could believe that the archbishop thanked God heartily for the taking of the Bastille? Nothing had changed, neither men nor principles. The court was still the court, the enemy ever the enemy. What had been done was done. Neither the National Assembly nor the electors of Paris, with all their omnipotence, could alter the past. On the 14th of July, there had been a person conquered, who was the king, and the conqueror was the people. How then were they to undo that, cause that not to be, blot out history, change the reality of actual events, and dupe the king and the people, in such a manner that the former should consider himself happy in being beaten, and the latter, without distrust, should give themselves up again into the hands of a master so cruelly provoked?

Mounier, whilst relating on the 16th, in the National Assembly, the visit of the hundred deputies to the city of Paris, made the strange proposal (resumed on the morrow and voted at the Hôtel-de-Ville) to raise a statue to Louis XVI. on the site of the demolished Bastille. A statue for a defeat! that was something new and original. The ridicule of it was apparent.

Who was to be thus deceived? Was the victory indeed to be conjured away by thus allowing the vanquished to triumph?

The obstinacy of the king throughout the whole of the 14th of July, made the most simple perceive that his conduct on the 15th was by no means spontaneous. At the very moment the Assembly was conducting him back to the castle, amid this enthusiasm, feigned or real, a woman fell at his knees, and was not afraid to say: "Oh! Sire, are you really sincere? Will they not make you change?"

The population of Paris was full of gloomy ideas. They could not believe that with forty thousand men about Versailles, the court would make no attempt. They believed the king's conduct to be only intended to lull them into security, in order to attack with greater advantage. They distrusted the electors; two of the latter, deputed to Versailles on the 15th, were brought back, menaced as traitors, and in great danger. The French Guards were afraid of some ambush in their barracks, and refused to return to them. The people persisted in believing, that if the court dared not fight, it would be revenged by some dark plot, that it might have somewhere a mine to blow Paris into the air.

Fear was not ridiculous, but confidence most certainly was. Why should they have felt secure? The troops, in spite of the promise, did not withdraw. The baron de Falckenheim, who commanded at Saint-Denis, said he had no orders. Two of his officers who had come to reconnoitre, had been arrested at the barrier. What was still more serious, was, that the lieutenant of police had given in his resignation. Berthier the intendant had escaped, and with him, all the persons charged with the administration of provisions. In a day or two, perhaps, the market would be without grain, and the people would go to the Hôtel-de-Ville to demand bread and the heads of the magistrates. The electors sent several of their body to fetch grain from Senlis, Vernon, and even from Hâvre.

Paris was waiting for the king. It thought that if he had spoken candidly and from his heart, he would leave his Versailles and his wicked advisers, and cast himself into the arms of the people. Nothing would have been better timed, or have had a greater effect on the 15th:—he should have departed for Paris, on leaving the Assembly, and have trusted himself, not in words only, but truly, and with his person, boldly entering the crowd, and mingling with that armed population. The emotion, still so great, would have turned entirely in his favour.

That is what the people expected, what they believed and talked of. They said so at the Hôtel-de-Ville, and repeated it in the streets. The king hesitated, consulted, postponed for one day, and all was lost.

Where did he pass that irreparable day? From the evening of the 15th to the morning of the 16th, he was still shut up with those same ministers, whose audacious folly had filled Paris with bloodshed, and shaken the throne for ever. At that council, the queen wanted to fly, carry off the king, put him at the head of the troops, and begin a civil war. But, were the troops very sure? What would happen if war broke out in the army itself, between the French soldiers and the foreign mercenaries? Was it not better to temporise, gain time, and deceive the people? Louis XVI., between these two opinions, had none of his own,—no will; [10] he was ready to follow either indifferently. The majority of the council were for the latter opinion; so the king remained.

A mayor and a commandant of Paris appointed by the electors without the king's consent, those places accepted by men of such importance as Bailly and Lafayette, and their nominations confirmed by the Assembly, without asking the king for any permission, was no longer an insurrection, but a well and duly organized Revolution. Lafayette, "not doubting but all the *communes* would be willing to intrust their defence to armed citizens," proposed to call the citizen militia *National Guards* (a name already invented by Sieyès). This name seemed to

---

[10] The *Histoire Parlementaire* is wrong in quoting a pretended letter from Louis XVI. to the Count d'Artois (v. ii., p. 101), an apocryphal and ridiculous letter, like most of those published by Miss Williams, in the *Correspondance inédite,* so well criticised and condemned by MM. Barbier and Beuchot.

generalize, and extend the arming of Paris to all the kingdom, even as the blue and red cockade of the city, augmented with white, the old French colours, became that of all France.

If the king remained at Versailles, if he delayed, he risked Paris. Its attitude was becoming more hostile every moment. On the districts being engaged to join their deputies to those of the Hôtel-de-Ville, in order to go and thank the king, several replied, "There was no occasion yet to return thanks."

It was not till the evening of the 16th, that Bailly having happened to see Vicq-d'Azyr, the queen's physician, gave him notice that the city of Paris wished for and expected the king. The king promised to go, and the same evening wrote to M. Necker to engage him to return.

On the 17th, the king departed at nine o'clock, very serious, melancholy, and pale; he had heard mass, taken the communion, and given to *Monsieur* his nomination as lieutenant-general, in case he was killed or detained prisoner; the queen, in his absence, wrote, with a trembling hand, the speech she would go and pronounce at the Assembly, if the king should be detained.

Without guards, but surrounded by three or four hundred deputies, he arrived at the (city) barrier at three o'clock. The mayor, on presenting him the keys, said: "These are the same keys that were presented to Henri IV.; he had reconquered his people, now the people have re-conquered their king."

Those last words, so true and so strong, the full meaning of which was not perceived, even by Bailly, were enthusiastically applauded.

The Place Louis XV. presented a circle of troops, with the French Guards, drawn up in a square battalion, in the centre. The battalion opened and formed into file, displaying cannon in the midst (perhaps those of the Bastille). It put itself at the head of the procession, dragging its cannon after it—and the king followed.

In front of the king's carriage rode Lafayette, the commandant, in a private dress, sword in hand, with the cockade and plume in his hat. Everything was obedient to his slightest gesture. There was complete order and silence too; not one cry of *Vive le Roi*.[11] Now and then, they cried *Vive la Nation*. From the *Point-du-Jour* to Paris, and from the barrier to the Hôtel-de-Ville, there were two hundred thousand men under arms, more than thirty thousand guns, fifty thousand pikes, and, for the others, lances, sabres, swords, pitchforks, and scythes. No uniforms, but two regular lines, throughout that immense extent, of three, and sometimes of four or five men deep.

A formidable apparition of the nation in arms. The king could not misunderstand it; it was not a party. Amid so many weapons and so many different dresses, there was the same soul and the same silence!

Everybody was there; all had wanted to come; nobody was missing at that solemn review. Even ladies were seen armed beside their husbands, and girls with their fathers. A woman figured among the conquerors of the Bastille.

Monks, believing also that they were men and citizens, had come to take their part in that grand crusade. The Mathurins were in their ranks under the banner of their order, now become the standard of the district of that name. Capucins were there shouldering the sword or the musket. The *ladies of the Place-Maubert* had put the revolution of Paris under the protection of Saint Geneviève, and offered on the preceding evening a picture wherein the saint was encouraging the destroying angel to overthrow the Bastille, which was seen falling to pieces with broken crowns and sceptres.

Two men only were applauded, Bailly and Lafayette, and no others. The deputies marched surrounding the king's carriage, with sorrowful, uneasy looks; there was something gloomy about that procession. Those strange looking weapons, those

---

[11] Save one mishap; one gun went off, and a woman was killed. There was no bad intention towards the king. Everybody was royalist, both the Assembly and the people: even Marat was till 1791. In an unpublished letter of Robespierre's (which M. De George communicated to me at Arras), he seems to believe in the good faith of Louis XVI., whose visit to the city of Paris is therein related, (23rd of July, 1789).

pitchforks and scythes, were not pleasing to the eye. Those cannon reclining so quietly in the streets, silent, and bedecked with flowers, seemed as though they would awake. Above all the apparent signs of peace hovered a conspicuous and significant image of war,—the tattered flag of the Bastille.

The king alights, and Bailly presents to him the new cockade of the colours of the city, which had become those of France. He begs of him to accept "that distinguishing symbol of Frenchmen." The king put it in his hat, and, separated from his suite by the crowd, ascended the gloomy stairs of the Hôtel-de-Ville. Overhead, swords placed crosswise formed a canopy of steel; a singular honour, borrowed from the masonic customs, which seemed to have a double meaning, and might lead to suppose that the king was passing under the yoke.

There was no intention to cause either humiliation or displeasure. On the contrary, he was received with extraordinary emotion. The great hall, crowded with a confused mass of notables and men of every class, presented a strange spectacle; those in the middle remained kneeling, in order not to deprive the others of the happiness of seeing the king, and all had their hands raised towards the throne, and their eyes full of tears.

Bailly, in his speech, had pronounced the word *alliance* between the king and the people. The president of the electors, Moreau de Saint Méry (he who had been chairman during the great days, and given three thousand orders in thirty hours) ventured a word that seemed to engage the king: "You *come to promise* your subjects that the authors of those disastrous councils shall surround you no longer, and that Virtue, too long exiled, shall remain your support." Virtue meant Necker.

The king, from timidity or prudence, said nothing. The city proctor then made a proposal to raise a statue on the Place de la Bastille; it was voted unanimously.

Next, Lally, always eloquent, only too tender-hearted and lachrymose, avowed the king's *chagrin, and the need he had of consolation.* This was showing him as conquered, instead of associating him with the victory of the people over the ministers who were departing. "Well, citizens, are you satisfied! Behold the king," &c. That *Behold*, thrice repeated, seemed like a sad parody of Ecce Homo.

Those who had noticed that similitude found it exact and complete, when Bailly showed the king at the window of the Hôtel-de-Ville, with the cockade in his hat. He remained there a quarter of an hour, serious and silent. On his departure it was intimated to him, in a whisper, that he ought to say something himself. But all they could get from him was the ratification of the citizen guard, the mayor, and the commandant, and the very laconic sentence: "You may always rely on my affection."

The electors were satisfied, but not so the people. They had imagined that the king, rid of his bad advisers, had come to fraternize with the city of Paris. But, what! not one word, not one gesture! Nevertheless, the crowd applauded on his return; they seemed to desire to give vent at length to their long restrained feelings. Every weapon was reversed in sign of peace. They shouted *Vive le Roi*, and he was carried to his carriage. A market-woman flung her arms round his neck. Men with bottles stopped his horses, poured out wine for his coachman and valets, and drank with them the health of the king. He smiled, but still said nothing. The least kind word, uttered at that moment, would have been re-echoed and celebrated with immense effect.

It was past nine in the evening when he returned to the castle. On the staircase he found the queen and his children in tears, who came and threw themselves into his arms. Had the king then incurred some alarming danger in going to visit his people? Was his people his enemy? And what more would they have done for a king set at liberty, for John or Francis I., returning from London or Madrid?

On the same day, Friday, the 17th, as if to protest that the king neither said nor did anything at Paris but by force and constraint, his brother the Count d'Artois, the Condés, the Contis, the Polignacs, Vaudreuil, Broglie, Lambesc, and others, fled France. It was no easy matter. They found everywhere their names held in detestation, and the people rising against them. The Polignacs and Vaudreuils were only able to escape by declaiming along their road against Vaudreuil and Polignac.

The conspiracy of the court, aggravated with a thousand popular accounts, both strange and horrible, had seized upon every imagination, and rendered them incurably suspicious and distrustful. Versailles, excited at least as much as Paris, watched the castle night and day as the centre of treason. That immense palace seemed a desert. Many dared no longer enter it. The north wing, appropriated to the Condés, was almost empty; the south wing, that of the Count d'Artois, and the seven vast apartments of the ladies Polignac were shut up for ever. Several of the king's servants would have liked to forsake their master. They were beginning to entertain strange ideas about him.

For three days, says Besenval, the king had scarcely anybody about him but M. de Montmorin and myself. On the 19th, every minister being absent, I had entered the king's apartment to ask him to sign an order to have horses given to a colonel who was returning. As I was presenting that order a footman placed himself between the king and me, in order to see what he was writing. The king turned round, perceived the insolent fellow, and snatched up the tongs. I prevented him from following that impulse of very natural indignation; he clasped my hand to thank me, and I perceived tears in his eyes.

II

Popular Judgments

ROYALTY remains alone. The privileged class go into exile or submit; they declare they will henceforth vote in the National Assembly and be subject to the majority. Being isolated and laid bare, royalty appears what it had been fundamentally for a long time: a nonentity.

That nonentity was the ancient faith of France; and that faith deceived now causes her distrust and incredulity; it makes her excessively uneasy and suspicious. To have believed and loved, and to have been for a century always deceived in that love, is enough to make her no longer believe in anything.

Where will faith be now? At that question, they experience a feeling of terror and solitude, like Louis XVI. himself in the corner of his lonely palace. There will no longer be faith in any mortal power.

The legislative power itself, that Assembly beloved by France, is now so unfortunate as to have absorbed its enemies, five or six hundred nobles and priests, and to contain them in its bosom. Another evil is, that it has conquered too much; it will now be the authority, the government, the king—when a king is no longer possible.

The electoral power, which likewise found itself obliged to govern, feels itself expiring at the end of a few days, and entreats the districts to create its successor. During the cannonade of the Bastille, it had shuddered and doubted. Men of little faith! But perfidious? No. That *bourgeoisie* of 1789, imbued with the philosophy of that grand age, was certainly less egotisti-

199

cal than our own. It was wavering and uncertain, bold in principle, but timid in application; it had been so long in bondage!

It is the virtue of the judiciary power, when it remains entire
and strong, to compensate for every other; but itself is compen-
sated for by none. It was the mainstay and the resource of our
ancient France, in her most terrible moments. In the fourteenth
and sixteenth centuries, it sat immutable and firm, so that the
country, almost lost in the tempest, recovered and found itself
still in the inviolable sanctuary of civil justice.

Well! even that power is shattered. Shattered by its inconsistency and contradictions. Servile and bold at once, for the
king and against the king, for the pope and against the pope,
the defender of the law and the champion of privilege, it speaks
of liberty and resists for a century every liberal progress. It
also, and as much as the king, deceived the hope of the people.
What joy, what enthusiasm, when the *parlement* returned from
exile, on the accession of Louis XVI.! And it was in answer
to that confidence that it joined the privileged class, stopped all
reform, and caused Turgot to be dismissed! In 1787, the people
sustained it still, and, by way of recompense, the *parlement*
demanded that the Estates-General should be restored in imitation of the old form of 1614, that is to say useless, powerless,
and derisive.

No, the people cannot confide in the judiciary power.

What is most strange, is, that it was this power, the guardian of order and the laws, that began the riot. Disturbances
first begin about the *Parlement,* at every *lit de justice.* They
were encouraged by the smiles of the magistrate. Young counsellors, such as d'Esprémesnil or Duport, mindful of the *Fronde,*
would willingly have imitated Broussel and the Coadjutor. The
organised Basoche furnishes an army of clerks. It has its king,
its judgments, its provosts, old students, as was Moreau at
Rennes, or brilliant orators and duellists, like Barnave at Grenoble. The solemn prohibition that the clerks should not wear a
sword, did but make them the more pugnacious.

The first club was the one opened by counsellor Duport
at his house in the Rue du Chaume in the Marais. There

he assembled the most forward of the *parlement* people, advocates and deputies, especially the Bretons. The club being transferred to Versailles, was called the *Breton Club*. On its return to Paris with the Assembly, and changing its character, it took up its quarters at the convent of the Jacobins.

Mirabeau went but once to Duport's; he used to call Duport, Barnave, and Lameth, the *Triumgueusal*.[12] Sieyès also went but would not return there. "It is a den of political banditti, said he; they take outrages for expedients." Elsewhere he designates them still more harshly: "One may imagine them to be a set of wicked blackguards, ever in action, shouting, intriguing, and rioting lawlessly, recklessly, and then laughing at the mischief they had done. To them may be attributed the greater part of the errors of the Revolution. Happy would it have been for France, if the subaltern agents of those early perturbators, on becoming leaders in their turn, by a sort of customary hereditary right in long revolutions, had renounced the spirit by which they had been so long agitated!"

These subalterns alluded to by Sieyès, who will succeed their leaders (and who were far superior to them), were especially two men,—two revolutionary levers, Camille Desmoulins and Danton. Those two men, one the king of pamphleteers, the other the thundering orator of the Palais Royal, before he was that of the Convention, cannot be further mentioned in this place. Besides, they are about to follow us, and will soon never leave us. In them, or in nobody, are personified the comedy and tragedy of the Revolution.

Presently they will let their masters form the club of the Jacobins, and will go and found the *Cordeliers*. At the present, all is mingled together: the grand club of a hundred clubs, among the *cafés*, the gaming-houses, and women, is still the Palais Royal. There it was that on the 12th of July, Desmoulins cried: To arms! And there, on the night of the 13th, sentence was passed on Flesselles and De Launey. Those

---

[12] Meaning the Three Knaves,—a parody, of course, on triumvirate.— C. C.

passed on the Count D'Artois, the Condés and the Polignacs, were forwarded to them; and they had the astonishing effect, hardly to be expected from several battles, of making them depart from France. Hence arose a fatal predilection for the means of terror which had so well succeeded. Desmoulins, in the speech which he attributes to the lamp (lanterne) of La Grève, makes it say, "That strangers gaze upon it in an ecstasy of astonishment; that they wonder that a lamp should have done more in two days than all their heroes in a hundred years." [13]

Desmoulins renews ever with inexhaustible wit the old jokes that filled all the middle ages on the gallows, the rope, and the persons hanged. That hideous, atrocious punishment, which renders agony visible, was the usual text of the most joyous stories, the amusement of the vulgar, the inspiration of the Basoche. This found all its genius in Camille Desmoulins. That young lawyer of Picardy, with a very light purse and a still lighter character, was loitering briefless at the *Palais,* when the Revolution made him suddenly plead at the Palais Royal. A slight impediment in his speech did but render him the more amusing. His lively sallies playing about his embarrassed lips, escaped like darts. He followed his comic humour without much considering whether it might not end in tragedy. The famous judgments of the Basoche, those judicial farces which had so much amused the old *Palais,* were not more merry than the judgments of the Palais Royal,[14] the difference was that the latter were often executed in La Grève (the place of execution).

What is most strange, and a subject for reflection, is, that Desmoulins, with his roguish genius and mortal jests, and that bull of a Danton, who bellows murder, are the very men who, four years later, perish for having proposed *The Committee of Clemency!*

---

[13] Camille Desmoulins, *Discours de la Lanterne aux Parisiens,* p. 2. He insinuates, however, rather adroitly, that those rapid condemnations are not without inconvenience, that they are liable to cause mistakes, &c.

[14] See the judgment of Duval d'Esprémesnil, related by C. Desmoulins in his letters.

Mirabeau, Duport, the Lameths, and many others more moderate, approved of the acts of violence; several said they had advised them. In 1788, Sieyès demanded the death of the ministers. On the 14th of July, Mirabeau demanded De Broglie's head! Desmoulins lodged in his house. He marched willingly between Desmoulins and Danton; and, being tired of his Genevese, preferred these men, directing the former to write, and the latter to speak.

Target, a very moderate, prudent, cool-headed man was intimate with Desmoulins, and gave his approbation to the pamphlet *De la Lanterne*.

This deserves an explanation: Nobody believed in justice, save in that of the people.

The legists especially despised the law, the jurisprudence of that time, in contradiction to all the ideas of the age. They were well acquainted with the tribunals, and knew that the Revolution had no more passionate adversaries than the *Parlement*, the High Court of Justice (*le Châtelet*), and the judges in general.

Such a judgment-seat was the enemy. To give up the trial of the enemy to the enemy, and charge it to decide between the Revolution and its adversaries, was to absolve the latter, render them stronger and more haughty, and send them to the armies to begin a civil war. Were they able to make one? Yes, in spite of the enthusiasm of Paris and the taking of the Bastille. They had foreign troops, and all the officers were for them; they had especially a formidable body, which then constituted the glory of France, the officers of the navy.

The people alone, in that rapid crisis, were able to seize and strike such powerful criminals. But if the people should mistake? This objection did not embarrass the partisans of violence. They recriminated. "How many times," would they reply, "have not the *Parlement* and the Châtelet made mistakes?" They quoted the notorious mistakes in the cases of Calas and Sirven; they reminded their opponents of Dupaty's terrible memorial for three men condemned to the wheel,—that memorial burnt by the *Parlement* that was unable to answer it.

What popular trials, would they again say, can ever be more

barbarous than the procedure of the regular tribunals, just as they now are, in 1789?—Secret proceedings, made entirely on documents that the defendant is not allowed to see; the accusations uncommunicated, the witnesses non-confronted, save that last short moment when the defendant, but just emerging from the utter darkness of his dungeon, bewildered by the light of day, comes to sit on his bench, replies or not, and sees his judges for the two minutes during which he hears himself condemned.[15] —Barbarous procedure, more barbarous sentences, execrable punishments!—We shudder to think of Damiens torn with pincers, quartered, sprinkled with molten lead.—Just before the Revolution, a man was burned at Strasbourg. On the 11th of August 1789, the *Parlement* of Paris, itself expiring, once more condemned a man to be broken on the wheel.

Such punishment, which was torture even for the spectator, wounded the souls of men, made them furious, mad, confounded every idea of justice, and subverted justice itself; the criminal who suffered such torture seemed no longer guilty; the guilty party was the judge; and a world of maledictions was heaped upon him. Sensibility was excited into fury, and pity grew ferocious. History offers several instances of this sort of furious sensibility which often transported the people beyond all the bounds of respect and fear, and made them rack and burn the officers of justice in place of the criminal.

A fact, too little noticed, but which enables us to understand a great many things, is, that several of our terrorists were men of an exquisite feverish sensibility, who felt cruelly the sufferings of the people, and whose pity turned into fury.

This remarkable phenomenon chiefly showed itself in nervous men, of a weak and irritable imagination, among artists of every kind: the artist is a man-woman.[16] The people whose nerves are stronger followed that impulse, but in the earlier

---

[15] A truly eloquent passage in Dupaty's memorial for three men condemned to be broken on the wheel, p. 117 (1786, in 4to.).

[16] I mean a complete man, who, having both sexes of the mind, is fruitful; however, having almost always the sense of irritation and choler predominant.

period never gave it. The acts of violence proceeded from the Palais Royal, where the citizens, lawyers, artists, and men of letters were predominant.

Even among these men, nobody incurred the whole responsibility. A Camille Desmoulins might start the game and begin the hunt; a Danton hunted it to death—in words, of course. But there was no lack of mute actors for the execution, of pale furious men to carry the thing to La Grève, where it was urged on by inferior Dantons. In the miserable crowd surrounding the latter, were strange looking figures, like beings escaped from the other world; spectral looking men, mad with hunger, delirious from fasting, and who were no longer men. It was stated that several, on the 20th of July, had not eaten for three days. Occasionally, they were resigned, and died without injuring anybody. The women were not so resigned; *they had children.* They wandered about like lionesses. In every riot they were the most inveterate and furious; they uttered cries of frenzy, and made the men ashamed of their delays; the summary judgments of La Grève were ever too long for them. They hanged straightaway.[17]

England has had in this century her poetry of hunger.[18] Who will give its history to France? A terrible history in the last century, neglected by the historians, who have reserved their pity for the artisans of famine. I have attempted to descend into the regions of that hell, guided nearer and nearer by deep groans of agony. I have shown the land more and more sterile in proportion as the exchequer seized and destroyed the cattle, and that the earth devoid of manure is condemned to a perpetual fast. I have shown how, as the nobles, the exempt from taxes, multiplied, the impost weighed ever more heavily on an ever declining land. I have not sufficiently shown how food became, from its very scarcity, the object of an eminently productive traffic. The profits were so

---

[17] They hanged thus on the 5th of October the honest *abbé* Lefebvre, one of the heroes of the 14th of July; luckily the rope was cut.

[18] Ebenezer Elliott, *Corn-law Rhymes* (Manchester, 1834), &c., &c.

obvious, that the king wished also to take a part. The world saw with astonishment a king trafficking with the lives of his subjects, a king speculating on scarcity and death,—a king the assassin of his people. Famine is no longer only the result of the seasons,—a natural phenomenon; it is neither rain nor hail. It is a deed of the civil order: people starve by order of the king.

The king here is the system. The people were starving under Louis XV., and they starve under Louis XVI.

Famine was then a science, a complicated art of administration and commerce. Its parents are the exchequer and monopoly. It engenders a race apart, a bastard breed of contractors, bankers, financiers, revenue-farmers, intendants, counsellors, and ministers. A profound expression on the alliance between the speculators and politicians was uttered from the bowels of the people: *compact of famine.*

Among those men was one who had long been famous. His name *Foulon* (very expressive,[19] and which he strove to justify) was in the mouth of the people as early as 1756. He had begun his career as an intendant of the army, and in the enemy's country. Truly terrible to Germany, he was even more so to our soldiers. His manner of victualling was as fatal as a battle of Rosbach. He had grown fat on the destitution of the army, doubly rich by the fasting of the French and the Germans.

Foulon was a speculator, financier, and contractor on one hand, and on the other a member of the Council which alone judged the contractors. He expected certainly to become minister. He would have died of grief, if bankruptcy had been effected by any other than he. The laurels of the *abbé* Terray did not allow him to sleep. He had the fault of preaching his system too loudly; his tongue counteracted his doings and rendered it impossible. The Court relished very much the idea of not paying, but it wanted to borrow, and calling the apostle of bankruptcy to the ministry was not the way to entice lenders.

---

[19] As if *foulons:* let us trample (on the people).—C. C.

Foulon was already an old man, one from the *good old days* of Louis XV., one of that insolent school that gloried in its rapine, boldly showing it, and which, for a trophy of depredation, built on the boulevard the Pavillon of Hanover. For his part, he had erected for himself, in the most frequented thoroughfare, at the corner of the Rue du Temple, a delightful mansion, which was still admired in 1845.

He was convinced that in France, as Figaro Beaumarchais says, "Everything ends in a song;" therefore he must assume a bold face, brave and laugh at public opinion. Hence those words which were re-echoed everywhere: "If they are hungry, let them browse grass. Wait till I am minister, I will make them eat hay; my horses eat it." He is also stated to have uttered this terrible threat: "France must be mowed." *Il faut faucher la France.*

The old man believed, by such bravado, to please the young military party, and recommend himself for the day he saw approaching, when the Court, wanting to strike some desperate blow, would look out for a hardened villain.

Foulon had a son-in-law after his own heart, Berthier, the intendant of Paris, a clever, but hard-hearted man, as admitted by the royalists,[20] and unscrupulous, since he had espoused a fortune acquired in such a manner.

Of humble extraction, being descended from a race of provincial attorneys or petty magistrates, he was hard-working, active, and energetic. A libertine at the age of fifty, in spite of his numerous family, he purchased, on all sides, so it was said, little girls twelve years of age. He knew well that he was detested by the Parisians, and was but too happy to find an opportunity of making war upon them. With old Foulon, he was the soul of the three days' ministry. Marshal de Broglie expected no good of it: he obeyed.[21] But Foulon and Berthier were very ardent. The latter showed a diabolical activity in collecting arms, troops, everything together, and in manu-

---

[20] According to Beaulieu's confession, *Mémoires,* ii., p. 10.
[21] Alex. de Lameth, *Hist. de l'Assemblée constituante,* i., p. 67.

facturing cartridges. If Paris was not laid waste with fire and sword, it was not his fault.

People feel astonished that persons so wealthy, so well-informed, of mature age and experience, should have cast themselves into such mad proceedings. The reason is, that all great financial speculators partake of the manner of gamblers; they have their temptations. Now, the most lucrative affair they could ever find, was thus to undertake to effect bankruptcy by military execution. That was hazardous. But what great affair is without risk? A profit is made on storm and fire; why not then on war and famine? Nothing risk, nothing gain.

Famine and war, I mean Foulon and Berthier, who thought they held Paris fast, were disconcerted by the taking of the Bastille.

On the evening of the 14th, Berthier attempted to reassure Louis XVI.; if he could but get from him the slightest order, he could even then pour down his Germans upon Paris.

Louis XVI. neither said nor did anything. From that moment, those two ministers felt they were dead men. Berthier fled towards the north, escaping by night from place to place; he passed four nights without sleeping, or even stopping, and yet had reached only Soissons. Foulon did not attempt to fly: first of all, he spread the report everywhere that he had not wished to be minister; next, that he was struck with apoplexy, and lastly pretended he was dead. He had himself buried with great pomp (one of his servants having died at the right moment.) This being done, he repaired very quietly to the house of his worthy friend Sartine, the former lieutenant of police.

He had good reason to be afraid: the movement was terrible. Let us go back a little. As early as the month of May, famine had exiled whole populations, driving them one upon the other. Caen and Rouen, Orleans, Lyons, and Nancy, had witnessed struggles for grain. Marseilles had seen at her gates a band of eight thousand famished people who must pillage or die; the whole town, in spite of the Government, in spite of the *Parlement* of Aix, had taken up arms, and remained armed.

The movement slackened a moment in June. All France, with eyes fixed on the Assembly, was waiting for it to conquer: no other hope of salvation. The most extreme sufferings were for a moment silent; one thought was predominant over all others.

Who can describe the rage, the horror of hope deceived, on the news of Necker's dismissal? Necker was not a politician; he was, as we have seen, timid, vain-glorious, and ridiculous. But in what concerned subsistence, it is but justice to say, that he was an indefatigable, ingenious administrator, full of industry and resources.[22] What is far better, he showed himself to be an honest, good, kind-hearted man; when nobody would lend to the state, he borrowed in his own name, and engaged his own credit as far as two millions of francs, the half of his fortune. When dismissed, he did not withdraw his security; but wrote to the lenders that he maintained it. In a word, if he knew not how to govern, he nourished the people, and fed them with his own money.

Necker and subsistence were words that had the same sound in the ears of the people. Necker's dismissal and famine, hopeless, irremediable famine, was what France felt on the 12th of July.

The provincial Bastilles, that of Caen and that of Bordeaux, either surrendered, or were taken by force, at the same time as that of Paris. At Rennes, Saint Malo, and Strasbourg, the troops sided with the people. At Caen there was a fight among the soldiers. A few men of the Artois regiment were wearing the patriotic symbols; those of the Bourbon regiment, taking advantage of their being unarmed, tore them away. It was thought that Major Belzunce had paid them to offer this insult to their companions. Belzunce was a smart, witty officer, but impertinent, violent, and haughty. He was loud in expressing his contempt for the National Assembly, for the people, the *canaille;* he used to walk in the town, armed to the teeth, with

---

[22] See Necker, *Oeuvres,* vi., pp. 298–324.

a ferocious-looking servant.[23] His looks were provoking. The people lost patience, threatened, and besieged the barracks; an officer had the imprudence to fire; and then the people ran to fetch cannon; Belzunce surrendered, or was given up to be conducted to prison; he could not reach it; he was fired upon and killed, and his body torn piece-meal: a woman ate his heart.

There was blood-shed at Rouen and Lyons: at Saint Germain, a miller was beheaded: a monopolist baker was near being put to death at Poissy; he was saved only by a deputation of the Assembly, who showed themselves admirable for courage and humanity, risked their lives, and preserved the man only after having begged him of the people on their knees.

Foulon would perhaps have outlived the storm, if he had not been hated by all France. His misfortune was to be so by those who knew him best, by his vassals and servants. They did not lose sight of him, neither had they been duped by the pretended burial. They followed and found the dead man alive and well, walking in M. de Sartine's park: "You wanted to give us hay," said they, "you shall eat some yourself!" They put a truss of hay on his back, and adorn him with a nosegay of nettles, and a collar of thistles. They then lead him on foot to Paris, to the Hôtel-de-Ville, and demand his trial of the electors, the only authority that remained. The latter must then have regretted they had not hastened the popular decision which was about to create a real municipal power, give them successors, and put an end to their royalty. Royalty is the word; the French Guards mounted guard at the royal palace of Versailles only on orders received (strange to say) from the electors of Paris.

That illegal power, invoked for everything, but powerless in all things, weakened still further by its fortuitous association with the former municipal magistrates, having nobody for its head but the worthy Bailly, the new mayor, and for its arm only Lafayette, the commander of a scarcely organised national

---

[23] *Mémoires de Dumouriez*, ii., p. 53.

guard, was now about to find itself in face of a terrible necessity.

They heard almost at the same time that Berthier had been arrested at Compiègne, and that Foulon was being conducted back again. For the former, they assumed a responsibility both serious and bold (fear is so sometimes), that of telling the people of Compiègne: "That there was no reason for detaining M. Berthier." They replied that he would then be assuredly killed at Compiègne, and that he could only be saved by conducting him to Paris.

As to Foulon, it was decided: That henceforth delinquents of that description should be lodged in the Abbaye, and that these words should be inscribed over the door: "Prisoners entrusted to the care of the nation." This general measure, taken in the interest of one man, secured for the ex-counsellor his trial by his friends and colleagues, the former magistrates, the only judges of that time.

All that was too evident; but also well watched by keen-sighted men, the attorneys and the Basoche, by investors, enemies of the minister of bankruptcy, and lastly, by many men who held public securities and were ruined by the fall in the funds. An attorney filed an indictment against Berthier, for his deposits of guns. The Basoche maintained that he had moreover one of those deposits with the abbess of Montmartre, and obliged a search to be made. La Grève was full of men, strangers to the people, *"of a decent exterior,"* and some very well dressed. The Stock Exchange was at La Grève.

People came at the same time to the Hôtel-de-Ville, to denounce Beaumarchais, another financier, who had stolen some papers from the Bastille. They ordered them to be taken back.

It was thought that the poor, at all events, might be kept silent by filling their mouths; so they lowered the price of bread: by means of a sacrifice of thirty thousand francs per day, the price was fixed at thirteen sous and a half the four pounds (equal to twenty sous at the present time).

The multitude of La Grève did not vociferate the less. At two, Bailly descends; all demand justice. "He expatiated on principles," and made some impression on those who were within hearing. The others shouted: "Hang! Hang him!" Bailly prudently withdrew, and shut himself up in the *Bureau des Subsistances*. The guard was strong, said he, but M. de Lafayette, who relied on his ascendancy, had the imprudence to lessen it.

The crowd was in a terrible fever of uneasiness lest Foulon should escape. He was shown to them at a window; nevertheless, they broke open the doors: it became necessary to place him in a chair in front of the bureau, in the great hall of Saint-Jean. There, they began to preach to the crowd again, to "expatiate on principles," that he must be judged. "Judged instantly, and hanged!" cried the crowd. So saying, they appointed judges, among others two *curés*, who refused. "Make room there for M. de Lafayette!" He arrives, speaks in his turn, avows that Foulon is a villain, but says it is necessary to discover his accomplices; "Let him be conducted to the Abbaye!" The front ranks, who heard him, consented; not so the others. "You are joking," exclaimed a well-dressed man, "does it require time to judge a man who has been judged these thirty years?" At the same time, a shout is heard, and a new crowd rushes in; some say: "It is the faubourg," others: "It is the Palais Royal." Foulon is carried off and dragged to the lamp opposite; they make him demand pardon of the nation. Then hoist him.—The rope breaks twice. They persist, and go for a new one. At length, having hanged him, they chop off his head, and carry it through Paris.

Meanwhile, Berthier has just arrived by the Porte Saint-Martin, through the most frightful mob that was ever seen: he had been followed for twenty leagues. He was in a cabriolet, the top of which they had broken to pieces in order to see him. Beside him sat an elector, Etienne de la Rivière, who was twenty times near being killed in defending him, and shielding him with his body. A furious mob was dancing on before him; others flung black bread into the carriage:—"Take that, brigand, that is the bread you made us eat!"

What had also exasperated all the population about Paris was, that amid the scarcity, the numerous cavalry collected by Berthier and Foulon, had destroyed or eaten a great quantity of young green wheat. This havoc was attributed to the orders of the intendant, to his firm resolution to prevent there being any crop and to starve the people.

To adorn that horrible procession of death, they carried before Berthier, as in the Roman triumphs, inscriptions to his glory:—"He has robbed the king and France. He has devoured the substance of the people. He has been the slave of the rich, and the tyrant of the poor. He has drunk the blood of the widow and the orphan. He has cheated the king. He has betrayed his country." [24]

At the fountain Maubuée, they had the barbarity to show him Foulon's head, livid, with the mouth full of hay. At that sight his eyes were glazed; he smiled a ghastly smile.

They forced Bailly at the Hôtel-de-Ville to interrogate him. Berthier alleged superior orders. The minister was his father-in-law, it was the same person. Moreover, if the hall of Saint-Jean was inclined to listen a little, La Grève neither listened nor heard; the vociferations were so dreadful, that the mayor and the electors felt more uneasy every moment. A new crowd of people having forced its way through the very mass, it was no longer possible to hold out. The mayor, on the advice of the board, exclaimed: "To the Abbaye!" adding that the guards were answerable for the prisoner. They could not defend him; but, seizing a gun, he defended himself. He was stabbed with a hundred bayonets; a dragoon, who imputed his father's death to him, tore out his heart, and ran to show it at the Hôtel-de-Ville.

The spectators in La Grève, who had watched from the windows the skill of the leaders in urging and exciting the mob, believed that Berthier's accomplices had taken their measures well, in order that he might not have the time to make any revelation. He alone, perhaps, possessed the real intentions

---

[24] *Histoire de la Révolution de '89, par deux amis de la liberté* (*Kerverseau et Clavelin, jusqu'au* t. 7,) t. 2, p. 130. See also the account of Etienne de la Rivière, in the *Procès-verbal des Électeurs.*

of the party. They found in his portfolio the description of the persons of many friends of liberty, who, doubtless, had no mercy to expect, if the court conquered.

However this may be, a great number of the comrades of the dragoon declared to him, that having dishonoured the company he must die, and that they would all fight him till he was killed. He was killed the same evening.

III

France in Arms

THE vampires of the *ancien régime,* whose lives had done so much harm to France, did still more by their death.

Those people, whom Mirabeau termed so well "the refuse of public contempt," are as if restored to character by punishment. The gallows becomes their apotheosis. They are now become interesting victims, the martyrs of monarchy; their legend will go on increasing in pathetic fictions. Mr. Burke canonized them and prayed on their tomb.

The acts of violence of Paris, and those of which the provinces were the theatre, placed the National Assembly in a difficult position, from which it could not well escape.

If it did not act, it would seem to encourage anarchy and authorise murder, and thus furnish a text for eternal calumny.

If it attempted to remedy the disorder, and raise fallen authority, it restored, not to the king, but to the queen and the court, the sword that the people had shivered in their hands.

In either hypothesis, despotism and caprice were about to be re-established, either for the old royalty or the royalty of the mob. At that moment they were destroying the odious symbol of despotism—the Bastille; and behold another Bastille—arbitrary rule—again springing up.

England rubs her hands with glee at this, and is grateful to the *Lanterne.* "Thank God," says she, "the Bastille will never disappear."

What would you have done? Tell us, you officious counsellers, you friendly enemies, sages of European aristocracy, you who so carefully pour calumny on the hatred you have planted. Sitting at your ease on the dead bodies of Ireland, Italy, and Poland, deign to answer; have not your revolutions of interest cost more blood than our revolutions of ideas?

What would you have done? Doubtless what was advised on the eve and the morrow of the 22nd of July, by Lally-Tollendal, Mounier, and Malouet; to re-establish order, they wished that power should be restored to the king. Lally put his whole trust in the king's virtues. Malouet wanted them to entreat the king to use his power and lend a strong hand to the municipal authority. The king would have armed, and not the people; no national guard. Should the people complain, why then let them apply to the *Parlement* and the Attorney-General. Have we not magistrates? Foulon was a magistrate. So Malouet would send Foulon to the tribunal of Foulon.

It is necessary, they very truly said, to repress disturbances. Only it was necessary to come to a right understanding. This word comprehended many things:

Thefts, other ordinary crimes, pillaging committed by a starving population, murders of monopolists, irregular judgment pronounced on the enemies of the people, resistance offered to their plottings, legal resistance, resistance in arms. All comprised in the word *troubles.* Did they wish to suppress all with an equal hand? If royal authority was charged to repress the disturbances, the greatest in its estimation was, most certainly, the taking of the Bastille; it would have punished that first.

This was the reply made by Buzot and Robespierre on the 20th of July, two days before the death of Foulon; and this was what Mirabeau said, in his journal, after the event. He set this misfortune before the Assembly in its true light,—the absence of all authority in Paris, the impotency of the electors, who, without any lawful delegation of power, continued to exercise the municipal functions. He wished municipalities to be organised, invested with strength, and authorized to undertake the maintenance of order. Indeed what other means were there than to strengthen the local power, when the central power was so justly suspected?

Barnave said three things were necessary: well-organized municipalities, citizen guards, and a legal administration of the law that might reassure the people.

What was that legal administration to be? A deputy-substitute, Dufresnoy, sent by a district of Paris, demanded sixty jurymen, chosen from the sixty districts. This proposition, supported by petition, was modified by another deputy, who wished magistrates to be added to the jurymen.

The Assembly came to no decision. An hour after midnight, being weary of contention, it adopted a proclamation, in which it claimed the prosecution of crimes of *lèse-nation, reserving to itself* the right *to indicate in the constitution the tribunal that should judge.* This was postponing for a long time. It invited to peace, for this reason: That the king had acquired *more rights than ever to the confidence* of the people, that there existed a *perfect accord,* &c.

Confidence! And yet there never was any confidence again! At the very moment the Assembly was speaking of confidence, a sad light burst forth, and fresh dangers were seen. The Assembly had been wrong; the people had been right. However willing the poeple might be to be deceived, and believe all was ended, common sense whispered that the *ancien régime* being conquered, would wish to have its revenge. Was it possible that a power which had possessed, for ages, all the forces of the country, administration, finances, armies, and tribunals, that still had everywhere its agents, its officers, its judges, without any change, and for compulsory partisans, two or three hundred thousand nobles or priests, proprietors of one-half or two-thirds of the kingdom,—could that immense and complicated power, which covered all France, die like one man, at once, by a single blow? Had it fallen down dead, shot by a cannon-ball of July? That is what the most simple child could not have been induced to believe.

It was not dead. It had been struck and wounded; morally

it was dead; physically it was not. It might rise again. How would that phantom reappear? That was the whole question put by the people!—the one that troubled the imagination. Common sense here assumed a thousand forms of popular superstition.

Everybody went to see the Bastille; all beheld with terror the prodigious rope ladder by which Latude descended the towers. They visited those ominous towers, and those dark, deep, fetid dungeons, where the prisoner, on a level with the common sewers, lived besieged and menaced by rats, toads, and every kind of foul vermin.

Beneath a staircase they found two skeletons, with a chain and a cannon-ball which one of those unfortunates had doubt-less to drag after him. Those dead bodies indicated crime. For the prisoners were never buried within the fortress; they were always carried by night to the cemetery of Saint Paul, the church of the Jesuits (the confessors of the Bastille); where they were buried under names of servants, so that nobody ever knew whether they were alive or dead. As for those two, the workmen who found them gave them the only reparation the dead could receive; twelve among them, bearing their imple-ments, and holding the pall with respect, carried and buried them honourably in the parish church.

They were even hoping to make other discoveries in that old cavern of kings. Outraged humanity was taking its revenge; people enjoyed a mingled sentiment of hatred, fear, and curiosity,—an insatiable curiosity, which, when everything had been seen, hunted and searched for more, wished to penetrate further, suspected something else, imagined prisons under prisons, dungeons under dungeons, into the very bowels of the earth.

The imagination actually sickened at that Bastille. So many centuries and generations of prisoners who had there suc-ceeded each other, so many hearts broken by despair, so many tears of rage, and heads dashed against the stones. What! had nothing left a trace! At most, some poor inscription, scratched

218

with a nail, and illegible? Cruel envy of time, the accomplice of tyranny, conniving with it to efface every vestige of the victims!

They could see nothing, but they listened. There were certainly some sounds, groans, and hollow moans. Was it imagination? Why, everybody heard them. Were they to believe that wretched beings were still buried at the bottom of some secret dungeon known only to the governor who had perished? The district of the Ile Saint-Louis, and others, demanded that they should seek the cause of those lamentable groans. Once, twice, nay, several times, the people returned to the charge; in spite of all these searches, they could not make up their minds: they were full of trouble and uneasiness for those unfortunates, perhaps buried alive.

Then again, if they were not prisoners, might they not be enemies? Was there not some communication, under the faubourg, between the subterraneous passages of the Bastille and those of Vincennes? Might not gunpowder be passed from one fortress to the other, and execute what De Launey had conceived the idea of doing, to blow up the Bastille, and overwhelm and crush the faubourg of liberty?

Public searches were made, and a solemn and authentic inquiry, in order to tranquillise the minds of the people. The imagination then transported its dream elsewhere. It transferred its plot and its fears to the opposite side of Paris, into those immense cavities whence our monuments were dug, those abysses whence we have drawn the Louvre, Notre Dame, and other churches. There, in 1786, had been cast, without there being any appearance of it (so vast are those caverns) all who had died in Paris for a thousand years, a terrible mass of dead bodies, which, during that year, were transported by night in funeral cars, preceded by the clergy, to seek, from the Innocents to the Tombe Issoire, a final repose and complete oblivion.

Those dead bodies were calling for others, and it was doubtless there that a volcano was preparing; the mine, from the Pantheon to the sky, was going to blow up Paris, and letting it fall again, would confound the shattered and disfigured members of the living and the dead,—a chaos of palpitating limbs, dead bodies, and skeletons.

Those means of extermination seemed unnecessary; famine was sufficient. A bad year was followed by a worse; the little grain that had grown up about Paris was trodden, spoilt, or eaten by the numerous cavalry that had been collected. Nay, the grain disappeared without horse-soldiers. People saw, or fancied they saw, armed bands that came by night and cut the unripe grain. Foulon, though dead, seemed to return on purpose to perform to the letter what he had promised: "Mow France." To cut down the green grain and destroy it in the second year of famine, was also to mow down men.

Terror went on spreading; the couriers, repeating those rumours, spread it every day from one end of the kingdom to the other. They had not seen the brigands, but others had; they were at such and such places, marching forwards, numerous, and armed to the teeth; they would arrive probably that night or on the morrow without fail. At such a place, they had cut down the grain in broad daylight, as the municipality of Soissons wrote in despair to the National Assembly, demanding assistance; a whole army of brigands were said to be marching against that town. They hunted for them; but they had disappeared in the mists of evening or in the morning fog.

What is more real, is, that to the dreadful scourge of famine, some had conceived the idea of adding another, which makes us shudder, when we do but remember the hundred years of warfare which, in the fourteenth and fifteenth centuries, made a cemetery of our unfortunate country, They wanted to bring the English into France. This has been denied; yet why? It is more than likely, since it was solicited at a subsequent period; attempted, and foiled at Quiberon.

But then, the question was not to bring their fleet on a shore difficult of access and destitute of defence, but to establish them firmly in a good, defensible place, to hand over to them the naval arsenal, wherein France, for a whole century, had expended her millions, her labours, and her energies; the head, the prow of our great national vessel, and the stumbling-block of England. The question was to give up Brest.

Ever since France had assisted in the deliverance of America, and cut the British empire asunder, England had desired not its misery, but its ruin and utter destruction; that some strong autumnal tide would raise the ocean from its bed, and cover with one grand flood all the land from Calais to the Vosges, the Pyrenees, and the Alps.

But, there was something still more desirable to be seen, which was, that this new inundation should be one of blood, the blood of France, drawn by herself from her own veins, that she should commit suicide and tear out her intestines.

The conspiracy of Brest was a good beginning. Only, there was reason to fear that England, by making friends with the villains who were selling her their native land, might unite against her all France reconciled in one common indignation, and that there should be no longer any party.

Another thing might have sufficed to restrain the English government, which is, that, in the first moments, England, in spite of her hate, smiled upon our Revolution. She had no suspicion of its extent; in that great French and European movement, which was no less than the advent of eternal right, she fancied she perceived an imitation of her own petty insular and egotistical revolution of the seventeenth century. She applauded France as a mother encourages the child that is trying to walk after her. A strange sort of mother, who was not quite sure whether she would rather the child should walk or break its neck.

Therefore, England withstood the temptation of Brest. She was virtuous, and revealed the thing to the ministers of Louis XVI., without mentioning the names of the parties. In that half revelation, she found an immense advantage, that of perplexing France, to complete the measure of distrust and suspicion, have a terrible hold on that feeble government, and take a mortgage upon it. There was every chance of its not inquiring seriously into the plot, fearful of finding more than it wished and of smiting its own friends. And if it did not inquire, if it kept the secret to itself, England was able at any time to unveil the awful mystery. It kept that sword suspended over the head of Louis XVI.

Dorset, the English ambassador, was an agreeable man; he never stirred from Versailles; many thought he had found favour in the eyes of the queen, and had been well received. Nevertheless, this did not prevent him, after the taking of the Bastille, the importance of which he fully appreciated, as well as the weight of the blow that the king had received, from seizing every opportunity of ruining Louis, as far as lay in his power.

A rather equivocal letter from Dorset to the Count d'Artois having been intercepted by chance, he wrote to the minister that they were wrong in suspecting him of having in the least influenced the disturbances of Paris; far from it, added he quietly, your Excellency knows well the eagerness I evinced in imparting to you the infamous conspiracy of Brest, *in the beginning of June,* the horror felt by my court, and the renewed assurance of its sincere attachment for the king and the nation. And then he entreated the minister to communicate his letter to the National Assembly.

In other words, he begged him to hang himself. His letter *of the 26th of July* stated, and published to the world, that the court, for two whole months, had kept the secret, without either acting or adopting, apparently reserving that plot as a last weapon in case of civil war,—the dagger of mercy (*poignard de miséricorde*), as they called it in the middle ages, which the warrior always kept, so that, when vanquished, thrown on the ground, and his sword broken, he might, whilst begging his life, assassinate his conqueror.

The minister Montmorin, dragged by the English into broad daylight, before the National Assembly, had but a very poor explanation to give, namely, that, not having the names of the guilty parties, they had been unable to prosecute. The Assembly did not insist; but the blow was struck, and was but so much the heavier. It was felt by all France.

Dorset's affirmation, which might have been believed to be

false, a fiction, a brand cast at random by our enemies, appeared confirmed by the imprudence of the officers in the garrison of Brest, who, on the news of the taking of the Bastille, made a demonstration of intrenching themselves in the castle, menacing to subject the town to martial law, if it should stir. This it instantly did, taking up arms, and overpowering the guard of the port. The soldiers and sailors, bribed in vain by their officers, sided with the people. The noble corps of the marine was very aristocratic, but certainly anything but English. Suspicions nevertheless extended even to them, and even further, to the nobles of Brittany. In vain were the latter indignant, and vainly did they protest their loyalty.

This irritation carried to excess made people credit the foulest plots. The prolonged obstinacy of the nobility in remaining separate from the Third in the Estates-General, the bitter, desperate dispute which had arisen on that occasion in every town, large or small, in villages and hamlets, often in the same house, had inculcated an indelible idea in the people, that the noble was an enemy.

A considerable portion of the higher nobility, illustrious and memorable in history, did what was necessary to prove that this idea was false, not at all fearful of the Revolution, and believing that, do what it might, it could not destroy history. But the others, and smaller gentry, less proud of their rank, more vain-glorious or more frank, moreover piqued every day by the new rising of the people whom they saw approaching nearer them, and who incommoded them more, declared themselves boldly the enemies of the Revolution.

The new nobles and the *Parlement* people were the most furious; the magistrates had become more warlike than the military; they spoke of nothing but battles, and vowed death, blood, and ruin. Those among them who had been till then the vanguard in opposing the wishes of the court, who had the most relished popularity, the love and enthusiasm of the public, were astounded and enraged, to see themselves suddenly indifferent or hated. They hated with a boundless hate. They often sought the cause of that very sudden change in the artful machination of their personal enemies, and political enmities were still further envenomed by ancient family feuds. At Quimper, one Kersalaun, a member of the *Parlement* of Brittany, one of the friends of Chalotais, and very lately the ardent champion of parliamentary opposition, becoming suddenly a still more ardent royalist and aristocrat, would walk gravely among the hooting crowds, who, however, dared not touch him, and naming his enemies aloud, used to say: "I shall judge them shortly, and wash my hands in their blood." [25]

One of these *Parlement* people, M. Memmay de Quincey, a noble *seigneur* in Franche-Comté, did not confine himself to threats. Envenomed probably by local animosity, and with his mind in a fever of frenzy, urged likewise perhaps by that fatal propensity of imitation which causes one infamous crime very often to engender many others, he realized precisely what De Launey had wanted to do,—what the people of Paris believed they had still to fear. He gave out at Vesoul, and in the neighbourhood, that by way of rejoicings for the good news, he would give a feast and keep open house. Citizens, peasants, soldiers, all arrive, drink, and dance. The earth opens, and a mine bursts, shatters, shivers, and destroys at random; the ground is strewn with bleeding members. The whole was attested by the *curé*, who confessed a few of the wounded who survived, attested by the *gendarmerie*, and brought on the 25th of July before the National Assembly. The Assembly being exasperated, obtained leave from the king that every power should be written to, in order to demand that the guilty should be delivered up.[26]

---

[25] Duchatellier, *La Révolution en Bretagne*, i., p. 175.

[26] Later, M. de Memmay was restored on the pleading of M. Courvoisier. He maintained that the accident had been occasioned by the barrel of gunpowder, left *by chance* beside some drunken men. Three things had contributed to create another suspicion: 1st. M. de Memmay's absence on the day of the feast; he was unwilling to be present, he said, wishing to give full scope to the rejoicings; 2ndly, his entire disappearance; 3rdly, the *Parlement*, of which he was a former member, would not allow the ordinary tribunals to make an inquiry, called the affair before a higher court, and reserved the trial to itself.

An opinion was gaining ground and growing stronger, that the brigands who used to cut down the grain, in order to starve the people, were not foreigners, as had been first supposed, not Italians or Spaniards, as Marseilles believed in May, but Frenchmen, enemies to France, furious enemies of the Revolution, their agents, their servants, and bands whom they paid.[27]

The horror of them increased, everybody believing he had exterminating demons about him. In the morning, they would run to the field, to see whether it was not laid waste. In the evening, they were uneasy, fearing they might be burned in the night. At the very name of these brigands, mothers would snatch up their children and conceal them.

Where then was that royal protection, on the faith of which the people had so long slept? Where that old guardianship which had so well re-assured them that they had remained minors, and had, as it were, grown up without ceasing to be children? They began to perceive that, no matter what sort of man Louis XVI. might be, royalty was the intimate friend of the enemy.

The king's troops, which, at other times, would have appeared a protection, were precisely a subject of dread. Who were at their head? The more insolent of the nobles, those who the least concealed their hate. They used to excite, to bribe when necessary the soldiers against the people, and to intoxicate their Germans; they seemed to be preparing an attack.

Man was obliged to rely on himself, and on himself alone. In that complete absence of authority and public protection, his

---

[27] The historians all affirm, without the least proof, that these alarms and accusations, all that great commotion, proceeded from Paris, from such and such persons. Doubtless, the leaders influenced the Palais Royal; the Palais Royal, Paris; and Paris, France. It is not less inexact to attribute everything to the Duke of Orleans, like most of the royalists; or to Duport, like M. Droz; to Mirabeau, like Montgaillard, &c. See the very wise answer of Alexandre de Lameth. What he ought to have added is, that Mirabeau, Duport, the Lameths, the Duke of Orleans, and most of the men of that period, less energetic than is believed, were delighted in being thought to possess so much money, such vast influence. They replied but little to such accusations, smiled modestly, leaving such to believe as would, that they were great villains.

duty as a father of a family constituted him the defender of his household. He became, in his house, the magistrate, the king, the law, and the sword to execute the law, agreeably to the old proverb: "The poor man in his home is king."

The hand of Justice, the sword of Justice: that king has his scythe in default of gun, his mattock, or his iron fork. Now let those brigands come! But he does not wait for them. Neighbours unite, villagers unite, and go armed into the country to see whether those villains dare come. They proceed and behold a band. Do not fire however. Those are the people of another village, friends and relations, who are also hunting about.[28]

France was armed in a week. The National Assembly learn every moment the miraculous progress of that Revolution; they find themselves, in an instant, at the head of the most numerous army ever seen since the crusades. Every courier that arrived astonished and almost frightened them. One day, somebody came and said: "You have two hundred thousand men." The next day, another said: "You have five hundred thousand men," Others arrived: "A million men have armed this week,—two millions, three millions."

And all that great armed multitude, rising suddenly from the furrow, asked the Assembly what they were to do.

Where then is the old army? It seems to have disappeared. The new one, being so numerous, must have stifled it without fighting, merely by crowding together.

People have said *France is a soldier,* and so she has been from that day. On that day a new race rose from the earth,— children born with teeth to tear cartridges, and with strong indefatigable limbs to march from Cairo to the Kremlin, and with the admirable gift of being able to march and fight without eating, of having only "their good spirits to feed and clothe them."

Relying on their good spirits, joy and hope! Who then has a right to hope, if it be not he who bears in his bosom the enfranchisement of the world?

---

[28] Montlosier, *Mémoires,* i., p. 233. Toulongeon, i., p. 56, &c., &c.

Did France exist before that time? It might be denied. She became at once a sword and a principle. To be thus armed is *to be*. What has neither idea nor strength, exists but on sufferance.

They *were* in fact; and they wanted *to be* by right.

The barbarous middle ages did not admit their existence, denying them as men, and considering them only as things. That period taught, in its singular school-divinity, that souls redeemed at the same price are all worth the blood of a God; then debased those souls, thus exalted, to brutes, fastened them to the earth, adjudged them to eternal bondage, and annihilated liberty.

This lawless right they called conquest, that is to say, ancient injustice. Conquest, would it say, made the nobles, the lords. "If that be all," said Sieyès, "we will be conquerors in our turn."

Feudal right alleged, moreover, those hypocritical acts, wherein it was supposed that man stipulated against himself: wherein the weaker party, through fear or force, gave himself up without reserving anything, gave away the future, the possible, his children unborn, and future generations. Those guilty parchments, a disgrace to nature, had been sleeping with impunity for ages in the archives of the castles.

Much was said about the grand example given by Louis XVI., who had enfranchised the last serfs of his domains. An imperceptible sacrifice that cost the treasury but little, and which had scarcely any imitator in France.

What! it will be said, were the *seigneurs* in '89 hard-hearted, merciless men?

By no means. They were a very varied class of men, but generally feeble and physically decayed, frivolous, sensual, and sensitive, so sensitive that they could not look closely at the unfortunate.[29] They saw them in idyls, operas, stories, and romances, which caused them to shed tears of compassion; they wept with Bernardin Saint-Pierre, with Grétry and Sedaine, Berquin and Florian; they found merit in their tears, and would say to themselves: "I have a good heart."

---

[29] This is confessed by M. De Maitre, in his *Considérations sur la Révolution* (1796).

Thus weak-hearted, easy, open-handed, and incapable of withstanding the temptation of spending, they required money, much money, more than their fathers. Hence the necessity of deriving large profits from their lands, of handing the peasant over to men of money, stewards, and agents. The more feeling the masters possessed, the more generous and philanthropic they were at Paris, and the more their vassals died of hunger; they lived less at their castles, in order not to see this misery, which would have been too painful for their sensibility.

Such was in general that feeble, worn-out, effeminate society. It willingly spared itself the sight of oppression, and oppressed only by proxy. However, there were not wanting provincial nobles, who prided themselves on maintaining in their castles the rude feudal traditions, and governed their family and their vassals harshly. Let us merely mention here the celebrated *Ami des hommes,* Mirabeau's father, the enemy of his family, who would lock up all his household, wife, sons, and daughters, people the state-prisons, have law-suits with his neighbours, and reduce his people to despair. He relates that, on giving a *fête,* he was himself astonished at the moody, savage aspect of his peasants. I can easily believe it; those poor people were probably afraid lest the *Ami des hommes* should take them for his children.

We must not be surprised if the peasant, having once taken up arms, made use of them, and had his revenge. Several lords had cruelly vexed their districts, who remembered it when the time had come. One of them had walled up the village well, and monopolised it for his own use. Another had seized on the common lands. They perished. Several other murders are recorded, which, doubtless, were acts of revenge.

The general arming of the towns was imitated in the rural districts. The taking of the Bastille encouraged them to attack their own bastilles. The only subject of astonishment, when one knows what they underwent, is, that they began so late. Sufferings and promises of revenge had accumulated by delay, and been stored up to a frightful height. When that monstrous avalanche, long pent up in a state of ice and snow, suddenly thawed, such a mass gave way, that everything was overwhelmed in its fall.

It would be necessary to distinguish, in that immense scene of confusion what appertains to the *wandering bands* of pillagers,—people driven about by famine, from what the *domiciled peasants*, the *communes*, did against their lord.

The evil has been carefully collected, but not so the good. Several lords found defenders in their vassals: for instance, the Marquis de Montfermeil, who, in the preceding year, had borrowed a hundred thousand francs in order to relieve them. Nay, the most furious sometimes stopped short in presence of weak adversaries. In Dauphiné, for instance, a castle was respected, because they found in it only a sick lady, in bed, with her children; they merely destroyed the feudal archives.

Generally, the peasant marched at once to the castle to demand arms; then, more daring, he burned the acts and titles. The greater part of those instruments of bondage, those which were the most immediate and oppressive, were much oftener in the register offices, with the attorneys and notaries. The peasant rarely went there. He preferred attacking the antiquities,—the original charters. Those primitive titles, on fine parchments, adorned with triumphant seals, remained in the treasury of the castle to be shown on grand days. They were stored away in sumptuous cases, in velvet portfolios at the bottom of an oaken ark,—the glory of the turret. No important feudal manor but showed, near its feudal dove-cote, its tower of archives.

Our country people went straight to the tower. There, in their estimation, was the Bastille, tyranny, pride, insolence, and the contempt of mankind; for many centuries, that tower had seemed to sneer at the valley, sterilizing, blighting, and oppressing it with its deadly shadow. A guardian of the country in barbarous times, standing there as a sentinel, it became later an object of horror. In 1789, what was it but the odious witness of bondage, a perpetual outrage, to repeat every morning to the man trudging to his labour, the everlasting humiliation of his race! "Work, work on, son of serfs, earn for another's profit; work, and without hope."

Every morning and every evening, for a thousand years, perhaps more, that tower had been cursed. A day came when it was to fall.

O glorious day, how long you have been in coming! How long our fathers expected and dreamed of you in vain! The hope that their sons would at length behold you, was alone able to support them; otherwise, they would no longer have consented to live; they would have died in their agony. And what has enabled me, their companion labouring beside them in the furrow of history, and drinking their bitter cup, to revive the suffering middle ages, and yet not die of grief? Was it not you, O glorious day, first day of liberty? I have lived in order to relate your history!

IV

The Rights of Man

ABOVE all that great commotion, in a region more serene, the National Assembly, without allowing itself to be molested by noise and clamour, was buried in thought and meditation.

The violence of party spirit which had divided it, seemed awed and restrained by the great discussion with which its labours began. Then people plainly saw how profoundly that aristocracy, the natural adversary of the interests of the Revolution, had been wounded in its ideas. They were all Frenchmen, after all, all sons of the eighteenth century and philosophy.

Either side of the Assembly, preserving its opposition, nevertheless entered upon the solemn examination of the *declaration of rights* with due solemnity.

The question was not a petition of rights, as in England, an appeal to the written law, to contested charters, or to the true or false liberties of the Middle Ages.

The question was not, as in America, to go seeking from state to state the principles which each of them acknowledged, to sum up and generalize them, and construct with them (*à posteriori*) the total formula which the confederation would accept.

The question was to give from above, by virtue of a sovereign, imperial, pontifical authority, the *credo* of the new age. What authority? Reason, discussed by a whole century of philosophers, profound thinkers, accepted by every mind and penetrating social order, and lastly, fixed and reduced to a formula by the logicians of the Constituent Assembly. The question was to impose as authority on reason what reason had found at the bottom of free inquiry.

It was the philosophy of the age, its legislator, its Moses, descending from the mount, with the rays of glory on its brow, and bearing the tables of the law in its hands.

There have been many disputations for and against the declaration of rights, but nothing to the point.

First of all, we have nothing to say to such as Bentham and Dumont, to utilitarians and quacks, who acknowledge no law but the written law, who know not that right is right only so far as it is conformable to right, to absolute reason. Mere attorneys, nothing more, in the garb of philosophers; what right have they to despise practical men? Like them, who write the law upon paper and parchment, we would engrave ours on tables of eternal right, on the rock that bears the world: invariable justice and indestructible equity.

To answer our enemies, let us confine ourselves to them and their contradictions. They sneer at the Declaration, and submit to it; they wage war against it for thirty years, promising their people the liberties which it consecrates. When conquerors in 1814, the first word they address to France they borrow from the grand formula which she laid down.[30] Conquerors did I say? No, conquered rather, and conquered in their own hearts; since their most personal act, the treaty of the Holy Alliance, reproduces the right that they have trampled on.

The Declaration of *Rights* attests the Supreme Being, the guarantee of human morality. It breathes the sentiment of *duty*. Duty, though not expressed, is no less everywhere present; everywhere you perceive its austere gravity. A few words borrowed from the language of Condillac, do not prevent us from recognising in the *ensemble* the true genius of the Revolution,— a Roman gravity and a stoic spirit.

---

[30] And very voluntarily borrowed; since it was done by all the kings of Europe at the head of eight hundred thousand soldiers. They acknowledge that every people has the right of choosing its government. See Alexandre de Lameth, p. 121.

Right was the first thing to be spoken of at such a moment,[31] it was rights that it was necessary to attest and claim for the people. People had believed till then that they had only *duties*.

However high and general such an act may be, and made to last for ever, can one reasonably expect it to bear no marks of the troublous period of its birth, no sign of the storm?

The first word was uttered three days before the 14th of July and the taking of the Bastille; the last, a few days before the people brought the king to Paris (the 6th of October). A sublime apparition of right between two storms.

No circumstances were ever more terrible, nor any discussion more majestic or more serious, even in the midst of emotion. The crisis afforded specious arguments to both parties.

Take care, said one, you are teaching man his rights, when he perceives them but too plainly himself; you are transporting him to a high mountain, and showing him his boundless empire. What will happen, when, on descending, he will find himself stopped by the special laws that you are going to make, when he will meet with boundaries at every step? [32]

There was more than one answer, but certainly the strongest was the state of affairs. The crisis was then at its height, and the combat still doubtful. It was impossible to find too high a mountain whereon to fix the standard. It was necessary to place that flag, if possible, so high that the whole world might behold it, and that its tricolor streamer might rally the nations. Recognised as the common standard of humanity, it became invincible.

There are still people who think that great discussion excited and armed the people, that it put the torch in their hand, and promoted warfare and conflagration. The first stumbling-block to that argument is, that the acts of violence began previous to the discussion. The peasants did not need metaphysical formula in order to rise in arms. Even afterwards it had but little influence. What armed the rural districts was, as we have already

---

[31] Of right and liberty alone: nothing more at first in that charter of enfranchisement. I explain myself more fully in the Introduction, and in the other volumes.

[32] *Discours de Malouet.*

said, the necessity of putting down pillage; it was the contagion of cities taking up arms; and, above all, it was the frenzy and enthusiasm caused by the taking of the Bastille.

The grandeur of that spectacle and the variety of its terrible incidents troubled the vision of history. It has mixed together and confounded three distinct and even opposite facts which were taking place at the same time.

1st. The excursions of the famished vagrants, who cut down the grain at night, and cleared the earth like locusts. Those bands, when strong, would break open lone houses, farms, and even castles.

2ndly. The peasant, in order to repel those bands, was in need of arms, and demanded and exacted them from the castles. Once armed and master, he destroyed the charters, in which he beheld an instrument of oppression. Woe to detested nobles! Then they did not attack his parchments alone, but his person also.

3rdly. The cities, the arming of which had brought about that of the rural districts, were obliged to repress them. The National Guards, who then had nothing aristocratic about them, since they included everybody, marched forth to restore order; they went to the succour of those castles which they detested. They often brought the peasants back to town as prisoners, but soon released them.[33]

I speak of the peasants domiciled in the neighbourhood. As for the bands of lawless strollers, pillagers, and brigands, as they were called, the tribunals, and even the municipalities, often treated them with extreme severity: a great number of them were put to death. Security was at length restored, and agriculture protected. If the depredations had continued, cultivation must have ceased, and France would have been starved to death the following year.

A strange situation for an Assembly to be discussing, calculating, weighing syllables, at the summit of a world in flames.

---

[33] All this is very much embroiled by historians, according to their passions. I have consulted old men, especially my illustrious and venerable friends M M. Béranger and de Lamennais.

Danger on the right and on the left. To repress the disorder, they have, one would think, but one means: to restore the ancient order, which is but a worse disorder.

It is commonly supposed that they were impatient to lay hold of power; that is true of certain of the members, but false, very false, with respect to the great majority. The character of that Assembly, considered in the mass, its originality, like that of the period, was a singular faith in the power of ideas. It firmly believed that truth, once found, and written in the formula of laws, was invincible. It would require but two months (such was the calculation, however, of very serious men); in two months the constitution was made; it would, by its omnipotent virtue, overawe authority and the people: the Revolution was then completed, and the world was to bloom again.

Meanwhile, the position of affairs was truly singular; Authority was in one place destroyed, in another very strong; organised on such a point, in complete dissolution on another, feeble for general and regular action, though formidable still to corruption, intrigue, and perhaps to violence. The accounts of those latter years, which appeared later, sufficiently show what resources were possessed by the court, and how they employed them,—how they tampered with the press, the newspapers, and even with the Assembly. Emigration was beginning, and with it an appeal to foreigners,—to the enemy,—a persevering system of treason and calumny against France.

The Assembly felt it was sitting upon a volcano. For the general safety, it was obliged to descend from the heights where it was making laws, and take a nearer view of what was passing on the earth. A stupendous descent! Solon, Lycurgus, or Moses, debased to the miserable cares of public *surveillance*, forced to watch over spies, and become an inspector of police!

The first hint was given by Dorset's letters to Count d'Artois, by his still more alarming explanations, and the notice of the conspiracy of Brest, so long concealed by the court. On the 27th of July, Duport proposed to create a committee of inquiry, composed of four persons. He uttered these ominous words: "Allow me to refrain from entering into any discussion. Plots are forming. There must not be any question of sending before the tribunals. We must acquire horrible and indispensable information."

The number four reminded them too much of the three inquisitors of State. It was therefore raised to twelve.

The spirit of the Assembly, in spite of its necessities, was by no means one of police and inquisition. A very serious discussion took place as to whether the secrecy of letters was to be violated, whether they ought to open that suspected correspondence, addressed to a prince, who, by his precipitate flight, declared himself an enemy. Gouy d'Arcy and Robespierre wished them to be opened. But the Assembly, on the opinion of Chapelier, Mirabeau, and even of Duport, who had just demanded a sort of State inquisition, magnanimously declared the secrecy of letters inviolable, refused to open them, and caused them to be restored.

This decision restored courage to the partisans of the court. They made three bold attempts. On Sieyès being proposed for president, they opposed to him the eminent legist of Rouen, Thouret, a man much esteemed, and very agreeable to the Assembly. His merit in their estimation was his having voted, on the 17th of June, against the title of *National Assembly*, that simple formula of Sieyès which contained the Revolution. To bring into opposition these two men, or rather those two systems, in the question of the presidency, was putting the Revolution on trial, and attempting to see whether it could not be made to retrograde to the 16th of June.

The second attempt was to prevent the trial of Besenval. That general of the queen against Paris had been arrested in his flight. To judge and condemn him was to condemn also the orders according to which he had acted. Necker, in returning, had seen him on his journey, and given him hopes. It was not difficult to obtain from his kind heart the promise of a solemn appeal to the city of Paris.[34] To obtain a general amnesty, in the

---

[34] He says expressly that he was speaking in the name of the king. See his speech, *Hist. de la Révolution, par deux amis de la liberté,* ii., p. 235.

joy of his return, end the Revolution, restore tranquillity, and appear as after the deluge, the rainbow in the heavens, was most charming to the vanity of Necker.

He went to the Hôtel-de-Ville, and obtained everything of those who happened to be there,—electors, representatives of districts, simple citizens, a mixed, confused, multitude, without any legal character. The joy of the people was extreme, both in the hall and in the public square. He showed himself at the window, with his wife on his right, and his daughter on his left, both weeping and kissing his hands. His daughter, Madame de Staël, fainted with delight.[35]

That done, nothing was done. The districts of Paris justly protested; this clemency filched from an Assembly lost in emotion, granted in the name of Paris by a crowd without authority, a national question, settled at once by a single town, —by a few of its inhabitants,—and that at the moment the National Assembly was creating a committee of inquiry and preparing a tribunal,—this was unprecedented and audacious. In spite of Lally and Mounier, who defended the amnesty, Mirabeau, Barnave, and Robespierre obtained a decision for a trial. The court were again defeated; however, they had one great consolation, worthy of their usual wisdom: they had compromised Necker, and destroyed the popularity of the only man who had any chance of saving them.

The court failed in the affair of the Presidency. Thouret, alarmed at the exasperation of the people, and the menaces of Paris, retired.

A third and far more serious attempt of the royalist party was made by Malouet; this was one of the strangest and most dangerous trials that the Revolution had met with in her perilous route, where her enemies were every day laying stumbling-blocks, and digging pits at every step.

The reader may remember the day, when, before the Orders had yet united, the clergy had gone hypocritically to show the Third Estate the black bread which the people had to eat, and to engage them, in the name of charity, to lay aside useless

---

[35] Staël, *Considerations*, 1st part, cn. xxiii. See also Necker, t. vi., ix.

disputes, in order to undertake with them the welfare of the poor. This is precisely what was done by Malouet, in other respects an honourable man, but a blind partisan of a royalty then all but destroyed.

He proposed to organise a vast poor-relief system, bureaus for relief and work, the first funds of which should be furnished by the establishments of charity, the rest by a general tax on all, and by a loan—a noble and honourable proposal, countenanced at such a moment by pressing necessity, but giving the royalist party a formidable political initiative. It placed in the hands of the king a three-fold fund, the last portion of which, the loan, was unlimited; it made him the leader of the poor, perhaps the general of the beggars against the Assembly. It found him dethroned, and placed him upon a throne, far more absolute, more solid, by making him king of famine, reigning by what is most imperious, food and bread.

What became of liberty?

For the thing to create less alarm, and appear a mere trifle, Malouet lowered the number of the poor to four hundred thousand,—a figure evidently false.

If he did not succeed, he nevertheless derived a great advantage, that of giving his party, the king's, a fine colouring in the eyes of the people,—the glory of charity. The majority, which would be too much compromised by refusing, was about compulsorily to follow and obey, and to place that great popular machine in the hands of the king.

Malouet proposed, lastly, to consult the Chambers of Commerce and the manufacturing towns, in order to aid the workmen, "to augment work and wages."

A sort of opposition bidding was about to be established between the two parties. The question was to obtain or to bring back the people. The proposal of *giving* to the indigent could only be met by one to authorise workmen *to pay taxes no longer,*—one, at least, to authorise country labourers no longer to pay the most odious of taxes, the feudal tributes.

Those rights were in great jeopardy. In order to destroy them the more effectually and annihilate the acts by which they were

consecrated, they burned even the castles. The large proprietors, who were sitting in the Assembly, were full of uneasiness.
A property so detested and so dangerous, which compromised
all the rest of their fortune, began to appear to them a burden.
To save those rights, it was necessary either to sacrifice a part,
or to defend them by force of arms, rally all the friends, clients,
and domestics they might possess, and begin a terrible war
against the whole people.

Except an inconsiderable number of old men who had served
in the Seven Years War, and young men who had taken a part
in that of America, our nobles had taken part in no campaigns
save garrison maneuvers. They were, however, individually
brave in private quarrels. The petty nobles of Vendée and
Brittany, till then so unknown, suddenly stood forth and
showed themselves heroic. Many nobles and emigrants distinguished themselves also in the great wars of the empire.
Perhaps, if they had acted in concert and rallied together,
they might for some time have arrested the Revolution. It
found them dispersed, isolated, and weak in their loneliness.
Another cause of their weakness, very honourable for them,
was, that many of them were at heart against themselves,—
against the old feudal tyranny, and that they were at the same
time its heirs and its enemies; educated in the generous ideas
of the philosophy of the time, they applauded that marvellous
resuscitation of mankind, and offered up prayers for it, even
though it cost their own ruin.

The richest *seigneur* in feudal properties, after the king, was
the Duke d'Aiguillon.[36] He possessed royal prerogatives in
two provinces of the South: all of odious origin, and which his
grand-uncle Richelieu had conferred upon himself. His father,
the colleague of Terray, minister of bankruptcy, had been
despised even more than he was detested. The young Duke
d'Aiguillon felt the more keenly the necessity of making himself popular; he was, with Duport and Chapelier, one of the
leaders of the *Breton Club*. There he made the generous and

---

[36] Alex. de Lameth, *Histoire de l'Assemblée Constituante*, i., p. 96.

shrewd proposition of building a backfire in that great conflagration, to throw down a part of the building in order to save
the rest; he wished, not to sacrifice the feudal rights (many
nobles had no other fortune), but to offer to the peasant *to
purchase his exemption at a moderate price.*

Viscount de Noailles was not at the club, but he got scent of
the proposal, and filched away the honour of being the first
proposer. A younger son, and possessing no feudal rights, he
was still more generous than the Duke d'Aiguillon. He proposed not only to permit a redemption from rights, but to
abolish without redemption seigneurial statute-labour (*cor-
vées*) and other personal bondage.

This was considered as an attack, a threat,—nothing more.
About two hundred deputies applauded the proposition. They
had just read a projected decree in which the Assembly
reminded people of the duty of respecting properties, of paying
rent, &c.

The Duke d'Aiguillon produced a very different effect. He
said that in voting, on the preceding evening, rigorous measures against those who attacked the castles, a scruple had
arisen in his mind, and he had asked himself whether those
men were really guilty. And he continued to declaim warmly,
violently, against feudal tyranny, that is to say, against himself.

That 4th of August, at eight in the evening, was a solemn
hour in which feudality, after a reign of a thousand years, ab-
dicates, abjures, and condemns itself.

Feudality has spoken. It is now the turn of the people. M. Le
Guen de Kerengal, a Bas-Breton, in the costume of his region,
an unknown deputy, who never spoke either before or after,
ascends the tribune, and reads some twenty lines of an accusing,
menacing character. He reproached the Assembly with singular
energy and authority for not having prevented the burning of
the castles, by breaking, said he, the cruel arms they contain,—
those iniquitous acts which debase man to the brute, which
yoke man and beast to the plough, which outrage decency.
"Let us be just; let them bring to us those titles, monuments of
the barbarity of our fathers. Who among us would not make an

expiatory pile to burn those infamous parchments? You have not a moment to lose; a delay of one day occasions new conflagrations; the downfall of empires is announced with far less uproar. Would you give laws only to France in ruins?" This made a deep impression. Another Breton did but weaken it by calling to mind several strange, cruel, incredible rights: the right that the lord of the manor had had to cut open the bellies of two of his vassals on returning from hunting, and of thrusting his feet into their bleeding bodies.

A provincial nobleman, M. de Foucault, making an attack on the great lords who had begun this lamentable discussion, demanded that, before anything else, the great should sacrifice their pensions and salaries,—the prodigious donations they drew from the king, doubly ruining the people, both by the money they extorted, and by the neglect into which the province fell, all the rich following their example, deserting their lands, and crowding about the court. MM. de Guiche and de Montemart believed the attack to be personal, and replied sharply that the persons alluded to would sacrifice everything.

Enthusiasm gained ground. M. de Beauharnais proposed that penalties should henceforth be the same for all, nobles and plebeians, and employments open to all. One asked for gratuitous justice; another, for the abolition of seigneurial justice, the inferior agents of which were the scourge of the rural districts.

M. de Custine said that the conditions of redemption proposed by the Duke d'Aiguillon were difficult, that those difficulties ought to be removed, and succour granted to the peasant.

M. de la Rochefoucault, extending the benevolence of France to the human race, demanded an amelioration for negro slavery.

Never did the French character shine forth more charmingly in its benevolence, vivacity, and generous enthusiasm. These men who had required so much time and study to discuss the Declaration of Rights, counting and weighing every syllable, having now an appeal made to their disinterestedness, replied unhesitatingly; they trod money under foot, and those rights of nobility which they loved more than money. A grand example which the expiring nobility bequeathed to our citizen aristocracy!

Amid the general enthusiasm and emotion, there was also a proud carelessness, the vivacity of a noble gamester who takes delight in flinging down his gold. All those sacrifices were made by rich and poor, with equal good humour, sometimes with archness (like Foucault's motion), and lively sallies.

"And what have I to offer?" said Count de Virieu. "At least the sparrow of Catullus." He proposed the destruction of the destroying pigeons, of the feudal dove-cot.

The young Montmorency demanded that all those prayers should be immediately converted into laws. Lepelletier de Saint-Fargeau desired that the people should immediately enjoy those benefits. Himself immensely rich, he wished that the rich, the nobles, the exempt from taxes, should assess themselves for this purpose.

Chapelier, the president, on being pressed to put the question to the vote, archly observed that none of *Messieurs* the clergy having yet been able to obtain a hearing, he should have to reproach himself with having shut them out from the tribune.[37]

The Bishop of Nancy then expressed, in the name of the ecclesiastical lords, a wish that the price of redemption from feudal rights should not accrue to the present possessor, but be invested as funds useful to the benefice itself.[38]

This was economy and husbandry rather than generosity. The Bishop of Chartres, a sensible man, who spoke next, found

---

[37] Omitted in the *Moniteur* and the *Histoire Parlementaire*. See the *Histoire des deux Amis de la Liberté*, ii., p. 321.

[38] Arranged and disfigured in the *Moniteur* and the historians who wish to conceal the egotism of the clergy. The *Procès-verbal* says only: He adhered, *in his own name and in the name of several* members of the clergy, to this system of redeeming the feudal rights, by submitting (by the incumbents) to the lodging and use of the funds arising from them.— *Archives du Royaume. Procès-verbaux de l'Assemblée Nationale. 4 Août,* '89. B. 2.

a way of being generous at the expense of the nobility. He sacrificed the game rights (*droits de chasse*), very important for the nobles, but of little value for the clergy.

The nobles did not shrink; they demanded the consummation of this renunciation. Several were reluctant. The Duke du Châtelet said, smiling at his neighbours: "The bishop deprives us of hunting; I will take away his tithes." And he proposed that tithes in kind should be converted into pecuniary dues redeemable at pleasure.

The clergy allowed those dangerous words to fall without observation, and followed their usual tactics of putting forward the nobility; the archbishop of Aix spoke forcibly against feudality, demanding that in future every kind of feudal convention should be prohibited.

"I wish I had land," said the Bishop of Uzès, "I should delight in giving it into the hands of the peasants. But we are only depositaries."

The Bishop of Nimes and Montpellier gave nothing, but demanded that the artisans and labourers should be exempt from charges and taxation.

The poorer ecclesiastics were alone generous. Some *curés* declared that their conscience did not allow them to have more than one benefice. Others said: "We offer our fees." Duport objected that the deficiency must then be made up to them. The Assembly was affected, and refused to accept the widow's mite.

Emotion and enthusiasm had gradually increased to an extraordinary degree. Nothing was heard in the Assembly but applause, congratulations, and expressions of mutual benevolence. Foreigners, present at that meeting, were struck with astonishment; then, for the first time, they beheld France, and all the goodness of her heart. What ages of struggles had not effected in their countries, she had just done in a few hours by disinterestedness and sacrifice. Money and pride trodden under foot, together with the old hereditary tyranny, antiquity, tradition itself,—the monstrous feudal oak, felled by one blow,— that accursed tree, whose branches covered the whole earth with a deadly shade, whilst its innumerable roots shot forth into the obscurest regions, probing and absorbing life, preventing it from rising to the light of day.

Everything seemed finished. But a scene no less grand was then beginning.

After the privileges of classes, came those of provinces. Such as were called state provinces (*pays d'état*), which had privileges of their own, divers advantages for liberties and taxation, were ashamed of their egotism; they wanted to be France, in spite of what it might cost their personal interest and their old fond reminiscences.

As early as 1788, Dauphiné had magnanimously offered to surrender its privileges, and advised the other provinces to do the same. It renewed that offer. The most obstinate, the Bretons, though bound by their mandates, and tied down by the ancient treaties of their province with France, nevertheless manifested the desire of uniting. Provence said the same, next Burgundy and Bresse, Normandy, Poitou, Auvergne, and Artois. Lorraine, in affecting language, said that it would not regret the domination of its adored sovereigns who were the fathers of the people, if it had the happiness of uniting with its brethren, and of entering with them all together into the maternal mansion of France,—into that vast and glorious family.

Next came the turn of the cities. Their deputies came in crowds to lay their privileges upon the altar of their native land.

The officers of justice were unable to pierce the crowd surrounding the tribune, to bring their tribute. A member of the *Parlement* of Paris imitated their example, renouncing the hereditary succession of offices,—transmissible nobility.

The archbishop of Paris demanded that they should remember God on that great day, and sing a Te Deum.

"But the king, gentlemen," said Lally, "the king who has convoked us after the long lapse of two centuries, shall he not have his reward? Let us proclaim him the restorer of French liberty!"

The night was far advanced: it was two o'clock. That night

dispelled for ever the long and painful dream of the thousand years of the middle ages. The approaching dawn was that of liberty!

Since that marvellous night, no more classes, but Frenchmen; no more provinces, but one France!

God save France!

V

The Clergy and the People

THE resurrection of the people who at length burst their sepulchre, feudality itself rolling away the stone by which it had kept them immured, the work of ages in one night, such was the first miracle—the divine and authentic miracle—of this new Gospel!

How applicable here are those words pronounced by Fauchet over the skeletons found in the Bastille! "Tyranny had sealed them within the walls of those dungeons which she believed to be eternally impenetrable to the light. *The day of revelation is come!* The bones have arisen at the voice of French liberty; they depose against centuries of oppression and death, prophesying the regeneration of human nature, and the life of nations!" [39]

Noble language of a true prophet. Let us cherish it in our hearts, as the treasure of hope. Yes, they will rise again! The resurrection begun on the ruins of the Bastille, continued through the night of the 4th of August, will display in the light of social life those crowds still languishing in the shadows of death. Day dawned in 1789; next, the morn arose shrouded in storms; then, a dark, total eclipse. The sun will yet shine out. "Solem quis dicere falsum audeat?"

---

[39] Printed at the end of Dussaulx's *Oeuvre des Sept Jours*. He says admirably on another occasion: "We have reached the middle of time. Tyrants are ripe." See his three speeches on liberty, spoken at Saint-Jacques, Sainte-Marguerite, and Notre-Dame.

It was two hours after midnight when the Assembly concluded its important work, and separated. In the morning (August 5th), Fauchet was making, at Paris, his funeral oration over the citizens killed before the Bastille. Those martyrs of liberty had just gained, that very night, in the destruction of the great feudal Bastille, their palm, and the price of their blood.

Fauchet there found once more words worthy of eternal remembrance: "How those false interpreters of divine oracles have injured the world! They have consecrated despotism, and made God the accomplice of tyrants. What says the Gospel? 'You will have to appear before kings; they will order you to act unrighteously, and you shall resist them till death.' False doctors triumph, because it is written: *Give unto Caesar the things that are Caesar's*. But must they also give unto Caesar what is not Caesar's? Now liberty is not Caesar's; it belongs to human nature."

Those eloquent words were still more so in the mouth of him who, on the 14th of July, had shown himself doubly heroic by courage and humanity. Twice had he attempted, at the peril of his life, to save the lives of others, and stop the effusion of blood. A true Christian and true citizen, he had wished to save all, both men and doctrines. His blind charity defended at the same time ideas hostile to one another, and contradictory dogmas. He united the two Gospels in one bond of love, without any attention to the difference of their principles, or to their opposite characters. Spurned and excluded by the priests, he looked upon what had caused his persecution as something, for that very reason, that he ought to respect and cherish. Who has not fallen into the very same error? Who has not cherished the hope of saving the past by hastening the future? Who would not have wished to quicken the spirit without killing the old form?—to rekindle the flame without molesting the dead ashes? Vain endeavour! In vain would we withhold our breath. It expands in the air, and flies to the four quarters of the world.

Who was then able to see all that? Fauchet was mistaken,

and so were many others. They endeavoured to believe the struggle ended, and peace restored; they wondered to find that the Revolution had been already in the Gospel. The heart of every one who heard those glorious words leaped with joy. The impression was so strong, the emotion so poignant, that they crowned the apostle of liberty with a civic wreath. The people and the armed population, the conquerors of the Bastille and the citizen guard, with drums beating in front, led him back to the Hôtel-de-Ville; a herald carried a crown before him.

Was this the last triumph of the priest, or the first of the citizen? Will those two characters, here confounded, be able to blend together? The tattered raiment, glorified by the bullets of the Bastille, allow us here to perceive the new man; in vain would he extend that robe in order to cover the past.

A new creed is advancing towards us, and two others are departing (how can it be helped?)—the Church and Royalty.

Of the three branches of the antique oak,—Feudality, Royalty, Church,—the first fell on the 4th of August; the two others totter to and fro; I hear a loud wind in the branches; they struggle, and resist strongly; their leaves are scattered on the ground; nothing can withstand that storm. Let what is doomed perish!

No regret, no useless tears! Gracious God! how long had that which imagines it is now dying, been sterile, dead and useless!

What bears an overwhelming testimony against the Church in 1789, is the state of utter neglect in which she had left the people. For two thousand years she alone had the duty of instructing them; and how had she performed it? What was the end and aim of the pious foundations in the middle ages? What duties did they impose on the clergy? The salvation of souls, their religious improvement, the softening of manners, the humanising of the people. They were your disciples, and given to you alone. Masters, what have you taught them?

Ever since the twelfth century, you have continued to speak to them a language no longer theirs, and the form of worship has ceased to be a mode of instructing them. The deficiency was supplied by preaching; but gradually it became silent, or spoke for the rich alone. You have neglected the poor, disdained the coarse mob. Coarse? Yes, through you. Through you, two people exist: the upper, civilised and refined to excess; the lower, rude and savage, much further removed from the other than in the beginning. It was your duty to fill up the interval, to be ever raising the lowly, and of the two to make one people. Now the crisis has come; and I see no cultivation acquired, no softening of manners among the classes of which you made yourselves the masters; what they possess, they have naturally, from the instinct of Nature, from the sap that she implants within us. The good is innate; and to whom must I attribute the evil, the anarchy, but to those who were answerable for their souls, and yet abandoned them?

In 1789, what are your famous monasteries, your antique schools? The abode of idleness and silence. Grass grows there, and the spider spins her web. And your pulpits? Mute. And your books? Empty.

The eighteenth century passes away, an age of attacks, in which, from time to time, your adversaries summon you in vain to speak and to act, if you be still alive.

One thing alone might be urged in your defence; many of you believe it, though not one will avow it. It is, that, for a long time past, doctrine was exhausted, that you no longer said anything to the people, having nothing to say, that you had lived your ages, an age of teaching,—an age of disputation— that everything passes and changes; the heavens themselves will pass away. Powerfully attached to outward forms, unable to separate the spirit from them, not daring to aid the phoenix to die to live again, you remained dumb and inactive in the sanctuary, occupying the place of the priest. But the priest was no longer there.

Depart from the temple. You were there for the people, to give them light. Go, your lamp is extinct. They who built those churches, and lent them to you, now demand them. Who were they? The France of those times; restore them to the France of to-day.

To-day (August, 1789,) France takes back the tithes, and to-morrow (November 2nd), she will take back the estates. By what right? A great jurisconsult has said: "By the right of *default of heirs*." The dead church has no heirs. To whom does her patrimony revert? To her author, to that PATRIA, whence the new church shall rise.

On the 6th of August, when the Assembly had been long discussing a loan proposed by Necker, and which, as he confessed, would not suffice for two months, a man who till then had seldom spoken, suddenly ascended the tribune; this time he said but these words: "The ecclesiastical estates belong to the nation."

Loud murmurs. The man who had so frankly stated the position of things was Buzot, one of the leaders of the future Gironde party: his youthful, austere, fervent, yet melancholy countenance,[40] was one of those which bear impressed upon their brow the promise of a short destiny.

The attempted loan failed, was again proposed, and at length carried. It had been difficult to get it voted, and it was more difficult to get it completed. To whom were the public going to lend? To the *ancien régime* or the Revolution? Nobody yet knew. A thing more sure, and clear to every mind, was the uselessness of the clergy, their perfect unworthiness, and the incontestable right that the nation had to the ecclesiastical estates. Everybody was acquainted with the morals of the prelates and the ignorance of the inferior clergy. The *curés* possessed some virtues, a few instincts of resistance, but no information; wherever they ruled they were an obstacle to every improvement of the people, and caused them to retrograde. To quote but one example, Poitou, civilised in the sixteenth century, became barbarous under their influence; they were preparing for us the civil war of Vendée.

The nobility saw this as plainly as the people; in their resolutions they demand a more useful employment of such and such church estates. The kings also had plainly seen it; several times they had made partial reforms, the reform of the

---

[40] See a description of him in the *Mémoires* of Madame Roland, t. ii.

Templars, that of the Lazarists, and that of the Jesuits. There remained something better to be done.

It was a member of the nobility, the Marquis de Lacoste, who, on the 8th of August, was the first to propose in precise formula: 1st. The ecclesiastical estates belong to the nation. 2ndly. Tithes are suppressed (no mention of redeeming them). 3rdly. The titularies are pensioned. 4thly. The salaries of the bishops and curates shall be determined by the provincial Assemblies.

Another noble, Alexandre de Lameth, supported the proposition by lengthened reflections on the matter and the right of foundations, a right so well examined already by Turgot as early as 1750, in the *Encyclopédie*. "Society," said Lameth, "may always suppress every noxious institution." He concluded by giving the ecclesiastical estates in pledge to the creditors of the State.

All this was attacked by Grégoire and Lanjuinais. The Jansenists, though persecuted by the clergy, did none the less defend them.

This is most remarkable, as it shows that privilege is very tenacious, even more so than the tunic of Nessus, and could not be torn off without tearing away the flesh! The greatest minds in the Assembly, Sieyès and Mirabeau, absent on the night of the 4th of August, deplored its results. Sieyès was a priest, and Mirabeau a noble. Mirabeau would have wished to defend the nobility and the king, unhesitatingly sacrificing the clergy. Sieyès defended the clergy sacrificed by the nobility.[41]

He said that tithes were a real property. How so? By their having been at first a voluntary gift, a valid donation. To which they were able to reply in the terms of law, that a donation is revocable *for cause of ingratitude,* for the forgetting or neglecting the end for which it was given; that end was the instruction of the people, so long abandoned by the clergy.

Sieyès urged adroitly that, in every case, tithes could not

---

[41] He attempts to justify this, in his *Notice* on his life, but does not succeed.

benefit the present possessors, who had purchased with the knowledge, prevision, and deduction of the tithes. This would be, said he, to make them a present of an income of seventy millions (of francs). The tithes were worth more than a hundred and thirty. To give them to the proprietors, was an eminently political measure, engaging for ever the cultivator, the firmest element of the people, in the cause of the Revolution.

That onerous, odious impost, variable according to the provinces, which often amounted to one-third of the harvest! which caused war between the priest and the peasant, which obliged the former, in harvest-time, to make a contemptible investigation, was nevertheless defended by the clergy, for three whole days, with obstinate violence. "What!" exclaimed a *curé*, "when you invited us to come and join you, *in the name of the God of peace!* was it to cut our throats!" So tithes were then their very life,—what they held most precious. On the third day, seeing everybody against them, they made the sacrifice. Some fifteen or twenty *curés* renounced, throwing themselves on the generosity of the nation. The great prelates, the Archbishop of Paris, and Cardinal De Larochefoucauld, followed that example, and renounced, in the name of the clergy. Tithes were abolished without redemption *for the future,* but maintained for the present, till provision had been made for the support of the pastors (August 11th).

The resistance of the clergy could not be availing. They had almost the whole Assembly against them. Mirabeau spoke three times; he was more than usually bold, haughty, and often ironical, yet using respectful language. He knew well the assent he must meet with both in the Assembly and among the people. The great theses of the eighteenth century were reproduced, as things consented to, admitted beforehand, and incontestable. Voltaire returned there, a terrible, rapid conqueror. Religious liberty was consecrated, in the Declaration of Rights, and not *tolerance,* a ridiculous term, which supposes a right to tyranny. That of *predominant* religion, *predominant* worship, which the clergy demanded, was treated as it deserved. The great orator, in this the organ both of the century and of France, put this word under the ban of every legislation. "If you write it," said he, "have also a *predominant* philosophy, and *predominant* systems. Nothing ought to be predominant but right and justice."

Those who know by history, by the study of the middle ages, the prodigious tenacity of the clergy in defending their least interest, may easily judge what efforts they would now make to save their possessions, and their most precious possession, their cherished intolerance.

One thing gave them courage; which is, that the provincial nobility, the *Parlement* people, all the *ancien régime,* had sided with them in their common resistance to the resolutions of the 4th of August. More than one who, on that night, proposed or supported them, was beginning to repent.

That such resolutions should have been taken by their representatives,—by nobles, was more than the privileged classes could comprehend. They remained confounded, beside themselves with astonishment. The peasants who had commenced by violence, now continued by the authority of the law. It was the law that was levelling, throwing down the barriers, breaking the seigneurial boundary, defacing escutcheons, and opening the chase throughout France to people in arms. All armed, all sportsmen, and all nobles! And this very law which seemed to ennoble the people and *disennoble* the nobility, had been voted by the nobles themselves!

If privilege was perishing, the privileged classes, the nobles and priests, preferred to perish also; they had for a long time become identified and incorporated within equality and intolerance. Rather die a hundred times than cease to be unjust! They could accept nothing of the Revolution, neither its principle, written in its Declaration of Rights, nor the application of that principle in its great social charter of the 4th of August. However irresolute the king might be, his religious scruples caused him to be on their side, and guaranteed his obstinacy. He would, perhaps, have consented to a diminution of the regal power; but tithes—that sacred property—and then the jurisdiction of the clergy, *their right of ascertaining secret transgressions,* disavowed by the Assembly, and the liberty of religious opinions proclaimed, that timorous prince could not admit.

They might be sure that Louis XVI. would, of his own accord, and without needing any outward impulse, reject, or at least attempt to elude, the Declaration of Rights, and the decrees of the 4th of August.

But between that and his being made to act and fight, the distance was still great. He abhorred bloodshed. It might be possible to place him in such a position as to oblige him to make war; but to obtain it directly, or to get from him resolution or order, was what nobody could ever think of.

The queen had no assistance to expect from her brother Joseph, too much occupied about his Belgium. From Austria she received nothing but counsels, those of the ambassador, M. Mercy d'Argenteau. The troops were not sure. What she possessed, was a very great number of officers, of the navy and others, and Swiss and German regiments. For her principal forces, she had an excellent select army of from twenty-five to thirty thousand troops in Metz and its environs, under M. de Bouillé, a devoted, resolute officer, who had given proofs of great vigour. He had kept those troops in severe discipline, inculcating in them aversion and contempt for citizens and the mob.

The queen's opinion had ever been to depart, to throw themselves into M. de Bouillé's camp, and begin a civil war.

Being unable to prevail upon the king, what remained but to wait, to wear out Necker, to compromise him; to wear out Bailly and Lafayette, to allow disorder and anarchy to continue; to see whether the people, whom they supposed to act by the instigation of others, would not grow tired of their leaders who left them to die of hunger. The excess of their miseries must at length calm, wear out, and dispirit them. They expected from day to day, to see them ask for the restoration of the *ancien régime,* the good old time, and entreat the king to resume his absolute authority.

"You had bread, when under the king: now that you have twelve hundred kings, go and ask them for some!" These words, attributed to a minister of those days,[42] were, whether uttered or not, the opinion of the court.

This policy was but too well aided by the sad state of Paris. It is a terrible but certain fact, that, in that city of eight hundred thousand souls, there was no public authority for the space of three months, from July to October.

No municipal power:—That primitive, elementary authority of societies was as it were dissolved. The sixty districts discussed but did nothing. Their representatives at the Hôtel-de-Ville were just as inactive. Only, they impeded the mayor, prevented Bailly from acting. The latter, a studious man, recently an astronomer and academician, quite unprepared for his new role, always remained closeted in the *bureau des subsistances*, uneasy, and never knowing whether he could provision Paris.

No police:—It was in the powerless hands of Bailly. The lieutenant of police had given in his resignation, and was not replaced.

No justice:—The old criminal justice was suddenly found to be so contrary to ideas and manners, and appeared so barbarous, that M. de Lafayette demanded its immediate reform. The judges were obliged to change their old customs suddenly, learn new forms, and follow a more humane but also a more dilatory mode of procedure. The prisons became full, and crowded to excess; what was henceforth the most to be feared, was to be left there and forgotten.

No more corporation authorities:—The deans, syndics, &c., and the regulations of trades, were paralysed and annulled by the simple effect of the 4th of August. The most jealous of the trades, those the access to which had till then been difficult; the butchers, whose shops were a sort of fief; the printers, and the peruke-makers, multiplied exceedingly. Printing, it is true,

---

[42] See the partial but curious article *Saint-Priest*, in the *Biographie Michaud*, evidently written from information given by his family.

was increasing to an immense extent. The peruke-makers, on the contrary, beheld at the same time their number increasing, and their customers disappearing. All the rich were leaving Paris. A journal affirms that in three months sixty thousand passports were signed at the Hôtel-de-Ville.[43]

Vast crowds of peruke-makers, tailors, and shoemakers, assembled at the Louvre and in the Champs Élysées. The National Guard would go and disperse them, sometimes roughly and unceremoniously. They addressed complaints and demands to the town impossible to be granted,—to maintain the old regulations, or else make new ones, to fix the price of daily wages, &c. The servants, left out of place by the departure of their masters, wanted to have all the Savoyards sent back to their country.

What will always astonish those who are acquainted with the history of other revolutions is, that in this miserable and famished state of Paris, denuded of all authority, there were on the whole but very few serious acts of violence. One word, one reasonable observation, occasionally a jest, was sufficient to check them. On the first days only, subsequent to the 14th of July, there were instances of violence committed. The people, full of the idea that they were betrayed, sought for their enemies haphazard, and were near making some cruel mistakes. M. de Lafayette interposed several times at the critical moment, and was listened to: he saved several persons.[44]

When I think of the times that followed, of our own time, so listless and self-seeking, I cannot help wondering that extreme misery did not in the least dispirit this people, nor drew from

---

[43] *Révolutions de Paris*, t. ii., No. 9, p. 8.

[44] On those occasions, M. de Lafayette was truly admirable. He found in his heart, in his love for order and justice, words and happy sayings above his nature, which was, we must say, rather ordinary. Just as he was endeavouring to save Abbé Cordier, whom the people mistook for another, a friend was conducting Lafayette's young son to the Hôtel-de-Ville. He seized the opportunity, and turning towards the crowd: "Gentlemen," said he, "I have the honour to present you my son." The crowd, lost in surprise and emotion, stopped short. Lafayette's friends led the abbé into the Hôtel and he was saved. See his *Mémoires*, ii., p. 264.

them one regret for their ancient slavery. They could suffer and fast. The great deeds achieved in so short a time, the oath at the Jeu-de-Paume, the taking of the Bastille, the night of the 4th of August, had exalted their courage, and inspired everybody with a new idea of human dignity. Necker, who had departed on the 11th of July, and returned three weeks after, no longer recognised the same people. Dussaulx, who had passed sixty years under the *ancien régime,* can find old France nowhere. Everything is changed, says he, deportment, costume, the appearance of the streets, and the signs. The convents are full of soldiers; and stalls are turned into guard-houses. Everywhere are young men performing military exercises; the children try to imitate them, and follow them, stepping to time. Men of fourscore are mounting guard with their great-grandchildren: "Who would have believed," say they to me, "that we should be so happy as to die free men?"

A thing little noticed is, that in spite of certain acts of violence of the people, their sensibility had increased; they no longer beheld with *sang froid* those atrocious punishments which under the old government had been a spectacle for them. At Versailles, a man was going to be broken on the wheel as a parricide; he had raised a knife against a woman, and his father throwing himself between them, had been killed by the blow. The people thought the punishment still more barbarous than the act, prevented the execution, and overthrew the scaffold.

The heart of man had expanded by the youthful warmth of our Revolution. It beat quicker, was more impassioned than ever, more violent, and more generous. Every meeting of the Assembly presented the touching, interesting spectacle of patriotic donations which people brought in crowds. The National Assembly was obliged to become banker and receiver; there they came for everything, and sent everything, petitions, donations, and complaints. Its narrow enclosure was, as it were, the mansion of France. The poor especially would give. Now, it was a young man who sent his savings, six hundred francs, painfully amassed. Then, again, poor artisans' wives, who

brought whatever they had,—their jewels and ornaments that
they had received at their marriage. A peasant came to declare
that he gave a certain quantity of grain. A schoolboy offered
a purse collected and sent to him by his parents, his New-
year's gift perhaps, his little reward. Donations of children and
women, generosity of the poor, the widow's mite, so small, and
yet so great before their native land!—before God!

Amid the commotion of ambition and dissension, and the
moral sufferings under which it laboured, the Assembly was
affected and transported beyond itself by this magnanimity of
the people. When M. Necker came to expose the misery and
destitution of France, and to solicit, in order to live at least
two months longer, a loan of thirty millions, several deputies
proposed that he should be guaranteed by their estates,—by
those of the members of the Assembly. M. de Foucault, like a
true nobleman, made the first proposition, and offered to pledge
six hundred thousand francs, which constituted his whole fortune.

A sacrifice far greater than any sacrifice of money, is that
which all, both rich and poor, made for the public welfare,—
that of their time, their constant thoughts, and all their activity.
The municipalities then forming, the departmental administra-
tions which were soon organized, absorbed the citizen entirely,
and without exception. Several of them had their beds carried
into the offices, and worked day and night.[45]

To the fatigue add also the danger. The suffering crowds
were ever distrustful; they blamed and threatened. The
treachery of the old administration caused the new one to be
treated with suspicion. It was at the peril of their lives that
those new magistrates worked for the salvation of France.

But the poor! Who can tell the sacrifices of the poor? At
night, the poor man mounted guard; in the morning, at four
or five o'clock, he took his turn (*à la queue*) at the baker's
door; and late, very late, he got his bread. The day was partly

---

[45] As did the administrators of Finistère. See, for what relates to this
truly admirable activity, Duchatellier's *Révolution en Bretagne, passim.*

lost, and the workshop shut. Why do I say workshop? They were almost all closed. Why do I say the baker? Bread was wanting, and still more often the money to buy bread. Sorrowful and fasting, the unfortunate being wandered about, crawled along the streets, preferring to be abroad to hearing at home the complaints and sobs of his children. Thus the man who had but his time and his hands wherewith to gain his living and feed his family, devoted them in preference to the grand business of public welfare. It caused him to forget his own.

O noble, generous nation! Why must we be so imperfectly acquainted with that heroic period? The terrible, violent, heart-rending deeds which followed, have caused a world of sacrifices which characterised the outset of the Revolution to be forgotten. A phenomenon more grand than any political event then appeared in the world; the power of man, by which man is God—the power of sacrifice had augmented.

VI

The Veto

THE situation was growing worse and worse. France, between two systems, the old and the new, tossed about without advancing; and she was starving.

Paris, we must say, was living at the mercy of chance. Its subsistence, ever uncertain, depended on some arrival or other, on a convoy from Beauce or a boat from Corbeil. The city, at immense sacrifices, was lowering the price of bread; the consequence was, that the population of the whole environs, for more than ten leagues round, came to procure provisions at Paris. Thus it was a whole vast area that had to be fed. The bakers profited by selling in underhanded fashion to the peasant, and afterwards, when the Parisians found their shops empty, they laid the blame on the administration for not provisioning Paris. The uncertainty of the morrow, and vain alarms, further augmented the number of difficulties; everybody reserved, stored up, and concealed provisions. The administration, put to its last resources, sent in every direction, and bought up by fair means or by force. Occasionally, loads of flour on the road were seized and detained on their passage by the neighbouring localities whose wants were pressing. Versailles and Paris shared together; but Versailles kept, so it was said, the finest part, and made a superior bread. This was a great cause of jealousy. One day, when the people of Versailles had been so imprudent as to turn aside for themselves a supply intended for the Parisians, Bailly, the honest and respectful

Bailly, wrote to M. Necker, that if the flour was not restored, thirty thousand men would go and fetch it on the morrow. Fear made him bold. His head was in danger if provisions failed. It often happened that at midnight he had but the half of the flour necessary for the morning market.[46]

The provisioning of Paris was a kind of war. The national guard was sent to protect such an arrival, or to secure certain purchases; purchases were made by force of arms. Being incommoded in their trade, the farmers would not thrash any longer, neither would the millers grind any more. The speculators were afraid. A pamphlet by Camille Desmoulins designated and threatened the brothers Leleu, who had the monopoly of the royal mills at Corbeil. Another, who passed for the principal agent of a company of monopolists, killed himself, or was killed, in a forest near Paris. His death brought about his immense frightful bankruptcy, of more than fifty millions of francs. It is not unlikely, that the court, who had large sums lodged in his hands, suddenly drew them to pay a multitude of officers who were invited to Versailles, and perhaps to be carried off to Metz: without money they could not begin the civil war. This was already war against Paris, and the very worst perhaps, from their keeping the town in such a state of peace. No work,—and famine!

"I used to see," says Bailly, "good tradespeople, mercers and goldsmiths, who prayed to be admitted among the beggars employed at Montmartre in digging the ground. Judge what I suffered." He did not suffer enough. We see him, even in his *Mémoires,* too much taken up with petty vanities—questions of precedence, to know by what honorary forms the speech for the consecration of the flags should begin, &c.

Neither did the National Assembly suffer enough from the sufferings of the people. Otherwise it would not have prolonged the eternal debate of its political *scolastique.* It would have understood that it ought to hasten on the movement of reforms, remove every obstacle, and abridge that mortal transi-

---

[46] *Mémoires de Bailly, passim.*

tion where France remained between the old order and the new. Everybody saw the question, yet the Assembly saw it not. Though endowed with generally good intentions and vast information, it seemed to have but little perception of the real state of things. Impeded in its progress by the opposition of its royalist and aristocratic members, it was still more so by those habits of the bar or of the Academy, which its most illustrious members, men of letters or advocates, still preserved.

It was necessary to insist and obtain at once, at any price, without wasting time in talking, the sanction of the decrees of the 4th of August, and to bury the feudal world; it was necessary to deduce from those general decrees political laws, and those administrative laws which should determine the application of the former; that is to say, to organise, to arm the Revolution, to give it form and power, and make it a living being. As such it became less dangerous than by being left floating, overflowing, vague, and terrible, like an element,—like a flood, or a conflagration.

It was especially necessary to use dispatch. It was a thunderbolt for Paris to learn that the Assembly was occupied only with the inquiry whether it would recognise in the King the *absolute right of preventing* (absolute veto), or *the right of adjourning,* of suspending for two years, four years, or six years. For such pressing, mortal evils, this prospect was despair itself, a condemnation without appeal. Four years, six years, good God! for people who knew not whether they should live till the morrow.

Far from progressing, the Assembly was evidently receding. It made two retrograde and sadly significant choices. It named as president La Luzerne, the bishop of Langres, a partisan of the *veto,* and next Mounier, once more a partisan of the *veto.*

The warmth with which the people espoused this question has been treated with derision. Several, so it was stated, believed that the *veto* was a person, or a tax.[47] There is nothing laughable in this but the sneerers themselves. Yes, the *veto* was

___

[47] See Ferrières, Molleville, Beaulieu, &c.

equal to a tax, if it prevented reforms and a diminution of the taxes. Yes, the *veto* was eminently personal; a man had but to say, *I forbid,* without any reason; it was quite enough.

M. de Sèze thought to plead skilfully for this cause, by saying that the question was not about a person, but a *permanent will,* more steady than any Assembly.

Permanent? According to the influence of courtiers, confessors, mistresses, passions, and interests. Supposing it permanent, that will may be very personal and very oppressive, if, whilst everything is changing about it, it neither change nor improve. How will it be if one same policy, one self-same interest, pass on with generation and tradition throughout a whole dynasty?

The *cahiers,* written under very different circumstances, granted to the King the sanction and the refusal of sanction. France had trusted to the royal power against the privileged classes. But now that that power was the auxiliary of privilege, were the *cahiers* still to be followed? As well restore the Bastille.

The sheet-anchor left with the privileged classes was the royal *veto.* They hugged and embraced the King in their shipwreck, wishing him to share their fate, and be saved or drowned with them.

The Assembly discussed the question as if it had been a mere struggle of systems. Paris perceived in it less a question than a crisis, the grand crisis and the total cause of the Revolution, which it was necessary to save or destroy: *To be or not to be,* nothing less.

And Paris alone was right. The revelations of history, and the confessions of the court party, authorise us now in this decision. The 14th of July had wrought no change; the true minister was Breteuil, the Queen's confidant. Necker was there only for show. The Queen was ever looking forward to flight and civil war; her heart was at Metz, in Bouillé's camp. Bouillé's sword was the only *veto* that pleased her.

The Assembly might have been supposed not to have perceived there was a Revolution. Most of the speeches would have served just as well for another century or any other people. One alone will live, that of M. Sieyès, who rejected the veto. He stated perfectly well that the real remedy for the reciprocal encroachments of the powers, was not thus to constitute the executive power an arbiter and a judge, but to make an appeal to the constituent power which is in the people. An Assembly may be mistaken; but how many more chances has not the irrevocable depositary of an hereditary power of being mistaken, wittingly or unwittingly, of following some dynastic or family interest?

He defined the *veto* as a simple *lettre-de-cachet* flung by an individual against the general will.

One sensible thing was said by another deputy, which is, that if the Assembly were divided into two Chambers, each having a *veto*, there would be little fear of an abuse of the legislative power; consequently, it was not necessary to oppose to it a new barrier, by giving the *veto* to the King.

There were five hundred votes for a single Chamber; and the dividing into two Chambers could obtain only one hundred. The multitude of nobles who had no chance of entering the upper Chamber, took good care not to create for the grand lords a peerage in the English fashion.

The arguments of the Anglomaniacs, which were then presented with ability by Lally, Mounier, &c., and subsequently obstinately reproduced by Madame de Staël, Benjamin Constant, and so many others, had been annihilated beforehand by Sieyès, in a chapter of his book on the *Third Estate*. This is truly admirable. That accomplished logician, by the sole power of his mind, not having seen England, and but little acquainted with her history, had already found those results which we obtain from a minute study of her past and present history! [48] He

---

[48] Her past, in my "History of France," wherein I meet with her every moment; her present, in the fine work of Léon Faucher. That book has given the English school a blow from which it will never recover. (See especially towards the end of the second volume). The English themselves (Bentham, Bulwer, Senior, &c.) agree to-day that their famous balance of the three powers is only a theme for schoolboys.

saw perfectly well that that famous balance of the three powers, which, if real, would prevent any progress whatsoever, is a pure comedy, a mystification, for the profit of one of the powers (aristocratic in England, monarchical in France). England has ever been, is, and will be an aristocracy. The art of that aristocracy, what has perpetuated its power, is not its giving a share to the people, but in finding an exterior field for their activity, to provide outlets for them;[49] it is thus it has spread England all over the globe.

As for the *veto*, Necker's opinion which he addressed to the Assembly, (and which, in any case, it had independently arrived at), was to grant the *veto* to the King,—the suspensive *veto;* the right of adjourning as far as the second legislature which should follow the one proposing the law.

That Assembly was ripe for dissolution. Created before the great Revolution which had just taken place, it was profoundly heterogeneous and confused, like the chaos of the *ancien régime,* whence it sprang. In spite of the name of National Assembly, with which it had been baptized by Sieyès, it remained feudal, and was nothing else but the old Estates-General. Ages had passed over it, from the 5th of May to the 31st of August. Elected in the antique form, and according to barbarous law, it represented some two or three hundred thousand nobles or priests just as much as the nation. By uniting them to itself, the Third Estate had grown weak and feeble. At every instant, even without being aware of it, it was compromising with them. It adopted scarcely any measures but such as were prejudicial, illegitimate, powerless, and dangerous. The privileged classes, who were manoeuvring outside

---

[49] England would have died, had she not found, from century to century, an exterior diversion for her interior evil (aristocratic injustice): in the sixteenth and seventeenth, North America and the spoliation of Spain; in the eighteenth, the spoliation of France and the conquest of India; in the nineteenth, a new colonial extension, and an immense manufacturing development.

with the court to undo the Revolution, obstructed it still more certainly in the very bosom of the Assembly.

That Assembly, full as it was of talent and science, was nevertheless monstrous, through the irremediable discordance of its elements. What fecundity, what act of procreation can be expected from a monster?

Such was the language of common sense and reason. The moderate who ought, one would think, to have been more keen-sighted and less dazzled, saw nothing of this. Strange enough, passion took a better view; it perceived that everything was danger and obstacle in this twofold situation, and strove to get clear of it. But as passion and violence it inspired infinite distrust, and met with immense difficulties; it became still more violent in order to surmount them, and that very energy created new obstacles.

The monster of the time, I mean the discord of the two principles, their impotency for creating anything vital, must, to be well perceived, be seen in one man. That unity of person, that lofty combination of faculties which is called genius, is of no use, if, in that man—that genius—ideas are warring together, if principles and doctrines carry on a furious struggle in his bosom.

I know not a more melancholy spectacle for human nature than that now presented by Mirabeau. At Versailles he speaks for the absolute *veto*, but in such obscure terms that nobody distinctly understands whether he be for or against it. At Paris his friends maintain, on the same day, at the Palais Royal, that he has opposed the *veto*. He inspired so much personal attachment in the young men about him, that they did not hesitate to lie boldly in order to save him. "I loved him like a mistress," said Camille Desmoulins. It is well known that one of Mirabeau's secretaries tried to commit suicide at his death.

Those liars, exaggerating, as it often happens, falsehood to obtain the more credit, affirmed that on leaving the Assembly he had been waited for, followed, and wounded, having been stabbed with a sword! All the Palais Royal exclaimed that a guard of two hundred men must be voted to guard poor Mirabeau!

In that strange speech [50] he had maintained the old sophism, that the royal sanction was a guarantee of liberty; that the King was a sort of tribune of the people; their representative—an irrevocable, irresponsible representative—one who is never to be called to account!

He was sincerely a royalist, and, as such, made no scruple to receive later a pension to keep open house for the deputies. He used to say to himself that after all he did but defend his own opinion. One thing, we must confess, corrupted him more than money, a thing which was the least to be suspected in that man so proud in his deportment and his language. What was it? Fear!

Fear of the rising, growing Revolution. He beheld that young giant then prevailing over him, and which subsequently carried him off like another man. And then he cast himself back upon what was called the old order—true anarchy and a real chaos. From that fruitless struggle he was saved by death.

---

[50] He had received it from a dreamer named Cazeaux. He had not even read it. On reading it at the tribune, he found it so bad that he was bathed in a cold perspiration, and skipped half of it.—Etienne Dumont's *Souvenirs*, p. 155.

VII

The Press

WE have just seen two things: the situation of affairs was intolerable, and the Assembly incapable of remedying it.

Would a popular movement settle the difficulty? That could take place only on condition that it was truly a spontaneous, vast, unanimous movement of the people, like that of the 14th of July.

The fermentation was great, the agitation lively, but as yet partial. From the very first day that the question of the *veto* was put (Sunday, August 30), all Paris took alarm, for the absolute *veto* appeared as the annihilation of the sovereignty of the people. However, the Palais Royal alone stood forward. There it was decided that they should go to Versailles, to warn the Assembly that they perceived in its bosom a league for the *veto,* that they knew the members, and that, unless they renounced, Paris would march against them. A few hundred men accordingly set forth at ten in the evening; a pertinacious violent man, the Marquis de Saint-Hururge, a favourite with the crowd on account of his herculean strength and stentorian voice, had placed himself at their head. Having been imprisoned under the old government on the demand of his wife (a pretty coquette who possessed some credit), Saint-Hururge, as may be conceived, was already a furious enemy of the *ancien régime,* and an ardent champion of the Revolution. On reaching the Champs-Elysées, his band, already greatly diminished, met with some national guards sent by Lafayette, who prevented their further progress.

The Palais Royal dispatched, one after the other, three or four deputations to the city authorities, to obtain leave to pass. They wanted to make the riot legal, and with the consent of the authority. It is superfluous to say that the latter did not consent.

Meanwhile another attempt, far more serious, was preparing in the Palais Royal. This attempt, whether successful or not, would at least have one general result; to start discussion of the great question of the day by the people as a whole. There was, then, no longer any possibility of its being suddenly decided, or carried by surprise, at Versailles; Paris was observing and watching the Assembly, both by the press and by its own assembly—the great Parisian assembly, united, though divided into its sixty districts.

The author of the proposition was a young journalist. Before relating it, we ought to give an idea of the movement operating among the Press.

This sudden awaking of a people, called all at once to a knowledge of their rights and to decide on their destiny, had absorbed all the activity of the time in journalism. The most speculative minds had been hurried to the field of the practical. Every science, every branch of literature, stood still; political life was everything.

Every great day in 1789 was accompanied with an eruption of newspapers:—

1st. In May and June, at the opening of the Estates-General, a multitude of them spring forth. Mirabeau patronised the *Courrier de Provence;* Gorsas, the *Courrier de Versailles;* Brissot, the *Patriote Français;* Barère, the *Point du Jour,* &c. &c.

2ndly. On the night before the 14th of July, appeared the most popular of all the newspapers, *Les Révolutions de Paris,* edited by Loustalot.

3rdly. On the eve of the 5th and 6th of October appeared the *Ami du Peuple* (Marat) and the *Annales Patriotiques* (Carra and Mercier). Soon after, the *Courrier de Brabant,* by

Camille Desmoulins, certainly the most witty of all; next, one of the most violent, the *Orateur du Peuple,* by Fréron.

The general character of that great movement, and which renders it the more admirable, is, that, in spite of shades of opinion, there is almost unanimity. Except one conspicuous newspaper, the Press presents the appearance of one vast council, in which everybody speaks in his turn, and all being engaged in a common aim, avoid every kind of hostility.

The Press, at that early age, struggling against the central power, has generally a tendency to strengthen the local powers, and to exaggerate the rights of the *commune* against the State. If the language of after-times might be here employed, we should say, that at that period they all seem *fédéralistes.* Mirabeau is as much so as Brissot or Lafayette. This goes so far as to admit the independence of the provinces, if liberty become impossible for all France. Mirabeau would be contented to be Count of Provence; he says so in plain terms.

Notwithstanding all this, the Press, struggling against the King, is generally royalist. "At that time," says Camille Desmoulins at a later period, "there were not ten of us republicans in France." We must not allow ourselves to mistake the meaning of certain bold expressions. In '88, the violent d'Eprémesnil had said: "We must *unbourbonise* France." But it was only to make the *Parlement* king.

Mirabeau, who was destined to complete the sum of contradictions, caused Milton's violent little book against kings to be translated and printed in his name in 1789 at the very moment when he was undertaking the defence of royalty. It was suppressed by his friends.

Two men were preaching the Republic: one of the most prolific writers of the period, the indefatigable Brissot, and the brilliant, eloquent, and bold Desmoulins. His book *La France libre* contains a violently satirical brief history of the monarchy. Therein he shows that principle of order and stability to have been, in practice, a perpetual disorder. Hereditary royalty, in order to redeem itself from so many inconveniences which are evidently inherent, has one general reply to everything: peace, the maintenance of peace; which does not prevent it from having, by minorities and quarrels of succession, kept France in an almost perpetual state of war:—wars with the English, wars with Italy, wars about the succession in Spain, &c.[51]

Robespierre said that the Republic crept in between the parties, without anybody having suspected it. It is more exact to say that royalty itself introduced the Republic, and urged it upon the minds of men. If men refuse to govern themselves, it is because royalty offers itself as a simplification which facilitates things, removes impediments, and dispenses with virtue and efforts. But what if royalty itself is the obstacle? It may be boldly affirmed that royalty showed the way to the Republic, bore along a France that was far removed from it, distrusted it or ignored it.

To return, the first of the journalists of that day was neither Mirabeau, Camille Desmoulins, Brissot, Condorcet, Mercier, Carra, Gorsas, Marat, nor Barère. They all published newspapers, and some to a great extent. Mirabeau used to print ten thousand copies of his famous *Courrier de Provence*. But of the *Révolutions de Paris* there were (of some numbers) as many as *two hundred thousand* copies printed. This was the greatest publicity ever obtained. The editor's name did not appear. The printer signed:—Prudhomme. That name has become one of the best known in the world. The unknown editor was Loustalot.

Loustalot, who died in 1792 at the age of twenty-nine, was a serious, honest, laborious young man. A writer of mediocrity, but grave, of an impassioned seriousness; his real originality was his contrast with the frivolity of the journalists of the time. In his very violence we perceive an effort to be just. He was the writer preferred by the people. Nor was he unworthy of the

---

[51] Sismondi has shown, by an exact calculation on a period of 500 years, how much longer and more frequent wars have been in hereditary than in elective monarchies: this is the natural effect of minorities, quarrels of succession, &c. Sismondi, *Etudes sur les Constitutions des Peuples libres*, i., 214–221.

preference. He gave, in the outbreak of the Revolution, more than one proof of courageous moderation. When the French guards were delivered by the people, he said there was but one solution for the affair; that the prisoners should betake themselves to prison again, and that the electors and the National Assembly should petition the king to pardon them. When a mistake of the crowd had placed good Lasalle, the brave commandant of the city, in peril, Loustalot undertook his defence, justified him, and restored him to favour. In the affair of the servants who wanted the Savoyards to be driven away, he showed himself firm and severe as well as judicious. A true journalist, he was the man of the day, and not of the morrow. When Camille Desmoulins published his book, *La France libre*, wherein he suppresses the king, Loustalot, whilst praising him, finds him extravagant, and calls him a man of feverish imagination. Marat, then little known, had violently attacked Bailly in the *Ami du Peuple*, both as a public character and as a man. Loustalot defended him. He considered journalism as a public function, a sort of magistracy. No tendency to abstractions. He lives wholly and entirely in the crowd, and feels their wants and sufferings; he applies himself especially to the problem of provisions, and to the great question of the moment: bread. He proposes machines for grinding wheat more expeditiously. He visits the unfortunate beings employed at work at Montmartre. And those miserable objects, whose extreme wretchedness had almost divested them of the human form,—that deplorable army of phantoms or skeletons, who inspire rather fear than pity,—wound Loustalot to the heart, and he addresses them in words of affection and tenderest compassion.

Paris could not remain in that position. It was necessary either to restore absolute royalty or found liberty.

On Monday morning, August 31st, Loustalot, finding the minds of the multitude more calm than on the Sunday evening, harangued in the Palais Royal. He said the remedy was not to go to Versailles, and made a less violent yet a bolder proposition. It was to go to the city authorities, obtain the convocation of the districts, and in those assemblies to put these questions:—1st. Does Paris believe that the king has the right to block action? 2ndly. Does Paris confirm or revoke its deputies? 3dly. If deputies be named, will they have a special mandate to refuse the *veto?* 4thly. If the former deputies be confirmed, cannot the Assembly be induced to adjourn the discussion?

The measure proposed, though eminently revolutionary and illegal (unconstitutional if there had been a constitution), nevertheless was so perfectly adapted to the necessities of the day, that it was, a few days later, reproduced, at least the principal part of it, in the Assembly itself, by one of its most eminent members.

Loustalot and the deputation of the Palais Royal were very badly received, their proposition rejected at the Hôtel-de-Ville, and the next morning accused in the Assembly. A threatening letter, received by the president and signed Saint-Hururge (who, however, maintained it was a forgery), completed the general irritation. They caused Saint-Hururge to be arrested, and the National Guard took advantage of a momentary tumult to shut up the Café de Foy. Meetings in the Palais Royal were forbidden and dispersed by the municipal authority.

The piquant part of the affair is that the executor of these measures, M. de Lafayette, was, at that time and always, a republican at heart. Throughout his life he dreamed of the republic and served royalty. A democratic royalty, or a royal democracy, appeared to him a necessary transition. To undeceive him it required no less than two experiments.

The court trifled with Necker and the Assembly. It did not deceive Lafayette; and yet he served it, and kept Paris in check. The horror of the former acts of violence of the people, and the bloodshed, made him recoil before the idea of another 14th of July. But would the civil war which the court was preparing have cost less blood? A serious and delicate question for the friend of humanity.

He was acquainted with everything. On the 13th of September, whilst receiving old Admiral d'Estaing, the commander of the National Guards of Versailles, to dinner at his house, he told him news of Versailles of which he was ignorant. That honest man, who thought he was very deep in the confidence of the king and the queen, now learned that they had returned to the fatal project of taking the king to Metz, that is to say, of beginning a civil war; that Breteuil was preparing everything in concert with the ambassador of Austria; that they were bringing towards Versailles the musketeers, the *gendarmes,* nine thousand of the king's household, two thirds of whom were noblemen; that they were to seize on Montargis, where they would be joined by the Baron de Vioménil, a man of action. The latter, who had served in almost all the wars of the century, recently in that of America, had cast himself violently into the counter-revolution party, perhaps out of jealousy for Lafayette, who seemed to be playing the first part in the Revolution. Eighteen regiments, and especially the *Carabiniers,* had not taken the oath. That was enough to block up all the roads to Paris, cut off its supplies, and famish it. They were no longer in want of money; they had collected it, raked it in from all sides; they made sure of having fifteen hundred thousand francs a month. The clergy would supply the remainder; a steward of the Benedictins was bound, for himself alone, in the sum of one hundred thousand crowns.

The old Admiral wrote to the queen on the Monday (14th): "I have always slept well the night before a naval battle, but since this terrible revelation, I have not been able to close my eyes." On hearing it at M. de Lafayette's table, he shuddered lest any one of the servants should hear it: "I remarked to him that one word from his mouth might become a death warrant." To which Lafayette, with his American coolness, replied: "That it would be advantageous for *one* to die for the salvation of all." The only head in peril would have been the queen's.

The Spanish ambassador said as much to d'Estaing; he knew it all from an eminent man who had been asked to sign a membership list circulated by the court.

Thus, this profound secret, this mystery, was spread through the salons on the 13th, and about the streets from the 14th to the 16th. On the 16th, the grenadiers of the French Guards, now become a paid national guard, declared they would go to

Versailles to resume their old duties, to guard the Château and the king. On the 22nd, the great plot was printed in the *Révolutions de Paris,* and read by all France.

M. de Lafayette, who believed himself *strong, too strong,* according to his own expressions, wished on one hand to check the Court by making them afraid of Paris, and on the other hand, to check Paris, and repress agitation by his National Guards. He used and abused their zeal, in quieting the rabble, imposing silence on the Palais Royal, and preventing mobs; he carried on a petty police warfare of annoyance against a crowd excited by the fears which he himself shared; he knew of the plot, and yet he dispersed and arrested those who spoke of it. He managed so well that he created the most fatal animosity between the National Guards and the people. The latter began to remark that the chiefs, the commanders, were nobles, rich men, people of consequence. The National Guards in general, reduced in number, proud of their uniform and their arms, new to them, appeared to the people a sort of aristocracy. Being citizens and merchants, they were great sufferers by the riots, receiving nothing from their country estates, and gaining nothing; they were every day called out, fatigued, and jaded; every day, they wanted to bring matters to an end, and they testified their impatience by some act of brutality which set the crowd against them. Once, they drew their swords against a mob of peruke-makers, and there was bloodshed; on another occasion, they arrested some persons who had indulged in jokes about the National Guard. A girl, having said she cared not a rap for them, was taken and whipped.

The people were exasperated to such a degree, that they brought against the National Guard the strangest accusation— that of favouring the Court, and being in the plot of Versailles.

Lafayette was no hypocrite, but his position was equivocal. He prevented the grenadiers from going to Versailles to resume their duties as the king's guards, and gave warning to the minister, Saint-Priest (September 17th). His letter was turned to advantage. They showed it to the municipality of Versailles, making them take an oath of secrecy, and inducing them to ask that the regiment of Flanders should be sent for. They solicited the same step from a part of the National Guards of Versailles, but the majority refused.

That regiment, strongly suspected, because it had hitherto refused to take the new oath, arrived with its cannon, ammunition, and baggage, and entered Versailles with much noise. At the same time, the Château detained the body guards, who had concluded their service, in order to have double the number. A crowd of officers of every grade were daily arriving *en poste,* as the old nobility used to do on the eve of a battle, fearing to arrive too late.

Paris was uneasy. The French Guards were indignant; they had been tried and tampered with without any other result than to put them on their guard. Bailly could not help speaking at the Hôtel-de-Ville. A deputation was sent, headed by the good old Dussaulx, to convey to the king the alarms of Paris.

The conduct of the Assembly in the meantime was strange. Now it seemed to be asleep, and then it would suddenly start up; one day violent, on the next moderate and timid.

One morning, the 12th of September, it remembers the 4th of August, and the great social revolution it had voted. It was five weeks since the decrees had been given; all France spoke of them with joy; but the Assembly said not one word about them. On the 12th, whilst a decree was being proposed in which the judicial committee demanded *that the laws should be put in force conformably to a decision of the 4th of August,* a deputy of Franche-Comté broke the ice and said: *"Steps are being taken to prevent the promulgation of those decrees of the 4th of August; it is said they are not to appear. It is time they should be seen, furnished with the royal seal. The people are waiting."* Those words were quickly taken up. The Assembly was roused. Malouet, the orator of the moderate party —of the constitutional royalists,—even he (singularly enough) supported the proposition, and others with them. In spite of the Abbé Maury, it was decided that the decrees of the 4th of August should be presented for the king's sanction.

This sudden movement, this aggressive disposition of even

the moderates, inclines one to suppose that the most influential members were not ignorant of what Lafayette, the Spanish ambassador, and many others, were saying at Paris.

The Assembly seemed on the morrow astonished at its vigour. Many thought that the Court would never let the king sanction the decrees of the 4th of August, and foresaw that his refusal would provoke a terrible movement—a second fit of the Revolution. Mirabeau, Chapelier, and others, maintained that these decrees, not being properly laws, but constitutional principles, had no need of the royal sanction; that the promulgation was sufficient. A bold, yet timid opinion: bold, in doing without the king; timid, in dispensing with his examining, sanctioning, or refusing: no refusal, no collision. Things would have been decided *ipso facto*, according as either party was predominant in this or that province. Here, they would have applied the decisions of the 4th of August, as decreed by the Assembly; there, they would have eluded them, as not sanctioned by the king.

On the 15th, the royal inviolability, hereditary right, was voted by acclamation, as if to dispose the king in their favour. They nevertheless received from him a dilatory, equivocal reply relative to the 4th of August. He sanctioned nothing, but discussed, blaming this, commending that, and admitting scarcely any article without some modification. The whole bore the impress of Necker's usual style, his tergiversation, blunders, and half measures. The Court, that was preparing something very different, apparently expected to captivate public attention by this empty answer. The Assembly was in great agitation. Chapelier, Mirabeau, Robespierre, Pétion, and others usually less energetic, affirmed that in demanding the sanction for these preliminary articles, the Assembly expected only a pure and simple promulgation. Then, a great discussion, and an unexpected, but very sensible motion from Volney: "This Assembly is too mixed in interests and passions. Let us determine the new conditions of election, and retire." Applause, but nothing more. Mirabeau objects that the Assembly has sworn not to separate before having formed the constitution.

On the 21st, the king being pressed to promulgate, laid aside all circumlocution; the Court apparently believed itself stronger. He replied that *promulgation* applied only to laws so drafted as to require execution (he meant to say sanction); that he was going to order the *publication,* and that he did not doubt but the laws which the Assembly would decree, would be such as he could *sanction.*

On the 24th, Necker came to make his confession to the Assembly. The first loan, thirty millions, had given but *two.* The second, eighty, had given but *ten.* The *general of finance,* as Necker's friends called him in their pamphlets, had been able to do nothing; the credit which he expected to control and restore had perished in spite of him. He came to appeal to the devotion of the nation. The only remedy was for the nation to sacrifice itself: let everyone tax himself at a fourth of his income.[52]

Necker had now ended his part. After having tried every reasonable means, he trusted himself to the faith, the miracle, the vague hope that a people unable to pay less was about to pay more, and that they would tax themselves with the monstrous impost of a quarter of their revenue. The chimerical financier brought forward as the last word of his balance-sheet, as cash, a Utopia which the good Abbé of Saint-Pierre would not have proposed.

The impotent willingly believes in the impossible; being incapacitated from acting himself, he imagines that chance, or some unknown and unforeseen accident, will act for him. The Assembly, no less impotent than the minister, shared his credulity. A wonderful speech from Mirabeau overcame all their doubts, and transported them out of their senses. He showed them bankruptcy, a hideous bankruptcy opening its monstrous abyss beneath them, and ready to devour both themselves and France. They voted. If the measure had been serious, if money had come in, the effect would have been

---

[52] Necker, ever generous, for his own part exceeded the quarter; he taxed himself at one hundred thousand francs.

singular: Necker would have succeeded in raising up those who were to drive Necker out of office, the Assembly would have paid for a war designed to dissolve the Assembly. Impossibility, contradiction, a perfect stand-still in every direction, was fundamentally the state of things for every man and every party. To sum up all in one word: *nobody can act.*

The Assembly can do nothing. Discordant in elements and principles, it was naturally incapable; but it becomes still more so in presence of tumult, at the entirely novel noise of the press which drowns its voice. It would willingly cling to the royal power which it has demolished; but its ruins are hostile: they would like to crush the Assembly. Thus Paris makes them afraid, and so does the Château. After the king's refusal, they dare no longer show their anger for fear of adding to the indignation of Paris. Except the responsibility of the ministers which they decree, they do nothing at all consonant with the situation of affairs; the dividing of France into departments, and the criminal law, are discussed in empty space; the hall is thinly attended; scarcely do six hundred members assemble, and it is to give the presidency to Mounier, a personification of immobility; to him who expresses best all the difficulties of acting, and the general paralysis.

Can the Court do anything? It thinks so at that moment. It sees the nobility and clergy rallying around it. It perceives the Duke of Orleans unsupported in the Assembly; [53] it beholds him, at Paris, spending much money, and gaining but little ground; his popularity is surpassed by Lafayette.

All were ignorant of the situation, all overlooked the general force of things, and attributed events to some person or other, ridiculously exaggerating individual power. According to its hatred or its love, passion believes miracles, monsters, heroes. The Court accuse Orleans or Lafayette of everything. Lafayette himself, though naturally firm and cool-headed, becomes imagi-

---

[53] In regulating the succession, the Assembly spared its rival the King of Spain, declaring it in no way prejudged the renunciations of the Bourbons of Spain to the crown of France.

native; he is not far from believing likewise that all the disturbances are the work of the Palais Royal. A visionary arises in the press, the credulous, blind, furious Marat, who will vent accusations dictated at random by his dreams, designating one to-day, and to-morrow another to death; he begins by affirming that the whole famine is the work of one man; that Necker buys up grain on every side, in order that Paris may have none.

Marat is only beginning, however; as yet he has but little influence. He stands conspicuously apart from all the press. The press accuses, but vaguely; it complains, and is angry, like the people, without too well knowing what ought to be done. It sees plainly in general that there will be "a second fit of the Revolution." But how? For what precise object? It cannot exactly say. For the prescription of remedies, the press,—that young power, suddenly grown so great through the impotency of the others,—the press itself is powerless.

It does but little during the interval previous to the 5th of October; the Assembly does little, and the Hôtel-de-Ville little. And yet everybody plainly perceives that some great deed is about to be achieved. Mirabeau, on receiving one day his bookseller of Versailles, sends away his three secretaries, shuts the door, and says to him: "My dear Blaisot, you will see here soon some great calamity—bloodshed. From friendship, I wished to give you warning. But be not afraid; there is no danger for honest men like you."

VIII

The People Go to Fetch the King
(October 5th, 1789)

On the 5th of October, eight or ten thousand women went to Versailles, followed by crowds of people. The National Guard forced M. de Lafayette to lead them there the same evening. On the 6th, they brought back the king, and obliged him to inhabit Paris.

This great movement is the most general, after the 14th of July, that occurs in the Revolution. The one of October was unanimous, almost as much so as the other; at least in this sense, that they who took no part in it wished for its success, and all rejoiced that the king should be at Paris.

Here we must not seek the action of parties. They acted, but did very little.

The real, the certain cause, for the women and the most miserable part of the crowd, was nothing but hunger. Having dismounted a horseman at Versailles, they killed and ate his horse almost raw.

For the majority of the men, both the people and the National Guards, the cause of the movement was honour, the outrage of the Court against the Parisian cockade, adopted by all France as a symbol of the Revolution.

Whether the men, however, would have marched against Versailles, if the women had not preceded them, is doubtful. Nobody before them had the idea of going to fetch the king.

The Palais Royal, on the 30th of August, departed with Saint-Hururge, but it was to convey complaints and threats to the Assembly then discussing the *veto*. But here, the people alone are the first to propose; alone, they depart to take the king, as alone they took the Bastille. What is most *people* in the people, I mean most instinctive and inspired, is assuredly the women. Their idea was this: "Bread is wanting, let us go and fetch the king; they will take care, if he be with us, that bread be wanting no longer. Let us go and fetch *the baker!*"

A word of simple yet profound meaning! The king ought to live with the people, see their sufferings, suffer with them, and be of the same household with them. The ceremonies of marriage and those of the coronation used to coincide in several particulars; the king espoused the people. If royalty is not tyranny, there must be marriage and community, and the couple must live, according to the low but energetic motto of the middle ages, "With one loaf and one pot."

Was not the egotistical solitude in which the kings were kept, with an artificial crowd of gilded beggars in order to make them forget the people, something strange and unnatural, and calculated to harden their hearts? How can we be surprised if those kings become estranged, hard-hearted, and barbarous? How could they, without their isolated retreat at Versailles, ever have attained that degree of insensibility? The very sight of it is immoral: a world made expressly for one man! There only could a man forget the condition of humanity, and sign, like Louis XIV., the expulsion of a million men; or, like Louis XV., speculate on famine.

The unanimity of Paris had overthrown the Bastille. To conquer the king and the Assembly, it was necessary that it should find itself once more unanimous. The National Guard and the people were beginning to divide. In order to re-unite them, and make them concur for the same end, it required no less than a provocation from the Court. No political wisdom would have brought about the event; an act of folly was necessary.

That was the real remedy, the only means of getting rid of the intolerable position in which everybody seemed entangled.

This folly would have been done by the queen's party long before, if it had not met with its chief stumbling-block and difficulty in Louis XVI. Nobody could be more averse to a change of habits. To deprive him of his hunting, his workshop, and his early hour of retiring to rest; to interrupt the regularity of his meals and prayers; to put him on horseback *en campagne,* and make an active partisan of him, as we see Charles I., in the picture by Vandyck, was not easy. His own good sense likewise told him that he ran much risk in declaring himself against the National Assembly.

On the other hand, this same attachment to his habits, to the ideas of his education and childhood, made him against the Revolution even more than the diminution of the royal authority. He did not conceal his displeasure at the demolition of the Bastille.[54] The uniform of the National Guards worn by his own people; his valets now become lieutenants—officers; more than one musician of the chapel chanting mass in a captain's uniform; all that annoyed his sight: he caused his servants to be forbidden "to appear in his presence in such an inappropriate costume." [55]

It was difficult to move the king, either one way or the other. In every deliberation, he was very fluctuating, but in his old habits, and in his rooted ideas, insuperably obstinate. Even the queen, whom he dearly loved, would have gained nothing by persuasion. Fear had still less influence upon him; he knew he was the anointed of the Lord, inviolable and sacred; what could he fear?

Meanwhile, the queen was surrounded by a whirlwind of passions, intrigues, and interested zeal; prelates and lords, all that aristocracy who had spoken so ill of her, and now were trying to effect a reconciliation, crowded her apartments, fervently conjuring her to save the monarchy. She alone, if they were to be believed, possessed genius and courage; it was time that she, the daughter of Maria-Theresa, should show herself.

---

[54] Alexandre de Lameth.
[55] Campan, ii.

The queen derived courage, moreover, from two very different sorts of people; on one hand, brave and worthy chevaliers of Saint-Louis, officers or provincial noblemen, who offered her their swords; on the other, plotters and schemers, who showed plans, undertook to execute them, and warranted success. Versailles was as if besieged by these Figaros of royalty.

It was necessary to make a holy league, and for all honest people to rally round the queen. The king would then be carried away in the enthusiasm of their love, and unable to resist any longer. The revolutionary party could make but one campaign; once conquered, it would perish: on the contrary, the other party, comprising all the large proprietors, was able to suffice for several campaigns, and maintain the war for many years. For such arguments to be good, it was only necessary to suppose that the unanimity of the people would not affect the soldier, and that he would never remember that he also was the people.

The spirit of jealousy then rising between the National Guard and the people doubtless emboldened the Court, and made them believe Paris to be powerless; they risked a premature manifestation which was destined to ruin them. Fresh body guards were arriving, for their three months' service; these men, unacquainted with Paris or the Assembly, strangers to the new spirit, good provincial royalists, imbued with all their family prejudices, and paternal and maternal recommendations to serve the king, and the king alone. That body of guards, though some of its members were friends of liberty, had not taken the oath, and still wore the white cockade. Attempts were made to use them to entice away the officers of the regiment of Flanders, and those of a few other troops. In order to bring them all together, a grand dinner was given, to which were admitted a few officers selected from the National Guard of Versailles, whom they hoped to attach to their cause.

We must know that the town in France which had the greatest detestation for the Court, was the one that saw most of it, namely, Versailles. Whoever was not a servant or an *employé* belonging to the Château was a revolutionist. The constant sight of all that pomp, of those splendid equipages, and those haughty, supercilious people, engendered envy and hatred. This disposition of the inhabitants had caused them to name one Lecointre, a linendraper, a firm patriot, but otherwise a spiteful, virulent man, as lieutenant-colonel of their National Guard. The invitation sent to a few of the officers was but little flattering to them, and a cause of great dissatisfaction to the others.

A regimental dinner might have been given in the Orangerie or anywhere else; but the king (an unprecedented favour) granted the use of his magnificent theatre, in which no *fête* had been given since the visit of the emperor Joseph II. Wines are lavished with royal prodigality. They drink the health of the king, the queen, and the dauphin; somebody, in a low, timid voice, proposed that of the nation; but nobody would pay any attention. At the dessert, the grenadiers of the regiment of Flanders, the Swiss, and other soldiers are introduced. They all drink and admire, dazzled by the fantastic brilliancy of that singular fairy scene, where the boxes, lined with looking-glasses, reflect a blaze of light in every direction.

The doors open. Behold the king and the queen! The king has been prevailed on to visit them on his return from the chase. The queen walks round to every table, looking beautiful, and adorned with the child she bears in her arms. All those young men are delighted, transported out of their senses. The queen, we must confess, less majestic at other periods, had never discouraged those who devoted their hearts to her service; she had not disdained to wear in her head-dress a plume from Lauzun's helmet.[56] There was even a tradition that the bold declaration of a private in the body guards had been listened to without anger; and that, without any other punishment than a benevolent irony, the queen had obtained his promotion.

So beautiful, and yet so unfortunate! As she was departing

---

[56] What does it signify whether Lauzun offered it, or she had asked for it? See *Mémoires de Campan*, and Lauzun (*Revue rétrospective*), &c.

with the king, the band played the affecting air: "O Richard, O my king, abandoned by the whole world!" Every heart melted at that appeal. Several tore off their cockades, and took that of the queen, the black Austrian cockade, devoting themselves to her service. At the very least, the tricolor cockade was turned inside out, so as to appear white. The music continued, ever more impassioned and ardent: it played the *March des Hulans*, and sounded the charge. They all leaped to their feet, looking about for the enemy. No enemy appeared; for want of adversaries they scaled the boxes, rushed out, and reached the marble court. Perseval, aide-de-camp to d'Estaing, scales the grand balcony, and makes himself master of the interior posts, shouting, "They are our prisoners." He adorns himself with the white cockade. A grenadier of the regiment of Flanders likewise ascends, and Perseval tore off and gave him a decoration which he then wore. A dragoon wanted also to ascend, but being unsteady, he tumbled down, and would have killed himself in his despair.

To complete the scene, another, half drunk and half mad, goes shouting about that he is a spy of the Duke of Orleans and inflicts a slight wound upon himself; his companions were so disgusted that they kicked him almost to death.

The frenzy of that mad orgy seemed to infect the whole court. The queen, on presenting flags to the National Guards of Versailles, said "that she was still enchanted by it." On the 3rd of October, another dinner; they grow more daring, their tongues are untied, and the counter-revolution showed itself boldly; several of the National Guards withdrew in indignation. The costume of National Guard is no longer received in the palace. "You have no feeling," said one officer to another, "to wear such a dress." In the long gallery, and in the apartments, the ladies no longer allow the tricolor cockade to circulate. With their handkerchiefs and ribands they make white cockades, and tie them themselves. The damsels grow so bold as to receive the vows of these new chevaliers, and allow them to kiss their hands. "Take this cockade," said they, "and guard it well; it is the true one, and alone shall be triumphant." How could they refuse, from such lovely hands, that symbol, that *souvenir?* And yet it is civil war and death: to-morrow, La Vendée! That fair and almost childlike form, standing by the aunts of the king, will be Madame de Lescure and de La Rochejaquelein.[57]

The brave National Guards of Versailles had much ado to defend themselves. One of their captains had been, willingly or unwillingly, decked out by the ladies with an enormous white cockade. His colonel, Lecointre, the linendraper, was furious. "Those cockades," said he, firmly, "shall be changed, and within a week, or all is lost." He was right. Who could mistake the omnipotence of the symbol? The three colours were the 14th of July and the victory of Paris, the Revolution itself. Thereupon a chevalier of Saint-Louis runs after Lecointre, declaring himself the champion of the white cockade against all comers. He follows, lies in wait for him, and insults him. This passionate defender of the *ancien régime* was not, however, a Montmorency, but simply the son-in-law of the queen's flower-girl.

Lecointre marches off to the Assembly, and requests the military committee to require the oath from the body guard. Some old guards there present declared that it could never be obtained. The committee did nothing, fearful of occasioning some collision and bloodshed; but it was precisely this prudence that occasioned it.

Paris felt keenly the insult offered to its cockade; it was said to have been ignominiously torn to pieces and trodden under foot. On the very day of the second dinner (Saturday evening, the 3rd) Danton was thundering at the club of the Cordeliers. On Sunday, there was a general onslaught on black or white cockades. Mixed crowds of commoners and bourgeois, coats side by side with jackets, assembled in the cafés and before the cafés, in the Palais Royal, at the Faubourg Saint-Antoine, at the ends of the bridges, and on the quays. Terrible rumours were

---

[57] She was then at Versailles. See the novel, true in this particular, which M. de Barante has published in her name.

in circulation about the approaching war; on the league of the
queen and the princes with the German princes; on the foreign
uniforms, red and green, then seen in Paris; on the supplies of
flour from Corbeil, which came now only every other day; on
the inevitably increasing scarcity, and on the approaching severe winter. There is no time to be lost, said they; if people
want to prevent war and famine, the king must be brought
here; otherwise the Court will carry him off.

Nobody felt all that more keenly than the women. The family, the household, had then become a scene of extreme suffering. A lady gave the alarm on the evening of Saturday, the 3rd.
Seeing her husband was not sufficiently listened to, she ran to
the Café de Foy, there denounced the anti-national cockades,
and exposed the public danger. On Monday a young girl took
a drum into the markets, beat the call to arms, and marched
off all the women in the quarter.

Such things are seen only in France; our women are brave,
and make others so. The country of Joan of Arc, Joan of Mont-
fort, and Joan Hachette, can cite a hundred heroines. There
was one at the Bastille, who afterwards departed for war, and
was made captain in the artillery; her husband was a soldier.
On the 18th of July, when the king went to Paris, many of the
women were armed. The women were in the van of our Revolution. We must not be surprised; they suffered more.

Great miseries are ferocious; they strike the weak rather
than the strong; they ill-treat children and women rather than
men. The latter come and go, boldly hunt about, set their wits
to work, and at length find at least sufficient for the day.
Women, poor women, live, for the most part, shut up, sitting,
knitting or sewing; they are not fit, on the day when everything is wanting, to seek their living. It is cruel to think that
woman, the dependent being, who can live only in company,
is more often alone than man. He finds company everywhere,
and forms new connexions. But she is nothing without family.
And yet her family overwhelms her; all the burden falls upon
her. She remains in her cold, desolate, unfurnished lodging,
with her children weeping, or sick and dying, who will weep

no more. A thing little remarked, but which gives perhaps the greatest pang to the maternal heart, is, that the child is unjust. Accustomed to find in the mother a universal all-sufficient providence, he taxes her cruelly, unfeelingly, for whatever is wanting, is noisy and angry, adding to her grief a greater agony.

Such is the mother. Let us take into account also many lonely girls, sad creatures, without any family or support, who, too ugly, or virtuous, have neither friend nor lover, know none of the joys of life. Should their little work be no longer able to support them, they know not how to make up the deficiency, but return to their garret and wait; sometimes they are found dead, chance revealing the fact to a neighbour.

These unfortunate beings possess not even enough energy to complain, to make known their situation, and protest against their fate. Such as act and agitate in times of great distress, are the strong, the least exhausted by misery, poor rather than indigent. Generally, the intrepid ones, who then make themselves conspicuous, are women of a noble heart, who suffer little for themselves, but much for others; pity, inert and passive in men, who are more resigned to the sufferings of others, is in women a very active, violent sentiment, which occasionally becomes heroic, and impels them imperatively towards the boldest achievements.

On the 5th of October, there was a multitude of unfortunate creatures who had eaten nothing for thirty hours.[58] That painful sight affected everybody, yet nobody did anything for them; everybody contented himself with deploring the hard necessity of the times. On Sunday evening (4th) a courageous woman, who could not behold this any longer, ran from the quarter Saint-Denis to the Palais Royal, forced her way through a noisy crowd of orators, and obtained a hearing. She was a woman of thirty-six years of age, well dressed and respectable,

---

[58] See the depositions of the witnesses, *Moniteur,* i., p. 568, col. 2. This is the principal source. Another, very important, abounding in details, and which everybody copies, without quoting it, is the *Histoire de deux Amis de la Liberté,* t. iii.

but powerful and intrepid. She wants them to go to Versailles, and she will march at their head. Some laugh at her; she boxes the ears of one of them for doing so. The next morning she departed among the foremost, sword in hand, took a cannon from the city, sat astride on it, and, with the match ready lit, rode off to Versailles.

Among the failing trades which seemed to be perishing with the *ancien régime* was that of carvers of wood. There used to be much work of that kind, both for the churches and apartments. Many women were sculptors. One of them, Madeleine Chabry, being quite out of work, had set up as a flower-girl (*bouquetière*) in the quarter of the Palais Royal, under the name of Louison; she was a girl of seventeen, handsome and witty. One may boldly venture to state that it was not hunger that drove her to Versailles. She followed the general impulse and the dictates of her good courageous heart. The women placed her at their head and made her their orator.

There were many others who were not driven by hunger: shopwomen, portresses, prostitutes, compassionate and charitable, as they so often are. There was also a considerable number of market-women; the latter were strict Royalists, but they wanted so much the more to have the king at Paris. They had already been to see him, on some occasion or other, some time before; they had spoken to him with much affection, with a laughable yet touching familiarity, which showed a perfect sense of the situation of affairs: "Poor man," said they, looking at the king, "poor dear man, good papa!" And to the queen more seriously: "Madam, madam, take compassion,—let us be free with each other. Let us conceal nothing, but say frankly what we have to say."

These market-women are not those who suffer much from misery: their trade consisting of the necessaries of life is subject to less variation. But they see wretchedness more than anybody, and feel it; passing their lives in the public streets, they do not, like us, escape the scenes of suffering. Nobody is more compassionate or kinder towards the wretchedly poor. With their clownish forms and rude and violent language, they have often a noble heart overflowing with good nature. We have seen our women of Picardy, poor fruitwomen of the market of Amiens, save the father of four children, who was going to be guillotined. It was at the time of the coronation of Charles X.; they left their business and their families, went off to Reims, made the king weep with compassion, obtained the pardon, and on their return, taking up a sizable collection among themselves, sent away the father, with his wife and children, safe and loaded with presents.

On the 5th of October, at seven in the morning, they heard the beating of a drum, and could no longer resist. A little girl had taken a drum from the guard-house, and was beating the call to arms. It was Monday; the markets were deserted, and all marched forth. "We will bring back," said they, *"the baker and the baker's wife.* And we shall have the pleasure of hearing *our little mother* Mirabeau."

The market people march forth, and the Faubourg Saint-Antoine, on the other hand, was likewise marching. On the road, the women hurry along with them all they happen to meet, threatening such as are unwilling that they will cut their hair off. First they go to the Hôtel-de-Ville. There a baker had just been brought who used to give false weight of seven ounces in a two pound loaf. The lamp was lowered. Though the man was guilty on his own confession, the National Guard contrived to let him escape. They presented their bayonets to the four or five hundred women already assembled. On the other side, at the bottom of the square, stood the cavalry of the National Guard. The women were by no means daunted. They charged infantry and cavalry with a shower of stones; but the soldiers could not make up their minds to fire on them. The women then forced open the Hôtel-de-Ville, and entered all the offices. Many of them were well dressed: they had put on white gowns for that grand day. They inquired curiously into the use of every room, and entreated the representatives of the districts to give a kind reception to the women they had forced to accompany them, several of whom were *enceinte,* and ill, perhaps from fear. Others, ravenous and wild, shouted out *Bread and arms!*—that the men were cowards,—and they would show them what courage was.—That the people of the Hôtel-de-Ville were only fit to be hanged,—that they must burn their writings and waste paper. And they were going to do so, and to burn the building perhaps. A man stopped them,—a man of gigantic stature, dressed in black, and whose serious countenance seemed more sombre than his dress. At first they were going to kill him, thinking he belonged to the town, and calling him a traitor. He replied he was no traitor, but a bailiff by profession, and one of the conquerors of the Bastille. It was Stanislas Maillard.

Early that morning, he had done good service in the Faubourg Saint-Antoine. The volunteers of the Bastille under the command of Hullin, were drawn up on the square in arms. The workmen who were demolishing the fortress believed they were sent against them. Maillard interposed and prevented the collision. At the Hôtel-de-Ville, he was lucky enough to prevent its being burnt. The women even promised they would not allow any men to enter: they had left armed sentinels at the grand entrance. At eleven o'clock, the men attacked the small door which opened under the arcade Saint-Jean. Armed with levers, hammers, hatchets, and pick-axes, they broke open the door, and forced the magazine of arms. Among them was a French guardsman, who had wanted in the morning to ring the tocsin, and had been caught in the act. He had, he said, escaped by miracle; the moderate party, as furious as the others, would have hanged him had it not been for the women; he showed his bare neck, which they had relieved from the rope. By way of retaliation, they took a man of the Hôtel-de-Ville in order to hang him. It was the brave Abbé Lefebvre, who had distributed the gunpowder on the 14th of July. Some women, or men disguised as women, hanged him accordingly to the little steeple; one of them cut the rope, and he fell, alive and only stunned, into a room twenty-five feet below.

Neither Bailly nor Lafayette had arrived. Maillard repaired to the aide-major-general and told him there was only one way of ending the business, which was that he, Maillard, should lead the women to Versailles. That journey will give time to collect the troops. He descends, beats the drum, and obtains a hearing. The austere tragical countenance of that tall man in black was very effective in La Grève; he appeared a prudent man, and likely to bring matters to a successful issue. The women, who were already departing with the cannon of the town, proclaimed him their captain. He put himself at their head with eight or ten drums; seven or eight thousand women followed, with a few hundred armed men, and a company of the volunteers of the Bastille brought up the rear.

On arriving at the Tuileries, Maillard wanted to follow the quay, but the women wished to pass triumphantly under the clock, through the palace and the garden. Maillard, an observer of ceremony, told them to remember that it was the king's house and garden; and that to pass through without permission was insulting the king.[59] He politely approached the Swiss guard, and told him that those ladies merely wished to pass through, without doing any mischief. The Swiss drew his sword and rushed upon Maillard, who drew his. A portress gave a lucky stroke with a stick; the Swiss fell, and a man held his bayonet to his breast. Maillard stopped him, coolly disarmed them both, and carried off the bayonet and the swords.

The morning was passing, and their hunger increased. At Chaillot, Auteuil, and Sèvres, it was very difficult to prevent the poor starving women from stealing food. Maillard would not allow it. At Sèvres the troop was exhausted; there, there was nothing to be had, not even for money; every door was closed except one, that of a sick man who had remained; Maillard contrived to buy of him a few pitchers of wine. Then, he chose seven men, and charged them to bring before him the bakers of Sèvres, with whatever they might have. There were eight loaves in all, thirty-two pounds of bread for eight thousand persons. They shared them among them and crawled further. Fatigue induced most of the women to lay aside their arms. Maillard, moreover, made them understand that as they

---

[59] *Déposition de Maillard, Moniteur,* i., p. 572.

wished to pay a visit to the king and the Assembly, and to move and affect them, it was not proper to arrive in such a warlike fashion. The cannon were placed in the rear, and in a manner concealed. The sage bailiff wished it to be an *amener sans scandale,* as they say in courts of law. At the entrance of Versailles, in order to hint their pacific intention, he gave a signal to the women to sing the air of Henri IV.

The people of Versailles were delighted, and cried *Vivent nos Parisiennes!* Foreigners among the spectators saw nothing but what was innocent in that crowd coming to ask the king for succour. The Genevese Dumont, a man unfriendly to the Revolution, who was dining at the palace *Des Petites-Écuries,* looking out of window, says himself: "All that crowd only wanted bread."

The Assembly had been that day full of stormy discussions. The king, being unwilling to *sanction* either the declaration of rights, or the decrees of the 4th of August, replied that constitutional laws could be judged only in their *ensemble;* that he *acceded,* however, in consideration of the alarming circumstances, and on the express condition that the executive power would resume all its force.

"If you accept the king's letter," said Robespierre, there is no longer any constitution, nor any right to have one." Duport, Grégoire, and other deputies speak in the same manner. Pétion mentions and blames the orgy of the body guards. A deputy, who had himself served among them, demands, for their honour, that the denunciation be stated in a regular form, and that the guilty parties be prosecuted. "I will denounce," cried Mirabeau, "and I will sign, if the Assembly declare that the person of the king is *alone* inviolable." This was designating the queen. The whole Assembly recoiled from the motion, which was withdrawn. On such a day, it would have provoked assassination.

Mirabeau himself was not free from uneasiness for his backsliding, and his speech on the *veto.* He approached the president, and said to him in an undertone: "Mounier, Paris is marching against us,—believe me or not, forty thousand men are marching against us. Feign illness, go to the palace, and give them this notice; there is not a moment to be lost." "Is Paris marching?" said Mounier, drily (he thought Mirabeau was one of the authors of the movement). "Well! so much the better! we shall have a republic the sooner."

The Assembly decide that they will send to the king to request the mere and simple acceptation of the Declaration of Rights. At three o'clock, Target announces that a crowd had appeared before the doors on the *Avenue de Paris*.

Everybody was acquainted with the event, except the king. He had departed for the chase that morning as usual, and was hunting in the woods of Meudon. They sent after him. Meanwhile, they beat the call to arms, the body guards mounted their horses on the *Place d'Armes*, and stood with their backs to the iron gates; the regiment of Flanders below, on their right, near the *Avenue de Sceaux*. M. d'Estaing, in the name of the municipality of Versailles, orders the troops to act in concert with the National Guard, and oppose the rioters. The municipality had carried their precaution so far as to authorize d'Estaing *to follow the king*, if he went far, on the singular condition of *bringing him back* to Versailles as soon as possible. D'Estaing adhered to the latter order, went up to the Château, and left the National Guard of Versailles to manage as it pleased. M. de Gouvernet, the second in command, likewise left his post, and placed himself among the body guards, preferring, he said, to be with people who know how to fight and use the sword. Lecointre, the lieutenant-colonel, remained alone to command.

Meanwhile, Maillard arrived at the National Assembly. All the women wanted to enter. He had the greatest trouble to prevail on them to send in only fifteen of their number. They placed themselves at the bar, having at their head the French guardsman of whom we have spoken, a woman who carried a tambourine at the end of a pole, and the gigantic bailiff in the midst, in his tattered black coat, and sword in hand. The soldier began by pertly telling the Assembly that, on no bread being found at the baker's that morning, he had wanted to ring the tocsin; that he had near been hanged, and owed his safety to the ladies who accompanied him. "We come," said he, "to demand bread, and the punishment of the body guard who have insulted the cockade. We are good patriots; on our road we have torn down the black cockades, and I will have the pleasure of tearing one before the Assembly."

To which the other gravely added: "Everybody must certainly wear the patriotic cockade." This was received with a few murmurs.

"And yet we are all brethren!" cried the sinister apparition.

Maillard alluded to what the municipal council of Paris had declared the day before: that the tricolor cockade, having *been adopted as a symbol of fraternity*, was the only one that ought to be worn by citizens.

The women, being impatient, shouted together, "Bread! Bread!" Maillard then began to speak of the horrible situation of Paris, of the supplies being intercepted by the other towns, or by the aristocrats. "They want," said he, "to starve us. A miller has received from somebody two hundred francs to induce him not to grind, with a promise that he should receive as much every week." The Assembly exclaimed, "Name him." It was in the Assembly itself that Grégoire had spoken of that current report; and Maillard had heard of it on the road.

"Name him!" some of the women shouted at random: "It is the archbishop of Paris."

At that moment, when the lives of many men seemed hanging by a thread, Robespierre took a serious step. Alone, he supported Maillard; said that Abbé Grégoire had spoken of the fact, and would doubtless give some information.[60]

Other members of the Assembly tried threats and caresses. A deputy of the clergy, an *abbé*, or a prelate, offered his hand to one of the women to kiss. She flew into a passion, and said, "I was not made to kiss a dog's paw." Another deputy, a military

---

[60] All this has been disfigured and curtailed by the *Moniteur*. Luckily, it gives later the depositions (at the end of the 1st volume). See also the *Deux Amis de la Liberté*, Ferrières, &c. &c.

man, and wearing the cross of Saint-Louis, hearing Maillard say that the clergy were the grand obstacle to the constitution, exclaimed, in a passion, that he ought instantly to be punished as an example. Maillard, nothing daunted, replied that he inculpated no member of the Assembly; that the Assembly were doubtless ignorant of all; and that he thought he was doing them a service in giving them this information. For the second time, Robespierre supported Maillard, and calmed the anger of the women. Those outside were growing impatient, fearing for the safety of their orator. A report was spreading among them that he had perished. He went out for a moment, and showed himself.

Maillard, then resuming his speech, begged the Assembly to engage the National Guards to make atonement for the insult offered to the cockade. Some deputies gave him the lie. Maillard insisted in unceremonious language. Mounier, the president, reminded him of the respect due to the Assembly; and added, foolishly, that they who wished to be citizens were perfectly at liberty to be so. This gave an advantage to Maillard; he replied: "Everybody ought to be proud of the name of citizen; and if, in that august assembly, there were anybody who considered it a dishonour, he ought to be excluded." The Assembly started with emotion, and applauded: "Yes," cried they, "we are all citizens!"

At that moment a tricolored cockade was brought in, sent by the body guard. The women shouted, "God save the king and the body guard!" Maillard, who was not so easily satisfied, insisted on the necessity of sending away the regiment of Flanders.

Mounier, then hoping to be able to get rid of them, said that the Assembly had neglected nothing to obtain provisions, neither had the king; that they would try to find some new means, and that they might withdraw in peace. Maillard did not stir, saying, "No, that is not enough."

A deputy then proposed to go and inform the king of the miserable state of Paris. The Assembly voted it, and the women, eagerly seizing that hope, threw their arms round the necks of the deputies, and embraced the president in spite of his resistance.

"But where is our Mirabeau?" said they, once more; "we should like to see our Count de Mirabeau."

Mounier, surrounded, kissed, and almost stifled, then moodily set out with the deputation and a crowd of women, who insisted on following him. "We were on foot," says he, "in the mud, and it was raining in torrents. We had to pass through a ragged noisy multitude, armed in a fantastic manner. Body guards were patrolling and galloping about. Those guards on beholding Mounier and the deputies, with their strange *cortège* of honour, imagined they saw there the leaders of the insurrection, and wanting to disperse that multitude, galloped through them." [61] The *inviolable* deputies escaped as they could, and ran for their lives through the mud. It is easy to conceive the rage of the people, who had imagined that, with them, they were sure of being respected!

Two women were wounded, and even by swords, according to some witnesses.[62] However, the people did nothing. From three till eight in the evening, they were patient and motionless, only shouting and hooting whenever they beheld the odious uniform of the body guard. A child threw stones.

The king had been found; he had returned from Meudon, without hurrying himself. Mounier, being at length recognised, was allowed to enter with twelve women. He spoke to the king of the misery of Paris, and to the ministers of the request of the Assembly, who were waiting for the pure and simple acceptation of the Declaration of Rights and other constitutional articles.

Meanwhile the king listened to the women with much kindness. The young girl, Louison Chabry, had been charged to speak for the others; but her emotion was so great in presence of the king, that she could only articulate "Bread!" and fell

---

[61] See Mounier, at the end of the *Exposé justificatif.*

[62] If the king forbade the troops to act, as people affirm, it was at a later period, and too late.

down in a swoon. The king, much affected, ordered her to be taken care of; and when, on departing, she wanted to kiss his hand, he embraced her like a father.

She ran out a Royalist, and shouting *"Vive le Roi!"* The women, who were waiting for her in the square, were furious, and began saying she had been bribed; in vain did she turn her pockets inside out, to show that she had no money; the women tied their garters round her neck to strangle her. She was torn from them, but not without much difficulty. She was obliged to return to the Château, and obtain from the king a written order to send for grain, and remove every obstacle for the provisioning of Paris.

To the demands of the president, the king had coolly replied: "Return about nine o'clock." Mounier had nevertheless remained at the castle, at the door of the council, insisting on having an answer, knocking every hour, till ten in the evening. But nothing was decided.

The minister of Paris, M. de Saint-Priest, had heard the news very late (which proves how indecisive and spontaneous the departure for Versailles had been). He proposed that the queen should depart for Rambouillet, and that the king should remain, resist, and fight if necessary; the departure of the queen alone would have quieted the people and rendered fighting unnecessary. M. Necker wanted the king to go to Paris, and trust himself to the people; that is to say, that he should be sincere and frank, and accept the Revolution. Louis XVI., without coming to any resolution, dismissed the council, in order to consult the queen.

She was very willing to depart, but with him, and not to leave such an indecisive man to himself; the name of the king was her weapon for beginning the civil war. Saint-Priest heard, about seven o'clock, that Lafayette, urged by the National Guard, was marching against Versailles. "We must depart immediately," said he; "the king at the head of the troops will pass without any difficulty." But it was impossible to bring him to any decision. He believed (but very wrongly) that, if he departed, the Assembly would make the Duke of Orleans king. He was also adverse to flight; he strode to and fro, repeating from time to time: "A king a fugitive! a king a fugitive!" [63] The queen, however, having insisted on departing, the order was given for the carriages. It was too late.

[63] See Necker, and his daughter, Madame de Staël's *Considérations*.

IX

The King Brought Back to Paris

ONE of the Paris militia, whom a crowd of women had taken, in spite of himself, for their leader, and who excited by the journey, had shown himself at Versailles more enthusiastic than all the others, ventured to pass behind the body guard there: seeing the iron gate shut, he began insulting the sentinel stationed within, and menacing him with his bayonet. A lieutenant of the guard and two others drew their swords, and galloped after him. The man ran for his life, tried to reach a shed, but tumbled over a tub, still shouting for assistance. The horseman had come up with him, just as the National Guard of Versailles could contain themselves no longer: one of them, a retail wine-merchant, stepped from the ranks, aimed, fired, and stopped him short; he had broken the arm that held the uplifted sabre.

D'Estaing, the commander of this National Guard, was at the castle, still believing that he was to depart with the king. Lecointre, the lieutenant-colonel, remained on the spot demanding orders of the municipal council, who gave none. He was justly fearful lest that famished multitude should overrun the town and feed themselves. He went to them, inquired what quantity of provisions was necessary, and entreated the council to give them; but could only obtain a little rice, which was nothing for such a multitude. Then he caused a search to be made in every direction, and, by his laudable diligence, gave some relief to the people.

At the same time, he addressed himself to the regiment of Flanders, and asked the officers and soldiers whether they would fire. The latter were already under a far more powerful influence. Women had cast themselves among them, entreating them not to hurt the people. A woman then appeared among them, whom we shall often see again, who seemed not to have walked in the mire with the others, but had, doubtless, arrived later, and who now threw herself at once among the soldiers. This was a handsome young lady, Mademoiselle Théroigne de Méricourt, a native of Liège, lively and passionate, like so many of the women of Liège who effected the Revolution of the fifteenth century,[64] and fought valiantly against Charles the Bold. Interesting, original, and strange, with her riding-habit and hat, and a sabre by her side, speaking and confounding equally French and the *patois* of Liège, and yet eloquent. She was laughable, yet irresistible. Théroigne, impetuous, charming, and terrible, was insensible to every obstacle. She had had amours; but then she felt but one passion,—one violent and mortal, which cost her more than life,[65] her love for the Revolution; she followed it with enthusiasm, never missed a meeting of the Assembly, frequented the clubs and the public places, held a club at her own house, and received many deputies. She would have no more lovers, and declared that she would have none but the great metaphysician, the abstract, cold Abbé Sieyès, ever the enemy of women.

Théroigne, having addressed that regiment of Flanders, bewildered, gained them over, and disarmed them so completely that they gave away their cartridges like brothers to the National Guard of Versailles.

D'Estaing then sent word to the latter to withdraw. A few departed; others replied that they would not go till the body guards had first moved. The latter were then ordered to file off. It was eight o'clock, and the evening was dark. The people

---

[64] See my *Histoire de France*, t. vi.

[65] A tragical story, terribly disfigured by Beaulieu and all the royalists. I entreat the people of Liège to defend the honour of their heroine.

followed, pressed upon the body guards, and hooted after them. The guards force their way sword in hand. Some who were behind, being more molested than the rest, fired their pistols: three of the National Guard were hit, one in the face; the two others received the bullets in their clothes. Their comrades fire also by way of answer; and the body guard reply with their musquetoons.

Other National Guards entered the court-yard, surrounded d'Estaing, and demanded ammunition. He was himself astonished at their enthusiasm and the boldness they displayed amid the troops: "True martyrs of enthusiasm," said he subsequently to the queen.[66]

A lieutenant of Versailles declared to the guard of the artillery, that if he did not give him some gunpowder, he would blow his brains out. He gave him a barrel which was opened on the spot; and they loaded some cannon which they pointed opposite the balustrade, so as to take in flank the troops which still covered the castle, and the body guards who were returning to the square.

The people of Versailles had shown the same firmness on the other side of the Château. Five carriages drew up to the iron gates in order to depart; they said it was the queen, who was going to Trianon. The Swiss opened, but the guards shut. "It would be dangerous for her Majesty," said the commandant, "to leave the Château." The carriages were escorted back. There was no longer any chance of escape. The king was a prisoner.

The same commandant saved one of the body guard whom the crowd wanted to tear to pieces, for having fired on the people. He managed so well that they left the man; they were satisfied with tearing the horse to pieces; and they began roasting him on the *Place D'Armes;* but the crowd were too hungry to wait, and devoured it almost raw.

It was a rainy night. The crowd took shelter where they could; some burst open the gates of the great stables, where

---

[66] See one of his letters at the end of vol. i., of *Deux Amis de la Liberté.*

the regiment of Flanders was stationed, and mixed pell-mell with the soldiers. Others, about four thousand in number, had remained in the Assembly. The men were quiet enough, but the women were impatient at that state of inaction: they talked, shouted, and made an uproar. Maillard alone could keep them quiet, and he managed to do so only by haranguing the Assembly.

What contributed to incense the crowd, was that the body guards came to the dragoons, who were at the doors of the Assembly, to ask whether they would assist them in seizing the cannon that menaced the Château. The people were about to rush upon them, when the dragoons contrived to let them escape.

At eight o'clock, there was another attempt. They brought a letter from the king, in which, without speaking of the Declaration of Rights, he promised in vague terms to allow grain to circulate freely. It is probable that, at that moment, the idea of flight was predominant at the Château. Without giving any answer to Mounier, who still remained at the door of the council, they sent this letter to engage the attention of the impatient crowd.

A singular apparition had added to the affright of the Court. A young man enters, ill-dressed, like one of the mob, and quite aghast.[67] Everybody was astonished; it was the young Duke of Richelieu who, in that disguise, had mingled with the crowd, a fresh swarm of people who had marched from Paris; he had left them half way on the road in order to give warning to the royal family; he had heard horrible language, atrocious threats, which made his hair stand on end. In saying this, he was so livid, that everybody turned pale.

The king's heart was beginning to fail him; he perceived that the queen was in peril. However agonizing it was to his conscience to consecrate the legislative work of philosophy, at ten o'clock in the evening he signed the Declaration of Rights.

Mounier was at last able to depart. He hastened to resume

---

[67] Staël, *Considérations*, 2nd part, ch. xi.

his place as president before the arrival of that vast army from Paris, whose projects were not yet known. He re-entered the hall; but there was no longer any Assembly; it had broken up: the crowd, ever growing more clamorous and exacting, had demanded that the prices of bread and meat should be lowered. Mounier found in his place, in the president's chair, a tall fine well-behaved woman, holding the bell in her hand, and who left the chair with reluctance. He gave orders that they were to try to collect the deputies again; meanwhile, he announced to the people that the king had just accepted the constitutional articles. The women crowding about him, then entreated him to give them copies of them; others said: "But, M. President, will this be very advantageous? Will this give bread to the poor people of Paris?" Others exclaimed: "We are very hungry. We have eaten nothing to-day." Mounier ordered bread to be fetched from the bakers'. Provisions then came in on all sides. They all began eating in the hall with much clamour.

The women, whilst eating, chatted with Mounier: "But, dear President, why did you defend that villainous *veto?* Mind the lanterne!" Mounier replied firmly, that they were not able to judge,—that they were mistaken; that, for his part, he would rather expose his life than betray his conscience. This reply pleased them very much, and from that moment they showed him great respect and friendship.[68]

Mirabeau alone would have been able to obtain a hearing, and silence the uproar. He did not care to do so. He was certainly uneasy. According to several witnesses, he had walked about in the evening among the people, with a large sabre, saying to those he met, "Children, we are for you." Afterwards, he had gone to bed. Dumont, the Genevese, went in quest of him, and brought him back to the Assembly. As soon as he arrived, he called out, in his voice of thunder, "I should like to know how people have the assurance to come and trouble our meeting. M. President, make them respect the Assembly!" The

---

[68] Mounier, at the end of the *Exposé justificatif.*

women shouted "Bravo!" They became more quiet. In order to kill time, they resumed the discussion on the criminal laws.

"I was in a gallery (says Dumont) where a fish-woman was acting as commander-in-chief, and directing about a hundred women, especially girls, who, at a signal from her, shouted or remained silent. She was calling the deputies familiarly by their names, or else would inquire, 'Who is that speaking yonder? Make that chatterbox hold his prating! That is not the question! The thing is to have bread! Let them rather hear our little mother Mirabeau!' Then all the women would shout, 'Our little mother Mirabeau!' But he would not speak." [69]

Lafayette, who had left Paris between five and six in the evening, did not arrive till after twelve. We must now go back, and follow him from noon to midnight.

About eleven, being informed that the Hôtel-de-Ville was invaded, he repaired thither, found the crowd dispersed, and began dictating a despatch for the king. La Grève was full of the paid and unpaid National Guards, who were muttering from rank to rank that they ought to march to Versailles. Many French ex-guards, especially, regretted having lost their ancient privilege of guarding the king, and wanted to recover it. Some of them went to the Hôtel-de-Ville, and knocked at the bureau, where Lafayette was dictating. A handsome young grenadier, who spoke admirably, said to him firmly:

"General, the people are without bread; misery is extreme. The committee of subsistence either deceives you, or are themselves deceived. This state of things cannot last; there is but one remedy: let us go to Versailles. They say the king is a fool; we will place the crown on the head of his son; a council of regency shall be named, and everything will go on better."

Lafayette was very firm and obstinate, but the crowd was still more so. He believed very properly in his influence over the people: he was, however, able to see that he had overrated it. In vain did he harangue the people; in vain did he remain several hours in the Grève on his white horse, some-

---

[69] Etienne Dumont, *Souvenirs*, p. 181.

times speaking, sometimes imposing silence with a gesture, or else, by way of having something to do, patting his horse with his hand. The difficulty was growing more urgent; it was no longer his National Guards who pressed him, but bands from the Faubourgs Saint-Antoine and Saint-Marceau,—men who would listen to nothing. They spoke to the general by eloquent gestures, preparing a noose for him, and taking aim at him. Then he got down from his horse, and wanted to re-enter the Hôtel-de-Ville; but his grenadiers barred the passage: "*Morbleu!* general," said they, "you shall stay with us; you would not abandon us!"

Luckily, a letter is brought down from the Hôtel-de-Ville; they authorise the general to depart, "seeing it is impossible to refuse." "Let us march," said he, though he did so with regret. The order was received with shouts of joy.

Of the thirty thousand men of the National Guard, fifteen thousand marched forth. Add to this number a few thousands of the people. The insult offered to the national cockade was a noble motive for the expedition. Everybody applauded them on their passage. An elegantly-dressed assemblage on the terrace by the water-side looked on and applauded. At Passy, where the Duke of Orleans had hired a house, Madame de Genlis was at her post, shouting, and waving her handkerchief, doing all she could to be seen. The bad weather caused them to march rather slowly. Many of the National Guards, so eager before, now began to cool. This was not like the fine weather on the 14th of July. They were drenched with a cold October rain. Some of them stopped on the road; others grumbled, and walked on. "It is disagreeable," said the rich tradesmen, "for people who go to their country-houses in fine weather only in coaches, to march four leagues in the rain." Others said, "We will not do all this drudgery for nothing." And they then laid all the blame on the queen, uttering mad threats, and appearing very malignant. The Château had been expecting them in the greatest anxiety. They thought that Lafayette only pretended that he was forced, but that really he availed himself willingly of the opportunity. They wanted to see whether, at eleven o'clock, the crowd being then dispersed, the carriages could pass through the Dragon gates. The National Guard of Versailles was on the watch, and blocked the passage.

The queen, however, would not depart alone. She rightly judged that there was no safe refuge for her, if she separated from the king. About two hundred noblemen, several of whom were deputies, offered themselves to defend her, and asked her for an order to take horses from her stables. She authorised them, in case, she said, the king should be in danger.

Lafayette, before entering Versailles, made his troops renew their oath of fidelity to the law and the king. He sent him notice of his arrival, and the king replied: "that he would see him with pleasure, and that he had just accepted *his* Declaration of Rights."

Lafayette entered the Château alone, to the great astonishment of the guards and everybody else. In the *oeil-de-boeuf*, one of the courtiers was so foolish as to say: "There goes Cromwell." To which Lafayette replied very aptly, "Sir, Cromwell would not have entered alone."

"He appeared very calm," says Madame De Staël (who was present); "nobody ever saw him otherwise; his modesty suffered from the importance of his position." The stronger he appeared, the more respectful was his behaviour. The outrage, moreover, to which he had been subjected, made him more of a Royalist than ever.

The king intrusted to the National Guard the outer posts of the castle; the body guards preserved those within. Even the outside was not entirely intrusted to Lafayette. On one of his patrols wishing to pass into the park, the entrance was refused. The park was occupied by body guards and other troops; till two in the morning [70] they awaited the king, in case he should at last resolve to fly. At two o'clock only, having been pacified by Lafayette, they told them they might go to Rambouillet.

The Assembly had broken up at three o'clock. The people

---

[70] Till that hour, they still thought of doing so, if we may believe the testimony of M. de la Tour-du-Pin.—*Mémoires* de Lafayette, ii.

had dispersed, and retired to rest, as they could, in the churches and elsewhere. Maillard and many of the women, among whom was Louison Chabry, had departed for Paris, shortly after the arrival of Lafayette, carrying with them the decrees on grain and the Declaration of Rights.

Lafayette had much trouble to find lodging for his National Guards; wet, and worn out, they were trying to dry themselves and to get food. At last, believing everything quiet, he also went to the Hôtel de Noailles, and slept, as a man sleeps after twenty hours' fatigue and agitation.

Many people did not sleep: especially those who having come from Paris in the evening, had not undergone the fatigue of the preceding day. The first expedition, in which the women were predominant, being very spontaneous, natural as it were, and urged by necessity, had not cost any bloodshed. Maillard had had the glory of maintaining some sort of order in that disorderly crowd. The natural *crescendo* ever observable in such insurrections, scarcely left room to hope that the second expedition would pass off as quietly. True, it had been formed before the eyes of the National Guard, and as if in concert with it. Nevertheless there were men there who were determined to act without them; many were furious fanatics, who would have liked to kill the queen; [71] others who pretended to be so, and seemed to be the most violent, were simply a class of men ever superabundant when the police is weak, namely, thieves. The latter calculated the chances of breaking into the Château. They had not found much in the Bastille worth taking. But, what a delightful prospect was opened for pillage in the wonderful palace of Versailles, where the riches of France had been amassed for more than a century!

---

[71] I do not see in the *Ami du peuple* how Marat can be accused of having been the first to suggest sanguinary violence. What is certain is he was very restless: "M. Marat flies to Versailles, returns like lightning and makes alone as much noise as the four trumpets of the Day of Judgment, shouting: 'O death! arise!'"—Camille Desmoulins, *Révolutions de France et de Brabant,* iii., p. 359.

At five in the morning, before daylight, a large crowd was already prowling about the gates, armed with pikes, spits, and scythes. They had no guns. Seeing some body guards as sentinels at the gates, they forced the National Guards to fire on them; the latter obeyed, taking care to fire too high.

In that crowd, wandering or standing round fires that had been made in the square, was a little hump-backed lawyer, Verrières, mounted on a large horse; he was considered very violent; they had been waiting for him ever since the preceding evening, saying they would do nothing without him. Lecointre was likewise there, going to and fro haranguing the crowd. The people of Versailles were perhaps more stirred up than the Parisians, having been long enraged against the court and the body guards; they had lost an opportunity, the night before, of falling on them, which they regretted, and wanted now to pay them what they owed them. Among them were several locksmiths and blacksmiths, (of the manufactory of arms?) rough men, who strike hard, and who, moreover, ever thirsty at the forge, are also hard drinkers.

About six o'clock, this crowd, composed of Parisians and people of Versailles, scale or force the gates, and advance into the courts with fear and hesitation. The first who was killed, if we believe the Royalists, died from a fall, having slipped in the marble court. According to another and a more likely version, he was shot dead by the body guard.

Some took to the left, toward the queen's apartment, others to the right, toward the chapel stairs, nearer the king's apartment. On the left, a Parisian running unarmed, among the foremost, met one of the body guard, who stabbed him with a knife. The guardsman was killed. On the right, the foremost was a militia-man of the guard of Versailles, a diminutive locksmith, with sunken eyes, almost bald, and his hands chapped by the heat of the forge.[72] This man and another, without answering the guard, who had come down a few steps

---

[72] Deposition of Miomandre, one of the body guards.—*Moniteur*, i., p. 566.

and was speaking to him on the stairs, strove to pull him down by his belt, and hand him over to the crowd rushing behind. The guards pulled him towards them; but two of them were killed. They all fled along the grand gallery, as far as the *oeil-de-boeuf*, between the apartments of the king and the queen. Other guards were already there.

The most furious attack had been made in the direction of the queen's apartment. The sister of her *femme-de-chambre* Madame de Campan, having half opened the door, saw a guardsman covered with blood, trying to stop the furious rabble. She quickly bolted that door and the next, put a petticoat on the queen, and tried to lead her to the king. An awful moment! The door was bolted on the other side! They knock again and again. The king was not within; he had gone round by another passage to reach the queen. At that moment a pistol was fired, and then a gun, close to them. "My friends, my dear friends," cried the queen, bursting into tears, "save me and my children." They brought her the dauphin. At length the door was opened, and she rushed into the king's apartment.

The crowd was knocking louder and louder to enter the *oeil-de-boeuf*. The guards barricaded the place, piling up benches, stools, and other pieces of furniture; the lower panel was burst in. They expected nothing but death; but suddenly the uproar ceased, and a kind clear voice exclaimed: "Open!" As they did not obey, the same voice repeated: "Come, open to us, body guard; we have not forgotten that you men saved us French Guards at Fontenoy."

It was indeed the French Guards, now become National Guards, with the brave and generous Hoche, then a simple sergeant-major—it was the people, who had come to save the nobility. They opened, threw themselves into one another's arms, and wept.

At that moment, the king, believing the passage forced, and mistaking his saviours for his assassins, opened his door himself, by an impulse of courageous humanity, saying to those without: "Do not hurt my guards."

The danger was past, and the crowd dispersed; the thieves

alone were unwilling to be inactive. Wholly engaged in their own business, they were pillaging and moving away the furniture. The grenadiers turned that rabble out of the castle.

A scene of horror was passing in the court. A man with a long beard was chopping with a hatchet to cut off the heads of two dead bodies,—the guards killed on the stairs. That wretch, whom some took for a famous brigand of the south, was merely a *modèle* who used to sit at the Academy of Painting; for that day, he had put on the picturesque costume of an antique slave, which astonished everybody, and added to their fear.[73]

Lafayette, awakened but too late, then arrived on horseback. He saw one of the body guards whom they had taken and dragged near the body of one of those killed by the guards, in order to kill him by way of retaliation. "I have given my word to the king," cried Lafayette, "to save his men. Cause my word to be respected." The man was saved; not so Lafayette. A furious fellow cried out: "Kill him!" He gave orders to have him arrested, and the obedient crowd dragged him accordingly towards the general, dashing his head against the pavement.

He then entered the castle. Madame Adelaide, the king's aunt, went up to him and embraced him: "It is you," cried she, "who have saved us." He ran to the king's cabinet. Who

---

[73] His name was Nicolas. According to his landlord, the man had never given any proof of violence or ill-nature. Children used to take that terrible man by the beard. He was in fact a vain half-silly person who fancied he was doing something grand, audacious, and original, and perhaps wanted to realize the bloody scenes he had beheld in pictures or at the theatre. When he had committed the horrible deed, and everybody had recoiled from him, he suddenly felt the dreariness of that strange solitude, and sought, under different pretexts, to get into the conversation, asking a servant for a pinch of snuff, and a Swiss of the castle for some wine, which he paid for, boasting, and trying to encourage and comfort himself.—See the depositions in the *Moniteur*. The heads were carried to Paris on pikes; one by a child. According to some, they departed the same morning; others say, a little before the king, and, consequently, in presence of Lafayette, which is not likely. The body guard had killed five men of the crowd or National Guards of Versailles, and the latter seven body guards.

would believe that etiquette still subsisted? A grand officer stopped him for a moment, and then allowed him to pass: "Sir," said he seriously, "the king grants you *les grandes entrées.*"

The king showed himself at the balcony, and was welcomed with the unanimous shout of "God save the King! *Vive le Roi!*"

"The King at Paris!" was the second shout, which was taken up by the people, and repeated by the whole army.

The queen was standing near a window with her daughter beside her, and the dauphin before her. The child, playing with his sister's hair, cried: "Mamma, I am hungry!" O hard reaction of necessity! Hunger passes from the people to the king! O Providence! Providence! Pardon! This one is but a child!

At that moment several voices raised a formidable shout: "The queen!" The people wanted to see her in the balcony. She hesitated: "What!" said she, "all alone?" "Madam, be not afraid," said Lafayette. She went, but not alone, holding an admirable safeguard,—in one hand her daughter, in the other her son. The court of marble was terrible, in awful commotion, like the sea in its fury; the National Guards, lining every side, could not answer for the centre; there were fire-arms, and men blind with rage. Lafayette's conduct was admirable: for that trembling woman, he risked his popularity, his destiny, his very life; he appeared with her on the balcony, and kissed her hand.[74]

The crowd felt all that; the emotion was unanimous. They saw there the woman and the mother, nothing more. "Oh!

---

[74] By far the most curious deposition is that of the woman La Varenne,—the valiant portress of whom we have spoken. Therein we may perceive how a legend begins. This woman was an eye-witness,—had a hand in the business; she received a wound in saving one of the body guard; and she sees and hears whatever is uppermost in her mind; she adds it honestly: "The queen appeared in the balcony; M. de Lafayette said: 'The queen has been deceived. She *promises to love her people,* to be attached to them, as Jesus Christ is to his Church.' And as a token of approval, the queen, shedding tears, twice raised her hand. The king asked pardon for his guards," &c.

how beautiful she is! What! is that the queen? How she fondles her children!" Noble people! may God bless you for your clemency and forgetfulness!

The king was trembling with fear, when the queen went to the balcony. The step having succeeded: "My guards," said he to Lafayette, "could you not also do something for them?" "Bring one forward." Lafayette led him to the balcony, told him to take the oath, and show the national cockade in his hat. The guard kissed it, and the people shouted: "*Vivent les gardes-du-corps!*" The grenadiers, for more safety, exchanged caps with the guards so that, by this mixture of costume, the people could no longer fire on the guards without running the risk of killing the grenadiers.

The king was very reluctant to quit Versailles. To leave the royal residence was in his estimation the same thing as to abandon royalty. A few days before, he had rejected the entreaties of Malouet and other deputies, who in order to be further from Paris, had begged him to transfer the Assembly to Compiègne. And now, he must leave Versailles to go to Paris,—pass through that terrible crowd. What would befall the queen? He shuddered to think.

The king sent to entreat the Assembly to meet at the Château. Once there, the Assembly and the king being together, and supported by Lafayette, some of the deputies were to beseech the king not to go to Paris. That request was to have been represented to the people as the wish of the Assembly. All that great commotion would subside; fatigue, lassitude, and hunger would gradually disperse the people; they would depart of their own accord.

The Assembly, which was then forming, appeared wavering and undecided.

Nobody had any fixed resolution or determination. That popular movement had taken all by surprise. The most keen-sighted had expected nothing of this. Mirabeau had not foreseen it, neither had Sièyes. The latter said pettishly, when he received the first tidings of it: "I cannot understand it; it is going all wrong."

314

I think he meant to say: "contrary to the Revolution." Sièyes, at that time, was still a revolutionist, and perhaps rather favourably inclined towards the branch of Orleans. For the king to quit Versailles, his old court, and live at Paris among the people, was, doubtless, a fine chance for Louis XVI. to become popular again. If the queen (killed, or in exile) had not followed him, the Parisians would, very probably, have felt an affection for the king. They had, at all times, entertained a predilection for that fat, good-tempered man, whose very corpulency gave him an air of pious paternal good-nature, quite to the taste of the crowd. We have already seen that the market-women used to call him *a good papa:* that was the very idea of the people.

This removal to Paris, which so much frightened the king, frightened, in a contrary manner, such as wanted to strengthen and continue the Revolution, and, still more, those who, for patriotic or personal views, would have liked to make the Duke of Orleans lieutenant-general (or something better.)

The very worst thing that could have happened for the latter, who was foolishly accused of wishing to kill the queen, was, that the queen should have been killed, and that the king, freed from that living cause of unpopularity, should return to Paris, and fall into the hands of such men as Bailly or Lafayette.

The Duke of Orleans was perfectly innocent of the movement of the 5th of October. He could neither help it, nor take advantage of it. On the 5th and the following night, he went restlessly from place to place. Depositions prove that he was seen everywhere between Paris and Versailles, but that he did nothing.[75] Between eight and nine in the morning of the 6th, so soon after the massacre, that the court of the castle was

---

[75] All that he appears to have done, was to authorise the purveyor of the Assembly, on the evening of the 5th, to furnish provisions to the people who were in the hall. There is nothing to show that he acted, to any extent, from the 15th of July to the 5th of October, except in an awkward and weak attempt which Danton made in his favour with Lafayette.—See the *Mémoires* of the latter.

still stained with blood, he went and showed himself to the people, with an enormous cockade in his hat, laughing, and flourishing a switch in his hand.

To return to the Assembly. There were not forty members who repaired to the castle. Most of them were already in the entrance hall, and rather undecided how to act. The crowds of persons who thronged the tribunes increased their indecision. At the first word said about sitting at the Château, they began vociferating. Mirabeau then arose, and, according to his custom of disguising his obedience to the people in haughty language, said, "that the liberty of the Assembly would be compromised if they deliberated in the palace of kings; that it did not become their dignity to quit their usual place of meeting; and that a deputation was sufficient." Young Barnave supported the motion. Mounier, the president, opposed it, but in vain.

At length, they heard that the king had consented to depart for Paris; the Assembly, on Mirabeau's proposition, voted, that, for their present session, they were inseparable from the king.

The day was advancing. It was not far from one o'clock. They must depart, and quit Versailles. Farewell to ancient monarchy!

A hundred deputies surround the king; a whole army,—a whole people. He departs from the palace of Louis XIV., never to return.

The whole multitude begins to move: they march off towards Paris, some before the king, and some behind. Men and women, all go as they can, on foot or on horseback, in coaches and carts, on carriages of cannon, or whatever they could find. They had the good fortune to meet with a large convoy of flour,—a blessing for the famished town. The women carried large loaves on pikes, others, branches of poplar, already tinted by autumn. They were all very merry, and amiable in their own fashion, except a few jokes addressed to the queen. "We are bringing back," cried they, "the baker, his wife, and the little shop-boy." They all thought they could never starve, as long as they had the king with them. They were all still royalists, and full of joy at being able at length to put their *good papa* in good keeping: he was not very clever; he had broken his word; it was his wife's fault; but, once in Paris, good women would not be wanting, who would give him better advice.

The whole spectacle was at once gay, melancholy, joyous, and gloomy. They were full of hope, but the sky was overcast, and the weather unfortunately did not favour the holiday. The rain fell in torrents; they marched but slowly, and in muddy roads. Now and then, several fired off guns, by way of rejoicing, or to discharge their arms.

The royal carriage, surrounded by an escort, and with La-fayette at the door, moved like a hearse. The queen felt uneasy. Was it sure she should arrive? She asked Lafayette what he thought, and he inquired of Moreau de Saint-Méry, who, having presided at the Hôtel-de-Ville on the famous days of the taking of the Bastille, was well acquainted with the matter. He replied in these significant words: "I doubt whether the queen could arrive alone at the Tuileries; but, once at the Hôtel-de-Ville, she will be able to return."

Behold the king at Paris, in the place where he ought to be, in the very heart of France. Let us hope he will be worthy of it.

The Revolution of the 6th of October, necessary, natural, and justifiable, if any ever was; entirely spontaneous, unforeseen, and truly popular; belongs especially to the women, as that of the 14th of July does to the men. The men took the Bastille, and the women took the king.

On the 1st of October, everything was marred by the ladies of Versailles; on the 6th, all was repaired by the women of Paris.

BOOK III

OCTOBER 6, 1789, TO JULY 14, 1790

I

Unanimity to Revive the Kingly Power (October, 1789)

EARLY in the morning of the 7th of October, the Tuileries were crowded with an excited multitude, impatient to see their king. Throughout the day, whilst he was receiving the homage of the constituted authorities, the crowd was watching without, and anxiously expecting to behold him. They saw, or thought they saw him through the distant windows; and whenever any one was happy enough to catch a glimpse of him, he pointed him out to his neighbour, exclaiming, "Look! there he is!" He was obliged to show himself in the balcony, where he was received with unanimous acclamations; nay, he felt obliged to descend even into the gardens, to make a still closer demonstration of sympathy for the enthusiasm of the people.

His sister, Madame Elizabeth, an innocent young person, was so affected by it, that she caused her windows to be opened, and supped in presence of the multitude. Women with their children drew near, blessing her, and extolling her beauty.

On the very preceding evening, that of the 6th of October, everybody had felt quite reassured about that people of whom they had been so much afraid. When the king and the queen appeared by torch-light at the Hôtel-de-Ville, a roar like thunder arose from La Grève,—shouts of joy, love, and gratitude, towards the king who had come to live among them. The men wept like children, shook hands, and embraced each other.[1]

"The Revolution is ended," cried they; "here is the king delivered from that Palace of Versailles, from his courtiers and advisers." And indeed that pernicious charm which for more than a century had held royalty captive, remote from mankind, in a world of statues and automata still more artificial, was now, thank heaven, dissolved. The king was restored again to true nature,—to life and truth. Returning from that long exile, he was restored to his home; he resumed his proper place, and found himself re-established in the kingly element,—which is no other than the people. And where else could a king ever breathe and live?

Live amongst us, O king, and be at length free; for, free you have never been; but have ever acted, and let others act, against your will. Every morning you have been made to do what you repented of before night; yet you obeyed every day. After having been so long the slave of caprice, reign at length according to the law; for this is royalty,—this is liberty; and such is the kingdom of God.

Such were the thoughts of the people, generous and sympathetic, without either rancour or distrust. Mingling, for the first time, in the crowd of lords and elegant ladies, they behaved towards them with great respect. Nay, they looked kindly upon the body-guards themselves, as they walked along arm in arm with the brave French guards, their friends and protectors. They cheered them both, in order to reassure and console their enemies of the preceding day.

Let it be for ever remembered that at this period, so falsely described, or perverted by hate, the heart of France was full of magnanimity, clemency, and forgiveness. Nay, even in the acts of resistance, provoked on all sides by the aristocracy,—in those energetic measures whereby the people declare them-

---

[1] All this, and the following, is quoted from royalist writers, Weber, i., 257; Beaulieu, ii., 203, &c. Their testimony is conformable to that of the *Amis de la liberté*, iv., 2–6.

selves ready to strike, they threaten but forgive. Metz denounces its rebellious *Parlement* to the National Assembly, and then intercedes for it. Brittany, in the formidable federation that she formed in the middle of winter (January), showed herself both strong and merciful. One hundred and fifty thousand armed men there engaged themselves to withstand the enemies of the law; and the youthful commander, who, at the head of their deputies, swore with his sword on the altar, added to his oath: "If they become good citizens, we will forgive them."

Those great federations,[2] which were formed throughout France for eight or nine months, are the characteristic feature, the stamp of originality, of that period. They had at first a defensive character, being formed for mutual protection against unknown enemies, the *brigands,* and against the aristocracy. Next, these brothers being up in arms together, wished also to live together; they sympathised with the wants of their fellow-citizens, and pledged themselves to secure a free circulation for grain, and to forward provisions from one province to another, from those who had but little to those who had none. At length, confidence is restored, and food is less scarce; but the federations continue, without any other necessity than that of the heart: *To unite,* as they said, *and love one another.*

The towns at first unite together, in order to protect themselves against the nobles. Next, the nobles being attacked by the peasants, or by wandering bands of paupers, and the castles burnt; the townsmen sally forth in arms, and hasten to protect the castles and defend the nobles, their enemies. These nobles go in crowds to take refuge in the towns, among those who have saved them, and take the civic oath (February and March).

Struggles between town and country places are happily of short duration. The peasant soon perceives the course of events, and, in his turn, confederates for order and the consti-

---

[2] Spontaneously-organized associations of citizens or towns, as expressions of national unity (Ed. note).

tution. I have now before me the *procès-verbaux* of a number
of those rural federations, and I perceive in them the patriotic
spirit, in spite of the simple language in which it is expressed,
bursting forth as energetically as in the towns, and perhaps
even more so.

There is no longer any rampart between men. One would
think that the walls of cities had fallen. Great federations of
the cities often hold their meetings in the country; and often
the peasants, in orderly bands, with the mayor or *curé* at their
head, go and fraternise with the inhabitants of the towns.

All were orderly, and all armed. The National Guard, at that
period (a circumstance worthy of memory), was generally
composed of everybody.[3]

Everybody is in motion and all march forth as in the time
of the Crusades. Whither are they all marching thus in groups
of cities, villages, and provinces? What Jerusalem attracts thus
a whole nation, attracting it not abroad, but uniting it, concentrating it within itself . . . It is one more potent than that

---

[3] Everybody *without exception* in the rural districts. Amid the panic
terrors renewed every moment for more than a year, everybody was armed,
at least with agricultural implements, and appeared thus armed at the
reviews and most solemn festivals. In towns, the organisation varied; the
permanent committees which formed there, on the news of the taking of
the Bastille, opened registers in which the well-disposed of every class of
men went and wrote their names; wherever there was any danger, these
volunteers were absolutely everybody without exception. The unlucky
question about the uniform first gave rise to divisions; then select bodies
were formed, much disliked by all the others. The uniform was exacted
very early at Paris, and the National Guard there became reduced to some
thirty thousand men. But everywhere else there were but few uniforms; at
most facings were added varying in colour, according to each town. At
length the blue and red became predominant. The proposition to require
a uniform throughout France was not made till July 18th, 1790. On the
28th of April, 1791, the Assembly limited the title of national guard to
active citizens, or primary electors; the number of these electors (who, as
proprietors, or tenants, paid taxes to the value of three days' labour, or
three francs at most) amounted to four million four hundred thousand
men. And even of this number the majority, being workmen and living
from hand to mouth by daily labour, were unable to continue the
enormous sacrifice of time which the service of the national guard then
required.

of Judea; it is the Jerusalem of hearts, the holy unity of fraternity, the great living city, made of men. It was built in less than
a year, and since then has been called *Patrie*.

Such is my course in this third book of the Revolution;
obstacles of every kind, outcries, acts of violence, and bitter
disputes may delay me, but shall not deter me from my task.
The 14th of July has proved to me the unanimity of Paris, and
another 14th of July will presently show me the unanimity of
France.

How was it possible that the king, the ancient object of the
people's affection, should alone be forgotten in this universal
brotherly embrace? On the contrary, he was its first object. In
spite of his being accompanied by the ever melancholy, hard-
hearted, and rancorous queen; and notwithstanding the abject
thraldom in which he was evidently held by his bigoted
scruples, and the bondage also in which his affection for his
wife enabled the latter to keep him, the people were obstinately bent on placing all their hopes in the king.

A fact ridiculous to state, is, that the dread inspired by the
events of the 6th of October had created a multitude of royalists. That terrible surprise, that nocturnal phantasmagoria, had
seriously startled the imagination; and people became more
closely attached to the king. The Assembly, especially, had
never felt so well disposed in his favour. They had been
frightened; and even ten days later it was with great repugnance that they went to assemble in that moody Paris of October, amid that stormy multitude. One hundred and fifty
deputies preferred to take passports; and Mounier and Lally
escaped.

The two first men in France, Lafayette and Mirabeau, one
the most popular, the other the most eloquent, were royalists
on their return to Paris.

Lafayette had been mortified at being led to Versailles,
though apparently the leader of the people. He was piqued
about his involuntary triumph almost as much as the king himself. He effected two measures on his return: he emboldened
the municipality to prosecute Marat's sanguinary newspaper at

the Châtelet (tribunal); and he went in person to the Duke of Orleans, intimidated him, spoke to him in strong and resolute terms, both at his house and before the king, giving him to understand that after the 6th of October, his presence at Paris was troublesome, furnished pretexts, and excluded tranquillity. By these means he induced him to go to London; but when the duke wanted to return, Lafayette sent him word that, the day after his return, he would have to fight a duel with him.

Mirabeau, thus deprived of his duke, and plainly perceiving that he should never be able to derive any advantage from him, turned, with all the assurance of superior power, like an indispensable person whom it is impossible to reject, and went over to the side of Lafayette. (October 10th–20th). He frankly proposed to him to overthrow Necker, and to share the government between themselves.[4] This was certainly the only chance of safety that remained to the king. But Lafayette neither liked nor esteemed Mirabeau; and the Court detested them both.

For a moment, a brief moment, the two remaining centers of strength, popularity and genius, reached agreement to the advantage of royalty. An accident that happened just at the door of the Assembly, two or three days after they arrived in Paris, alarmed them, and induced them to desire order, cost what it would. A cruel mistake caused a baker to lose his life (October 21).[5] The murderer was immediately judged and hanged. This was an opportunity for the municipality to demand a law of severity and force. The Assembly decreed martial law, which armed the municipalities with the right of calling out the troops and citizen guard for dispersing the mob. At the same time, they decreed that crimes of lèse-nation should be tried by an old royal tribunal, at the Chatêlet,—a

---

[4] Consult the three principal witnesses—Mirabeau, Lafayette, and Alexandre de Lameth.

[5] This crime, committed at the door of the Assembly, and which caused them to vote forthwith coercive laws, could not have benefited any but the royalists. I am, however, of opinion that it was the mere result of accident, and of the distrust and animosity engendered by misery.

petty tribunal for so great a mission. Buzot and Robespierre said it was necessary to create a high national court. Mirabeau ventured so far as to say that all these measures were useless, but *that it was necessary to restore strength to the executive power,* and not allow it to take advantage of its own annihilation.

This happened on the 21st of October. What progress since the 6th! In the course of a fortnight, the king had recovered so much ground, that the bold orator frankly placed the safety of France in the strength of the kingly power.

Lafayette wrote to the fugitive Mounier in Dauphiné, where he was lamenting the king's captivity, and inciting people to civil war: [6] that the king was by no means captive, that he would habitually inhabit the capital, and that he was about to recommence his hunting parties. This was not a falsehood. Lafayette in fact entreated the king to go forth and show himself, and not give credit to the report of his captivity by a voluntary seclusion.[7]

No doubt but Louis XVI. could, at that period, have easily withdrawn either to Rouen, as Mirabeau advised him, or to Metz, and the army commanded by Bouillé, which the queen desired.

---

[6] M. de Lally has himself assured us that his friend Mounier used to say, "I think we must fight for it."—See Bailly, iii., 223, *note.*

[7] Lafayette, ii., 418, *note.*

II

Resistance—The Clergy

(October to November, 1789)

THE gloomy winter on which we are now entering was not horribly cold like that of 1789; God took compassion on France. Otherwise, there would have been no possibility either of enduring it or of living. The general misery had increased: there was no labour, no work. At that period, the nobles were emigrating, or at least quitting their castles and the country, then hardly safe, and settling in the towns, where they remained close and quiet, in the expectation of events; several of them were preparing for flight, and quietly packing up their trunks. If they acted on their estates, it was to demand money and not to give relief; they collected in haste whatever was owing, the arrears of feudal rights. Hence, a scarcity of money, a cessation of labour, and a frightful increase of beggars in every town,—nearly two hundred thousand in Paris! Others would have come, by millions, if the municipalities were not obliged to keep their own paupers. Each of them, throughout the winter, drained itself in feeding its poor, till every resource was exhausted; and the rich, no longer receiving any pensions, descended almost to the level of paupers. Everybody complains and implores the National Assembly. If things remain in this state, its task will be no less than to feed the whole nation.

But the people must not die. There is, after all, one resource, a patrimony in reserve, which they do not enjoy. It was on their account and to feed them that our charitable ancestors exhausted their fortunes in pious foundations, and endowed the ecclesiastics, the dispensers of charity, with the best part of their possessions. The clergy had so well kept and augmented the property of the poor, that at length it comprised one-fifth of the lands of the kingdom, and was estimated at four thousand millions of francs (160,000,000*l.*)

The people, these paupers really so rich, now go and knock at the door of the church, their own mansion, to ask for a part of a property the whole of which is their own—*Panem! propter Deum!* [8].—It would be cruel to let this proprietor, this member of the family, this lawful heir, starve on the threshold.

Give, if you are Christians; the poor are the members of Christ. Give, if you are citizens; for the people are the living city. Pay back, if you are honest; for this property was only a deposit.

Restore, and the nation will give you more. The question is not to cast yourselves into an abyss in order to fill it up; you are not asked to sacrifice yourselves, as new martyrs, for the people. On the contrary, the question is to come to your own assistance and to save yourselves.

In order to understand this, it must be remembered that the body of the clergy, monstrously rich in comparison to the nation, was also, in itself, a monster of injustice and inequality. Though the head of that body was enormously swollen and bloated, its lower members were meagre and starving: whilst one priest possessed an income of a million, another had but two hundred francs a year.

In the project of the Assembly, which did not appear till the spring, this was all altered. The country curates and vicars were to receive from the state about sixty millions, and the bishops only three. Hence their cry: religion is destroyed; Jesus is angry; the Virgin is weeping in the churches of the south, and in La Vendée; and hence all the phantasmagoria necessary to incite the peasants to rebellion and slaughter.

---

[8] "Bread! for the love of God!"

The Assembly wished also to give pensions of thirty-three millions to the monks and nuns, and twelve millions to separate ecclesiastics, &c. They would have carried the general pay of the clergy to the enormous sum of one hundred and thirty-three millions; which, by suppressions, would have been reduced to half. This was acting most generously. The most insignificant curate was to have (exclusive of house, presbytery, and garden) at least twelve hundred francs a year. To tell the truth, the whole of the clergy (except a few hundred men) would have risen from misery to comfort; so that what was called the spoliation of the clergy, was really a donation.

The prelates made a grand, heroic resistance. It was necessary to return to the point three times and make three distinct attacks (October, December, and April), to get from them what was only justice and restitution. It is very easy to see upon what these men of God had set their life and heart: *their property!* They defended it, as the early Christians had defended the faith!

Their arguments failed them, but not so their rhetoric. Now, they indulged in threatening prophecies. If you touch a property holy and sacred beyond all others, they will all be in danger; the right of property expires in the mind of the people. To-morrow, the people will come to demand the agrarian law! Another added meekly: Even though you ruin the clergy, you would not gain much; the clergy, alas! are so poor, and in debt moreover; their estates, if no longer administered by them, would never cover their debts.

The debate had begun on the 10th of October. Talleyrand, bishop of Autun, who had done the business of the clergy, and now wanted to do business at their expense, was the first who broke the ice and ventured upon this slippery ground, and limped along avoiding the dangerous point of the question, saying only: "That the clergy were not proprietors in the same sense as other proprietors."

To which Mirabeau added: "Property belongs to the nation."

The legists of the Assembly proved superabundantly: first, that the clergy were *not proprietors* (able to use and abuse);

330

secondly, that they were *not possessors* (the canon law forbidding them to possess); thirdly, that they were *not even tenants*, but depositaries, administrators at most, and dispensers.

What produced more effect than the dispute of words was, that at the very moment when the axe was laid at the foot of the tree, dumb witnesses appeared, who, without making any deposition against it, showed all the injustice and barbarity that this fatal tree had covered with its shadow.

The clergy still possessed serfs in the time of the Revolution. The whole of the eighteenth century had passed away, together with all the liberators, both Rousseau and Voltaire, whose last thought was the enfranchisement of the Jura. Yet the priest had still his serfs!

Feudalism had blushed at its own misdeeds, and, in various ways, had abdicated those shameful rights. Much to its honour, it had rejected the last remnants on the night of the 4th of August. But the priest still possessed his serfs!

On the 22nd of October, one of them, named Jean Jacob, a peasant-tenant in mortmain of the Jura, a venerable man more than a hundred and twenty years old, was led forward by his children and requested the favour of thanking the Assembly for their decrees of the 4th of August. Great was the emotion. The National Assembly all arose in presence of that patriarch of mankind, and made him sit covered. A noble mark of respect paid to old age, and a reparation also to the poor serf, for so long an insult to the rights of humanity. This man had been a serf for half a century under Louis XIV., and for eighty years since then. And he still remained a serf: the decrees of the 4th of August were only in a state of general declaration; nothing had been executed. Bondage was not expressly abolished till March, 1790; and the old man died in December; so, this last of the serfs never saw the light of liberty.

On the same day (October 22nd) M. de Castellane, taking advantage of the emotion of the Assembly, demanded that the thirty-five prisons in Paris, and those of France, should be visited, and that prisons far more secret and horrible than the royal Bastilles, the ecclesiastical dungeons, should especially be opened. It was at length most necessary that on such a day of resurrection the sun should pierce through the veil of mystery, and that the beneficent light of the law should, for the first time, illumine those judgment-seats of darkness, those subterraneous dungeons, those *in pace*,[9] where often in their furious monastic hatred or jealousy, or on account of their amours, still more atrocious than their hatred, the monks buried their brethren alive.

Alas! what were convents altogether but so many *in pace*, in which families abandoned and forgot such of their members as happened to be a burden, and whom they sacrificed for the others? These persons were not able, like the serf of Jura, to crawl as far as the feet of the National Assembly to demand their liberty, and embrace the tribunal instead of the altar. At most, if they dared, they might with great difficulty, at a distance, and by letter, make known their complaints. A nun wrote on the 28th of October, timidly, and in general terms, asking nothing for herself, but entreating the Assembly to legislate on ecclesiastical vows. The Assembly dared not at that time come to any resolution; they merely suspended the pronouncing of vows, thus barring the entrance to fresh victims. But how would they have hastened to open the gates for the sad inhabitants of the cloisters, had they known the desperate state of misery to which they had been reduced! I have said in another book [10] how every kind of cultivation and intellectual amusement had been gradually withdrawn from the poor nuns, how the distrust of the clergy had deprived them of food for the mind. They were literally dying, without a breath of anything vital; the absence of religion was also as great as that of worldly things, perhaps even greater. Death, *ennui*, vacancy; nothing to-day; nothing to-morrow; nothing in the morning, and nothing in the evening; only a confessor occasionally, and

---

[9] Cells in which the superiors imprisoned for life.—C. C.
[10] *"Priests, Women, and Families,"* passim.

a little immorality. Or else they ran violently to the opposite extreme, from the cloister to Voltaire or Rousseau, into absolute Revolution. I have known some who were outright unbelievers. A few had a faith of their own; and theirs was so powerful that they could have walked through fire. Witness Charlotte Corday, nourished in the cloister, with the precepts of Plutarch and Rousseau, beneath the vaulted roof of Matilda and William the Conqueror.[11]

It was like a review of all the unfortunate; all the phantoms of the middle ages reappeared in their turn before the face of the clergy, the universal oppressor. The Jews came. After having been annually smitten on the cheek at Toulouse, or hanged between two dogs, they came modestly to ask whether they were men. These ancestors of Christianity, so harshly treated by their own sons, were also, in one sense, the ancestors of the French Revolution; the latter, as a reaction of Right, would necessarily bow down before that austere law, wherein Moses foresaw the future triumph of Right.

Another victim of religious prejudices, the poor community of actors, came also to claim their rights. O barbarous prejudices! The two first men of England and France, the author of *Othello* and the author of *Tartufe*, were they not actors? And was not the great man who spoke for them in the National Assembly, even Mirabeau, a sublime actor? "Action, action, action!" is what makes the orator, said Demosthenes.

The Assembly decided nothing for the actors, and nothing for the Jews. On the account of the latter, they granted to *non-catholics* access to civil employments. They also recalled from foreign countries our unfortunate brethren, the Protestants, driven away by the barbarous agents of Louis XIV., and promised to restore to them their property, as far as they were able. Several returned, after an exile of a century; but few recovered their fortune. This innocent and unjustly banished population

---

[11] At the Abbaye-aux-Dames at Caen.—See her Biography, by Paul Delasalle, Louis Dubois, &c.

did not find an indemnity of a milliard of francs (400,000*l.*), a sum so lavishly squandered on the guilty emigrants.[12]

What they found was equality, the most honourable rehabilitation, France restored to justice, and raised from the dead, and men of their belief in the foremost rank of the Assembly, Rabaut and Barnave at the tribune. Too just retribution! These two illustrious Protestants were members of the ecclesiastical committee, and were now judging their ancient judges, and deciding on the fate of those who banished, burnt, and broke their fathers on the wheel. By way of vengeance, they proposed to vote one hundred and thirty-three millions for the Catholic clergy!

Rabaut Saint-Etienne was, as is well known, the son of the old doctor, the persevering apostle and glorious martyr of Cévennes, who for fifty years knew no other roof than leaves and the canopy of heaven, hunted like a bandit, passing the winters on the snow among wolves, without any other weapon than his pen, with which he wrote his sermons in the woods. His son, after working many years at the task of religious liberty, had the happiness of voting it. It was he also who proposed and proclaimed the *unity* and *indivisibility* of France (August 9, 1791). A noble proposition, which all doubtless would have made, but which was to spring first from the heart of our Protestants, so long and so cruelly divorced from their native land. The Assembly raised Rabaut to the dignity of president, and he had the glorious happiness of writing to his venerable parent these words of solemn rehabilitation and honour for the proscribed: "The President of the National Assembly is at your feet."

---

[12] We must, however, make a distinction. There is the emigrant who goes to side with the enemy; and the emigrant, more than excusable, who departs through fear.

III

Resistance—The Clergy—The Parlements —The Provincial Estates

THE discussion on ecclesiastical estates began on the 8th of October; and on the 14th, the clergy raised the shout of civil war.

On the 14th, it was a bishop of Brittany; on the 24th, the clergy of the diocese of Toulouse: a tocsin in the west, and a tocsin in the south.

We must not forget that in this same month of October, the prelates and rich *abbés* of Belgium, whose estates were also in danger, were creating an army and appointing a general. Brabant and Flanders unfurled the banner of the blood-red cross. The Capuchin friars, and other monks, were exciting the peasantry, intoxicating them with savage sermons and furious processions, and forcing upon them swords and daggers against the Emperor. Our peasantry were less prompt in making the movement. Their judgment in general is healthy, and far more clear and sober than that of the Belgians. The old frolicsome spirit of the *fabliaux* [13] and of Rabelais, but little favourable to the clergy, is never entirely extinct in France. "*Monsieur le curé*, and his housekeeper," is ever an inexhaustible text of scandal for the long winter's evenings. The curate, however, was rather lampooned than hated; but the bishops (all nobles

---

[13] Satirical Poems.

at that time, Louis XVI. would elect no others) were, for the most part, far more scandalous. Without confining their amours to their provincial countesses, who used to do the honours of the episcopal palace, they had intrigues also with the actresses of Paris. These countesses, or marchionesses, mostly of the poorer ranks of the nobility, occasionally honoured their half-marriages by their real merit; more than one governed the bishopric, and better than the bishop could have done it. One of these women, not far from Paris, managed the elections of '89 in her diocese, and strove energetically to send two excellent deputies to the National Assembly.

An episcopacy so worldly, that remembered its religion only as soon as its estates were about to be touched, had really a difficult task in attempting to renew the ancient spirit of fanaticism in the rural districts. Even in Brittany, where the peasantry always belong to the priests, it was an imprudent blunder of the bishop of Tréguier to fling abroad the manifesto of civil war on the 14th of October; he fired too soon; and his gun missed fire. In his incendiary mandate he declared the king was a prisoner, and religion overthrown; that the priests would be nothing better than *clerks paid by brigands*—that is to say, the nation, the National Assembly. To be able to say such things on the 14th, it would have been necessary to be ready to make a civil war on the morrow. Indeed, a few giddy young nobles made an attempt to excite the peasantry. But the peasant of Brittany, so resolute when once on the road and bent on proceeding, is slow in making the first move; he found it difficult to understand that the question of church lands, though doubtless very serious, comprised all religion. Whilst the peasant was ruminating, and studying this knotty point, the town did not wait to reflect, but acted, and with terrible vigour, without consulting anybody. All the municipalities in the diocese invaded Tréguier, and proceeded without losing a day, against the bishop and the noble instigators; interrogated them, and took down the depositions of witnesses against them. The intimidation was so great, that the prelate and the others denied everything, assuring that they had neither said nor done anything to excite the country people to rebel. The municipalities sent the whole of the proceedings thus begun to the National Assembly, to the Keeper of the Seals; but, without waiting for the judgment, they pronounced at once a provisional sentence: "Whoever enlists for the nobles is a traitor to the commoners; and the nobles themselves are *unworthy of the protection of the nation,* if they attempt to obtain a rank in the national guard." [14]

The mandate came out on the 14th; and this violent retaliation took place on the 18th (at latest). During the week the sword was drawn. Brest having purchased some grain for provision, some of the peasantry were paid and urged to stop the grain-waggons, and the envoys of Brest, at Lannion; they were in imminent danger of their lives, and obliged to sign a shameful surrender. An army immediately marched forth from Brest, and from all the different towns at once. Such as were too remote, as Quimper, Lorient, and Hennebon, offered money and assistance. Brest, Morlaix, Landernau, and several others, marched in whole masses; on the road, they met all the communes arriving also in arms, and were obliged to send some of them back again. The wonder is that no violence was committed. This general mustering, rising like a storm along the whole country, arrived at the heights above Lannion, and there halted. The heroic manhood of Brittany was never more conspicuously displayed; she was firm against herself. They merely took back the purchased grain, and handed the guilty parties over to the judges, that is to say, their friends.

What rendered the privileged classes so easy to be conquered at that period, was that they did not act in concert. Several made an appeal to physical force at once; but the greater number did not despair of resisting by the law, by the old, and perhaps by the new, system.

The *parlements* had not yet acted. It was their vacation. They intended to act on their return to business in November.

The majority of the nobles and upper clergy did not yet act.

---

[14] Bailly, iii., 209. Duchatellier gives but little information in this matter.

They still entertained one hope. Being the proprietors of the greater part of the land, and predominant in the rural districts, they held in their dependency a whole race of servants and clients under different denominations. These country people being called to vote by Necker's universal election in the spring of 1789, had generally voted properly, because their patrons, for the most part, gloried in bringing about the Estates-General, which they considered a thing of no consequence. But ages had passed away in a year. The same patrons at the present time, the end of the year 1789, would certainly make desperate efforts to get the rural population to vote against the Revolution; they were going to make the farmer choose between his patriotism (still very young) and his daily bread, and to lead their submissive, trembling labourers, in bands, to the electoral urn, and make them vote by cudgel law. Things will presently change, when the peasant will be able to catch a glimpse of the way to acquire the church estates, and the lands of the manors, and when the Assembly will have created, by these sales, a legion of proprietors and free electors. At the present moment, however, there is nothing of the kind. The rural districts are still subject to electoral bondage: Necker's universal suffrage, if the Assembly had adopted it, would incontestably have given the victory to the old state of affairs.

On the 22nd of October, the Assembly decreed that nobody could be an elector unless he paid in direct taxes, as proprietor or tenant, the value of three days' labour, (that is to say, three francs, at most).

With that one line, they swept away from the hands of the aristocracy a million rural electors.

Of the five or six million electors produced by universal suffrage, there remained *four millions four hundred thousand* [15] proprietors or tenants.

Grégoire, Duport, Robespierre, and other worshippers of the ideal, objected, but in vain, that men were equal and ought

---

[15] This is, at least, the number found in 1791. We shall revert to this important point.

therefore all to vote according to the dictates of natural law. Two days previously, Montlosier, the royalist, had likewise proved that all men are equal.

In the crisis in which they then were, nothing could have been more futile and fatal than this thesis of natural law. These Utopists thus bestowed a million electors on the enemies of equality in the name of equality.

The glory of this truly revolutionary measure belongs to Thouret, the illustrious legist of Normandy, a practical Sieyès, who caused the Assembly to pass, or at least facilitated, the great measures which it then enacted. Without either eloquence or effect, he severed with the power of his logic those knotty questions with which the most intelligent, such as Sieyès and Mirabeau, seemed to be puzzled.

He alone ends the discussion on the ecclesiastical estates, by extricating it from the lower region of disputation, and boldly raising it to the light of philosophical right. All his arguments, in October and December, are summed up in this profound sentence: "How could you possess?" said he to the clergy, "*you do not exist.*

"You do not exist as a body. The moral bodies which the state creates are not bodies in the proper sense of the word, are not living beings. They have a moral ideal existence which is imparted to them by the will of the state, their creator. The state made them, and causes them to live. As useful, it maintained them; but having become noxious, it withdraws from them its will, which constitutes all their life and rational being."

To which Maury replied: "No, the state did not create us; we exist without the state." Which was equivalent to saying, We are a state within the state, a principle in opposition to a principle, a struggle, an organised warfare, permanent discord in the name of charity and union.

On the 3rd of November, the Assembly decreed that the property of the clergy *was at the disposal of the nation*. In December it further decreed, in the terms laid down by Thouret: That the clergy are no longer an order; *that they do not exist* (as a body).

The 3rd of November is a great day. It breaks up the *parlements* and even the provincial estates.

On the same day appeared Thouret's report on the organisation of departments, the necessity of dividing the provinces, of removing those false nationalities, so malevolent and hostile, in order to constitute a real nation in the spirit of unity.

Who was interested in maintaining those ancient divisions, all those feelings of bitter rivalry, to keep people Gascons, Provençaux, and Britons, and to prevent Frenchmen from being one France? Those who reigned in the provinces, the *parlements,* and the provincial estates; those false phantoms of liberty which for so long a time had made it but its shadow, a snare, and even impeded its birth.

Well then, on the 3rd of November, at the moment when it gives the first blow to the provincial estates, the Assembly adjourns the *parlements* for an indefinite period. Lameth made the proposal, and Thouret drew up the decree. "We have buried them alive," said Lameth on leaving the Assembly.

All the old magistracy had sufficiently proved what the Revolution had to expect from it. The tribunals of Alsace, Beaujolais, and Corsica; the prevosts of Champaign and Provence, took upon themselves to choose between the different laws; they were perfectly acquainted with such as favoured the king, but did not know the others. On the 27th of October, the judges sent to Marseilles by the *parlement* of Aix acted according to the ancient forms, with secret procedures, and all the old barbarous practices, without paying any attention to the contrary decree, sanctioned on the 4th of October. The *parlement* of Besançon openly refused to register any decree of the Assembly.

The latter had but to say one word to annihilate this insolence. The people were trembling with indignation around those rebellious tribunals. "Against those estates and *parlements,*" said Robespierre, "you need do nothing; the municipalities will act sufficiently."

On the 5th of November, the Assembly raised its arm to

strike. "Such tribunals as do not register within three days shall be prosecuted for illegal behaviour."

These bodies had had under the feeble government now expiring, a considerable power of resistance, both legal and seditious. The whimsical mixture of functions which they combined gave them abundant means of doing so.—Their sovereign, absolute, hereditary *jurisdiction,* which never forgot an injury, was dreaded by all; even ministers and great lords never dared exasperate judges who would remember the circumstance, perhaps fifty years afterwards, in some trial or other to ruin their families.—Their *refusal to register,* which gave them a kind of *veto* against the king, had at least the effect of affording a signal to sedition, and, in an indirect manner, of proclaiming it legal.—Their *administrative* usurpations, the superintendence of provisions in which they interfered, afforded them a thousand opportunities of causing a terrible accusation to impend over people in power.—Lastly, a part of the *police* was in their hands; that is to say, that they were charged to repress on one hand the troubles they excited on the other.

Was this dangerous power at least in safe hands that might provide security? The *parlement* men in the eighteenth century had been seriously corrupted by their intercourse with the nobility. Even those among them who, as Jansenists, were hostile to the court, devout, austere, and factious, were, in spite of their surly haughtiness, not the less flattered to behold duke or prince so-and-so in their antechamber. The great lords, who laughed at them in secret, courted and flattered them, and spoke subserviently to them in order to win unjust law-suits, especially to be able to usurp the lands of the commons with impunity. The meanness to which the courtiers stooped before those bigwigs, involved them no further. They themselves would laugh at it; occasionally, they condescended to marry their daughters,—their fortunes, in order to replenish their own. The younger of the parliamentarians, too much flattered by this acquaintance and these alliances with personages of higher rank, strove hard to imitate them—to be, after their example, good-natured profligates, and, like awkward imitators, they outstepped their masters. They would lay aside their red robes, and descend from the fleurs-de-lis to frequent houses of a lower order, fashionable suppers, and to take part in private theatricals.

O Justice, how low hast thou fallen! . . . O degrading history! In the middle ages it was material, in the land and in the race, in the fief and in the blood. The lord, or he who succeeds all others, the lord of lords, the king, would say: "Justice is mine; I can judge or cause to be judged." By whom? "No matter by whom; by any one of my lieutenants, by my servant, my steward, my porter. . . . Come here; I am pleased with you and give you a magistracy." This man says, to the same purpose: "I shall not be a judge myself, I shall sell this magistracy."—Then comes the son of a merchant, who purchases, to sell a second time, this most holy of sacred things; thus justice passes from hand to hand, like a parcel of goods, nay, passes into a heritage, a dowry . . . A strange marriage settlement for a young bride, the right of hanging and breaking a man on the wheel!

Hereditary right, venality, privilege, exception,—such were the names of justice. And yet how otherwise should we term injustice?—Privileges of *persons*, judged by whom they chose. Privilege of *time:* I judge thee, at my good pleasure, to-morrow, in ten years, or never.—And privilege of *place*. The *parlement* will summon from the distance of a hundred and fifty leagues or more some poor fellow who is pleading against his lord. I advise him to be resigned and give up his cause; let him abandon it altogether rather than come and waste years perhaps at Paris, in dirt and poverty, in soliciting a decree from the good friends of his lord.

The *parlements* of latter years had provided, by decrees, not promulgated, but avowed and faithfully executed, that none but men of noble birth or newly-made nobles could any longer be admitted among them.

Thence arose a deplorable decline of capacity. The study

of the law, debased in the schools,[16] weakened among the lawyers, was altogether wanting among the magistrates,—those
very men who applied the law for life or death. The lawyers'
corporation very seldom required the candidate to give proofs
of his science, if he proved his titles of nobility.

Thence also proceeded a line of conduct more and more
false and ambiguous. Those noble magistrates are constantly
advancing and retreating. They shout for liberty; Turgot becomes minister, and then they reject him. They raise a cry of
Estates-General! But the day they are given such a body, they
set out to render it null by organizing it on the lines of the old
powerless Estates.

On that day they expired.

When the Assembly decreed an indefinite vacation, they had
little expected such a blow. Those of Paris wanted to resist; [17]
but the Archbishop of Bordeaux, the Keeper of the Seals, entreated them not to do so. November would have renewed the
great October movement. They registered and made the somewhat dilatory offer to give judgment gratuitously.

Those of Rouen also enregistered; but they wrote secretly
and prudently to the king, that they did so provisionally, and
from motives of obedience to him. Those of Metz said as much,
publicly and boldly, in a general meeting of all the chambers,
resolutely grounding this act on the *non-liberty* of the king.
Those men were able to swagger, being protected by Bouillé's
artillery.

The timid Bishop, the Keeper of the Seals, was sore afraid.
He pointed out the danger to the king: how the Assembly
would retaliate, in anger, and let loose the people. The way to
save the *parlements,* was for the king to hasten to condemn
them himself. He would be in a better position to interfere and

---

[16] The venerable M. Berriat Saint-Prix has often related to me some
singular facts relating to this matter. Ignorance and routine were becoming
the character of the tribunals more and more every day. On their
systematic opposition to d'Aguesseau's attempts to restore unity to the law,
see M. La Ferrière's fine *Histoire du Droit Français.*

[17] See Sallier, the Parliamentarian, *Annales,* ii., p. 49.

intercede. Indeed, the cities of Rouen and Metz were already impeaching their *parlements* and demanding their punishment. Those proud bodies saw themselves alone, with the whole population against them: they retracted. Metz itself interceded for its guilty *parlement;* and the Assembly pardoned it (November 25th, 1789).

IV

Resistance—Parlements

—Movement of the Federations

THE most obstinate resistance was that of the *parlement* of Brittany. Three separate times it refused to register, and thought itself able to maintain its refusal. On one hand, it had the nobility, who were mustering at Saint-Malo, the numerous and very faithful servants of the nobles, its own members and clients in the towns, its friends in the religious establishments (*confréries*), and the corporations of trades; add, moreover, the facility of obtaining recruits in that multitude of workmen out of employ, and people wandering about the streets, dying of hunger. The towns beheld them busily engaged in preparing a civil war. Surrounded as they were by hostile or doubtful rural districts, they might be reduced to famine; they therefore resolved to settle the question at once. Rennes and Nantes, Vannes and Saint Malo, sent overwhelming accusations to the Assembly, declaring that they abjured all connection with the traitors. Without waiting for orders, the national guard of Rennes entered the castle and secured the cannon (December 18, 1789).

The Assembly took two measures. It summoned the *parlement* of Brittany to its bar; and it gave a favourable reception to the petition of Rennes soliciting the creation of other tribunals. It began its great work, the organisation of a system of justice worthy of the name, neither paid, purchased, nor hereditary, but sprung from the people and for the people. The first article of such an organisation was, of course, the suppression of the *parlements* (December 22, 1789).

Thouret, the author of the report, well laid down this maxim, sadly overlooked since then, that a revolution that wishes to be durable ought, before everything else, to deprive its enemies of the sword of justice.

It is a strange contradiction to say to the system overthrown: "Thy principle is adverse to me; I blot it out of the laws and government; but in all private matters, thou shalt apply it against me." How was it possible thus to disown the quiet, calm, but terrible omnipotence of the judicial power, which must inevitably absorb it. Every other power is in need of it; but it can do without the others. Give me but the judicial power, and keep your laws and ordinances, all that mountain-heap of paper; and I will undertake to establish triumphantly the system the most opposite to your laws. Those old parliamentary tyrants were obliged, in spite of themselves, to come and bow down to the National Assembly (January 8th). If they had not come by fair means, Brittany would even have raised an army on purpose to drag them thither. They appeared with an arrogant air and an ill-disguised contempt for that Assembly of lawyers, for whom they cared almost as little as they did in days of yore, when, with a lofty demeanour, they overwhelmed the bar with their severe lectures. But now the tables were turned. Besides, what did individuals matter? It was before reason that they had to reply, before principles, set forth for the first time.

Their haughtiness entirely disappeared, and they remained, as it were, nailed to the ground, when, from that Assembly of advocates, they listened to the following words: "You say Brittany is not represented; and yet she has, in this Assembly, sixty-six representatives. It is not in antiquated charters, in which cunning, combined with power, found means to oppress the people, that you must look for the rights of the nation; it is in

Reason; its rights are as ancient as time, and as sacred as nature."

The president of the *parlement* of Brittany had not defended the *parlement* which formed the matter of debate. He defended Brittany, which neither wished nor needed to be defended.

He alleged the clauses of the marriage of Anne of Brittany, a marriage that was no better than a divorce organised and stipulated for by Brittany and France. He pleaded for this divorce, as a right that was to be eternal. A hateful insidious defence, addressed not to the Assembly, but to provincial pride,—a provocation exciting civil war.

Had Brittany to fear she would become less by becoming France? Was it possible that such a separation should last forever? Was it not necessary that a more real alliance should be sooner or later effected? Brittany has gained enough in sharing the glory of so great an empire; and certainly this empire has also gained, we must frankly confess, in espousing that poor yet glorious country, its bride of granite, that mother of noble hearts and vigorous resistance.

Thus the defence of the *parlements*, being untenable, subsided into a defence of provinces and provincial estates. But these estates found themselves still weaker in one respect. The *parlements* were homogeneous organised bodies; but the estates were nothing better than monstrous and barbarous constructions, heterogeneous and discordant. The best to be said in their favour was that a few of them, those of Languedoc, for instance, had administered injustice wisely and prudently. Others, those of Dauphiné, under the able direction of Mounier, had made a noble beginning on the eve of the Revolution.

This same Mounier, a fugitive, and belonging to the reaction-party, had abused his influence over Dauphiné to fix an early convocation of the estates, "in which they would examine whether the king were really free." At Toulouse one or two hundred nobles and parliamentarians had made a show of assembling the estates. Those of Cambrésis, an imperceptible assembly in an imperceptible country, which termed themselves estates, had also claimed their privilege of not being France, and said, like those of Brittany, "We are a nation."

The false and faithless representatives of these provinces came boldly and spoke in their name; but they were violently contradicted at the very same moment. The municipalities, roused into life, and full of vigour and energy, came one after the other before the National Assembly to say to those Estates and *Parlements:* "Speak not in the name of the people; the people do not know you; you represent only yourselves,—venality, hereditary right, and Gothic privilege."

The municipality, a real living body (this we perceive from the violence of its blows), used towards those old artificial bodies, those ancient barbarous ruins, the equivalent of the language already expressed to the body of the clergy: "You do not exist!"

They appeared pitiable to the Assembly. All it did to those of Brittany was to declare them incapable of doing what they refused to do,—to interdict them from all public functions, until they had presented a request for leave to take the oath (January 11th).

The same indulgence was granted, two months later, to the *parlement* of Bordeaux, which, taking advantage of the troubles in the south, ventured so far as to make a kind of suit against the Revolution, declaring, in a public document, that it had done nothing but mischief, and insolently terming the Assembly *the deputies of the bailiwicks.*

The Assembly had but little occasion to act with severity: this was more than sufficiently carried out by the people. Brittany quelled her *parlement,* and that of Bordeaux was accused before the Assembly by the very city of Bordeaux which sent the ardent and youthful Fonfrède expressly to support the accusation (March 4th).

These attempts at resistance became quite insignificant amid the immense popular movement manifested on all sides. Never, since the Crusades, had there been so general and deep a commotion among all classes of the people. In 1790 it was the enthusiasm of fraternity; about to become the enthusiasm of war.

Where did this enthusiasm first begin? Everywhere. No precise origin can be assigned to these great spontaneous facts.

In the summer of 1789, from the general dread of *brigands*, solitary habitations, and even the hamlets felt alarmed at their isolated position: one hamlet united with another, their villages with villages, and even the town with the country. Federation, mutual assistance, brotherly friendship, fraternity,—such was the idea, the title of their covenants. Few, very few are yet written.

The idea of fraternity is at first rather limited. It implies only the neighbours, or at most the province. The great federation of Brittany and Anjou has still this provincial character. Convoked for the 26th of November, it was completed in January. At the central point of the peninsula, far from the roads, and in the solitary little town of Pontivy the representatives of a hundred and fifty thousand national guards assembled together. Those on horseback alone wore a common uniform, a red body with black facings; all the others, distinguished by rose, amaranth, or chamois facings, reminded one in their very union, of the diversity of the towns that deputed them. In their covenant of union, to which they invite all the municipalities in the kingdom, they insist nevertheless on always forming a family of Brittany and Anjou, "whatever be the new division of departments, necessary for the administration." They establish a system of correspondence between their cities. In the general disorganisation, in their continuing uncertainty about the success of the new order, they take measures that will ensure their own separate organization.

In less isolated places, in districts traversed by high roads, and especially on rivers, this brotherly covenant assumes a more extensive significance. The rivers which, under the old order of things, by the vast number of tolls and interior custom-house duties, were hardly anything better than barriers, obstacles, and impediments, become under the government of liberty, the principal means of circulation, and bring men into a correspondence of ideas and sentiments as much as of commerce.

It was near the Rhône, at the petty town Etoile, two leagues from Valence, that *the province was abjured* for the first time; fourteen rural communes of Dauphiné unite together and devote themselves to the grand unity of France (Nov. 29th, 1789),—a noble answer from these peasants to politicians like Mounier, who were making an appeal to provincial pride, to the spirit of dissension, and were endeavouring to arm Dauphiné against France.

This federation, renewed at Montélimart, is no longer that of Dauphiné alone, but composed of several provinces of either bank, Dauphiné and Vivarais, Provence and Languedoc; this time, therefore, they are *Frenchmen.*—Grenoble sends to it, of her own accord, in spite of her municipality and of politicians; she no longer cares about her position as a capital-town; she prefers being France.—All repeat together the sacred oath, which the peasants had already taken in November:—No more provinces! one native-land! and to give one another mutual aid and provisions, passing grain from one place to another by the Rhône (December 13th).

That sacred river, flowing by so many races of men, of different nation and language, seems to hasten to exchange different products, sentiments, and ideas; and is, in its varied course, the universal mediator, the sociable *Genius,* the bond of fellowship of the South. It was at its delightful and smiling point of junction with the Saône, that, in the reign of Augustus, sixty nations of the Gauls had raised their altar; and it is at the sternest point, at the deep, melancholy passage commanded by the copper mountains of the Ardèche, in the Roman province of Valence, seated beneath her eternal arc, that was organized, on the 31st of January, 1790, the first of our grand federations. Ten thousand men were up in arms, who must have represented several hundreds of thousands. There were thirty thousand spectators. In presence of that immutable antiquity, those everlasting mountains, and that noble river, ever changing yet ever the same, the solemn oath was taken. The ten thousand bending one knee, and the thirty thousand kneeling, swore all together the holy unity of France.

The whole was grand; both the time and place; and, what is more rare, the language was by no means inferior. It was full of the wisdom of Dauphiné and the simplicity of Vivarais, the whole being animated with the breath of Languedoc and Provence. At the commencement of a career of sacrifices which they clearly foresaw, at the moment they were beginning the great but difficult task, those excellent citizens recommended to one another to found liberty on its only solid base "virtue," on what renders devotion easy, "simplicity, sobriety, and pureness of heart."

I would also like to know what was said at Voute, almost opposite, on the other side of the Rhone, by the hundred thousand armed peasants who there cemented the union of the province of Vivarais. It was still the month of February, a rough season in those cold mountains; neither weather, misery, nor the horrible roads, prevented those poor people from arriving at the place of meeting. Neither torrents, ice, precipices, nor the thawing of the snow was able to arrest their march. A new breath of life was in the air which inspired them with a glow of enthusiasm; citizens for the first time, and summoned from their remote snowy regions by the unknown name of liberty, they set forth, like the kings and shepherds of the East at the birth of Christ, seeing clearly in the middle of night, and following unerringly, through the wintry mists, the dawn of spring, and the star of France.

Long before this, the fourteen towns of Franche-Comté, feeling uneasy between the castles and the pillagers forcing and burning the castles, had united at Besançon and promised one another mutual assistance.

Thus, far above the riots, dangers, and fears, I hear a great and mighty word, at once sweet and formidable, one that will restrain and calm everything. Fraternity, gradually rising and re-echoed by those imposing assemblies, each of which is a great people.

And in proportion as these associations are formed, they associate also one with another: like those great farandoles of the South, where each new company of dancers join hands with another, and the same dance transports whole populations.

At the same period, the noble heart of Burgundy displayed itself by two early illustrious examples.

In the very depth of winter, and during the general scarcity, Dijon calls upon all the municipalities of Burgundy to hasten to the assistance of starving Lyons.[18]

Lyons was starving, and Dijon grieves. Thus these words fraternity and national bond of fellowship, are not words only, but sincere sentiments, real and efficacious actions.

The same city of Dijon, joined to the federations of Dauphiné and Vivarais (themselves united to those of Provence and Languedoc) invites Burgundy to give her hand to the cities of Franche-Comté. Thus, the immense farandole of the southeast, joining and ever forming new links, advances as far as Dijon, which is connected with Paris.

All abandoning egotism, all wishing to do good to all and to feed one another, provisions begin to circulate easily, and plenty is again restored; it seemed as though, by some miracle of fraternity, a new harvest had been made in the dead of winter.

In all this, there is not a vestige of that spirit of exclusion and local isolation later designated by the name of federalism. On the contrary, there is here a covenant sworn for the unity of France. These federations of provinces look all towards the centre; all invoke, join, and devote themselves to the National Assembly, that is to say, to unity. They all thank Paris for its brotherly summons; one town demands its assistance, another to be affiliated to its national guard. Clermont had proposed to it in November a general association of municipalities. At

---

[18] Archives of Dijon. I owe this communication to the obliging service of M. Garnier.

that period, indeed, threatened by the Estates, the *Parlements*, and the Clergy, the rural districts being doubtful, all the safety of France seemed to depend on a close union of the cities. Thank heaven, the great federations gave a happier solution to this difficulty.

In their movement they transported, with the towns, an immense number of the rural population. This has been seen in the case of Dauphiné, Vivarais, and Languedoc.

In Brittany, Quercy, Rouergue, Limousin, and Périgord, the country places are less peaceful; in February there were several disturbances and acts of violence. The beggars, supported till then with great difficulty by the municipalities, gradually spread abroad over the whole country. The peasants begin again to force the castles, burn the feudal charters, and execute by main force the declarations of the 4th of August, the promises of the Assembly. Whilst the latter is ruminating, terror reigns in the rural districts. The nobles forsake their castles and remove to town to conceal themselves and seek safety among their enemies. And those enemies defend them. The national guards of Brittany, who have just sworn their league against the nobles, now arm in their favour, and go to defend those manors where they were conspiring against them.[19] Those of Quercy and the South in general were equally magnanimous.

The pillagers were checked, the peasantry kept in order, and gradually initiated and interested in the march of the Revolution. To whom, indeed, could it be more profitable than to them? It had delivered from tithes such of them as were pro-

---

[19] The National Guards of 1790 were by no means an aristocracy, as some writers, by a strange anachronism, have given us to understand. In most of the towns, they were, as I have said, literally *everybody*. All were interested in preventing the devastation of the rural districts, which would have rendered cultivation impossible, and famished France. Besides, those transient disturbances had by no means the character of a *Jacquerie*. In certain neighbourhoods of Brittany and Provence, the peasants themselves repaired the damage that had been committed. In a castle where they found only a sick lady with her children, they abstained from every kind of disturbance, &c.

prietors; and among the rest it was going to create proprietors by hundreds and thousands. It was about to honour them with the sword, to raise them in one day from serfs to nobles, to conduct them throughout the earth to glory and adventures, and to create from them princes and kings,—nay, more, heroes!

V

Resistance—The Queen and Austria (October to February)

FROM the sublime spectacle of fraternity, I fall, alas! to the earth, among intrigues and plots.

Nobody appreciated the immensity of the movement; nobody fathomed that rapid and invincible tide rising from October to July. Whole populations, till then unknown to one another, met and united. Distant towns and provinces, which even lately were still divided by an ancient spirit of rivalry, marched forth, as it were, to meet one another, embraced and fraternised. This novel and striking fact was scarcely noticed by the great thinkers of the age. If it had been possible for it to be noticed by the queen and the Court, it would have discouraged all useless opposition. For who, whilst the ocean is rising, would dare to march against it?

The queen deceived herself at the very outset; and she remained mistaken. She looked upon the 6th of October as an affair prepared by the Duke of Orleans, a trick played against her by the enemy. She yielded; but, before her departure, she conjured the king, in the name of his son, to go to Paris only to wait for an opportunity to escape.[20]

On the very first day, the Mayor of Paris, on entreating him to fix his residence there, and telling him that the centre of

---

[20] Beaulieu, ii., 203.

the empire was the natural abode of the kings, obtained from him only this answer: "That he would willingly make Paris his *most habitual* residence."

On the 9th appeared the king's proclamation, in which he announced that if he had not been in Paris, *he feared that there might have been great disorder;* that, the constitution being made, he would realise his project of going *to visit his provinces;* that he indulged in the hope of receiving from them proofs of their affection, of seeing them *encourage the National Assembly,* &c.

This ambiguous letter, which seemed to provoke Royalist addresses, decided the commune of Paris to write also to the provinces; it desired to comfort them, it said, against certain insinuations, *casting a veil over the plot* which had nearly overthrown the new order of things; and it *offered a sincere* fraternal alliance to all the communes in the kingdom.

The queen refused to receive the conquerors of the Bastille, who had come to present to her their homage. She gave an audience to the market-women (*dames de la Halle*), but at a distance, and as though separated and defended by the wide skirts of the ladies of the court, who placed themselves before her. By thus acting, she estranged from her a very royalist class; several of the market-women disavowed the 6th of October; and themselves arrested some female vagrants who were entering houses to extort money.

These sad mistakes committed by the queen were not calculated to increase confidence. And how indeed could it have existed amid the attempts of the Court, ever miscarrying and always discovered? Between October and March, a plot was discovered nearly every month (those of Augeard, Favras, Maillebois, &c.)

On the 25th of October, Augeard, the queen's keeper of the seals, was arrested, and at his house was found a plan to conduct the king to Metz.

On the 21st of November, in the Assembly, the committee of inquiry, provoked by Malouet, silences the latter by telling him there exists a new plot to carry off the king to Metz, and that he, Malouet, knows all about it.

On the 25th of December the Marquis de Favras, another agent for carrying off the king, was arrested; he had been recruiting partisans in Paris. If the purpose of all this had been to complete the job of stirring up the people's imagination, to drive them mad with distrust and fears by surrounding them with shady plots and snares, this would have been just the way to go about it. It would have been necessary to keep showing the people, through a series of clumsy conspiracies, the king in flight, the king at the head of the armies, the king returning to starve out Paris.

Doubtless, supposing liberty to have been firmly established and the opposition less vigorous, it would have been better to have allowed the king and the queen to escape, to have conducted them to their proper place,—the frontier, and made a present of them to Austria.

But, in the fluctuating and uncertain state in which our poor country then was, having for her director an assembly of metaphysicians, and against her men of execution and vigour, like M. de Bouillé, our naval officers, and the nobles of Brittany, it was very difficult to part with so great a hostage as the king, and thus bestow on all those powers that unity of which they were in want.

Therefore, the people kept watch night and day, prowling around the Tuileries, and trusting to nobody. They went every morning to see whether the king had not departed; and they held the national guard and its commander responsible for his presence. A thousand reports were in circulation, copied by violent furious newspapers, which were denouncing plots at random. The moderate party felt indignant, denied, and would not believe them . . . And yet the plot was none the less discovered the next day. The result of all this was that the king, who was by no means a prisoner in October, was so in November or December.

The queen had overlooked one admirable irreparable opportunity,—the moment when Lafayette and Mirabeau were united in her favour (the end of October).

She was unwilling to be saved by the Revolution, or men such as Mirabeau and Lafayette; this true princess of the house of Lorraine, courageous and rancorous, desired to conquer and be revenged.

She risked everything inconsiderately, evidently thinking, that after all, as Henrietta of England said in a tempest, queens could not be drowned.

Maria-Theresa had been on the point of perishing, and yet had not perished. This heroic remembrance of the mother had much influence over the daughter, though without reason; the mother had the people on her side, and the daughter had them against her.

Lafayette, though but little inclined to be a royalist before the 6th of October, had become so sincerely ever since. He had saved the queen and protected the king. Such actions form attachments. The prodigious efforts he was obliged to make for the maintenance of order, caused him to desire earnestly that the kingly power should resume its strength; and he wrote twice to M. de Bouillé, intreating him to unite with him for the safety of royalty. M. de Bouillé, in his memoirs, bitterly regrets his not having listened to him.

Lafayette had performed a service agreeable to the queen, by driving away the Duke of Orleans. He seemed to be acting the part of a courtier. It is curious to behold the general, the man of business, following the queen to the churches, and attending the service when she performed her Easter devotions.[21] For the sake of the queen and the king, Lafayette overcame the repugnance he felt for Mirabeau.

As early as the 15th of October, Mirabeau had offered his services, by a note, which his friend Lamarck, the queen's

---

[21] By so doing, Lafayette wanted, I think, to pay also his court to his devout and virtuous wife. He hastened to write and tell her this important event.

attendant, did not show even to the king. On the 20th came another note from Mirabeau; but this one was sent to Lafayette, who had a conversation with the orator, and conducted him to the house of the minister Montmorin.

This unexpected succour, though a god-send, was very badly received. Mirabeau would have wished the king to be satisfied with a million (of francs) for his whole expenditure; to withdraw, not to the army at Metz, but to Rouen, and thence publish ordinances more popular than the decrees of the Assembly.[22] Thus there would be no civil war, the king making himself more revolutionary than the Revolution itself.

A strange project, proving the confidence and easy credulity of genius! If the Court had accepted it for a day, if it had consented to act this borrowed part, it would have been to hang Mirabeau on the morrow.

He might have seen very plainly, as far back as November, what he had to expect from those whom he wished to save. He wanted to be minister, and to keep at the same time his predominant position in the National Assembly. For this purpose, he desired the Court to contrive to secure for him the support and connivance, or at least the silence, of the royalist deputies; but, so far from doing so, the Keeper of the Seals warned and animated several deputies, even in the opposition, against the project. In the ministry, and at the Jacobins (this club was scarcely open), they strove at the same time to disqualify Mirabeau for the ministry. Two upright men, Montlosier on the right side of the Assembly, and Lanjuinais on the left, spoke to the same effect. They proposed, and caused it to be decreed, "that no deputy, on duty, nor for three years afterwards, could accept any place in the government." Thus the Royalists succeeded in debarring from the ministry the great orator, who would have been the support of their party (November 7th).

The queen, as we have said, was unwilling to be saved by

---

[22] See the documents quoted in the *Histoire,* by M. Droz, and in the *Mémoires de Mirabeau.*

the Revolution, neither would she be so by the princes and the emigrant party. She had been too well acquainted with the Count d'Artois not to know that he was of very little value; and she very properly distrusted Monsieur as a person of a false and uncertain character.

What then were her hopes, her views, and her secret counsellors?

We must not reckon Madame de Lamballe,[23] a pretty, little, insignificant woman, and a dear friend of the queen's, but devoid of ideas and conversation, and little deserving the terrible responsibility laid to her charge. She seemed to form a centre, doing gracefully the honours of the queen's private salon, on the ground floor of the Pavilion of Flora (at the Tuileries). Many of the nobility would go there; an indiscreet, frivolous, inconsiderate race, who thought, as in the time of the Fronde, to gain the day by satirical verses, witticisms, and lampoons. There, they would read a very witty newspaper, called the *Acts of the Apostles,* and sing ditties about the king's captivity, which made everybody weep, both friends and enemies.

The connections of Marie-Antoinette were entirely with the nobles, very little with the priests. She was no more a bigot than her brother Joseph II.

The nobles were not a party; they were a numerous, divided, and disconnected class; but the priests were a party, a very close, and materially a very powerful body. The transient dissension between the curates and the prelates made it appear weak; but the power of the hierarchical system, the party spirit, the Pope, the voice of the Holy-See, would presently restore the unity of the clergy. Then, from its inferior members, it was about to derive incalculable powers in the land, and in the men of the land, the inhabitants of the rural districts; it was about

---

[23] Pretty is the proper expression; nothing could be farther from beauty: very small features, a very low forehead, and very little brain. Her hands were rather large, says Madame de Genlis. The portrait at Versailles shows very plainly her extraction and her country; she was a nice little Savoyard. Her hair, concealed by powder, was luxuriant and admirable. (Alas! this appeared but too plainly!)

to bring against the people of the Revolution a whole nation,—Vendée against France.

Marie-Antoinette saw nothing of all this. These great moral powers were to her a dead letter. She was meditating victory, physical force, Bouillé and Austria.

When the papers of Louis XVI. were found on the 10th of August in the iron chest, people read with astonishment that, during the first years of his marriage, he had looked upon his youthful bride as a mere agent of Austria.[24]

Having been married by M. de Choiseul, against his will, into that twice hostile house of Lorraine and Austria, and, obliged to receive into his palace the abbé de Vermond, spy of Maria-Theresa, he persevered so long in his distrust as to remain nineteen years without speaking to this Vermond.

It is well known how the pious empress had distributed among her numerous family their several parts, employing her daughters especially as the agents of her policy. By Caroline, she governed Naples; and by Marie-Antoinette she expected to govern France. The latter, a true Lorraine-Austrian, pestered Louis XVI. for ten years to oblige him to give the ministry to Choiseul, himself a Lorraine and the friend of the empress. She succeeded at least in making him accept Breteuil, who, like Choiseul, had been at first ambassador at Vienna, and, like him again, belonged entirely to that court. It was again the same influence (Vermond's over the queen) which, at a more recent period, overcame the scruples of Louis XVI., and made him take for his prime minister an atheist, the Archbishop of Toulouse.

The death of Maria-Theresa, and the severe language of Joseph II. on his sister and Versailles, would, one would think, have rendered the latter less favourable towards Austria. Yet it was at this very time that she persuaded the king to grant the millions which Joseph II. wanted to extort from the Dutch.

---

[24] He caused her correspondence with Vienna to be watched by Thugut, in whom she confided.—Letter dated October 17th, 1774, quoted by Brissot, *Mémoires*, iv., 120.

In 1789 the queen had three confidants,—three advisers,—Vermond, ever in the Austrian interest; Breteuil, no less so; and lastly, M. Mercy d'Argenteau, the Austrian ambassador. Behind this old man, we may perceive another urging him forward,—old Prince de Kaunitz, for seventy years a minister of the Austrian monarchy; these two coxcombs, or rather these old women, who seemed to be entirely occupied with toilet and trifles, directed the queen of France.

A fatal direction, a dangerous alliance! Austria was then in so bad a situation, that, far from serving Marie-Antoinette, she could only be an obstacle to her in acting, a guide to lead to evil, and impel her towards every absurd step that the Austrian interest might require.

That Catholic and devout Austria having become half philosophical in her ideas under Joseph II., had found means to have nobody on her side. Hungary, her own sword, was turned against her. The Belgian priests had robbed her of the Low-Countries, with the encouragement of the three Protestant powers, England, Holland, and Prussia. And what was Austria doing in the meantime? She was turning her back on Europe, marching through the deserts of the Turks, and exhausting her best armies for the advantage of Russia.

The emperor was in no better plight than his empire. Joseph II. was consumptive; he was dying and beyond the power of remedy. He had showed, in the Belgian business, a deplorable vacillation of conduct: first furious threats of fire and sword, and barbarous executions which excited horror throughout Europe; next (on the 25th of November) a general amnesty, which nobody would accept.

Austria would have been lost if the Revolution of Belgium had found support in the Revolution of France.[25]

---

[25] Any vigorous movement, even a counter-revolutionary one, might have been prejudicial to her. If our bishops, for instance, had been aided by the king in their attempts, and obtained any advantage, their success would have encouraged the Belgian prelates who had expelled Austria. She found it expedient for the time being to turn moderate, nay, liberal, in order to gain over the Belgian *progressists,* whose moderate liberal principles were

Here in France, everybody thought that the two revolutions were about to act in concert and march forward together. The most brilliant of our journalists, Camille Desmoulins, had, without awaiting events, united in one hope these sister countries by intitling his journal *Revolutions of France and Brabant.*

The obstacle to this was that the one was a revolution made by priests, and the other by philosophers. The Belgians, however, being aware that they could not rely upon their protectors, the three Protestant powers, applied to France. Vander Noot, the champion of the clergy of the Low-Countries, the great agitator of the Catholic mob, did not scruple to write to the Assembly and the king. The letter was sent back (December 10th). Louis XVI. showed himself the true brother-in-law of the emperor.[26] The Assembly despised a revolution made by abbés. The Tuileries, entirely governed by the ambassador of Austria, succeeded in lulling the honest Lafayette (and he the Assembly) into security.

The queen's agent, Lamarck, departed in December to offer his sword to the Belgians, his countrymen, against the Austrians. He had, however, the queen's consent, and consequently the Austrian ambassador's. They had hoped that Lamarck, a nobleman of pleasing manners and fond of novelty, might serve as a mediator, and perhaps induce the Belgians, then the conquering party, to accept a middle course that would reconcile everything,—a spurious constitution under an Austrian prince. With the word constitution, they lull Lafayette into security a second time.

Lamarck, very justly treated with suspicion by the party of

---

very similar to Lafayette's. If Lafayette had lent his support to those *progressists,* they would most certainly have rejected the alliance of Austria, and preferred the assistance of France. Therefore the interest of Austria was, that nothing should be done in France, either one way or the other.

[26] I do not think that the idea of making the Duke of Orleans King of Brabant was ever seriously entertained at the Tuileries, as some writers have stated. The surest way of being in the good graces of the Court was to testify much interest for the Emperor. This is also the line of conduct followed by Livarot, the commandant of Lille.—(*Correspondance inédite,* November 30th and December 13th, 1789.)

the Belgian priests and the aristocracy, succeeded better with those who were called *progressists*. Austria, in order to divide her enemies, was then giving out that she was a partisan of progress; and the accession of Leopold, the philanthropic re-former, contributed much to give credit to this falsehood (February 20th). In her indirect participation in all this, the queen did herself much harm. She ought to have allied herself more and more closely with the clergy. Austria, in her struggle with the clergy, had interests diametrically opposite.

Apparently she hoped that, if the Emperor, coming to terms with the Belgians, at length found himself free to act, she would be able to find shelter under his protection, show the Revolution a war ready to break out against France, and per-haps strengthen Bouillé's little army with a few Austrian troops.

This was a wrong calculation. All that required much time; and there was none to spare. Austria, extremely egotistical, was a very distant and very doubtful ally.

However this may be, the two brothers-in-law pursued exactly the same line of conduct. In the same month, Louis XVI. and Leopold both declared themselves the friends of liberty, the zealous defenders of constitutions, &c.

The same conduct in two situations diametrically opposite. Leopold was acting very well to recover Belgium: he was dividing his enemies and strengthening his friends. Louis XVI., on the contrary, far from strengthening his friends, was casting them, by this parade, into utter discouragement; he was paralysing the clergy, the nobility, and the counter-revolution.

Necker, Malouet, and the moderate party, believed that the king, by making an almost revolutionary constitutional pro-fession of faith, might constitute himself the leader of the Rev-olution. It was thus that the counsellors of Henry III. had induced him to take the false step of calling himself the Leader of the League.

It is true the opportunity seemed favourable. The riots of January had excited much alarm on the subject of property. In presence of this great social interest, it was supposed that every political interest would appear of minor importance. The state of disorganisation was frightful; and the authority took care not to remedy it; in one place it was really extinct; in another it *pretended to be dead,* as one of the brothers Lameth used to say. Many people had had revolution enough, and more than enough; and from discouragement, would willingly have sacrificed their golden dreams for peace and unity.

At the same time (from the 1st to the 4th of February) there occurred two events of similar meaning:

First, the opening of the club of the *Impartial* (composed of Malouet, Virieu, &c.). Their impartiality consisted, as they tell us in their declaration, in *restoring power to the king,* and *preserving church property,* in submitting the alienation of the ecclesiastical estate to the will of the provinces.

On the 4th of February, the king unexpectedly presents himself before the Assembly, makes an affecting speech which filles everybody with surprise and emotion. It was incredible, marvellous! The king was secretly in love with that very constitution which stripped him of his power. He commands and admires, especially the beautiful division of the departments. Only, he advises the Assembly to postpone a part of the reforms. He deplores the disorders, and defends and consoles the clergy and the nobility; but, in short, he is, he declares, before everything else, the friend of the constitution.

He presented himself thus before the Assembly, then embarrassed about the means of restoring order, and seemed to say: You know not what to do? Well, give me back my power.

The scene had a prodigious effect. The Assembly lost its reason. Barère was drowned in tears. The king withdrew, and the Assembly crowded about him and escorted him back to the queen, who received the deputation, in presence of the Dauphin. Still haughty and gracious: "Here is my son," said she, "I will teach him to cherish liberty, and I hope he will be its support."

On that day she was not the daughter of Maria-Theresa, but the sister of Leopold. Shortly afterwards, her brother issued his hypocritical manifesto, in which he declared himself to be the friend of liberty and of the constitution of the Belgians; nay, he went so far as to tell them that after all they had the right to take up arms against him, their emperor.

To return; the Assembly seemed completely delirious, no longer knowing what it said. It arose in a mass and swore fidelity to the constitution which, as yet, did not exist. The galleries joined in those transports with inconceivable enthusiasm. Everybody began to take the oath, at the Hôtel-de-Ville, at La Grève, and in the streets. A *Te Deum* was sung; and Paris illuminated in the evening. And, indeed, why should they not rejoice? The Revolution is effected, and this time thoroughly.

From the 5th to the 15th of February, there was nothing but a succession of fêtes both at Paris and in the provinces. On all sides, and in every public thoroughfare, the people crowded together to take the oath. School-boys and children were led thither in procession; and the whole country was transported with joy and enthusiasm.

Many of the friends of liberty were frightened at this movement, thinking it might turn to the king's advantage. This was a mistake. The Revolution was so powerful in its nature, and so buoyant in its spirit, that every new event, whether for or against it, ever favoured it ultimately and impelled it still faster. This affair of the oath ended in what always happens in every strong emotion. In uttering words nobody attributed to them any other meaning than what he felt in his heart. Many a one who had taken the oath to the king, had meant nothing more than swearing fidelity to his native land.

It was remarked that at the *Te Deum*, the king had not gone to Notre-Dame; that he had not, as had been hoped, sworn at the altar. He was very willing to lie, but not to perjure himself.

On the 9th of February, whilst the fêtes still continued, Grégoire and Lanjuinais said that the cause of the riots was the non-execution of the decrees of the 4th of August; consequently, that they ought not to halt, but to proceed.

The attempts of the Royalists to restore power and military

force to royal authority, were not happy. Many attempted a ruse, saying that *at least in the rural districts*, it was necessary to allow the military to act without the authorisation of the municipalities. Cazalès tried audacity, and broached the strange advice to give the king a dictatorship *for three months;* —a clumsy trick. Mirabeau, Buzot, and several others, frankly declared that the executive power was not to be trusted. The Assembly would confide in none but the municipalities, gave them full power to act, and made them responsible for such disturbances as they were able to prevent.

The extraordinary audacity of Cazalès' proposal can only be accounted for by its date (February 20th). A sanguinary sacrifice had been made on the 18th, which appeared to answer for the good faith of the court.

It had at that time two suits, two trials on its hands, those of Besenval and Favras.

Besenval, accused for the events of the 14th of July, had after all only executed the orders of his superior, the minister —the king's own commands. However, his being considered innocent would seem to condemn the taking of the Bastille and even the Revolution. He was especially odious as being a queen's man, the ex-confidant of her parties at Trianon, an old friend of Choiseul's, and, as such, belonging to the Austrian cabal.

The Court was less interested about Favras. He was an agent of Monsieur; and had undertaken, in his name, to carry off the king. Monsieur, probably, was to have been lieutenant-general, perhaps regent, if the king had been suspended, as some of the Parliamentarians and friends of the princes had proposed. Lafayette says in his memoirs, that Favras was to have begun by killing Bailly and Lafayette.

On Favras being arrested in the night of the 25th of December, Monsieur, much alarmed, took the singular step of going to justify himself—(where do you suppose? Before what tribunal?)—before the city of Paris. The municipal magistrates were by no means qualified to receive such an act. Monsieur denied all association with Favras, said he had no knowledge of the business, and made a hypocritical parade of revolutionary sentiments and his love of liberty.

Favras displayed much courage, and ennobled his life by his death. He made a very good defence, compromising nobody any more than was necessary. He had been given to understand that it was necessary that he should die discreetly, and he did so. The long and cruel promenade to which he was condemned, the penance at Notre-Dame, &c., did not shake his resolution. At La Grève, he requested to depose once more, and was not hanged until dark, by torchlight (February 18th). It was the first time a nobleman had been hanged. The people testified a furious impatience, always believing that the Court would find means to save him. His papers, taken possession of by the magistrate in charge of civil cases, were (says Lafayette) given up by the daughter of this magistrate to Monsieur, on his succeeding to the throne as Louis XVIII., who burned them in great haste.

On the Sunday following the execution, the widow of Favras and her son attended in mourning at the public dinner of the king and queen. The Royalists thought they would exalt and welcome with affection the family of the victim. The queen dared not even raise her eyes.

Then they perceived the state of impotency to which the Court was reduced, and how little support they might expect who devoted their lives to its service.

As early as the 4th of February, the king's visit to the Assembly and his profession of patriotic faith had much discouraged them. The Viscount de Mirabeau withdrew in despair and broke his sword. For, indeed, what could he believe; or what could it mean? The Royalists had the alternative, either of believing the king to be a liar, a turn-coat, or a deserter from his own party. Was it true that the king was no longer a royalist? Or else, was he sacrificing his clergy and faithful nobility, in order to save a remnant of royalty?

Bouillé, left without orders, and absolutely ignorant of what he had to do, then fell into the deepest despondency. Such was also the feeling of many nobles, officers of the army or navy, who then abandoned their country. Bouillé himself requested permission to do the same, and serve abroad. The king sent him word to remain, because he should need him. People had begun to hope too soon. The Revolution was finished on the 14th of July; finished on the 6th of October; and finished on the 4th of February; and yet I begin to fear that in March it is not quite ended.

What matter! Liberty, mature and powerful even in her cradle, needs not be alarmed at her antagonists. In a moment, she has just overcome the most formidable disorder and anarchy. Those pillages in the rural districts, that warfare against the castles, which, extending further and further, was threatening the whole country with one immense conflagration; all subsides in a moment. The movement of January and February is already appeased in March. Whilst the king was presenting himself as the only guarantee of public tranquillity, and the Assembly was seeking but not finding the means of restoring it, France had created it herself. The enthusiastic transport of fraternity had outstepped the speed of legislation; the knotty point which nobody could solve, had been settled for ever by national magnanimity. The cities all in arms, had marched forth for the defence of the chateaux, and protected the nobles, their enemies.

The great meetings continue, and become more numerous every day, so formidable, that without acting, by their mere presence, they necessarily intimidate the two enemies of France; on one hand, anarchy and pillage, on the other the counter-revolution. They are no longer merely the more thin and scattered populations of the South that now assemble; but the massy and compact legions of the great provinces of the north; now it is Champaign with her hundred thousand men; now Lorraine with her hundred thousand; next, the Vosges, Alsace, and others. A movement full of grandeur, disinterested, and devoid of jealousy. All France is grouping, uniting, and gravitating towards union. Paris summons the provinces, and wishes to unite to herself every commune. And the provinces wish, of their own accord, without the least particle of envy, to unite still more closely. On the 20th of March, Brittany demands that France should send to Paris one man in every thousand. Bordeaux has already demanded a civic festival for the 14th of July. These two propositions presently will make but one. France will invite all France to this grand festival, the first of the new religion.

VI

Continuation—The Queen and Austria —The Queen and Mirabeau—The Army (March to May, 1790)

THE conspiracy of Favras was devised by Monsieur; that of Maillebois (discovered in March) belonged to the Count d'Artois and the emigrants. The Court, without being ignorant of these, seemed to follow rather the counsel in the memorial of Augeard, the queen's keeper of the seals: to refuse, wait, *feign confidence, and let five or six months slip away*. This same watchword was given at Vienna and at Paris.

Leopold was negotiating. He was putting the governments self-styled the friends of liberty—those spurious revolutionists (I mean England and Prussia)—to a serious trial: he was placing them opposite to the Revolution, and they were gradually unmasking. Leopold said to the English: "Does it suit you that I should be forced to yield to France a portion of the Low Countries?" and England drew back; she sacrificed, to that dread, the hope of seizing Ostend. To the Prussians and Germans in general, he said: "Can we abandon our German princes established in Alsace, who are losing their feudal rights?" As early as the 16th of February, Prussia had already spoken in their favour, and proclaimed the right of the empire to demand satisfaction of France.

The whole of Europe belonging to either party,—on one hand Austria and Russia, on the other England and Prussia, were gradually gravitating towards the self-same thought,—the hatred of the Revolution. However, there was this difference, that liberal England and philosophical Prussia needed a little time in order to pass from one pole to the other, to prevail upon themselves to give themselves the lie, to abjure and disown their principles, and avow that they were the enemies of liberty. This worthy struggle between decency and shame was to be treated delicately by Austria; therefore, by waiting, an infinite advantage would be obtained. A little longer, and all honest people would be agreed. Then, left quite alone, what would France do? . . . What an enormous advantage would Austria presently have over her, when assisted by all Europe!

Meanwhile, there was no harm in deluding the revolutionists of France and Belgium with fair words, in lulling them into security, and, if possible, in dividing them.

As soon as ever Leopold was made emperor (February 20th) and published his strange manifesto, in which he adopted the principles of the Belgian revolution, and acknowledged the legality of the insurrection against the emperor (March 2nd), his ambassador, M. Mercy d'Argenteau, prevailed upon Marie-Antoinette to master her repugnance and form an alliance with Mirabeau.

But, nothwithstanding the facility of the orator's character, and his eternal need of money, this alliance was difficult to execute. He had been slighted and rejected at the time when he might have been useful. And now they came to court him, when all was compromised, and perhaps even lost.

In November they had had an understanding with the most revolutionary deputies to exclude Mirabeau from the ministry forever; and now they invited him.

He was summoned for an enterprise that had become impossible, after so many acts of imprudence and three unsuccessful plots.

The ambassador of Austria himself undertook to recall from Belgium the man the most likely to prove the best mediator,

M. de Lamarck, Mirabeau's personal friend, and also personally devoted to the queen.

He returned. On the 15th of March he took to Mirabeau the overtures of the Court, but found him very cool; for his good sense enabled him to perceive that the Court merely proposed to him that they should sink together.

When pressed by Lamarck, he said that the throne could only be restored by establishing it upon the basis of liberty; that if the Court wanted anything else, he would oppose it instead of serving it. And what guarantee had he for this? He himself had just proclaimed before the Assembly how little confidence he put in the executive power. In order to pacify him, Louis XVI. wrote to Lamarck that he had never desired anything but a power limited by the laws.

Whilst this negotiation was pending, the Court was carrying on another with Lafayette. The king gave him a written promise of the most absolute confidence. On the 14th of April, he asked him his opinion on the royal prerogative, and Lafayette was simple enough to give it.

Now, seriously, what was it that the Court wanted? To gain time,—nothing more; to delude Lafayette, neutralise Mirabeau, annihilate his influence, keep him divided between opposite principles, and, perhaps, also to compromise him, as it had served Necker. The Court had ever shown its deepest policy in ruining and destroying its deliverers.

Exactly at the same period, and in the very same manner, the queen's brother, Leopold, was negotiating with the Belgian *progressists* and compromising them; then, when menaced by the people, denounced and prosecuted, they were at length induced to desire the invasion and the re-establishment of Austria.[27]

How can one believe that these precisely identical moves by the brother and the sister occurred purely by chance?

Mirabeau, indeed, had reason to reflect twice before he

---

[27] For the conduct of Leopold in Europe, and especially in Belgium, see Hardenberg, Borgnet, &c.

trusted himself to the Court. It was the time when the king, yielding to the importunate demands of the Assembly, gave up to it the famous *Red Book* (of which we shall presently speak) and the honour of so many persons; all the secret pensioners heard their names cried in the streets. Who could assure Mirabeau that the Court might not think proper, in a short time, to publish also his treaty with it? The negotiation was not very encouraging; offers were made, and then withdrawn: the Court put no confidence in him at all, but demanded his secrets and the opinions of his party.

But a man like Mirabeau was not to be deluded so easily. However great might be his tendency to royalty in his heart, it was impossible to blind so keen-sighted a person. Meanwhile, he proceeded in his usual course: as the organ of the Revolution, his voice was never wanting on decisive occasions; he might have been won over, but he was neither to be silenced, enervated, nor neutralised. Whenever the state of affairs was urgent, the vicious and corrupt politician instantly disappeared; the god of eloquence took possession of him, his native land acted by him, and thundered by his voice.

In the single month of April, whilst the Court was hesitating, bargaining, and concluding, the power of his eloquence smote it twice.

The first blow (which we postpone to the next chapter, in order to keep together whatever relates to the clergy) was his famous apostrophe on Charles IX. and the St. Bartholomew massacre, which is to be found in every memoir: "From hence I behold the window," &c. Never had the priests been stunned by so terrible a blow! (April 13th.)

The second affair, no less serious, was on the question whether the Assembly should dissolve; the powers of several deputies were limited to one year, and this year was drawing to a close. As far back as the 6th of October, a proposal had been made (and then very properly) to dissolve the Assembly. The Court was expecting and watching for the moment of dissolution,—the interregnum,—the ever perilous moment between the Assembly that exists no longer, and the one not yet formed.

Who was to reign in the interval but the king, by ordinances?
And having once resumed his power and seized the sword,
it would be his business to keep it.

Maury and Cazalès in forcible, but irritating and provoking,
speeches, asked the Assembly whether its powers were unlimited,—whether it considered itself a *National Convention;*
they insisted on this distinction between convention and legislative assembly. These subtleties provoked Mirabeau into one
of those magnificent bursts of eloquence which reached the sublime: "You ask," said he, "how, being deputies of bailiwicks,
we have made ourselves a convention? I will answer. The day
when, finding our assembly-room shut, bristling and defiled
with bayonets, we hastened to the first place that could contain us, and swore we would rather perish,—on that day, if we
were not a convention, we became one. Let them now go and
hunt out of the useless nomenclature of civilians the definition
of the words National Convention! Gentlemen, you all know
the conduct of that Roman who, to save his country from a
great conspiracy, had been obliged to outstep the powers conferred upon him by the laws. A captious tribune required from
him the oath that he had respected them. He thought, by that
insidious proposal, to leave the consul no alternative but per-
jury, or an embarrassing avowal. I swear, said that great man,
that I have saved the republic! Gentlemen, I swear also, that
you have saved the commonwealth!"

At that splendid oath, the whole Assembly arose, and decreed that there should be no elections till the constitution was
finished.

The Royalists were stunned by the blow. Several, nevertheless, thought that the hope of their party, the new election,
might even have turned against them; that it might, perhaps,
have brought about a more hostile and violent assembly. In
the immense fermentation of the kingdom, and the increasing
ebullition of public feeling, who could be sure of seeing his
way clearly? The mere organisation of the municipalities had
shaken France to her centre. Scarcely were they formed when,
by their side, societies and clubs were already organised to

watch over them: formidable, but useful societies; eminently useful in such a crisis; a necessary organ and instrument of public distrust, in presence of so many conspiracies.

The clubs will grow greater and greater; it must be so: the state of things requires it. This period is not yet that of their greatest power. For the rest of France, it is the period of federations; but the clubs already reign at Paris.

Paris seems to be watching over France, panting and on the alert; keeping its sixty districts permanently assembled; not acting, but ever ready. It stands listening and uneasy, like a sentinel in the neighbourhood of the enemy. The watch-word "Beware!" is heard every hour; and two voices are incessantly urging it forward,—the club of the Cordeliers, and that of the Jacobins. In the next book, I shall enter those formidable caverns; in this place I abstain. The Jacobins are not yet characterised, being in their infancy, or rather in a spurious constitutional age, in which they are governed by such men as Duport and the Lameths.

The principal character of those great laboratories of agitation and public surveillance, of those powerful machines (I speak especially of the Jacobins), is that, as in the case with all machinery, collective action was far more predominant than individual influence; that the strongest and most heroic individual there lost his advantage. In societies of this kind, active mediocrity rises to importance; but genius has very little weight. Accordingly, Mirabeau never willingly frequented the clubs, nor belonged exclusively to any; paying short visits, and passing an hour at the Jacobins, and another in the same evening at the club of 1789, formed in the Palais-Royal by Sieyès, Bailly, Lafayette, Chapelier, and Talleyrand (May 13).

This was a dignified and elegant club, but devoid of action: true power resided in the old smoky convent of the Jacobins. The dominion of intrigue and commonplace oratory, there sovereignly swayed by the triumvirate of Duport, Barnave, and Lameth, contributed not a little to render Mirabeau accessible to the suggestions of the Court.

This man was contradiction personified. What was he in real-

ity? A royalist, a noble in the most absolute sense. And what
was his action? Exactly the contrary; he shattered royalty with
the thunders of his eloquence.

If he really wished to defend it, he had not a moment to
lose; it was hourly declining. It had lost Paris; but it still possessed large scattered crowds of adherents in the provinces. By
what art could these be collected into a body? This was the
dream of Mirabeau. He meditated organising a vast correspondence, doubtless similar, and in opposition to that of the
Jacobins. Such was the groundwork of Mirabeau's treaty with
the Court (May 10th). He would have constituted in his house
a sort of ministry of public opinion. For this purpose, or under
this pretext, he received money and a regular salary; and as
he was accustomed to do everything, whether good or evil,
boldly and publicly, he established himself in grand style, kept
his carriage and open house in the little mansion which still
exists in the Chaussée d'Antin.

All this was but too manifest; and it appeared still clearer,
when, from the midst of the left of the Assembly, he was seen
to speak with the right in favour of royalty, to obtain for the
king the initiative of making peace or war.

The king had lost the management of the interior, and afterwards power in the law courts: the judges as well as the
municipal magistrates were being abstracted from his prerogative. If he was now to lose war, what would remain of royalty?
Such was the argument of Cazalès. Barnave and the opposite
side had a thousand ready answers without uttering a word
effectually. The truth was, that the king was distrusted; that
the Revolution had been made only by shattering the sword in
his hands; that of all his powers the most dangerous that they
could leave in his hands was war.

The occasion of the debate was this. England had been
alarmed at seeing Belgium offer its alliance to France. Like
the Emperor and Prussia, she began to be afraid of a vivacious
and contagious revolution which captivated both by its ardour
and a character of human (more than national) generality,
very contrary to the English genius. Burke, a talented, but pas-

sionate and venal Irishman, a pupil of the Jesuits of Saint Omer, vented, in parliament, a furious philippic against the Revolution, for which he was paid by his adversary Mr. Pitt. England did not attack France; but she abandoned Belgium to the Emperor, and then went to the other end of the world to seek a quarrel on the sea with Spain, our ally. Louis XVI. intimated to the Assembly that he was arming fourteen vessels.

Thereupon, there arose a long and complicated theoretical discussion on the general question,—to whom belonged the initiative of making war. Little or nothing was said on the particular question, which nevertheless commanded the other. Everybody seemed to avoid it—to be afraid of considering it.

Paris was not afraid of it, but considered it attentively. All the people perceived and said that if the king possessed the sword, the Revolution must perish. There were fifty thousand men at the Tuileries, in the Place Vendôme, and the Rue Saint Honoré, waiting with inexpressible anxiety, and greedily devouring the notes flung to them from the windows of the Assembly, to enable them to keep pace every moment with the progress of the discussion. They were all indignant and exasperated against Mirabeau. On his entering and leaving the Assembly, one showed him a rope, another a pair of pistols.

He demonstrated great coolness. Even at moments when Barnave was occupying the tribune with his long orations, thinking the time had come to overthrow him, Mirabeau did not even listen, but went out to take a walk in the garden of the Tuileries amid the crowd, and paid his respects to the youthful and enthusiastic Madame de Staël, who was there also waiting with the people.

His courage did not make his cause the better. He triumphed in speaking on the theoretical question, on the natural association (in the great act of war) between thought and power, between the Assembly and the king. But all this metaphysical language could not disguise the state of affairs.

His enemies took every unparliamentary means, akin to assassination, which might have caused him to be torn in pieces. During the night they caused an atrocious libel to be written, printed, and circulated. In the morning, on his way to the Assembly, Mirabeau heard on all sides the cry of "The discovery of the great treachery of Count de Mirabeau." The danger, as was always the case with him, inspired him admirably; he overwhelmed his enemies: "I knew well," cried he, "how short was the distance from the Capitol to the Tarpeian rock," &c.

He thus triumphed on the personal question. And even on the question in debate, he made a skilful retreat; at the first opportunity afforded him by the proposal of a less startling formula, he turned about, yielded on the form but gained the substance. It was decided that the king had the right to make the *preparations,* to *direct* the forces as he would, that he *proposed* war to the Assembly, which was to decide on nothing that was not *sanctioned* by the king (May 22nd).

On leaving the Assembly, Barnave, Duport, and Lameth, who were retiring in despair, were applauded and almost carried home by the people, who imagined they had gained the day. They had not the courage to tell them the truth. In reality the Court had the advantage.

It had just experienced on two occasions the power of Mirabeau,—in April against it, and in May in its favour. On the latter occasion, he had made superhuman efforts, sacrificed his popularity, and risked his life. The queen granted him an interview, the only one, in all probability, that he ever had.

There was another weak point in this man which cannot be dissembled. A few proofs of confidence, doubtless exaggerated by the zeal of Lamarck, who wished to bring them together, excited the imagination of the great orator—a credulous being, as such men ever are. He attributed to the queen a superiority of genius and character of which she never gave any proof. On the other hand, he easily believed, in his pride and the sense of his superiority, that he whom nobody could resist would easily captivate the mind of a woman. He would much rather have been the minister of a queen than of a king—the minister, or rather the lover.

The queen was then with the king at Saint Cloud. Surrounded by the national guard, generally disposed in their favour, they found themselves pretty free, in a sort of half captivity, since they used to go every day to take long walks, sometimes to the distance of several leagues, without guards. There were, however, many kind good-natured persons who could not bear the idea that a king and a queen should be the prisoners of their subjects. One day, in the afternoon, the queen heard a slight sound of lamentation in the solitary court of Saint Cloud; she raised the curtain and saw beneath her balcony about fifty persons, countrywomen, priests, and old chevaliers of Saint Louis, who were silently weeping and stifling their sobs.

Mirabeau could not be callous to such impressions. Having remained, in spite of all his vices, a man of ardent imagination and violent passion, he found some happiness in feeling himself the supporter, the defender, perhaps the deliverer of a handsome and captive queen. The mystery of the interview added to his emotion. He went, not in his carriage, but on horseback, in order not to attract any attention, and he was received, not at the castle, but in a very solitary spot, at the highest point in the private park, in a kiosk which crowned that fairy garden. It was at the end of May.

Mirabeau was then very evidently suffering from the malady that brought him to his grave. I do not allude to his excesses and prodigious fatigues. No, Mirabeau died of nothing but the hatred entertained towards him by the people. First adored and then execrated! To have had his prodigious triumph in Provence, where he felt himself pressed upon the bosom of his native land; next, in May, 1790, the people in the Tuileries demanding him that they might hang him! Himself facing the storm, without being sustained by a good conscience, laying his hand upon his breast and feeling there only the money received in the morning from the Court! All this, anger, shame, uncertain hope, were boiling in confusion in his troubled soul. With a dull, leaden, unhealthy complexion, sore red eyes, sunken cheeks, and symptoms of an unwieldy and unwholesome obesity, such appeared the violent Mirabeau, as he slowly wended his way on horseback through the avenue of Saint Cloud, injured and wounded, but not overthrown.

And how much also is that queen changed, who is waiting in her pavilion. Her thirty-five years begin to appear, that affecting age which Van-Dyck so often delighted to paint. Add, moreover, those delicate and faint purple hues which betoken profound grief—a malady, a deep-seated and incurable malady —of the heart and of the body. It is evidently an incessant internal struggle. Her carriage is haughty, and her eyes are dry; yet they show but too plainly that every night is passed in tears. Her natural dignity, and that of her courage and misfortune which constitute another royalty, forbid any kind of distrust. And much does he need to believe in her who now devotes himself to her service.

She was surprised to see that this man so detested and decried, this fatal man the first organ of the Revolution, this monster, in short, was still a man; that he possessed a peculiar charming delicacy, which the energy of his character would seem to exclude. According to every appearance, their conversation was vague and by no means conclusive. The queen had her own intentions, which she kept to herself, and Mirabeau his, which he took no pains to conceal,—to save at the same time the king and liberty. How were they to understand each other? At the close of the interview, Mirabeau addressing himself to the woman as much as to the queen by a gallantry at once respectful and bold: "Madam," said he, "when your august mother admitted one of her subjects to the honour of her presence, she never dismissed him without allowing him to kiss her hand." The queen held forth her hand. Mirabeau bowed; then, raising his head, he exclaimed in a tone of sincerity and pride, "Madam, the monarchy is saved!"

He withdrew, affected, delighted,—and deceived! The queen wrote to her agent in Germany. M. de Flachslanden, that they were making use of Mirabeau, but that there was nothing serious in their connection with him.

At the time he had just gained, at the price of his popularity, and nearly of his life, that dangerous decree which in reality restored to the king the right of making peace and war, the king was causing a search to be made in the archives of the *parlement* for the ancient forms of protestation against the Estates-General, wishing to make a secret one against all the decrees of the Assembly (May 23rd).[28]

Thank heaven the salvation of France did not depend on that great yet credulous man and that deceitful court. A decree restores the sword to the king; but that sword is broken. .The soldier becomes again one of the people, and mingles and fraternises with the people.

M. de Bouillé informs us in his Memoirs that he left nothing untried to set the soldiery and the people in opposition, and inspire the military with hatred and contempt for the citizens.

The officers had eagerly seized an opportunity of raising this hatred still higher, even to the National Assembly, and of calumniating its conduct towards the soldiery. One of the stanchest patriots, Dubois de Crancé, had expounded to the Assembly the lamentable composition of the army, recruited for the most part from vagabonds; and thence deduced the necessity of a new organisation which would make the army what it has been, the flower of France. Now it was this language, so well intentioned towards the military,—this attempt to reform and rehabilitate the army, that they abused. The officers went about saying and repeating everywhere to the soldiers that the Assembly had insulted them. This gave great hope to the Court; for it expected to be thus able to regain possession of the army. These significant words were written to the commandant of Lille from the office of the ministry: "Every day we are gaining ground a little. Only just forget us and reckon us as nothing, and soon we shall be everything" (December 8th, January 3rd).

Vain hope! Was it possible to believe that the soldier would

---

[28] The king sent thither the keeper of the seals himself, who, during the emigration, revealed the fact to Montgaillard. As to the queen's letter to Flachslanden, the original still exists in a private collection, and has been read, not by me, but by a very careful learned person, worthy of confidence, employed in the archives.

long remain blind, that he would see without emotion that intoxicating spectacle of the fraternity of France, that, at a moment when his native land was found again, he alone would obstinately remain outside his home, and that the barracks and the camp would be like an isle separated from the rest of the world?

It is doubtless alarming to see the army deliberating, distinguishing, and choosing in its obedience. Yet, in this case, how could it be otherwise? If the soldier were blindly obedient to authority, he disobeyed that supreme authority whence all others proceed; if docile to his officers, he found himself infallibly a rebel to the commander of his commanders,—the Law. Neither was he at liberty to abstain and remain neuter; the counter-revolution had no intention to do so; it commanded him to fire on the Revolution,—on France,—on the people,—on his father and his brother, who were holding forth their arms to embrace him.

The officers appeared to him what they were, the enemy,—a nation apart, becoming more and more of another race and a different nature. As inveterate hardened sinners bury themselves still deeper in sin on the approach of death, so the old system towards its close was more cruel and unjust. The upper grades were no longer given to any but the young men of the Court, to youthful *protégés* of noble ladies; Montbarry, the minister, has himself related the violent and shameful scene between himself and the queen in favour of a young colonel. The least important ranks, still accessible under Louis XIV. and Louis XV., were, in the reign of Louis XVI., given only to those who were able to prove four degrees of nobility. Fabert, Catinat, and Chevert, would have been unable to attain the rank of lieutenant.

I have said what was the budget for war (in 1784): forty-six millions for the officer, and forty-four for the soldier. Why say soldier? Beggar would be the proper term. The pay, comparatively high in the seventeenth century, is reduced to nothing under Louis XV. It is true that under Louis XVI. another pay was added, settled with the cudgel. This was to imitate the famous discipline of Prussia; and was supposed to contain the whole secret of the victories of Frederick the Great: man driven like a machine, and punished like a child. This is most assuredly the worst of all systems, thus uniting opposite evils, —a system at the same time mechanical and non-mechanical; on one hand fatally harsh, and on the other violently arbitrary.

The officers sovereignly despised the soldier, the citizen, and every kind of man; and took no pains to conceal this contempt. Yet, wherefore? What was their great merit? Only one, they were good swordsmen. That respectable prejudice which sets the life of a brave man at the discretion of the skilful consti- tuted for the latter a kind of tyranny. They even tried this sort of intimidation on the Assembly; in the chamber of the nobility, certain members fought duels to prevent others from uniting with the Third-Estate. Labourdonnaie, Noailles, Castries, Ca- zalès, challenged Barnave and Lameth. Some of them ad- dressed gross insults to Mirabeau, in the hope of getting rid of him; but he was immutable. Would to heaven that the greatest seaman of that time, Suffren, had been equally impassible! Ac- cording to a tradition which is but too probable, a young cox- comb of noble birth had the culpable insolence to call out that heroic man, whose sacred life belonged only to France: and he, already in years, was simple enough to accept, and received his death wound. The young man having friends at court, the affair was hushed up. Who rejoiced? England; for so lucky a stroke of the sword she would have given millions.

The people have never had the wit to understand this point of honour. Men like Belzunce and Patrice, who defied every- body, laboured in vain. The sword of the emigration broke like glass under the sabre of the Republic.

If our land officers, who had done nothing, were neverthe- less so insolent, good heavens! what were our officers of the navy! Ever since their late successes (which, after all, were only brilliant single fights of one vessel with another), they could no longer contain themselves; their pride had fretted into ferocity. One of them having been so remiss as to keep com- pany with an old friend, then a land officer, they forced him to fight a duel with him, to wash out the crime; and, horrible to relate, he killed him!

Acton, a naval officer, was as if King of Naples; the Vaudreuils surrounded the queen and the Count d'Artois with their violent counsels; other naval officers, the Bonchamps and Marignis, as soon as France had to face the whole of Europe, stabbed her behind with the poignard of La Vendée.

The first blow to their pride was given by Toulon. There commanded the very brave, but very insolent and hard-hearted Albert de Rioms, one of our best captains. He had thought he could lead both towns, the Arsenal and Toulon, in precisely the same manner, like a crew of galley-slaves, with a cat-o'-nine-tails, protecting the black cockade, and punishing the tricolour. He trusted to an agreement which his naval officers had made with those of the land, against the national guard. When the latter came to make their complaints, headed by the magistrates, he gave them the reception that he would have given to the galley-slaves in the Arsenal. Then a furious multitude besieged the commandant's hotel. He ordered the soldiers to fire, but nobody obeyed. At last, he was obliged to entreat the magistrates of the town to grant him their assistance. The national guard, whom he had insulted, had great difficulty in defending him; and were only able to save him by putting him in his own prison (November, December, 1789).

At Lille, an attempt was made in the same manner to bring the troops and the national guards to blows, and even to arm one regiment against another. Livarot, the commandant (as appears in his unpublished letters), urged them on by speaking to them of the alleged insult offered them by Dubois de Crancé in the National Assembly. The Assembly replied only by measures to improve the condition of the soldiery, testifying at least some interest for them, as far as it could, by the augmentation of a few deniers added to their pay. What encouraged them much more, was to see that, at Paris, M. de Lafayette had promoted all the subaltern officers to the superior grades. Thus the insurmountable barrier was at length destroyed.

Poor soldiers of the ancient system, who had so long suffered beyond all hope and in silence! . . . Without being the wonderful soldiers of the Republic and the empire, they were not unworthy of having also at last their day of liberty. All I read of them in our old chronicles, astonishes me with their patience, and affects me with the kindness of their hearts. I behold them, at La Rochelle, entering the famished city and giving their bread to the inhabitants. Their tyrants, their officers, who shut them out from every career, found in them only docility, respect, kindness, and benevolence. In some skirmish or other under Louis XV., an officer fourteen years of age, who had but just arrived from Versailles, was unable to march any further: "Pass him on to me," said a gigantic grenadier, "I will put him on my back; in case of a bullet, I will receive it for the child."

It was inevitable that there should be at length a day for justice, equality, and nature; happy were they who lived long enough to behold it: it was indeed a day of happiness for all. What joy for Brittany to find again the pilot of Duguay-Trouin, nearly a hundred years of age, still in his humble profession; he whose calm and resolute hand had steered the conqueror to battle. Jean Robin, of the Isle of Batz, was recognised at the elections, and with one accord placed by the side of the president. People blushed for France for so long a period of injustice, and wished, in the person of this venerable man, to honour so many heroic generations unworthily slighted and trampled upon, during their lives, by the insolence of those who profited by their services, and then, alas! condemned them to oblivion.

VII

A Religious Struggle:
The Passion of Louis XVI

IT was too evident that the soldier was not to be armed against the people; therefore, it became necessary to find a way of arming the people against themselves,—against a revolution made entirely on their account.

To the spirit of federation and union, to the new revolutionary faith, nothing could be opposed but the ancient faith, if it still existed.

In default of the old fanaticism, either extinct, or at least profoundly torpid, the clergy had a hold that has seldom failed them, the easy good-nature of the people, their blind sensibility, their credulity towards those whom they love, their inveterate respect for the priest and the king—the king, that ancient worship, that mystic personage, a compound of the two characters of the priest and the magistrate, with a gleam of the grace of God!

There the people had even addressed their prayers and their groans; and well do we know with what success,—what a sad return. In vain did royalty trample them underfoot and crush them, like a merciless machine; they still loved it as a person.

Nothing was easier to the priests than to make Louis XVI. appear in the light of a saint or a martyr. His sanctified, paternal, and heavy-looking countenance (uniting the characteristic features of the houses of Saxony and Bourbon) was that of a cathedral saint, ready made for a church-porch. His short-sighted air, and his indecision and insignificance, invested him precisely with that vague mystery so very favourable for every legend.

This was an admirable, pathetic text, well calculated to affect the hearts of men. He had loved the people, desired their welfare, and yet he was punished by them. Ungrateful madmen had dared to raise their hand against that excellent father, against God's anointed! The good king, the noble queen, the saint-like princess Elizabeth, and the poor little dauphin, were captives in that horrid Paris! How many tears flowed at such a narration; how many prayers, vows, and masses to heaven for their deliverance! What female heart was not bursting when, on leaving the church, the priest whispered: "Pray for the poor king!" Pray also for France,—is what they ought to have said; pray for a poor people, betrayed and delivered up to foreigners.

Another text, no less powerful for exciting civil war, was the opening of the convents, the order for making an inventory of the ecclesiastical possessions, and the reduction of the religious houses. This reduction was nevertheless conducted with the kindest solicitude. In every department, one house at least was reserved for every order, whither those who wished to remain might always retire. Whoever was willing to come out, came out and received a pension. All this was moderate, and by no means violent. The municipalities, very kindly disposed at that period, showed but too much indulgence in the execution of their orders. They often connived, and scarcely took an inventory, frequently noting only half the objects, and half the real value. No matter! Nothing was left untried to render their task both difficult and dangerous. The day of the inventory, the accursed day on which laymen were to invade the sacred cloisters, was clamorously noised abroad. To arrive even at the gate, the municipal magistrates were first obliged, at the peril of their lives, to pass through a collected mob, amid the screams of women, and the threats of sturdy beggars fed by the monasteries. The gentle lambs of the Lord confronted the men of the law, whose task was to execute the law, with refusals, delays, resistance, to the point of tearing them to pieces.

All that was prepared with much skill and remarkable address. If it were possible to give a complete history of it, with all its particulars, we should be very much edified on a curious subject of transcendental philosophy; how, at a period of indifference and incredulity, politicians can make and rekindle fanaticism? A grand chapter this would be to add to the book imagined by a philosopher,—"The Mechanism of Enthusiasm."

The clergy were devoid of faith; but they found for instruments persons who still possessed it, people of conviction, pious souls, ardent visionaries with poetical and whimsical imaginations, which are ever to be found, especially in Brittany. A lady, named Madame de Pont-Levès, the wife of a naval officer, published a fervent mystical little volume, called "The Compassion of the Virgin for France," a female composition well adapted to females, calculated to excite their imagination, and turn their brains.

The clergy had, moreover, another very easy means of acting on those poor populations ignorant of the French language. They allowed them to remain ignorant of the suppression of the tithes and collections, said not a word about the successive abolition of the indirect taxes, and plunged them in despair, by pointing out to them the burden of taxation which oppressed the land, and informing them that they were presently to be deprived of one-third of their goods and cattle.

The south offered other elements of anarchy no less favourable; men of feverish passion, active, fervent, and political, whose minds, full of intrigue and cunning, were well calculated not only to create a revolt, but to organise, regulate, and direct an insurrection.

The real secret of resistance, the only way that gave any serious chance to the counter-revolution, the idea of the future Vendée, was first reduced to a formula at Nimes: Against the Revolution, no result is possible without a religious war. In other words: Against faith, no other power but faith.

Terrible means, that make us shudder when we remember—

when we see the ruins and deserts made by ancient fanaticism. What would have happened, if all the South and the West, all France, had become a Vendée?

But the counter-revolution had no other chance. To the genius of fraternity only one could be opposed, that of the St. Bartholomew massacre.

Such was, in general terms, the thesis which, as early as January, 1790, was supported at Turin, before the general council of the emigration, by the fervent envoy of Nimes, a man sprung from the people, and possessed of little merit, but obstinate and intrepid, who saw his way clearly and frankly stated the question.

The man who, by special grace, was thus admitted to speak before princes and lords, Charles Froment, for such was his name, the son of a man accused of forgery (afterwards acquitted), was himself nothing more than a petty collector for the clergy and their factotum. After being a revolutionist at first, he had perceived that at Nimes there was more business to be done on the opposite side. He had at once found himself the leader of the Catholic populace, whom he let loose on the Protestants. He himself was much less fanatical than factious, a man fit for the period of the Gibelins. But he saw very plainly that the true power was the people,—an appeal to the faith of the multitude.

Froment was graciously received and listened to, but little understood. They gave him some money, and the hope that the commandant of Montpellier would furnish him with arms. Moreover, they were so little aware how very useful he might be, that subsequently, when he emigrated, he did not even obtain from the princes permission to join the Spaniards and put them in communication with his former friends.

"What ruined Louis XVI.," says Froment in his pamphlets, "was his having philosophers for ministers." He might have extended this still further, with no less reason. What rendered the counter-revolution generally powerless, was that it possessed within itself, at different degrees, but still it possessed at

390

heart, the philosophy of the age, that is to say, the Revolution itself.

I have said, in my Introduction, that everybody, even the queen, the Count d'Artois, and the nobility, was, at that time, though in a different degree, under the influence of the new spirit.

The language of ancient fanaticism was for them a dead letter. To rekindle it in the masses was for such minds an operation quite incomprehensible. The idea of exciting the people to rebel, even in their favour, gave them alarm. Besides, to restore power to the priests, was a thing quite contrary to the ideas of the nobility; they had ever been waiting and hoping for the spoils of the clergy. The interests of these two orders were adverse and hostile. The Revolution, which seemed likely to bring them together, had caused a wider separation. Nobles who were proprietors, in certain provinces, in Languedoc for instance, gained by the suppression of church tithes more than they lost by their feudal rights.

In the debate on the monastic vows (February), not one noble sided with the clergy. They alone defended the old tyrannical system of irrevocable vows. The nobles voted with their usual adversaries for the abolition of vows, the opening of the monasteries, and the liberty of the monks and nuns.

The clergy take their revenge. When the question is to abolish the feudal rights, the nobility cry out, in their turn, about violence, atrocity, &c. The clergy, or at least the majority of the clergy, let the nobility cry on, vote against them, and help to ruin them.

The advisers of the Count d'Artois, M. de Calonne and others, and the queen's Austrian advisers, were certainly, like the party of the nobility in general, very favourable to the spoliation of the clergy, provided it was performed by themselves. But rather than employ ancient fanaticism as a weapon, they much preferred making an appeal to foreigners. On his head they had no repugnance. The queen beheld in the foreigners her near relations; and the nobility had throughout Europe connexions of kindred, caste, and common culture, which rendered them very philosophical on the subject of the vulgar prejudices of nationality. What Frenchman was more a Frenchman than the general of Austria, the charming Prince de Ligne! And did not French philosophy reign triumphant at Berlin? As for England, for our most enlightened nobles, she was precisely the ideal, the classic land of liberty. In their opinion there were but two nations in Europe,—the polite and the impolite. Why should they not have called the former to France, to reduce the others to reason?

So, we have here three counter-revolutions in operation without being able to act in concert.

1st. The queen and the ambassador of Austria, her chief adviser, are waiting till Austria, rid of her Belgian affair, and securing the alliance of Europe, shall be able to threaten France, and subdue her (if necessary) by physical force.

2nd. The emigration party, the Count d'Artois, and the brilliant chevaliers of the Oeil-de Boeuf, who, tired to death of Turin and wanting to return to their mistresses and actresses, would like the foreign powers to act at once, and open for them a road to France, cost what it would; in 1790 they were already wishing for 1815.

3rd. The clergy are still less inclined to wait. Sequestrated by the Assembly, and gradually turned out of house and home, they would like at once to arm their numerous clients, the peasants and farmers;—at once, for to-morrow perhaps they would all grow lukewarm. How would it be if the peasant should think of purchasing the ecclesiastical lands? Why then the Revolution would have conquered irrevocably.

We have seen them in October firing before the word was given. In February, there was a new explosion even in the Assembly. It was the time when the agent of Nimes, on his return from Turin, was scouring the country, organising Catholic societies, and thoroughly agitating the South.

In the midst of the debate on the inviolability of vows, a member of the Assembly invoked the rights of nature, and repelled as a crime of ancient barbarity this surprising of man's

392

will, which, on a word that has escaped his lips or been extorted from him, binds him and buries him alive for ever. Thereupon loud shouts of "Blasphemy! blasphemy! He has blasphemed!" The Bishop of Nancy rushes to the tribune: "Do you acknowledge," cried he, "that the Catholic, Apostolic, and Roman Religion, is the religion of the nation?" The Assembly perceived the blow, and avoided it. The answer was, that the question of the suppression of the convents was especially one of finances; that there was nobody who did not regard the Catholic religion as the national religion; and that to confirm it by a decree would be to compromise it.

This happened on the 13th of February. On the 18th, they issued a libel, diffused in Normandy, wherein the Assembly was devoted to the hatred of the people, as assassinating at the same time religion and royalty. Easter was then approaching; the opportunity was not lost: they sold and distributed about the churches, a terrible pamphlet,—"The Passion of Louis XVI."

To this legend the Assembly was able to oppose another, of equal interest, which was, that Louis XVI., who, on the 4th of February, had sworn fidelity to the constitution, still kept a permanent agent with his brother, amid the mortal enemies of the constitution; that Turin, Treves, and Paris, were like the same court, kept and paid by the king.

At Treves was his military establishment, paid and maintained by him, with his grand and private stables, under Prince de Lambesc.[29] Artois, Condé, Lambesc, and all the emigrants were paid enormous pensions. And yet alimentary pensions of widows and other unfortunates of two, three, or four hundred francs were indefinitely postponed.

The king was paying the emigrants in defiance of a decree

---

[29] Everything was carried on exactly as at Versailles; it was a ministry that the king kept publicly abroad. Whatever was done at Paris was regulated at Treves. The accounts of expenses and other unpublished papers, show Lambesc signing the accounts, executing petitions sent from Paris, appointing *employés* for Paris, pages for the Tuileries, &c. Uniforms for the body-guards were made in France to be sent to Treves; and horses were brought over from England for the officers at that place. The king entreats Lambesc to be so good as to employ at least French horses.

by which the Assembly had, for the last two months, attempted to withhold this money which was thus passing over to the enemy; and this decree he had precisely forgotten to sanction. The irritation increased, when Camus, the severe reporter of the financial committee, declared he could not discover how a sum of sixty million francs had been expended. The Assembly enacted that, for every decree presented for royal sanction, the keeper of the seals should render an account *within eight days* of the royal sanction or refusal.

Great was the outcry and lamentation on this outrageous exaction against the royal will. Camus replied by printing the too celebrated "Red Book" (April 1), which the king had given up in the hope that it would remain a secret between him and the committee. This impure book, defiled at every page with the shameful corruption of the aristocracy, and the criminal weaknesses of royalty, showed whether people had been wrong in shutting up the filthy channel through which the substance of France was flowing away. A glorious book, in spite of all that! For it plunged the Revolution into the hearts of men.

"Oh! how rightly we have acted!" was the general cry; and how far people were, even in their most violent accusations, from suspecting the reality! At the same time, the faith grew stronger that this monstrous old system of things, contrary to nature and God, could never return. The Revolution, on beholding the hideous face of her adversary, unveiled and unmasked, felt strong, living, and eternal. Yes, whatever may have been the obstacles, delays, and villainies, she lives and will live for ever!

A proof of this strong faith is that in the universal distress, and during more than one insurrection against indirect taxation, direct taxes were punctually and religiously paid.

Ecclesiastical estates are set up for sale to the value of four hundred million francs; the city of Paris alone purchases the value of half, and all the municipalities follow this example.

This method was very good. Few individuals would have wished themselves to have expropriated the clergy; the municipalities alone were able to undertake this painful operation. They were to purchase, and then sell again. There was much hesitation, especially among the peasantry; for this reason, the cities were to give them the example in purchasing and selling again, first the ecclesiastical houses; after which would come the sale of the lands.

All those properties served as mortgage for the paper-money created by the Assembly. To each note a lot was assigned and affected; and these notes were called *assignats*. Every piece of paper was property,—a portion of land; and had nothing in common with those forged notes of the Regency, founded on the Mississippi, on distant and future possessions.

Here the pledge was tangible. To this guarantee, add that of the municipalities that had purchased of the State and were selling again. Being divided among so many hands, those lots of paper-money once given out and circulated, were about to engage the whole nation in this great operation. Everybody would have a part of this money, and thus both friends and enemies would be equally interested in the safety of the Revolution.

Nevertheless, the remembrance of Law, and the traditions of so many families ruined by his system, were no slight obstacle. France was far less accustomed than England or Holland to behold real values circulating in the form of paper. It was necessary for a whole nation to rise superior to their every-day habits; it was an act of mystical quality, of revolutionary faith, that the Assembly demanded.

The clergy were terrified on seeing that their spoils would thus be in the hands of the whole people; for after having been reduced to impalpable powder, it was very unlikely that they should ever come again into their possession. They endeavoured at first to liken these solid assignats, each of which was land, to the Mississippi rubbish: "I had thought," said the Archbishop of Aix in a perfidious manner, "that you had really renounced the idea of bankruptcy." The answer to this was too easy. Then, they had recourse to another argument. "All this," said they, "is got up by the Paris bankers; the provinces will not accept it." Then, they were shown addresses from the provinces demanding a speedy creation of assignats.

They had expected at least to gain time, and in the interval to remain in possession, ever waiting and watching to seize some good opportunity. But even this hope was taken from them: "What confidence," said Prieur, "will people have in the mortgage that founds the assignats, if the mortgaged estates are not really in our hands?" This tended to dispossess and dislodge the clergy immediately, and to put all the property into the hands of the municipalities and districts.

In vain did the Assembly offer them an enormous salary of a hundred millions: they were inconsolable.

The Archbishop of Aix in a whining discourse, full of childish and unconnected lamentations, inquired whether they would really be so cruel as to ruin the poor, by depriving the clergy of what was given for the poor. He ventured this paradox that a bankruptcy would infallibly follow the operation intended to prevent the bankruptcy; and he accused the Assembly of having meddled with spiritual things by declaring vows invalid, &c.

Lastly, he went so far as to offer, in the name of the clergy, a loan of four hundred millions, mortgaged upon their estates. Whereupon Thouret replied with his Norman impassibility: "An offer is made in the name of a body *no longer existing*." And again: "When the religion sent you into the world, did it say to you: go, prosper, and acquire?"

There was then in the Assembly a good-natured simple Carthusian friar, named Dom Gerles, a well-meaning short-sighted man,—a warm patriot, but no less a good Catholic. He believed (or very probably he allowed himself to be persuaded by some cunning ecclesiastic) that what gave so much uneasiness to the prelates, was solely the spiritual danger, the fear lest the civil power should meddle with the altar. "Nothing is more simple," said he; "in order to reply to persons who say that the Assembly wishes to have no religion, or that it is willing to admit every religion in France, it has only to decree: "That the Catholic, Apostolic, and Roman religion, is and shall ever be the religion

396

of the nation, and that its worship is the only one authorised"
(April 12, 1790).

Charles de Lameth expected to escape the difficulty, as on
the 13th of February, by saying that the Assembly, which, in
its decrees, followed the spirit of the Gospel, had no need to
justify itself in this manner.

But the word was not allowed to drop. The Bishop of Clermont bitterly rejoined, and pretended to be astonished that,
when there was a question of doing homage to the religion,
people should deliberate instead of replying by a hearty acclamation.

All the right side of the Assembly arose, and gave a cheer.

In the evening they assembled at the Capucins, and—to be
provided in case the Assembly should not declare Catholicism
the national religion—prepared a violent protest to be carried
in solemn procession to the king, and published in a vast
number of copies throughout France, in order to make the
people well understand that the National Assembly desired to
have no kind of religion.

VIII

Religious Struggle—Success of the Counter-Revolution (May, 1790)

THE motion made by that plain man had wonderfully changed the aspect of affairs. From a period of debate, the revolution appeared suddenly transported into an age of terror.

The Assembly had to contend with terror of two kinds. The clergy had a silent formidable argument, well understood; they exhibited to the Assembly a Medusa, civil war, the imminent insurrection of the west and the south, the probable resurrection of the old wars of religion. And the Assembly felt within itself the immense irresistible force of a revolution let loose, that was to overthrow everything,—a revolution which had for its principal organ the riots of Paris, thundering at its doors, and often drowning the voices of the deputies.

In this affair, the clergy had the advantage of position; first, because they seemed to be in personal danger; that very danger sanctified them: many an unbelieving, licentious, intriguing prelate suddenly found himself, under favour of the riots, exalted to the glory of martyrdom—a martyrdom nevertheless impossible, owing to the infinite precautions taken by Lafayette, then so strong and popular, at the zenith of his glory,—the real king of Paris.

The clergy had moreover in their favour the advantage of a

clear position, and the outward appearances of faith. Hitherto interrogated and placed at the bar by the spirit of the age, it is now their turn to question, and they boldly demand "Are you Catholics?" The Assembly replies timidly, in a disguised equivocal tone, that it cannot answer, that it respects religion too much to make any answer, that, by paying such a religion, it has given sufficient proof, &c.

Mirabeau said hypocritically: "Must we decree that the sun shines?" and another: "I believe the Catholic religion to be the only true one; I respect it infinitely. It is said the gates of hell shall not prevail against it. Are we then to confirm such language by some miserable decree?" &c. &c.

But d'Espremesnil tore away this mask of hypocrisy by his energetic language: "Yes," said he. "When the Jews crucified Jesus Christ, they said, 'Hail, king of the Jews!'"

Nobody replied to this terrible attack. Mirabeau remained silent, and crouched, like a lion about to make a spring. Then seizing the opportunity afforded by a deputy who was quoting, in favour of intolerance, some treaty or other made by Louis XIV.: "And how," cried he, "should not every kind of intolerance have been consecrated in a reign signalised by the revocation of the Edict of Nantes. If you appeal to history, forget not that hence, from this very tribune, I behold the window whence a king, armed against his people by an execrable faction, that disguised personal interest under the cloak of religion, fired his arquebuss, and gave the signal for the Saint Bartholomew!"

And, with his gesture and finger, he pointed to the window, which from that place it was impossible to perceive; but he mentally saw it, and everybody saw it.

The blow struck home. What the orator had said revealed precisely what the clergy wanted to do. Their plan was to carry to the king a violent protestation which would have armed believers, and to put the arquebuss into the king's hands, to fire the first shot.

Louis XVI. was not a Charles IX.; but, being very sincerely convinced of the right of the clergy, he would have accepted the peril for what he considered the safety of religion. However, three things prevented him: his natural indecision, the timidity of his ministry, and, lastly, more than all the rest, his fears for the life of the queen,—the terror of the 6th of October daily renewed, that violent menacing crowd beneath his windows, that ocean-multitude beating against his walls. At every resistance the queen seemed in peril. Moreover, she herself had other views and different hopes, far removed from the clergy.

An answer was returned, in the name of the king, that if the protest were brought to the Tuileries, it would not be received.

We have seen how the king, in February, had discouraged Bouillé, the officers, and the nobility. In April, his refusal to support the clergy would deprive them of courage if they could ever lose it when the question concerns their wealth. Maury said in a rage that people should know in France in what hands royalty found itself.

It now remained to act without the king. Were they to act with the nobility? And yet the clergy could not rely much even on their assistance. They still had the monopoly of all the officers' ranks; but, not being sure of the soldiers, they were afraid of an outbreak and were less impatient and less warlike than the priests. Froment, the agent of the clergy at Nimes, although he had obtained an order from the Count d'Artois, was unable to persuade the commandant of the province to allow him to make use of the arsenal, and yet the business was urgent. The great federations of the Rhône had intoxicated the whole country, and that of Orange in April had completed the general enthusiasm. Avignon no longer remembered that it belonged to the pope, but sent to Orange, with all the French towns. Had they waited a moment longer, it would have escaped them. If the chief towns of aristocracy and fanaticism, like Avignon and Arles, with which the clergy were ever threatening, themselves became revolutionary, the counter-revolution, held moreover in close quarters by Marseilles and

Bordeaux, had no longer any hope. The explosion must take place now or never.

We should not at all understand the eruptions of these old volcanoes of the South, if we did not previously examine that ever burning soil. The infernal flames of the stakes which were there kindled so many times, those contagious sulphurous flames seem to have gained the very soil, so that unknown conflagrations are there ever undermining the land. It is like those burning coal-pits in the Aveyron, the fire is not at the surface; but, if you plunge a cane into that yellow turf, it smokes, takes fire, and reveals the hell that is dormant at your feet.

May animosity ever decline!—But it is necessary that reminiscences should remain, that so many woes and sufferings be never lost for the experience of men. It is necessary that the first and most sacred of our liberties, religious freedom, go to strengthen itself and revive at the sight of the horrible ruins left by fanaticism.

The very stones speak in default of men. Two monuments especially deserve to be the objects of a frequent pilgrimage,—two opposite yet instructive monuments,—the one infamous, the other sacred.

The infamous one is the palace of Avignon, that Babel of the popes, that Sodom of legates, that Gomorrah of cardinals; a monstrous palace covering the whole brow of a mountain with its obscene towers, the scene of lust and torture, where priests showed to kings that, in comparison to them, they were mere novices in the abominable arts of sensuality. The originality of the construction is that the places of torture not being far removed from the luxurious alcoves, ball rooms, and festive halls, they might very easily have heard, amid the singing in the courts of love, the shrieks and groans of the tortured, and the breaking and cracking of their bones. Priestly prudence had provided against this by a scientific arrangement of the vaults, proper to absorb every kind of noise. The superb pyramidal hall where the flaming piles were erected (imagine

the interior of a cone of sixty feet) testifies a frightful knowledge of acoustics; only here and there a few traces of oily
soot still call to mind the burning of flesh.[30]

The other place, both holy and sacred, is the Bagne (for
galley-slaves) at Toulon, the Calvary of religious liberty, the
place where the confessors of the faith, the heroes of charity,
died a lingering death beneath the lash.

Be it remembered that several of these martyrs, condemned
to the galleys for life, were not Protestants, but men accused
of having allowed Protestants to escape!

Some were sold during the reign of Louis XV. For a fair
price (120*l.*), a galley-slave might be purchased. M. de
Choiseul, to pay his court to Voltaire, gave him one as a free
gift.

This horrible code, which our Reign of Terror copied without
ever being able to equal it, armed children against their fathers,
gave them their property beforehand, so that the son was
interested in keeping his father at Toulon.

What is more curious than to witness the Church, *the groaning dove*, groaning in 1682, when little children had just been
carried away from their heretical mothers—groaning to deliver
them? No, for the king to find laws more efficacious and severe.
Yet how could any ever be found more severe than these?

At every assembly of the clergy, the dove continues to groan.
Nay, even under Louis XVI., when they allowed the spirit of
the time to extort from them that glorious charter of enfranchisement which had always excluded the Protestants from
every public employment, the clergy address fresh groans to
the king by Loménie, an atheistic priest.

I entered full of trembling and respect into that holy bagne
of Toulon. There I sought for the vestiges of the martyrs of
religion and those of humanity, killed there with ill-treatment,
for having had manly hearts, for having alone undertaken to
defend innocence and perform the work of God!

---

[30] This pyramidal hall for burning victims, must not be confounded with
the Tour de la Glacière, of which I shall speak hereafter.

Alas! nothing remains. Nothing remains of those atrocious and superb galleys, gilded and sanguinary, more barbarous than those of Barbary, and which the lash watered with the blood of those saints. Even the registers, in which their names were inscribed, have for the most part disappeared. In the few that remain, there are only laconic indications, their entrance and their exit; and that exit was generally death.—Death which came more or less speedily, thus indicating the degrees of resignation or despair. A terrible brevity, two lines for a saint, two or three for a martyr. No note has been taken of the groans, the protestations, the appeals made to heaven, the silent prayers, or the psalms chanted in a low voice amidst the blasphemies of thieves and murderers.—Oh! all that must be elsewhere. "Be comforted! The tears of men are engraved for eternity in rock and marble!" said Christopher Columbus.

In marble? No, but in the human soul. In proportion as I studied and learned, I was consoled to see that indeed those obscure martyrs nevertheless bore their fruit,—admirable fruit: the amelioration of those who saw or heard them, a melting of the heart, a humanising of the soul in the eighteenth century, an increasing horror of fanaticism and persecution. In course of time, there remained nobody to enforce those barbarous laws. The intendant Lenain (de Tillemont), a nephew of the illustrious Jansenist, on being obliged to condemn to death one of the last of those Protestant martyrs, said to him: "Alas! sir, such are the king's orders." He burst into tears, and the convict tried to comfort him.

Fanaticism was expiring of itself. It was not without trouble and much labour, that, from time to time, politicians managed to rekindle the flame. When the *parlement,* accused of scepticism, jansenism, and anti-jesuitism, seized the opportunity afforded by Calas, to recover its former reputation, when, in concert with the clergy, it attempted to agitate the old fury of the people, it was found to be quite dormant.

It succeeded only by means of brotherhoods, generally composed of petty people, who, as tradespeople, or in some other manner, were the clients of the clergy. In order to trouble, bewitch, alarm, and inflame the minds of the people, they did what is done at the races, where a hot coal is inserted under the skin of a horse, which then becomes mad. Only the coal in this case was an atrocious comedy, a frightful exhibition. The brotherhoods, in their white ominous costume (the hood concealing their faces, with two holes for the eyes), solemnised a death festival for the son that Calas had killed, as they said, to prevent him from abjuring. Upon an enormous catafalque, surrounded with wax-candles, a skeleton was seen, moved by springs, holding in one hand the palm of martyrdom, and in the other a pen to sign the abjuration of heresy.

We know how the blood of Calas recoiled upon the fanatics, and the excommunication hurled upon the murderers, the false judges and wicked priests by the old pontiff of Ferney. On that day, struck by lightning, they began to tumble down a declivity where it is impossible to stop; they rolled down head foremost, the reprobates, till they plunged into the gulf of the Revolution.

And on the eve, at the very brink of the abyss, royalty, which they were dragging with them, in their fall, at length thought proper just to be humane. An edict appeared (1787) in which it was confessed that the Protestants were men; they were permitted to be born, to marry, and to die. In other respects, they were by no means citizens, being excluded from civil employments, and unable either to administer, to judge, or to teach; but admitted, as their only privilege, to pay the taxes and their persecutors, the Catholic clergy, and to maintain, with their money, the altar that cursed them.

The Protestants of the mountains cultivated their meagre country. The Protestants of the cities carried on trade, the only thing they were allowed to do, and, by degrees, as they felt themselves more safe, a few of the industrious arts. Having been kept down, in cruel subjection, out of every kind of employment, or influence, and excluded most especially for a hundred years from every military grade, they no longer had any resemblance with the hardy Huguenots of the sixteenth century; and Protestantism was reduced to its starting point of the middle ages,—industry and commerce. If we except the Cevenols, incorporated in their rocks, the Protestants in general possessed very little land; their riches, already considerable at this period, were houses and factories, but especially and essentially moveables, such as can always be transported.

The Protestants of the province of Gard, were, in 1789, rather more than fifty thousand male inhabitants (as in 1698, and also in 1840, the number has varied very little), consequently very weak, isolated, and totally unconnected with their brethren of the other provinces, lost like a point, an atom, in a vast multitude of Catholics, who were counted by millions. At Nimes, the only town where the Protestants were assembled in any considerable number, they were six thousand to twenty-one thousand men of the other religion. Of the six thousand, three or four thousand were workmen of manufactories, an unwholesome diminutive race, miserable, and subject, as the workman is everywhere, to frequent want of work.

But the Catholics were never out of work, being chiefly tillers of the ground, and their very mild climate admitting of that kind of labour in every season. Many of them had a bit of land, and cultivated at the same time for the clergy, the nobility, and the wealthy Catholic burgesses, who possessed the whole of the environs.

The Protestants of the towns, well-informed, moderate, and serious, confined to a sedentary life, and devoted to their reminiscences, having in each family a subject of grief and perhaps also of fear, were almost devoid of enterprise, and lost to all hope. When they beheld the glorious dawn of the first day of liberty, on the eve of the Revolution, they hardly dared indulge in hope. They let the *parlements* and the nobility advance boldly and speak in favour of the new ideas; but, generally, they themselves remained silent. They knew perfectly well that to impede the Revolution, it would have been sufficient to be seen expressing their sympathy.

It burst forth. The Catholics, be it said to their honour, the great majority of the Catholics, were delighted to see the Protestants at length become their equals. The unanimity was affecting, and one of the sights the most worthy to call down the blessing of God upon earth. In many parts, the Catholics went to the temple of the Protestants, and united with them to return thanks to Providence together. On the other hand, the Protestants attended the Catholic *Te Deum*. For, above all the altars, every temple, and every church a divine ray had appeared in heaven.

The 14th of July was welcomed by the South, as also by all France, as a deliverance wrought by God,—a departure from the land of Egypt; the people had crossed through the sea, and, safe on the opposite shore, were singing the song of praise. They were no longer Protestants and Catholics, but Frenchmen. It happened, without any intention or premeditation, that the permanent committee organised in the towns, was composed of persons of either religion; so likewise was the national militia. The officers were generally Catholics, because the Protestants, strangers to military service, would hardly have been able to command. To make amends, they constituted the cavalry almost entirely, many of them having horses for the necessities of their trade.

However, after the lapse of two or three months, a project was set on foot at Nimes and Montauban, to form new companies exclusively Catholic.

This glorious unanimity had disappeared. A serious and solemn question, that of the property of the clergy, had caused an entire change.

The clergy showed a remarkable power of organisation, and an intelligent activity in creating a civil war in a population that had no wish for it.

Three means were employed. First, the mendicant friars, the Capuchins and the Dominicans, who became the distributors and propagators of a vast number of *brochures* and pamphlets. Secondly, the publichouses (*cabarets*), and the petty retail winesellers, who, dependent on the clergy, the principal proprietors of vineyards, were on the other hand in communication with the lower orders of the Catholics, especially with the rural electors among the peasantry. The latter, on their way to town, used to halt at the cabaret; where they spent (and this includes our third article) twenty-four sous which the clergy gave them for every day they went to the elections.

Froment, the agent of the priests in all these doings, was more than a man; he was himself a legion,—acting at the same time by a vast number of hands, by his brother Froment (surnamed *Tapage*), his relations, and his friends. He had his bureau, his friends, his library of pamphlets and his lair at the elections, close by the church of the Dominicans; and his house communicated with a tower commanding the ramparts: an excellent position for civil war, which defied musketry and was afraid of nothing but artillery.

Before having recourse to arms, Froment undermined the Revolution by the Revolution itself,—by the National Guard and the elections. Assemblies held at night in the church of the White Penitents, prepared the municipal elections in such a manner as to exclude all Protestants. The enormous powers which the Assembly gave to the municipal authorities, the right of calling out the troops, proclaiming martial law, and hoisting the red flag, are thus found to be placed, at Nimes and Montauban, in the hands of the Catholics; and that flag will be hoisted for them, should they ever require it, and never against them.

The National Guard was next. It had been composed in July of the most fervent patriots, who hastened to enlist; of those also who, possessing no other wealth than moveables, were the most afraid of pillage; such were the merchants, for the most part Protestants. As for the rich Catholics, who were especially land proprietors, they could not lose their lands, and therefore were more slow in arming. When their castles were attacked, the National Guard, composed of Protestants and Catholics, took every care to defend them; that of Montauban saved a château belonging to Cazalès the royalist.

To change this state of affairs, it was necessary to awaken

envy and create a spirit of rivalry. This came soon enough of itself by the force of circumstances, apart from every difference of opinion and party. Every corps that seemed select, whether aristocratic, like the volunteers of Lyon and Lille, or patriotic, like the dragoons of Montauban and Nimes, was equally detested. They excited against the latter those petty people who formed the great mass of the Catholic companies, by spreading a report among them that the others called them *cébets* or onion-eaters. This was a gratuitous accusation; for why should the Protestants have insulted the poor? Nobody at Nimes was poorer than the Protestant workmen. And their friends and defenders of the mountain, in the Cévennes, who often have no other food than chestnuts, led a harder, poorer, and more abstinent life than the onion-eaters at Nimes, who eat bread also and often drink wine.

On the 20th of March, they heard that the Assembly, not satisfied with having opened to Protestants the road to public employment, had raised a Protestant, Rabaut Saint-Etienne, to the highest of all, a position then higher than the throne,—to the presidency of the nation. Nothing was yet ready,—few arms, if any; nevertheless, the impression was so strong that four Protestants were assassinated by way of expiation—a fact contested, but certain.

Toulouse did penance for the sacrilege of the Assembly, made a public confession of its sins, and offered up nine days' prayers to avert the wrath of God. It was the period of an execrable festival, an annual procession made in remembrance of the massacre of the Albigenses. The brotherhoods of every denomination repair in crowds to the chapel erected on the field of slaughter; and the most furious motions are made in the churches. Machinery is set to work in every direction. They fetch from their old lumber-rooms those instruments of fanaticism which played their parts at the time of the Dragonnades and the Saint-Bartholomew massacre: virgins who shed tears praying for murders, and Christs to nod, &c. &c. Add, moreover, a few more recent inventions; for instance, a Dominican to go about the streets of Nimes, in his white monk-dress, begging his bread and weeping over the decrees of the Assembly; at Toulouse, a bust of the captive king, the martyr-king, placed near the preacher and covered with a black veil, to be suddenly revealed at the pathetic moment in the sermon to ask assistance of the good people of Toulouse.

All that was too clear. It meant *blood!* And the Protestants understood it.

Isolated amidst a vast Catholic population, they saw themselves a small flock marked for slaughter. The terrible reminiscences treasured in each family, would return to their minds at night and frighten them out of their sleep. The effects of this panic were whimsical enough; the dread of the *brigands* which pervaded to rural districts, was often confounded in their imaginations with that of Catholic assassins; and they hardly knew whether they were in 1790 or in 1572. At Saint-Jean-de-la-Gardonnenque, a small trading town, some couriers entered one morning, crying: "Be on your guard! here they are!" They ring the alarm-bell, run to arms, the women cling to their husbands to prevent them from going out; they shut up their houses, put themselves in a state of defence, with paving-stones at the windows. And the town was indeed invaded, but by friends, the Protestants of the country, who had arrived by forced marches. Among them was seen a beautiful girl, armed, and carrying a gun, between her two brothers. She was the heroine of the day, and was crowned with laurel; all the tradespeople recovering from their panic, took up a collection for their lovely deliverer; and she returned to her mountains with her dowry in her apron.

Nothing could allay their fears but a permanent association between the communes, an armed federation. They formed one towards the end of March in a meadow of the Gard, a sort of island between a canal and the river, sheltered from every kind of surprise. Thousands of men repaired thither, and what was more comforting, the Protestants saw a great number of Catholics mingled with them under their banner. The peaceful

Roman ruins which crown the landscape filled their minds with loftier thoughts; they seemed to have survived in order to despise and see decline those miserable quarrels of religion, and to have the promise of a more noble age.

The two parties were drawn up in array and ready to act; Nimes, Toulouse, and Montauban were watching Paris and waiting. Let us compare dates. On the 13th of April, in the bosom of the Assembly, they obtain from it a spark to kindle all the South,—its refusal to declare Catholicism the predominant religion; on the 19th the clergy protest. As early as the 18th Toulouse protests with fire-arms; there they act the scene of the king's bust; the patriots shout "Long live the king and the law!" and the soldiers fire on them.

On the 20th, at Nimes, is a great and solemn *Catholic declaration* signed by three thousand electors, and backed with the signatures of fifteen hundred *distinguished persons*,—a declaration forwarded to all the municipalities in the kingdom, followed and copied at Montauban, Albi, Alais, Uzès, &c. This article, planned at the White Penitents, was written by Froment's clerks, and signed in his house by the populace. It amounted to a criminal accusation against the National Assembly; and gave it notice that it had to restore power to the king, and to bestow upon the Catholic religion the monopoly of public worship.

At the same time, they were striving to form new companies in every direction. These were strangely composed, consisting of ecclesiastical agents, peasants, marquises and domestics, nobles and porters. In default of guns, they had pitch-forks and scythes; they were also secretly fabricating a terrible murderous weapon,—pitchforks with edges like a saw.

The municipalities, created by the Catholics, pretended not to see all this; they seemed to be very busily engaged in strengthening the strong, and weakening the weak. At Montauban, the Protestants, six times less numerous than their adversaries, wanted to accede to the federative covenant which the Protestants of the rural districts had just formed; but the municipality would not allow it. They next attempted to disarm their animosity by withdrawing from the public employments to which they had been raised, and causing Catholics to be appointed in their stead. This was taken for weakness; and the religious crusade was not the less preached in the churches. The vicars-general excited the minds of the people still more by causing prayers of forty hours to be said for the safety of the religion in peril.

The municipality of Montauban at length threw off the mask by an affair that could not fail to bring about an explosion. For the execution of the decree of the Assembly ordering an inventory to be made in the religious communities, it chose precisely Rogation-Day, the 10th of May. It was also during a Spring festival that the Sicilian Vespers took place. The season added much to the general excitement. This festival of Rogation is the moment when the whole population is out of doors, and full of emotions aroused by worship and the season, feels that intoxicating influence of Spring, so powerful in the South. Though occasionally retarded by the hail-storms of the Pyrenees, it bursts out only with greater vigour. Everything seems then to be emerging and springing forth at once—man from his house, and the grass from the earth; and every creature leaps with joy; it is like a *coup d'état* of Providence—a revolution in nature.

And well did they know that the women who go whining about the streets their lachrymose canticles *Te rogamus, audi nos*—well did they know that they would urge their husbands to the fight, and cause them to be killed, rather than allow the magistrates to enter the convents.

The latter begin their march, but, as they might have foreseen, are stopped short by the impenetrable masses of the people, and by women sitting and lying before the sacred thresholds. It would be necessary to walk over them. They therefore withdraw, and the crowd becomes aggressive; it even threatens to burn down the house of the military commandant, a Catholic, but a patriot. It marches towards the Hôtel-de-Ville, in order to force the arsenal. If it succeeded in doing so; if, in that state of fury, it seized upon arms, the massacre of the Protestants and patriots in general must have begun.

The municipality had the power of calling out the regiment of Languedoc; but it declined doing so. The national guards march of their own accord and occupy the military post that covers the Hôtel-de-Ville, where they are soon besieged. Far from succouring them, assistance is sent to the furious populace, who are supported by the persons employed in the excise. Five or six hundred shots are fired against the windows. The unfortunate guards pierced with bullets, several being killed, a great number wounded, and being without ammunition, show a white handkerchief and ask them to spare their lives. The firing continues all the same, and the wall, their only defence, is demolished. Then the culpable municipality decides, *in extremis*, to do what it ought to have done before—to call out the regiment of Languedoc, which, for a long time, had desired to advance.

During this butchery, a noble lady had caused masses to be said.

Those who have not been killed are therefore at length able to go forth. But the fury of the populace was not exhausted. Their dress, the national uniform, is torn from them, as is also the cockade, which is trampled under foot. Bare-headed, holding tapers in their hands, and stripped to their shirts, they are then dragged along the streets, stained with their blood, as far as the cathedral, where they are made to kneel on the steps to do penance. . . In front marches the mayor, bearing a white flag.

For less cause, France had carried out the insurrection of the 6th of October; for a less outrage offered to the tri-coloured cockade, she had overthrown a monarchy.

We tremble for Montauban when we perceive the terrible exasperation that such an event would excite, and the strong fellowship which, even at that time, bound together the whole nation from north to south. If there had been nobody in the south to avenge such an affront, all the centre and the north,

412

the whole of France would have marched. The outrage was felt even in the most inconsiderable villages. I have now before me the threatening addresses of the populations of Marne and Seine-et-Marne on those indignities of the south.[31]

The north was able to remain quiet. The south was quite sufficient. Bordeaux was the first to march; then Toulouse, on which those of Montauban had relied; even Toulouse turned against them and demanded they should be chastised. Bordeaux advanced; and, its numbers increasing, on its passage through the different communes, was obliged to send many away, being unable to feed such crowds of soldiers. The prisoners of Montauban were put in the van to receive the first fire (the only way of defending themselves imagined by the assassins). But van there was none! The regiment of Languedoc fraternised with the people of Bordeaux.

Paris sent one of the king's commissioners, one of Lafayette's officers, a kind, and too indulgent person, who rather declared against his own party; he sent back the Bordeaux people and entered into terms with the rioters. There was no inquiry as to the bloodshed; the dead remained dead; the wounded kept their wounded; and the imprisoned remained in prison; the king's commissary thought of no other way of getting them out than causing the favour to be asked of him by the very persons who had placed them there.

Everything took place in the same manner at Nimes. The Catholic volunteers boldly wore the white cockade and shouted "Down with the nation!" The soldiers and subaltern officers of the regiment of Guienne were indignant, and sought to quarrel with them. A single regiment, isolated amidst so vast a multitude, having on its side only the Protestant portion of the population, was in a hazardous position. Observe that it had its own officers against it, they having declared themselves the

---

[31] I believe I have read everything relating far or near to these riots of Montauban, Nimes, &c., and have stated nothing till I had compared and weighed the testimony, and formed my conviction with the attention of a juryman.—This once for all. I quote but little, in order not to interrupt the unity of my narration.

partisans of the white cockade, and also the municipality, who refused to proclaim martial law. Many persons were wounded; and a grenadier was aimed at and killed by Froment's own brother.

The soldiers were imprisoned, and the assassin was allowed to go free. So the counter-revolution was as triumphant at Nimes as at Montauban.

In the last-mentioned town, the conquerors were not satisfied with this, but had the audacity to go and make a collection among the families of the victims, nay, even in the prisons where they still remained. Oh horror! They were not allowed their liberty till they had paid their assassins!

IX

A Religious Struggle
—The Counter-Revolution Quelled
in the South (June, 1790)

WHAT was the National Assembly doing at Paris at this time? It was following the clergy in the procession of Corpus-Christi.

Its more than Christian meekness, in all this, is a surprising spectacle. It was satisfied with a single concession which the ministers obtained from the king. He forbade the white cockade and condemned those who had signed the declaration of Nimes. The latter got off easily by substituting, in place of their cockade, the red tuft of the ancient Leaguers; and they boldly protested that they persisted for the king against the king's orders.

This was clear, simple, and vigorous; the clerical party knew very well what they wanted. The Assembly knew it not. It was then accomplishing a feeble, deceptive task, what was then called the civil constitution of the clergy.

Nothing was more fatal to the Revolution than to be self-ignorant from the view point of religion—not to know that it bore a religion in itself.

It neither knew itself nor Christianity; it knew not exactly whether it was conformable or contrary to it—whether it was to go back to it or march forward.

In its easy confidence, it welcomed with pleasure the sympathy shown towards it by the bulk of the lower clergy. It was told, and it expected that it was about to realise the promises of the Gospel; that it was called to reform and renew Christianity, and not to replace it. It believed this and marched in this direction; but, as its second step, it found that the priests had become priests again, the enemies of the Revolution; and the Church appeared what it really was—the obstacle, the main impediment, far more than even royalty.

The Revolution had done two services for the clergy: given them an existence and an easy livelihood, and liberty to the monks. And this is precisely what enabled Episcopacy to turn them against it; the bishops designating every priest friendly to the Revolution to the hatred and contempt of the people, as won, bought over, and corrupted by temporal interests. Honour and the spirit of party impelled the priests towards ingratitude; and they quitted Revolution, their benefactress, for Episcopacy, their tyrant!

Strange enough, it was to defend their prodigious fortunes, their millions, their palaces, horses, and mistresses, that the prelates imposed upon the priests the law of martyrdom. One, for example, who wanted to keep an income of eight hundred thousand livres denounced as shameful a salary of twelve hundred francs that a country curate accepted from the Assembly.

The lower clergy thus found themselves, from the very first, and for a question of money, forced to make a choice. The bishops did not allow them a moment for reflection; but declared to them that, if they were for the nation, they were against the Church,—out of the Catholic unity, beyond the communion of the bishops and the Holy See, contaminated, rejected, renegade, and apostate members.

What were those poor priests to do? Leave the old system, in which so many generations had lived; become suddenly rebels to that imposing authority, which they had ever respected, and quit the known world for another? And what other, what new system? It is necessary to have an idea, and a

416

faith in that idea, thus to leave the shore and embark in the future.

A truly patriotic curate, he of Saint-Etienne-du-Mont, who, on the 14th of July, marched under the banner of the people, at the head of his district, was overwhelmed and frightened at the cruel alternative in which he was placed by the bishops. He remained forty days in sackcloth, on his knees, before the altar; and though he had remained there for ever, he would not have found any answer to the insoluble question which now presented itself.

Whatever ideas the Revolution possessed, it owed to the eighteenth century, to Voltaire and Rousseau. During the twenty years that had passed between the great period of those two masters and the Revolution, between the thought and the execution, nobody had seriously continued their work.

Therefore the Revolution found the human mind at the point where they had left it: ardent humanity in Voltaire, fraternity in Rousseau; two foundations, assuredly religious, but merely laid, and with scarcely any superstructure.

The last testament of the century is in two pages of Rousseau, of a very opposite tendency.

In one, in the "Social Contract," he establishes and proves, that the Christian neither is, nor can be a citizen.

In the other, which is in "Emile," he yields to an affecting enthusiasm for the Gospel and Jesus, so far as to say, "His death is that of a God!"

This effusion of sentiment and affection was noted and stored up as a valuable avowal, a solemn self-denegation of the philosophy of the eighteenth century. Thence arose an immense misunderstanding, which still remains.

People began to read the Gospel again; and in that book of resignation, submission, and obedience to authority, they read every moment what they themselves had in their hearts,—liberty and equality. Indeed, they appear there in every page; only, we must not make a mistake, equality in obedience, as the Romans had made it for every nation; and liberty internal, inactive, entirely pent up in the soul, just as it was able to be conceived, when, every national resistance having ceased, the hopeless world saw the growing stability of the Eternal Empire.

Assuredly, if there be a situation of things opposite to that of 1789, it is this. Nothing could be more strange than to seek in that affecting legend of resignation, the code of a period when man had claimed his rights.[32]

The Christian is that resigned man of the ancient empire, who places no hope in his personal action, but believes he shall be saved solely and exclusively by Christ. There are very few Christians. There were three or four in the Constituent Assembly. At that period, Christianity (doubtless living and durable as a sentiment) was dead as a system. Many mistook this point; among others, numbers of the friends of liberty, who, being affected by the Gospel, imagined themselves, on that account, to be Christians. As to popular life, Christianity preserved only what it owes to its anti-Christian part, borrowed or imitated from paganism (I mean the idolatry of the Virgin and the Saints), and to the material and sensuous devotion of the Sacred-Heart.

The true Christian principle, that man is saved only by the grace of Christ, after being solemnly condemned by the Pope

---

[32] And from this false study of the Gospel, they passed on to a no less false interpretation of the whole Christian system. There also they found just what they had in their thoughts, liberty; they found that Christianity, which originates in a transgression committed by Adam, an abuse of liberty, is the religion *of liberty*. Yes, of liberty *lost;* that is what ought to have been added. Liberty appears at the starting-point of the system, but to perish irrevocably. The fatality of the first transgression carries with it the whole human race. The few that escape are saved, not by the use of liberty, but by the arbitrary grace of Christ. If you insist that man's free-will should be accounted as something, you lessen the merits of the Saviour; if you will have it that we are saved by free-will, Christ is no longer the Saviour.—To say all in one word: liberty is in every living system; therefore it is in Christianity; it is even its starting-point, but it is not its great, characteristic, and predominant law, that which constitutes the life of the system. The Christian dogma is not the dogma of liberty, but of a *powerless* liberty; it teaches the transmission of a liberty *lost;* it places salvation in grace, which is the free activity of God, but *not ours.* This explains why every kind of despotism, feudal, royal, no matter what, has grounded itself on Christianity.

towards the end of the reign of Louis XIV., has only pined away, its defenders ever diminishing in numbers, hiding, resigning themselves to their fate, and dying without either a complaint or a struggle. And it is by so doing that this party proves, as much as by its doctrine, that it is indeed and truly Christian. It lies hid, as I have said, though it still possesses men of a singular power, whom it might show to its great advantage.

I, who seek my faith elsewhere, and who turn my eyes towards the east, have nevertheless been unable to behold, without the deepest emotion, these men of another age silently becoming extinct. Forgotten by all men, except pagan-christian authority, which practises towards them, unknown to the world, the most cowardly persecution,[33] they will die in worthy fashion. I have had occasion to test them. One day, when in my lectures I was about to encounter their great men of Port-Royal, I expressed an intention of giving utterance to my thoughts, and of disburdening my heart; of saying that then and now, in these men as in Port-Royal, it was paganism persecuting Christianity. They entreated me to do nothing of the kind (and may they forgive me for having violated their secret): "No, sir," said they; "there are situations in which one must learn to die in silence." And, as I insisted from sympathy, they avowed to me ingenuously that, in their opinion, they had not long to suffer; that the great and last day, which will judge both men and doctrines, could not be far; the day when the world will begin to live and cease to die. . . . He who, in their name, told me these strange things, was a young man, serious and pale, prematurely old, who would not tell me his name, and whom I never saw afterwards. That apparition has remained upon my mind as a noble farewell with the past. I

---

[33] A truly cowardly persecution, which deals especially with females, the last surviving Jansenist sisters, whom they are harassing to a lingering death; cowardly also in its fury against the church of Saint Séverin. It has not been demolished, like Port-Royal, but transformed, abandoned to the paganism of the Sacred-Heart, and periodically polluted with Jesuitical preachers.

seemed to hear the last words of the Bride of Corinth: "We will go down into the tomb, to rejoin our ancient gods."

There were three such men in the Constituent Assembly; none of them possessed genius, none was an orator, and yet they exercised certainly a great,—too great influence. Heroic, disinterested, sincere, and excellent citizens, they contributed more than anybody to drive the Revolution into the old impracticable paths; and, as far as in them lay, they made it a reformer, and yet prevented its being a founder, innovator, a creator.

What was necessary to be done in 1790 and 1800? It was necessary at least to wait, and make an appeal to the living powers of the human mind.

Those powers are eternal, and in them is the inexhaustible fountain of philosophical and religious life. No period ought to be despaired of; the worst of modern times, that of the Thirty Years' War, nevertheless produced Descartes, the regenerator of the mind of Europe. It was necessary to appeal to life, and not organise death.

The three men who impelled the Assembly to commit this great blunder, were named Camus, Grégoire, and Lanjuinais.

Three men of unconquerable resolution. Those who saw Camus lay his hand on Dumouriez amidst his army, and those who, on the 31st of May, saw Lanjuinais, when hurled down from the tribune, rushing back to it and holding on, between daggers and pistols, know that few men would appear brave if compared to those two. As to Bishop Grégoire, after remaining in the Convention, during the whole of the reign of Terror, alone on his bench, in his violet robe, nobody daring to sit near him, he has left behind him the reputation of the firmest character that perhaps ever appeared. Terror recoiled before that inflexible priest. During the most stormy days and the most sombre nights of the Convention, it had in Grégoire the immutable image of Christianity, its dumb protest, and its threat of resurrection.

These men, so intrepid and pure, were none the less the supreme temptation of the Revolution; they led it to commit this serious blunder—to organise the Christian Church without believing in Christianity.

Under their influence, and that of the legists who followed their steps without perceiving the mistake, the Assembly, for the most part sceptical and Voltairian in its ideas, imagined that it might alter the exterior without changing the ground-work. It presented the strange spectacle of a Voltaire reforming the Church, and pretending to restore to it its apostolic severity.

But setting aside the incurable defect of this suspicious origin, the reformation was reasonable; it might be called a charter of deliverance for the Church and the clergy.

The Assembly wishes that the clergy should be in future the elect of the people, emancipated from the *Concordat,* a shameful covenant by which two thieves, the king and the pope, had shared the Church between them and cast lots for its vesture; —enfranchised, by their superior remuneration of a regular salary, from the odious necessity of exacting tithes, and such like casualties, and fleecing the people;—enfranchised from an unjust system of promotion and those petty court *abbés* who used to spring from boudoirs and alcoves into the episcopacy; —lastly, free from all locusts and big-bellied priests, and from the ridiculous cages for fattening prebendaries. Add a better division of the dioceses, henceforth of equal extent, with eighty-three bishoprics, the same number as that of the departments, the revenue fixed at seventy-seven million francs, and the clergy better paid with this sum than with its three hundred millions formerly, from which they derived so little advantage.

The debate was neither powerful nor profound. There was only one bold sentence pronounced, and that was said by the Jansenist Camus, and certainly it went beyond his meaning: "We are a National Convention," said he; *"we have assuredly the power to change the religion; but we shall not do so."* Then, being frightened at his own audacity, he added very quickly: "We could not abandon it without crime" (June 1st, 1790). Being legists and theologians, they invoked only texts and musty volumes: at every contested quotation they hastened to fetch their books, and were anxious to prove, not that their opinion was good, but that it was old: "Thus did the early Christians." A poor argument! It was very doubtful whether a thing proper at the age of Tiberius, remained so eighteen hundred years afterwards, in the reign of Louis XVI.

It was necessary, without any tergiversation, to examine, whether the right was above or below, in the king, the pope, or in the people.

What would election by the people produce? Doubtless this was unknown. But people knew perfectly well what was a clergy after the fashion of the king, the pope, and the lords.[34] What countenance would those loudly-protesting prelates have put on if they had been obliged to show by what oil and what hand they had been consecrated? The safest way for them was not to enter too closely into this question of origin. They declaimed by choice on the most temporal question, on the most foreign to the spiritual order, the division of the dioceses. In vain was it proved to them that this division, entirely imperial in its Roman origin, and made by the government, might be modified by another government. They would not listen to reason, but held fast. This division was the only thing, the holy of holies; no dogma of the Christian faith was more deeply implanted in their hearts. If a council were not convened, or if the matter were not referred to the pope, all was over; France was about to become schismatical, and from schismatical heretical; from heretical sacrilegious, athestic, &c.

These solemn farces, which at Paris only caused people to

---

[34] The right of advowson, in the hands of the lords, had very curious effects. One Samuel Bernard, a Jew, who had bought a certain seigneurial manor, had, by that very fact, the right of appointing to such a benefice; between title-deeds and sales, he acquired the Holy Ghost. The Holy Ghost would descend, alas! from doings still more sad. Such a one was bishop by the grace of Madame de Polignac; another was appointed by La Pompadour, whilst another owed his bishopric to the wanton sports of Madame Du Barry with Louis XV. A handsome young abbé of twenty, abbé de Bourbon, endowed with an income of a million francs, was the offspring of a noble young lady, sold by her parents and long brought up by the king for a momentary gratification.

shrug their shoulders with contempt, had nevertheless the intended effect in the West and the South. There they were
printed and distributed in an immense number of copies, with
the famous protest in favour of the property of the clergy,
which, in two months, reached the thirtieth edition. Being
repeated in the pulpit in the morning, commented in the confessional in the afternoon, and adorned with murderous annota-
tions, this text of hatred and discord continued more and more
to exasperate the women, rekindle religious strife, whet the
poignards, and sharpen the pitchforks and scythes.

On the 29th and 31st of May, the Archbishop of Aix and the
Bishop of Clermont (one of the principal leaders of the revolt,
and the king's confidential man) notified the ecclesiastical ulti-
matum to the Assembly: That no change could be made without the convocation of a council. And in the early part of the
month of June blood was flowing at Nimes.

Froment had armed his surest companies, and had, at great
expense, even dressed several of his men in the livery of the
Count d'Artois. They were the first of the notorious *verdets*
of the South. Being supported by an aide-de-camp of Prince de
Condé, and backed by several municipal officers, he had at
length extorted from the commandant of the province the
promise to open the arsenal and give guns to all the Catholic
companies: a last decisive act which the municipality and the
commandant could not commit without declaring themselves
frankly against the Revolution.

Let us wait a little longer, said the municipality; the elections
of the department begin at Nimes on the 4th; let us go on
gently till the voting, and manage to get places given to us.

Let us act, said Froment; the electors will vote better at the
sound of the musketry. The Protestants are being organised,
and they have established a powerful correspondence from
Nimes to Paris, and from Nimes to the Cévennes.

Was Nimes a very sure place for the clergy if they waited?
The town was about to feel, in its industry, an immediate
benefit from the Revolution, the suppression of the taxes on
salt, iron, leather, oil, soap, &c. And would the Catholic rural

districts, very catholic before harvest, be equally so afterwards, when the clergy had exacted the tithes?

A trial was pending against the assassins of May, against Froment's brother. That trial was coming on very slowly, but still it was in preparation.

A last and decisive reason that forced Froment to act, was that the Revolution of Avignon had been effected on the 11th and the 12th, and that it was about to demoralise his party, and cause its weapons to fall from its hands. Before news had spread, he attacked, in the evening of the 13th, a favourable day, the Sunday after the festival of Corpus-Christi, a great portion of the populace having been drinking and become excited.

Froment, and the historians of his faction, the conquered party, make this incredible statement: that the Protestants began the trouble, that they themselves disrupted the elections in which lay all their hopes; they maintain that it was the few who undertook to slaughter the many (six thousand men against twenty thousand odd, without counting the suburbs).

And was that small body so very warlike and terrible? It was a population that had remained for a century apart from every kind of military practice; merchants, excessively afraid of pillage; and feeble workmen, physically very inferior to the porters, vine-dressers, and labourers, whom Froment had armed. The dragoons of the National Guard, Protestants for the most part, tradespeople and their sons, were not men likely to stand against those strong hardy men who used to drink their fill in the wine cabarets belonging to the clergy.

In every place where the Protestants were the majority, these two forms of worship presented a spectacle of the most affecting fraternity. At Saint-Hippolyte, for instance, the Protestants had desired, on the 5th of June, to mount guard with the others, for the procession of Corpus-Christi.

On the day of the outbreak at Nimes, the patriots, to the number of fifteen hundred at least, and the most active, had assembled at the club, without arms, and were deliberating;

the galleries were full of women. Horrible was their panic on hearing the first discharge of musketry (June 13th, 1790).

At the opening of the elections, eight days before, trouble-makers had begun to insult and frighten the electors. They asked for a body of dragoons and patrols to disperse the threatening crowd. But that mob threatened the patrols still more; and then the complaisant municipality kept the dragoons in their quarters. In the evening of the 13th, men wearing red tufts come and tell the dragoons that if they do not march off, they are dead men. They remain, and receive a discharge of fire-arms. The regiment of Guienne was thirsting to march to their assistance; but the officers shut the doors and keep them to their quarters.

In presence of this unequal struggle, and seeing the elections so criminally disturbed, the municipality had a sacred duty to perform,—to display the red flag and call out the troops. But no municipality could be found. The electoral assembly of the department, in that hospitable town, is found to be abandoned by the magistrates, amid the firing of the musketry.

Among Froment's *Verdets* were even the domestics of several of the municipal officers mixed in with those of the clergy. The troops, the National Guard receiving no requisition, Froment had the town all to himself; his people were able to butcher freely, and had now begun to force open the houses of the Protestants. Had he only been able to keep his momentary advantage, he would have received from Sommières, only four leagues distant, a regiment of cavalry, whose colonel, a warm partisan, offered him his men, his purse, and his service.

The affair then assuming the appearance of a real revolution, the commandant of the province would at length have followed the orders he had received from the Count d'Artois, and have marched upon Nimes.

Contrary to every expectation, it was Nimes itself that spoilt the whole affair. Of the eighteen Catholic companies formed by Froment, only three followed him. The fifteen others never stirred. A great lesson, clearly showing the clergy how much they had mistaken the real state of the public mind. In the hour of bloodshed, the old spirit of fanatical hatred, though skilfully rekindled by social jealousy, was not quite strong enough.

The great and powerful city of Nimes, which they had expected to be able to drive so easily into rebellion, remained firm, like its indestructible monuments—its noble and eternal arena.

An infinitely small portion only of each party came to blows. The *Verdets* proved very brave, but furious and blind. Twice the municipal authorities, when they were at last found, were forced to confront them with the red flag; twice the *verdets* carried them all off, red flag and municipal authorities, in the very teeth of their enemies. They fired on the magistrates, the electors, and the king's commissioners; the next day, they fired on the attorney-general, and the royal magistrate for criminal cases, who were taking an inventory of the dead. These crimes, capital as they assuredly were, called for the most speedy and severe repression; and yet all that the municipality claimed from the troops was to serve as patrols!

If Froment had had more people, he would doubtless have occupied the great position of the arenas, then easy to defend. He left there a few men, and some others also in the convent of the Capucins. As for himself, he withdrew to his fort, on the ramparts, in the tower of the ancient castle. Once in his tower, in safety, and firing at his ease, he wrote to Sommières and Montpellier to obtain assistance. He sent also into the Catholic villages and caused them to ring their alarm-bells.

The Catholics were very slow, some even remained at home. But the Protestants were immediately on the alert. At the news of the danger in which the electors were placed, they marched all night, and between four and six o'clock the next morning, an army of Cevenols, with the tri-colour cockade, was at Nimes in battle array, shouting, *Vive la nation!*

Then the electors acted. Forming a military committee, by the help of a captain of artillery, they marched to the arsenal to procure some cannon. The entrance to it was by the street, or by the quarters of the regiment of Guienne. The officers, malevolently, told them to pass through the street. There, they were pierced with a volley of bullets, and withdrew; the officers, seeing their soldiers indignant, and about to turn against them, at length delivered up the cannon. The tower, being battered till a breach was made, was forced to parley. Froment, audacious to the last, sent an incredible missive, in which he offered *"to forget."*. . . Then, there was no longer any favour to be expected, the soldiery vowing death against the besieged. An attempt was made to save them; but they rushed upon their own ruin: they fired whilst capitulating. They were forced into their tower, taken by storm, pursued, and massacred.

The second day, and the third, they were pursued everywhere, or, at least, under this pretext, many old quarrels were avenged. The convents of the Capucins (the pamphlet warehouse, from which they had fired moreover), was also forced and everybody put to death. The case was the same with a celebrated cabaret, the head-quarters of the *Verdets;* and in this den they discovered two municipal magistrates. All this time, the two parties were firing at each other through the streets or from the windows. The savages from the Cévennes seldom gave any quarter; and in three days there were three hundred people killed. No church was pillaged, nor any woman insulted; they were temperate even in their fury. They would never have imagined flogging girls to death with a paddle bearing a fleur de lis, as the *verdets* of 1815 were to do.

This cruel affair of Nimes, perfidiously arranged by the counter-revolution, was curious, inasmuch as it destroyed its perpetrators. The snarer was caught in his own trap; it was the game hunting the huntsman!

Everything went wrong at once—at the moment of execution. They had reckoned on Montpellier; but the commandant dared not come. But the brave and patriotic National Guard, the future frame-work of the legion of victory, the 32nd demi-brigade came.

They had reckoned on Arles; and indeed Arles offered its

assistance; but it was to crush the counter-revolutionary party. And as for Pont-Saint-Esprit, it arrested Froment's envoys!

Go, now, and summon the Catholics of the Rhône. Try to puzzle their minds, and make them believe that in all this your religion is in peril. No, the question is about our native land.

The whole of Catholic Rhône declares against you, and becomes far more revolutionary than the Protestants. Your own saintly city of the Rhône, the petty Rome of the pope, even Avignon, joins the Revolution.

O Avignon! Why could France ever have taken thee, thou precious diamond, from her diadem! . . . O Vaucluse! O pure eternal remembrance of Petrarch, noble asylum of the great Italian who died of love for France, thou adorable symbol of the future union of the two countries, why didst thou ever fall into the polluted hands of the pope! . . . For money, and to obtain absolution for a murder, a woman sold Avignon and Vaucluse (1348)!

Avignon, without taking counsel, had, like France, made for itself a national militia, a municipality. On the 10th of June, all the nobility and partisans of the pope, being masters of the Hôtel-de-Ville and four pieces of cannon, shout: "Aristocracy forever!" Then thirty persons are killed or wounded. But then also the people begin to fight in earnest; they kill several, and take twenty-two prisoners. All the French communes, Orange, Bagnols, Pont-Saint-Esprit, hasten to assist Avignon, and save the prisoners. They receive them from the hands of the conquerors, and undertake to guard them.

On the 11th of June, they deface the arms of Rome, and those of France are set up in their place. Avignon sends a deputation to the bar of the National Assembly, and bestows itself on its real country, pronouncing these magnificent words, the testament of Roman genius: "Frenchmen, rule over the world."

Let us enter further into the causes, and complete and explain more clearly this rapid drama.

To make a religious war, people must be religious. The clergy were not sufficiently believers to fanaticise the people.

428

Neither were they very great politicians. That very year, 1790, when they stood so much in need of the people, whom they bribed on all sides, they still exacted from them the tithes abolished by the Assembly. In several places, insurrections took place against them, especially in the north, on account of those unfortunate tithes which they would not abandon.

That aristocratic clergy, without any comprehension of moral powers, thought that a little money, wine, the influence of the climate, and a single spark, would be sufficient. They ought to have been aware that to rekindle fanaticism, it required time, patience, secrecy, a country less observed, far from the high roads and larger cities. Most certainly, they might thus create a lasting agitation in the Bocage of La Vendée; but to act in the open day, before the anxious eyes of the Protestants, and in the neighbourhood of the great centres of civilisation, like Bordeaux, Marseilles, and Montpellier, who saw everything, and were able, at the slightest spark, to run and stamp out the fire, was a childish attempt.

Froment did all he could. He showed much audacity and decision; and he was abandoned.[35]

He began at the right moment, seeing that the affair at Avignon was about to spoil that of Nimes, not over-calculating his chances, but, like a brave man, trying to believe that the dubious parties who till then had not dared to declare in his favour, would at length make up their minds when they saw

---

[35] Froment escaped being massacred. However little disposed we may be in favour of the man and his party, it is impossible not to feel interested in his strange destiny. First, honoured, ennobled, and loaded with presents by the Count d'Artois, and the emigrants; then, in 1816, abandoned and disowned! The pamphlets which he then published, the proceedings of an old servant against an ungrateful and heartless master, have been everywhere carefully destroyed. Shall I add that this master went so far as to deprive him, after the law suit, of the miserable petty pension which he enjoyed? and that, after thirty years' gratuitous service, resolved that the man, ruined, worn out, and in debt on his account, should die in the street. Froment's pamphlets would deserve to be re-printed; so also would the "Memoirs of Vauban," the emigrant, now become so scarce; and M. Merilhou's very clever defence in favour of Froment (1823).

him engaged; and that they could not calmly see him annihilated.

The municipality; in other words, the Catholic citizen-class, was prudent; it dared not call upon the commandant of the province.

The nobility was prudent. The commandant, and the officers in general were unwilling to act without the proper and legal requisition of the municipality.

It was not that the officers were wanting in courage; but they were not sure of the soldiers. At the first extra-legal order, they might answer with their guns. And to give this first order, and make this dangerous experiment, it was necessary to have made, beforehand, a sacrifice of one's life. But to what idea, what faith? The majority of the nobility, though Royalists and Aristocrats, were not the less imbued with philosophical and Voltairian ideas, that is to say, in any one respect, won over to the new spirit.

The Revolution, growing more and more harmonised and in unison, appears every day more plainly what it is, a religion. And the Counter-Revolution, dissenting and discordant, attests the old faith in vain; it is not a religion.

It has no unity, no fixed principle. Its opposition is wavering, tending several ways at once. It staggers, like a drunken man, to the right and left. The king is for the clergy, and he refuses to support the ecclesiastical protest. The clergy pay and arm the people, and yet exact tithes of them. The nobility and officers wait for orders from Turin, and at the same time those of the Revolutionary authorities.

One thing is wanting in them all to render their action simple and strong; a thing that abounds in the other party—faith!

The other party is France; it has faith in the new faith, in the legitimate authority, the Assembly, the true voice of the nation.

On that side, everything is effulgent with light; on the other, everything is equivocal, all uncertainty, and darkness.

Why should there be any hesitation? All together, the soldier and the citizen, joining hands, will henceforth march with a firm step, and under the self-same flag. From April to June, almost all the regiments fraternize with the people. In Corsica, at Caen, Brest, Montpellier, Valence, as at Montauban and Nimes, the soldier declares for the people and the law. The few officers who resist are killed, and on them are found the proofs of their intelligence with the emigrants. As for the latter, the people are ready to receive them. The cities of the South do not slumber; Briançon, Montpellier, Valence, and lastly, great Marseilles, are willing to guard themselves; they seize on their citadels and fill them with their citizens. Now, let the emigrants and foreigners come, if they will!

One France, one faith, one oath! Here no doubtful man must remain. If you wish to remain wavering, depart from the land of loyalty, pass the Rhine, and cross over the Alps.

The king himself plainly perceives that his best sword, Bouillé, would at length find himself alone, if he did not take the oath like the others. The enemy of the federations, who had placed himself between the army and the people, is obliged to yield. People and soldiers, united in heart, are all present at that grand spectacle; even the inflexible is now obliged to give way; the king orders, and he obeys. He advances between them, sad and moody, and on his sword, devoted to royalty, takes the oath of fidelity to the Revolution.

X

The New Principle—

Spontaneous Organisation of France

(July, 1789 to July, 1790)

I HAVE related fully the resistance offered by the old principle,—the *parlements,* the nobility, and the clergy; and I am now going to expound, in a few words, the new principle, and state briefly the immense fact, by which their resistance was confounded and annihilated. The fact, admirably simple in its infinite variety, is *the spontaneous organisation of France.*

That is history, the real, the positive, and the durable; and the rest is nonentity.

It was, however, necessary to detail this nonentity at full length. Evil, precisely because it is nothing but an exception, an irregularity, requires, in order to be understood, a minute narration of particulars. Good, on the contrary, the natural, which springs forth of itself, is almost known to us beforehand by its conformity to the laws of our nature, by the eternal image of good which we possess within us.

The sources whence we derive history have preciously preserved the least worthy of preservation,—the negative accidental element, the individual anecdote, this or that petty intrigue or act of violence.

The great national facts, in which France has acted in con-

432

cord, have been accomplished by immense, invincible, and, for that very reason, by no means violent, powers. They have excited less attention, and passed almost unperceived.

All that we are furnished on these general facts, are the laws, which are derived from them, and have become their last expression. People are never tired of the discussion of the laws, and earnestly repeating the language of the Assemblies. But, as for the great and social movements which brought about those laws, which were their origin, the reason and necessity of their existence, there is scarcely a single line to recall them to our minds.

And yet this is the great climax to which everything else in this miraculous year from one July to the other tends: the law is everywhere forestalled by the spontaneous working of life and action,—an action which, among a few particular disturbances, contains nevertheless the new order of things and realises beforehand the law which will presently be made. The Assembly believes it is leading, but it follows; it is the recorder of France; what France does, it registers, more or less exactly, reduces to a formula, and writes under her dictation.

Let the scribes come here and learn; let them quit, for a moment, their den, the *Bulletin des Lois*, and throw aside those huge piles of stamped paper which have screened them from nature. If France could have been saved only by their pens and paper, she would have perished a hundred times.

Serious and infinitely interesting is the moment when nature recovers in time not to perish, when life, in presence of danger, follows instinct, its best guide, and finds therein its salvation.

A worn-out society, in this crisis of resurrection, affords us a spectacle of the origin of things. The civilians were musing over the cradle of infant nations. Wherefore muse? You have it before you.

Yes, it is the cradle of France that we now behold. May God protect that cradle! May He save and sustain it upon that great and boundless ocean where I tremble to behold it floating, upon the ocean of futurity!

France is born and started into life at the sound of the cannon of the Bastille. In one day, without any preparation or previous understanding, the whole of France, both cities and villages, is organised at the same time.

The same thing happens in every locality: the people go to the communal house, take the keys and assume the power in the name of the nation. The electors (everybody was an elector in 1789) form committees, like that of Paris, which will presently produce the regular municipalities.

The governors and administrators of cities (like those of the State) eschevins, notables, and others, withdraw and skulk away by the back door, bequeathing to the commune they had administered, debts as a souvenir.

The financial Bastille, which the oligarchy of notables had concealed so well from every eye, the administrative den, appears in broad daylight; [36] the shapeless instruments of that equivocal *régime*, the confusion of papers, the learned obscurity of calculations, are all brought to light.

The first cry of that liberty (which they call the spirit of disorder) is, on the contrary, order and justice.

Order, in broad daylight. France said to God, like Ajax: "Let me rather die in the light of heaven!"

What was most tyrannical in the old tyrannical system, was its obscurity: obscurity between the king and the people, between the city authorities and the town, and a no less profound obscurity between the land-proprietor and the tenant. What was a man bound in his conscience to pay to the State, to the Commune, and to the lord of the manor? Nobody could say. Most people paid what they were unable even to read. The utter ignorance in which the clergy, the privileged teachers of the people, had kept them, abandoned them blind and defenceless to those horrible cormorants, the limbs of the law. Every year, their stamped papers returned, still more blotted

---

[36] See, in Leber, the shameful picture of this ancient municipal administration, the gratifications exacted by the eschevins, &c. &c. Lyons was twenty-nine millions in debt!

434

and scribbled, with additional expenses, for the horror of the peasant. These mysterious and unknown extra-charges, whether understood or not, he was obliged to pay; but they remained stored up in his heart, as a treasure of vengeance, for which he should require an indemnity. In 1789, several persons stated that, in forty years, they had paid, with these extra-charges, more than the estates, of which they were then proprietors, were really worth.

In our rural districts, no damage was done to property except in the name of property. The peasant interpreted it in his own manner; but he never raised any doubt as to the idea of this right. The rural labourer knows what it is to acquire; the acquisition that he makes or sees made every day, by labour, inspires him with a sort of religious respect for property.

It was in the name of property, long violated and perverted by the agents of the lords of the manor, that the peasants erected those Maypoles on which they suspended the insignia of feudal and fiscal tyranny, the weathercocks of castles, the measures of raising rents unjustly, and the sieves which sifted the grain all to the advantage of the lord, and left only the refuse.

The committees of July 1789 (the origin of the municipalities of 1790) were, for the towns especially, the insurrection of *liberty*,—and for the villages that of property: I mean the most sacred property—man's *labour*.

The village associations were societies for protection,—first, against the legal agents; and secondly, against the brigands,—two words often synonymous.

They confederated against the stewards, collectors, managers, attorneys, and bailiffs,—against that horrible scrawl, which, by some magic process, had parched up the land, destroyed the cattle, and worn the peasant to the bone, reducing him to a skeleton.

They confederated also against those troops of pillagers, who were overrunning France, people starving for want of work, beggars turned thieves, who, at night, cut down the grain, even when unripe, thus destroying hope. If the villages had not taken up arms, a horrible famine must have been the result, a season like the year 1000 and several of the middle ages. Those wandering bands, difficult to seize, and everywhere expected, and which fear caused to appear everywhere present, filled with dismay our rural population, then less military than at the present day.

All the villages armed, and promised each other mutual protection. They agreed among themselves to unite, in case of alarm, at a given spot, in a central position, or one commanding the principal passage by land or by water.

One fact will serve to elucidate this subject. It reminds us, in some respects, of the panic at Saint-Jean-du-Gard, which I have already related.

Early one morning in summer, the inhabitants of Chavignon (Aisne) beheld, not without trepidation, their street full of armed men. They perceived, however, that, luckily, they were their neighbours and friends, the national guards of all the adjacent communes, who, under false alarm, had marched all night to come to defend them against the *brigands*. They had expected a fight, but they found a feast. All the inhabitants of Chavignon, overjoyed, went forth from their houses to welcome their friends. The women brought out and shared in common all the provisions they had; and casks of wine were opened. In the public square they displayed the flag of Chavignon, on which are delineated grapes and wheat with a naked sword,— a device that summed up very correctly the idea of the day: abundance and security, liberty, fidelity, and concord. The captain-general of the national guards that had come, made a very affecting speech on the eagerness of the communes to come to the defence of their brethren: "At the first word," said he, "we quitted our wives and children in tears; we left our ploughs and implements in the fields, and marched, without taking even the time to dress ourselves properly."

The inhabitants of Chavignon, in an address to the National Assembly, relate every circumstance, as a child would to its mother, and, full of gratitude, add this word from the heart: "What men, gentlemen, what men they have become, since you gave them a native land!"

These spontaneous expeditions were thus made, like family parties, with the curate marching at their head. At that of Chavignon, four of the communes that came were accompanied by their curates.

In certain districts, for instance in the Upper-Saône, the curates not only associated in these movements, but formed their centre, and were their leaders and directors. As early as the 27th of September, 1789, the rural communes, in the environs of Luxeuil, confederated under the direction of the curate of Saint Sauveur, and to him all the mayors took the oath.

At Issy-l'Evêque (also in Upper-Saône) there happened a more extraordinary fact. In the general annihilation of every kind of public authority, and seeing no longer any magistrate, a valiant *curé* assumed himself all the different powers: he enacted ordinances, re-judged law suits already tried, sent for the mayors of the neighbourhood, and promulgated in their presence the new laws which he gave to the country; then, arming himself, he marched forth, sword in hand, to set about sharing all the land into equal portions. It was necessary to check his zeal and remind him that there was still a National Assembly.

This is uncommon and remarkable. The movement in general was regular, and took place with more order than could have been expected under such circumstances. Though without laws, everybody obeyed a law,—that of preservation and safety.

Before the municipalities are organised, each village governs, guards, and defends itself, as an armed association of inhabitants of the same place.

Before there are any arrondissements and departments created by the law, common necessities, especially that of making the roads safe and transporting provisions, form associations between villages and villages, towns and cities, great federations for mutual protection.

We feel inclined to thank those dangers when we see how they force men to emerge from their isolated position, snatch them from their egotism, accustom them to feel themselves live in others, and awaken in their souls, that had remained dormant for so many centuries, the first spark of fraternity.

The law comes to acknowledge, authorise, and crown all this; but it does not produce it.

The creation of municipalities, and the concentrating into their hands even non-communal powers (taxation, superior police, the power of disposing of the military, &c.)—this concentration with which the Assembly has been reproached, was not the effect of a system, but the mere acknowledgment of a fact. Given the destruction of most agencies of public authority, given the wilful (and often perfidious) inactivity of those that remained, the instinct of self-preservation had produced the usual result: the interested parties had themselves taken their affairs in hand. And who is not interested in such a crisis? Even he who has no property, *who has nothing*, as people say, possesses, nevertheless, what is far dearer than any property,—a wife and children to defend.

The new municipal law created *twelve hundred thousand* municipal magistrates; and the judiciary organisation *a hundred thousand* judges (of whom five thousand were *juges-de-paix*, and eighty thousand assistants to the *juges-de-paix*). All these were chosen among the four million two hundred and ninety-eight thousand primary electors [37] (who, as proprietors or tenants, paid taxes to the value of three days' labour, or about three francs).

Universal suffrage had given six million votes; I shall explain hereafter this limitation of the electoral right, and the different principles which influenced the Assembly.

It is sufficient here to indicate the prodigious movement that France must then have made, in the spring of 1790, this crea-

---

[37] This is the number given in 1791 in the *Atlas National de France,* intended for public instruction and dedicated to the Assembly. The Bishop of Autun, in his speech of June 8, 1790, reckons only three million six hundred thousand active citizens. This small number would be too considerable if it meant only the proprietors, but it includes also those who pay taxes to the value of about three francs as *tenants.* The larger number is the more likely. Both, however, the larger and the smaller are doubtless only approximative.

tion of a multitude of judges and administrators,—*thirteen hundred thousand* at once arising from the election!

It may be said that before the military conscription, France had carried out a conscription of magistrates. A conscription of peace, order, and fraternity! What appears predominant here, in the judicial order, is this fine new element, unknown to all ages, the five thousand arbiters or justices of the peace, and their eighty thousand assistants; and, in the municipal order, it is the dependence in which the military force finds itself with respect to the magistrates of the people.

The municipal power inherited all the ruins of authority. Between the ancient system destroyed, and the new one then inactive, it alone remained standing. The king was disarmed, the army disorganised, every state and parlement demolished, the clergy dismantled, and the nobility about to be erased. The Assembly itself, the great apparent power, ordered rather than acted: it was a head without arms. But it had forty-four thousand hands in the municipalities, and it left almost everything to the twelve hundred thousand municipal magistrates.

The immensity of this number was a drawback to action; but, as an education of the people, as an initiation to public life, it was admirable. Being rapidly renewed, the magistracy would soon exhaust, in many localities, the class from which it was recruited (the four millions of proprietors or tenants who paid three francs taxes). It was necessary (and it was a fine necessity of this grand initiation) to create a new class of proprietors. The peasants of the clergy and the aristocracy, at first excluded from election as clients of the ancient system, would now, as purchasers of the estates set up for sale, find themselves proprietors, electors, municipal magistrates, assessors of justices of the peace, &c.; and, as such, become the stanchest supporters of the Revolution.

XI

The New Religion—Federations
(July, 1789 to July, 1790)

Nothing of all this existed in the winter of 1789: there were neither any regular municipalities nor any departments; no laws, no authority, no public power. Everything, one would think, is about to fall into chaos; and this is the hope of the aristocracy . . . "Ah! you wanted to be free! Look about you, and enjoy the order you have created." To this what reply is made by France? At that formidable crisis, she becomes her own law; and, without any assistance, springs, with a powerful will, over the chasm between one world and the other, passes, without stumbling, the narrow bridge over the abyss, without heeding the danger, with her eyes fixed on the goal. She advances courageously through that dark winter, towards the wished-for spring which promises a new light to the world.

What light? It is no longer, as in 1789 the vague love of liberty; but a determined object, of a fixed and settled form, which leads the whole nation, transporting and captivating the heart; at every new step, it appears more delightful, and the march is the more rapid. At length the shades of night disappear, the mist is dispelled, and France beholds distinctly what she had loved and followed, without ever having been able to attain it—the unity of the native land.

All that had been believed painful, difficult, and insurmountable, becomes possible and easy. People had asked themselves how the sacrifice of provincial sentiments, reminiscences, and inveterate prejudices, was to be accomplished. "How," said they, "will Languedoc ever consent to cease to be Languedoc, an interior empire governed by its own laws? How will ancient Toulouse descend from her capitol, her royalty of the South? And do you believe that Brittany will ever give way to France, emerge from her barbarous language and obstinate character? You will sooner see the rocks of Saint-Malo and Penmarck change their nature and become soft."

But lo! the native land appears to them on the altar, opening her arms and wishing to embrace them . . . And they all rush towards her and forget themselves, no longer knowing on that day to what province they belong . . . Like children gone astray, and lost till then, they have at length found a mother; they had been so humble as to imagine themselves Bretons, Provençaux. No, children, know well that you were the sons of France; she herself tells you so; the sons of that great mother, of her who is destined, in equality, to bring forth nations.

Nothing is more grand than to see this people advancing towards the light, without any law, but hand in hand. They advance, but do not act; neither do they feel any necessity of acting; they advance, that is sufficient; the mere sight of that immense movement causes everything to recoil before them; every obstacle vanishes, and all opposition is removed. Who would think of standing up against this pacific and formidable apparition of a great nation in arms?

The federations of November break up the provincial estates; those of January put an end to the struggle of the *parlements;* those of February put down the riots and pillages; in March and April, those masses are organised which stifle in May and June the first sparks of a war of religion; May, moreover, witnesses the military federations, the soldier becoming once more a citizen, and the sword of the counter-revolution, its last weapon, shattered to pieces . . . What remains? Fraternity has removed every obstacle, all the federations are about to confederate together, and union tends to unity.—No more federations! They are useless, only one now is necessary,—France; and it appears transfigured in the glory of July.

Is all this a miracle? Yes, and the greatest and most simple of miracles, a return to nature. The fundamental basis of human nature is sociability. It had required a whole world of inventions against nature to prevent men from living together.

Interior custom-duties, innumerable tolls on roads and rivers, an infinite diversity of laws and regulations, weights, measures, and money, and rivalry carefully encouraged and maintained between cities, countries, and corporations,—all these obstacles, these old ramparts, crumble and fall in a day. Men then behold one another, perceive they are alike, are astonished to have been able to remain so long ignorant of one another, regret the senseless animosity which had separated them for so many centuries, and expiate it by advancing to meet and embrace one another with a mutual effusion of the heart.

This is what rendered so easy and practicable the creation of departments, which had been believed to be entirely impossible. If it had been a mere geometrical conception, emanating from the brain of Sieyès, it would have possessed neither the power nor the durability which we now behold; it would not have survived the ruin of so many other revolutionary institutions. It was, generally speaking, a natural creation, a legitimate restoration of ancient relations between places and populations, which the artificial institutions of despotism and fiscality had kept divided. The rivers, for instance, which, under the ancient system, were scarcely better than obstacles (twenty-eight tolls on the Loire! to give only one example), the rivers, I say, became once more what nature intended them to be, the connecting bond of mankind. They formed and gave their names to the greater number of the departments; the Seine, the Loire, the Rhône, the Gironde, the Meuse, the Charente, the Allier, the Gard, and others, were like so many natural confederations between the two banks of the rivers, which the state acknowledged, proclaimed, and consecrated.

Most of the federations have themselves related their own

history. They wrote it to their parent, the National Assembly, faithfully and naturally, in a form often rustic and inexperienced; they spoke as they could; whoever knew how to write, wrote. It was not always possible to find in the rural districts a skilful scribe worthy of consigning such things to posterity. But good-will supplied the deficiency . . . Ye venerable monuments of youthful fraternity, shapeless, but spontaneous and inspired acts of France, you will remain for ever as witnesses of the hearts of our fathers, and of their transports, when they beheld for the first time the thrice blessed face of their native land!

I have found all that entire and glowing, as though made yesterday, when, sixty years afterwards, I lately opened those papers, which few persons had read. At the first I perused, I was overcome with respect; I perceived a singular, unparalleled fact, on which it is impossible to be mistaken: these enthusiastic documents addressed to the country (represented by the Assembly) are love-letters!

There is nothing official or constrained; it is evidently the language of the heart. The only art, rhetoric, or declamation that appears therein, is precisely the absence of art, the embarrassment of a youth who knows not how to express the most sincere sentiments, who employs the language of romance, for want of better, to confess his true passion.

But, from time to time, a word springing from the heart, protests against this being styled impotency of language, and causes us to perceive the real depth of the sentiment . . . And then the style is very verbose; for how, in such a moment, is it possible to say enough; or how ever to feel satisfied? . . . The material details likewise gave them much solicitude: no writing seemed handsome enough, no paper elegant enough, not to mention the sumptuous little tri-coloured ribbons to tie the papers with. When I saw them first, still gay and but little faded, they reminded me of what Rousseau says of the extraordinary care he took to write, embellish, and adorn, the manuscript of his "Julia." Such were also the thoughts, and such the care and solicitude of our fathers, when, from transient and

443

imperfect objects, their love aspired to eternal beauty!

What affected me, and filled me with emotion and admiration, is, that in so great a variety of men, characters, and localities, with so many divers elements, which, for the most part, were but yesterday strangers, nay, frequently hostile to one another, there is nothing but what breathes the pure love of unity.

Where, then, are the old distinctions of provinces and races of men? Where those powerful and geographical contrasts? All have disappeared: geography itself is annihilated. There are no longer any mountains, rivers, or barriers between men. Their language is still dissimilar, but their words agree so well that they all seem to spring from the same place,—from the same bosom. Everything has gravitated towards one point, and that point now speaks forth; it is a unanimous prayer from the heart of France.

Such is the power of love. To attain unity, nothing was able to prove an impediment, no sacrifice was considered too dear. All at once, and without even perceiving it, they have forgotten the things for which they would have sacrificed their lives the day before, their provincial sentiment, local tradition, and legends. Time and space, those material conditions to which life is subject, are no more. A strange *vita nuova*, one eminently spiritual, and making her whole Revolution a sort of dream, at one time delightful, at another terrible, is now beginning for France. It knew neither time nor space.

And yet it was antiquity, with its old habits, familiar objects, customary signs, and revered symbols, that had hitherto constituted life. All that now grows faint, or disappears. What remains, for instance, the ceremonies of the old religion, now called to consecrate these new festivals, is felt to be only an accessory. In those immense assemblies wherein people of every class and every communion have but one and the selfsame heart, there is something more sacred than an altar. No special form of worship can confer holiness on the most holy of holy things,—man fraternising in the presence of God.

444

All the old emblems grow pale, and the new ones that are tried have little significance. Whether people swear on the old altar, before the Holy Sacrament, or take the oath before the cold image of abstract liberty, the true symbol is elsewhere.

The beauty, the grandeur, the eternal charm of those festivals, is that the symbol is a living one.

This symbol for man is man. All the conventional world crumbling to pieces, a holy respect possesses him for the true image of God. He does not mistake himself for God: he has no vain pride. It is not as a ruler or a conqueror, but in far more affecting and serious attributes that man appears here. The noble harmonious sentiments of family, nature, and native land, are sufficient to fill these festivals with a religious, pathetic interest.

The president at first is some old man: the old man surrounded with children, has the whole nation for his family. He is conducted and escorted back with music. At the great federation of Rouen, where the national guards of sixty different towns attended, they brought from the remote Andelis, a venerable knight of Malta, eighty-five years of age, to preside over the Assembly. At Saint-Andéol, the honour of taking the oath at the head of all the people was conferred on two patriarchs, one ninety-three, and the other ninety-four,—one a noble and the colonel of the National Guard, the other a private labourer; they embraced at the altar, thanking heaven that they had lived to see that day. The people were full of emotion, believing they beheld in those venerable men the everlasting reconciliation of classes. They rushed into each other's arms, and joining hands, an immense farandole, comprising everybody, without exception, spread throughout the town, into the fields, across the mountains of Ardèche, and towards the meadows of the Rhône; the wine flowed in the streets, tables were spread, provisions placed in common, and all the people are together in the evening, solemnising this love-feast, and praising God.

There was everywhere an old man at the head of the people,

sitting in the first place, and presiding over the crowd, and around him were girls, like a garland of flowers. In all these solemnities, this lovely band marches dressed in white with sashes *à la nation* (that is to say, tri-coloured). Here, one of them pronounces a few noble charming sentences, which will create heroes to-morrow. Elsewhere (in the civic procession of Romans in Dauphiné), a beautiful girl marched along, bearing in her hand a palm with this superscription: *to the best citizen!* . . . Many returned from that procession lost in thought.

Dauphiné, the serious and valiant province which opened the Revolution, made numerous federations of the whole province, and of the towns and villages. The rural communes of the frontier nearest to Savoy, close to the emigrants, and tilling the ground in the neighbourhood of their guns, did but have still finer festivals. They had a battalion of children, another of women, and another of maidens, all armed. At Maubec they filed along in good order, headed by a banner, bearing and handling their naked swords with that graceful skill peculiar to the women of France.

I have related elsewhere [38] the heroic example of the women and maidens of Angers. They wanted to depart and follow the young army of Anjou and Brittany marching for Rennes, to take their share in that first crusade of liberty, to feed the combatants, and take care of the wounded. They swore they would never marry any but loyal citizens, love only the valiant, and associate for life only with those who devoted theirs to France.

They thus inspired the enthusiasm of 1788. And now in the federations of June and July, 1790, after the removal of so many obstacles, none were more affected in these festivals of victory; for, during the winter, in the complete absence of all public protection, what dangers had not the family incurred! In these great assemblages, so comforting in nature, they seized upon the hope of safety. Their poor hearts were, however, still heavy because of the past. And because of the future? But they

---

[38] Page 79.

wanted no future save the well-being of the country! They evinced, as we may perceive in every written document, more enthusiasm and fervour than even the men, and a greater impatience to take the civic oath.

Women are kept back from public life; and people are too apt to forget that they really have more right to it than any. The stake they venture is very different from ours; man plays only his life; but woman stakes her child. She is far more interested in acquiring information and foresight. In the solitary sedentary life which most women lead, they follow, in their anxious musings, the critical events of their country, and the movements of the armies. The mind of this woman, whom you believe to be entirely occupied with her household duties, is wandering in Algeria, sharing all the privations and marches of our young soldiers in Africa, and suffering and fighting with them. But, whether called or not, they took the most active part in the *fêtes* of the federations. In some village or other, the men had assembled alone in a large building, to make a common address to the National Assembly. The women draw near, listen, enter, and, with tears in their eyes, entreat to be allowed to join them. Then, the address is read to them, and they agree to it heartily. This affecting union of the family and the country filled every heart with an unknown sentiment. The *fête*, though quite accidental, was but the more touching on that account. It was short, like all human happiness, and lasted but one day. The account of the proceedings ends with a natural expression of melancholy and musing: "Thus passed away the happiest moment of our lives."

The reason was, they had to work on the morrow and rise early; for it was harvest time. The confederates of Etoile, near Valence, express themselves in words to this effect, after having mentioned their fire-works and farandoles: "We who, on the 29th of November, 1789, gave France the example of the first federation, have been able to devote to this festivity only one day; and we withdrew in the evening to rest ourselves in order to resume our labours on the morrow; for the labours of the field are urgent, and we are sorry for it.". . . Good husband-

447

men! They write all that to the National Assembly, convinced that it is thinking of them, and that, like God, it beholds and performs everything!

These memorials of rural communes are so many wild flowers that seem to have sprung up in the midst of the harvest. In reading them we seem to inhale the strong and vivifying perfume of the country at that glowing season of fecundity. It is like walking among the ripe grain.

And in fact it was in the open country that all this took place. No temple would have sufficed. The whole population went forth, every man, woman, and child; and with them they transported the old in their chairs, and infants in their cradles; whilst villages and whole towns were left in the custody of public faith. A few patrols, who cross through a town, depose that they saw nothing on their way but dogs. Any one who, on the 14th of July, 1790, had passed through those deserted villages, at noon, without seeing the country, would have taken them for Herculaneum and Pompeii.

Nobody was able to absent himself from the festival, for no one was a mere spectator; all were actors, from the centenarian to the new-born infant; and the latter more so than any.

He was carried like a living flower among the flowers of the harvest, offered by his mother, and laid upon the altar. But it was not the passive part of an offering alone that he had to perform; he was active also; he was accounted a person; took his civic oath by the lips of his mother; claimed his dignity as a man and a Frenchman; was put at once in possession of his native land, and received his share of hope.

Yes, the child, the future generation, was the principal actor. At a festival in Dauphiné, the commune itself is crowned, in the person of its principal magistrate, by a young child. Such a hand brings good fortune. These youths, whom I now behold under the anxious eye of their mother, will, in two years' time, at the age of fifteen or sixteen, depart in arms, full of military enthusiasm; the year 1792 will have summoned them, and they will follow their elders to Jemmapes. These again, still younger, whose arms appear so feeble, are the future soldiers

448

of Austerlitz. Their hand has brought good fortune; they have accomplished the good omen, and crowned their native land; and even to-day, though feeble and pale, France still wears that eternal crown, and overawes nations.

How great and happy the generation born amidst such things, and whose first gaze was gladdened by that sublime spectacle! Children brought and blessed at the altar of their native land, devoted by their weeping, but resigned and heroic mothers, and bestowed by them on France. Oh! those who are thus born can never die. You received on that day the cup of immortality. Even those among you whom history has not mentioned, nevertheless fill the world with your nameless living spirit, with that great unanimous idea which, sword in hand, they extended throughout the world.

I do not believe that the heart of man was at any period more teeming with a vast and comprehensive affection, or that the distinctions of classes, fortunes, and parties, were ever so much forgotten. In the villages, especially, there are no longer either rich or poor, nobles or plebeians; there is but one general table, and provisions are in common; social dissensions and quarrels have disappeared; enemies become reconciled; and opposite sects, believers and philosophers, Protestants and Catholics, fraternise together.

At Saint-Jean-du-Gard, near Alais, the Catholic curate and the Protestant minister embraced at the altar. The Catholics led the Protestants to church, and the minister was made to sit in the first place in the choir. Similar honours were done by the Protestants to the curate, who, seated among them in the most honourable place, listened to the minister's sermon. The religions fraternise on their old battle-field, at the entrance to the Cévennes, upon the tombs of their ancestors who killed one another, and on the still warm ashes of the faggots. God, so long accused, was at length justified. All hearts overflowed with love; prose was not sufficient; a burst of poetry could alone express so profound a sentiment. The curate composed and chanted a hymn to liberty; the mayor replied in stanzas, and his wife, a respectable mother of a family, at the moment when she presented her children at the altar, poured forth the feelings of her heart in a few pathetic verses.

The open air, the fields, and the immense valleys, where these festivals were generally held, seemed to contribute to this effusion of the heart. Man had not only reconquered his rights, but he had re-entered upon his possession of nature. Several of these writings testify the emotion which those poor people felt on beholding their country for the first time. Strange to relate! those rivers, mountains, and noble landscapes, where they were constantly passing, were discovered by them on that day: they had never seen them before.

An instinct of nature, the natural inspiration of the genius of the country, often caused them to choose for the scene of these festivals the very places which had been preferred by our ancient Gauls, the Druids. The islands held sacred by the ancestors, became sacred also for their posterity. In the departments of Gard, Charente, and elsewhere, the altar was erected on an island. That of Angoulême received the representatives of sixty thousand men; and there were, perhaps, as many upon the admirable amphitheatre on which this town is situated, above the river. In the evening, there was a banquet in the illuminated island, with a whole people for guests and spectators, from the top to the bottom of that gigantic coliseum.

At Maubec (in the department of Isère), where many rural communes assembled, the altar was erected in the middle of an immense plain, opposite to an ancient monastery, with a magnificent view, an unbounded horizon, and the reminiscence of Rousseau, who had lived there some time! In a speech glowing with enthusiasm, a priest extolled the glorious memory of the philosopher, who, in that very place, had mused and prepared that great day. In conclusion, he pointed to heaven, and called to witness the sun, then bursting from the clouds, as though to enjoy also that sublime and affecting spectacle.

We, worshippers of the future, who put our faith in hope, and look towards the east; we, whom the disfigured and perverted past, daily becoming more impossible, has banished from every temple; we who, by its monopoly, are deprived of temple and altar, and often feel sad in the isolated communion of our thoughts; we had a temple on that day,—such a temple as had never existed before! No artificial church, but the universal church; from the Vosges to the Cévennes, and from the Alps to the Pyrenees.

No conventional symbol! All nature, all mind, all truth!

Man who, in our old churches, never saw his fellows face to face, saw them here,—saw himself for the first time, and from the eyes of a whole people received a spark of God.

He perceived nature, seized it again, and found it still sacred: for in it he perceived his God.

And he called that people and that country by the name he had found,—Fatherland. And however large this *Patrie* may be, he enlarges his heart so as to embrace it all. He beholds it with the eyes of the mind, and clasps it with the longings of desire.

Ye mountains of our native land, which bound our sight, but not our thoughts, be witness that if we do not clasp in one brotherly embrace the great family of France, it is already contained in our hearts.

Ye sacred rivers, ye holy islands, where our altar was erected, may your waters, murmuring beneath the current of the spirit, go and proclaim to every sea and every nation, that, to-day, at the solemn banquet of liberty, we would not have broken bread, without having invited them, and that on this day of happiness, all humanity was present in the soul and wishes of France!

"Thus ended the happiest day of our life." This sentence, which the members of a village federation wrote, at the end of their memorial, on the evening of their festival, I was very near writing myself in concluding this chapter. It is ended, and nothing like it is in store for me. I leave here an irreparable moment of my life, a part of myself, which, I plainly feel, will remain here and accompany me no more: I seem to depart poor and needy. How many things that I wished to add, I have been obliged to sacrifice! I have not indulged in a single note; the least would have caused an interruption, and have been perhaps discordant, at this sacred moment. And yet it would have been necessary to give several; a number of interesting particulars presented themselves, and ought to have been inserted. Several of those memorials deserved to be printed entire (those of Romans, Maubec, Teste-de-Buche, Saint-Jean du Gard, &c.). The speeches are less valuable than the memorials; yet many of these are affecting; the text that recurs the most frequently, is that of the patriarch Simeon: "Now I may die." See among others the *procès-verbal* of Regnianwez (Renwez?) near Rocroi.

Each document taken singly is weak; but the whole possesses an extraordinary charm: *the greatest diversity* (provincial, local, urban, rural, &c.) *in the most perfect unity*. Each country performs this great act of unity with its special originality. The *fédérés* of Quimper crown themselves with the oak-leaves of Brittany; the inhabitants of Romans (in Dauphiné), on the confines of the South, place a palm in the hand of the handsome maiden who leads the procession. A courageous serenity, order, common sense, and a good heart, are very conspicuous in these confederations of Dauphiné.

In those of Brittany, there is a character of strength, of impassioned gravity, a seriousness allied to the tragic; they feel that this is not child's play, and that they are in presence of the enemy. In the mountains of Jura, in the country of the last of the serfs, the character is that of amazement, the delight of deliverance, on beholding themselves exalted from slavery to liberty, "more than free, citizens! Frenchmen! superior to all Europe." They founded an anniversary of the sacred night of the 4th of August.

What is extremely affecting is the prodigious effort of good will made by this people, so little prepared, to express the deep feeling that entirely filled their hearts. The inhabitants of Navarreins, in the Pyrenees, poor people, as they themselves say, lost in their mountains, devoid of every resource, not having even a community of language, lisp the French of the north, and offer to their country their hearts, their very impotency. One of the most clownish memorials (who would believe it?)

452

is that of a commune near Versailles and Saint-Germain. The rough common paper betokens extreme poverty, and the writing an utterly barbarous ignorance: most of these memorialists can make only a cross for their signatures; but yet they all sign one way or other; no one seems willing to be dispensed from signing; after the mother's name, you see the child's, the grand-daughter's, &c.

Their chief study, in general, in which they do not always happily succeed, is to find out visible signs,—symbols,—to express their new faith. At Dôle, the sacred fire, with which the priest was to burn incense on the altar of the country, was, by means of a burning-glass, extracted from the sun by the hand of a young maiden.

At Saint-Pierre (near Crépy), at Mello (Oise), and at Saint Maurice (Charente), they placed the law itself and the decrees of the Assembly upon the altar; at Mello, it was carried thither in an arch of alliance. At Saint Maurice, it was laid upon a map of the world which served to carpet the altar, and placed with the sword, the plough, and the scales, between two cannon-balls of the Bastille.

In other places, a happier inspiration leads them to choose entirely human symbols of union; marriages celebrated at the altar of the country, baptisms, or the adoption of children by communes or clubs. Often also, the women go to perform a funeral service for those who had been killed at the taking of the Bastille. Add to this immense sums given in charity, and distributions of provisions; or, far better than charity, provisions placed in common, and tables laid for everybody. The most touching proof of goodness of heart that I have met with, in a subscription (at Pleyssade, near Bergerac) raised by a few soldiers among themselves, amounting to the enormous sum (relatively to the means of these poor people) of one hundred and twenty francs! for a widow of a man killed at the Bastille! At Saint-Jean-du-Gard, the ceremony ends "with a solemn reconciliation of those who had quarrelled." At Lons-le-Saulnier, they drank to "All men, even our enemies, whom we swear to love and defend!"

XII

The New Religion—General Federation
(July 14, 1790)

THIS faith, this candour, this immense impulse of concord, after a whole century of dispute, was a subject of great astonishment for every nation; it was like a wonderful dream; and they all remained dumb and affected.

Several of our federations had imagined a touching symbol of union, that of celebrating marriages at the altar of the native land. Confederation itself, a union of France with France, seemed a prophetic symbol of the future alliance of nations, of the general marriage of the world.

Another symbol, no less affecting, appeared at these festivals. Occasionally they placed upon the altar a little child whom everybody adopted, and who, endowed with the gifts, the prayers, the tears of the whole assembly, became the relation of everybody.

That child upon the altar is France, with all the world surrounding her. In her, the common child of nations, they all feel themselves united, and all participating heartily in her future destiny, are anxiously praying around her, full of fear and hope. . . . Not one of them beholds her without weeping.

How Italy wept! and Poland! and Ireland! (Ah! sister sufferers, remember that day forever!) . . . Every oppressed nation, unmindful of its slavery at the sight of infant liberty, exclaimed: "In thee I am free!" [39]

In presence of that miracle, Germany remained lost in thought,—in an ecstatic revery. Klopstock was at prayers; and the author of "Faust," unable any longer to maintain the part of sceptical irony, found himself on the point of being converted to faith.

In a remote region of the northern seas, there then existed an extraordinary, powerful creature, a man, or rather a system, a living monument of scholastic science, callous and impenetrable,—a rock formed by adamant in the granite of the Baltic; on which every religion, every system of philosophy had struck and been shipwrecked. He alone remained immutable, and invulnerable to the outward world. His name was Emmanuel Kant; but he called himself Critic. For sixty years, this perfectly abstract being, devoid of all human connection, had gone out at precisely the same hour, and, without speaking to anybody, had taken precisely the same walk for a stated number of minutes; just as we see in the old town-clocks, a man of iron come forth, strike the hour and then withdraw. Wonderful to relate, the inhabitants of Koenigsberg (who considered this as an omen of the most extraordinary events) saw this planet swerve and depart from its long habitual course. . . . They followed him and saw him hastening towards the west, to the road by which they expected the courier from France!

O humanity! . . . To behold Kant moved and anxious, going forth on the road, like a woman, to inquire the news, was not that a surprising and wonderful change? Why, no; no change at all. That expansive intellect was following its course. What he had, till then, in vain sought for in science, *Spiritual Unity,* he now beheld forming itself by the heart and instinct.

Without any other guidance, the world seemed to be drawing towards that unity, its true goal, towards which it is ever

---

[39] These sentiments are to be found in a number of truly pathetic addresses, from men of every nation, especially in the ever-memorable address from the Belfast volunteers.

aspiring. "Ah! if I were *one*," says the world; "if I could at length unite my scattered members, and bring my nations together!" "Ah! If I were *one*," says man; "if I could cease to be the complex man that I am, rally my divided powers, and establish concord within me!" This ever impotent desire both of the world and the human soul, a nation seemed to be realising at that fugitive hour, playing that divine comedy of union and concord which we never behold but in our dreams.

Imagine, therefore, every nation watching attentively, and irresistibly attracted towards France, in heart and soul. And in France, also, behold every road thronged with men, travelling from every corner of the country towards the centre: union is gravitating towards unity.

We have already seen the unions forming, the groups rallying together, and, united, seeking a common centralisation. Each, a little France in itself, has tended towards its own Paris, and sought for it first in its own bosom. A considerable part of France believed, for a moment, it had found it at Lyons (May 30th). There, there was so prodigious a concourse of men, that it required no less than the wide plains of the Rhône to receive them. The whole of the east and the south had sent hither their representatives; the deputies of the national guard alone amounted to fifty thousand men. Some of them had travelled a hundred leagues, others two hundred, in order to be present. Deputies from Sarre-Louis there shook hands with those of Marseilles. Even a deputation from Corsica endeavoured to be present; but, in spite of all their haste, they did not arrive till the morrow.[40]

But it was not Lyons that was able to unite all France: it required Paris.

This fact caused great alarm among politicians on either side. Would it not be risking a fearful riot, pillage, and blood-

---

[40] I have now before me a splendid article, which, to my extreme regret, I am unable to insert, giving an account of this great Federation, and written (purposely for me) by an octogenarian, with the most fervent and affecting enthusiasm.—"Oh, what must the flame have been, since the ashes are so warm!"

shed, to bring those undisciplined crowds to Paris, the very centre of agitation? . . . And what would become of the king? Such was the language of the terrified royalists.

The king, said the Jacobins, the king will assuredly win over all those credulous people coming to us from the provinces. This dangerous union will deaden the public spirit, lull suspicion, and awaken once more their former idolatry: it will *royalize* France.

But neither party was able to prevent it.

The mayor and the commune of Paris, impelled and forced by the example and entreaties of the other towns, were absolutely obliged to go and ask the Assembly for a general confederation; and the Assembly, whether willing or not, was obliged to grant it. Nevertheless, it did all in its power to reduce the number of those who desired to come. The thing was decided very late, so that those who had to travel on foot from the uttermost parts of the kingdom, would be scarcely able to arrive in time: the expense also was to be defrayed by the several localities,—an obstacle likely to prove insurmountable for the poorer districts.

But how was it possible for obstacles to exist in so great a movement? People raised subscriptions as well as they could; and, as far as their means permitted, they equipped those who were to perform the journey: several however came without any uniform. Hospitality was universally and admirably displayed on every road; the people stopped the pilgrims of that great festival, and disputed the favour of entertaining them. They forced them to halt, to lodge, to eat, or at least to drink on their passage. None were considered strangers: all were regarded as relations, and forward they all went, national guards, soldiers, and sailors, marching all together. These bands, as they journeyed through the villages, presented an affecting spectacle. They who were thus invited to Paris were the oldest of the army and navy. Poor soldiers bent double by the Seven Years' War, gray-headed subaltern officers, brave officers of fortune, who had struggled through every hardship, old pilots worn out by tempests,—all these living ruins of the ancient system, had nevertheless determined to come. It was their holiday, their birthday! On the 14th of July, mariners eighty years old were seen marching for twelve hours together; they had recovered their strength, and felt themselves in the hour of death participating in the youthful vigour of France—the eternal spirit of their native land.

And as these bands of patriots tramped through the towns and villages, they chanted with all their might, and with heroic cheerfulness, a song which the inhabitants re-echoed from their thresholds. That song, the most national of all, with its emphatic and powerful rhymes, ever recurring in the self-same tone (like the commandments of God and the church), admirably sustained the weary steps of the traveller by shortening his journey, and the energy of the labourer by showing him the progress of his work. It faithfully kept time with the progress of the Revolution itself, using a more rapid movement when that terrible traveller increased her speed. Abridged, and comprised in a rondo of fury and madness, it became the murderous Ça ira! of 1793. That of 1790 was of a very different character:—

> Le peuple en ce jour sans cesse répète:
>   Ah! ça ira! ça ira! ça ira!
> Suivant les maximes de l'Evangile
>   (Ah! ça ira! ça ira! ça ira!)
> Du législateur tout s'accomplira;
> Celui qui s'élève, on l'abaissera;
> Et qui s'abaisse, on l'élèvera, &c.

For the traveller who was slowly journeying towards Paris, from the Pyrenees or the extremity of Brittany, under the burning sun of July, this song was a viaticum, a support, like the hymns chanted by the pilgrims who, in a revolutionary spirit, built up the cathedrals of Chartres and Strasbourg, in the middle ages. The Parisian sang it in quick time, and with violent energy, in digging up the Field of Mars, to prepare it for the field of the Federation. From being a flat plain, it was to assume the fine majestic form which we now behold. The city of Paris had sent thither a few thousand idle workmen who would have required years to execute so great a task. The people saw through this ill-will, and the whole population set to work. It was an extraordinary spectacle, to behold, both day and night, men of every class, and every age, even children, but all citizens,—soldiers, *abbés,* monks, actors, sisters of charity, noble ladies, market-women, all handling the pickaxe, rolling barrows, or driving carts. Children walked in front, bearing torches; perambulating musicians played to enliven the workmen; and they themselves, whilst levelling the earth, continued still to chant their levelling song: *"Ah ça ira! ça ira! ça ira!* He that exalteth himself shall be abased!"

The song, the work, and the workmen, was one and the same thing,—equality in action: the richest and the poorest were all united in work; but the poor, we must say, contributed the most. After their daily labour, it was a heavy task in July that the water-carrier, the carpenter, or the mason of the Bridge Louis XVI., which was then being constructed, had to perform in digging up the Field of Mars. Although it was harvest-time, the labourers did not excuse themselves from attending; but, though worn out and exhausted, repaired thither for recreation, and worked by torch-light.

This truly immense work, which converted a plain into a valley between two hills, was performed (who would believe it?) within a week!—having been begun precisely on the 7th of July and ended before the 14th.

The thing was executed with a hearty good-will, as though it had been a holy war. The authorities had hoped, by their calculated dilatoriness, to impede and prevent the festival of union; it was indeed becoming impossible. France was determined; and the thing was done.

Those wished-for guests were now arriving and filling every part of Paris. The inn-keepers and masters of furnished hôtels themselves reduced and fixed the moderate price at which they would receive that crowd of strangers. The majority were not allowed to go to the inns. The Parisians, though lodged, as is well known, in very close quarters, gladly put up with every inconvenience, in order to be able to receive the confederates.

When the Bretons, those eldest born of liberty, arrived, the conquerors of the Bastille advanced to meet them as far as Versailles, even to Saint-Cyr; and, after mutual congratulations and embraces, the two bodies united together, and forming but one, marched back to Paris.

Every heart expanded with an unknown sentiment of peace and concord, as we may judge from a fact, in my opinion, the most conclusive of all: the journalists ceased wrangling. Those fierce antagonists, those anxious guardians of liberty, whose habitual strife so embitters the hearts of men, rose superior to their inveterate habit; the emulation of the ancients, devoid of hatred and jealousy, took possession of their hearts, and, for a moment, dislodged the sad spirit of controversy. Loustalot, the honest and indefatigable author of the *Révolutions de Paris*, and the brilliant, fervent, but inconsistent, Camille Desmoulins, both gave utterance, at the same time, to an affecting and generous though impracticable idea,—*a confederative covenant between writers:* no more opposition and jealousy, no emulation but that for the public welfare.

The Assembly itself seemed won over by the universal enthusiasm. During a warm debate one evening in June, it felt once more for a moment its inspiration of 1789, its young excitement of the 4th of August. A deputy from Franche-Comté said that at a time when the confederates were arriving, they ought to be spared the humiliation of beholding provinces in chains at the feet of Louis XIV. on the *Place des Victoires*, and that those statues ought to be removed. A deputy from the South, taking advantage of the generous emotion which this proposal excited in the Assembly, asked for the abolition of all the pompous titles discordant with the idea of equality,— the names of counts, marquises, armorial bearings, and liveries. This motion, supported by Montmorency and Lafayette, was principally opposed by Maury (the son of a shoemaker, as is well known). The Assembly, without adjourning, abolished hereditary nobility (June 19th, 1790). Most of those who voted, regretted it on the morrow. This relinquishing of names of estates, and returning to family names almost forgotten, put everybody out of his element; Lafayette became an insignificant *M. Mottier,* and Mirabeau was enraged at being nothing more than *M. Riquetti.*

This change was not, however, the effect of chance, a mere caprice; but the natural and necessary application of the very principle of the Revolution. This principle is no other than Justice, which wishes that everybody should be answerable for his own works, whether for good or evil. Whatever your ancestors may have done is set down to your ancestors' account, not to yours. You have to act entirely for yourself! In this system, there can be no transmission of anterior merit, no nobility; but, at the same time, no transmission of previous transgressions. As early as the month of February, the barbarity of our laws condemning two youths to the gallows for forgery, the Assembly decided, on this occasion, that the families of culprits should not be at all disgraced by their execution. The public, touched with the youth and misfortune of these young men, comforted their respectable parents with a thousand proofs of sympathy; and several honourable citizens demanded their sisters in marriage.

No more transmission of merit; the abolition of nobility. *No more transmission* of evil; the scaffold no longer degrades the family or the children of the guilty.

The Jewish and Christian principle reposes precisely on the opposite idea, that crime is transmissible, and merit likewise; that of Christ, or that of the Saints, is profitable to the greatest undeservers.

On the day that the Assembly decreed the abolition of nobility, it had received an extraordinary deputation, which styled itself that of the deputies of the human race. A German of the Rhine, Anacharsis Clootz, (a whimsical character, to whom we shall have occasion to revert), presented, at the bar of the Assembly, a score of men from every nation in their national costumes,—Europeans and Asiatics. He demanded, in their name, to be allowed to take a part in the federation of the Field of Mars: "in the name of every people, that is to say, of the legitimate sovereigns, everywhere oppressed by kings."

Some deputies were affected, others laughed. And yet there was something serious in that deputation; it comprised men from Avignon, Liège, Savoy, and Belgium, who really desired at that time to become French; besides refugees from England, Prussia, Holland, and Austria, hostile to their governments, who, at that very moment, were conspiring against France. These refugees seemed a European committee, ready-formed against Europe, the first outline of those foreign legions which Carnot advised at a later period.

In opposition to the confederation of nations was formed one of kings. Indeed, the queen of France had reason to entertain hope, on seeing with what facility her brother Leopold had rallied Europe to Austria. German diplomacy, usually so slow, seemed to have found wings. The reason of this was that diplomatists were entirely left out of the affair, which was arranged personally by the kings themselves, without the knowledge of their ministers and ambassadors. Leopold had applied straight to the king of Prussia, pointed out to him their common danger, and opened a congress, in the very kingdom of Prussia, at Reichembach, in concert with England and Holland.

A dismal prospect for France: backed only by the powerless good-wishes of nations, and presently besieged by the armies and the malevolence of kings!

Neither did France seem safer at home: the Court winning over different members of the Assembly every day, and acting no longer by the right side, but even by the left, by the club of 1789, by Mirabeau and Sieyès, by corruption in different forms, treachery and intimidation. By these means it carried triumphantly a civil list of twenty-five millions, and for the queen a settlement of four. It obtained also coercive measures against the press, and was even so bold as to prosecute parties for the doings of the 5th and 6th of October.

Such was the state of things that the confederates beheld on arriving at Paris. Their idolatrous enthusiasm for the Assembly and the king was put to a very severe trial. Most of them had come inspired with a filial sentiment for their good *citizen king,* uniting in their emotion the past and the future,—royalty and liberty; and several, when admitted to an audience, fell upon their knees, and offered him their swords and their hearts. The king, timid by nature and by his false equivocal position, found little to say in answer to this warm and cordial expression of youthful emotion; and the queen still less. With the exception of *her faithful Lorrains,* the hereditary subjects of her family, she behaved generally very coolly towards the confederates.

At length arrived the great and long-desired day, the 14th of July, for which these good people had undertaken their arduous journey. Everything was in readiness. Even during the night, for fear of missing the festival, many of the people and the National Guard bivouacked in the Field of Mars. Daylight at length appears; but, alas! it rains! And heavy showers, with violent gusts of wind, continued throughout the day. "The weather is aristocratic," said the people, who took their places all the same; and their courageous persevering good humour seemed willing to avert the ill omen by a thousand mad jokes. One hundred and sixty thousand persons were seated upon the hillocks in the Field of Mars, and one hundred and fifty thousand remained standing; whilst, in the field itself about fifty thousand men, of whom fourteen thousand National Guards from the provinces, those of Paris, the deputies from the army, the navy, and others, were to perform maneuvers. The vast eminences of Chaillot and Passy were also crowded with spectators: a magnificent, immense amphitheatre, itself commanded by the more distant circus formed by Montmartre, Saint-Cloud, Meudon, and Sèvres; such a place seemed destined to receive the Estates-General of the world.

But, in spite of all this, it was raining! How slowly the hours seemed to pass in expectation! The confederates and the Parisian National Guards, who had been waiting ever since five in the morning along the boulevards, though drenched with rain, and dying of hunger, were still in good humour. Loaves, hams, and bottles of wine are sent down to them by ropes from the windows of the Rue Saint-Martin and the Rue Saint-Honoré.

They now arrive, crossing the river over a wooden bridge, built in front of Chaillot, and entering by a triumphal arch. In the middle of the Field of Mars arose the altar of the native land; and in front of the Military School the platforms to receive the king and the Assembly.

Again, all this was very tedious and trying to the patience. The first who arrived, to keep up their spirits in spite of the rain and the bad weather, bravely set to dancing. Their joyous farandoles, spreading further and further, in spite of the mud, form at length vast rondos, each of which is a province, a department, or several distinct races of men mingled together: Brittany is seen dancing with Burgundy, and Flanders with the Pyrenees. We beheld those groups commencing their merry rondos in the winter of 1789; and the immense farandole which has gradually formed itself of the whole of France, is now completed and ended at the Field of Mars . . . This is unity!

Farewell to the period of expectation, aspiration, and desire, when everybody dreamed and longed for this day . . . Here it is at last! What do we desire more? Why all this uneasiness? . . . Alas! the experience of the world teaches us this sad fact, so strange to tell, and yet so true, that union too often diminishes in unity. The wish to unite was already the union of hearts, perhaps the very best unity.

But, hush! The king has arrived and is seated; and so is the Assembly, and also the queen in a gallery that commands all the rest. Lafayette and his white horse have now reached the foot of the throne; and the commandant is alighting and receiving the king's orders. Amid two hundred priests, wearing tricoloured sashes, Talleyrand, Bishop of Autun, ascends, with a limping equivocal gait, towards the altar: who but he ought to officiate, when the ceremony is to take an oath?

Twelve hundred musicians were playing, but their music was scarcely heard. A dead silence ensues; but the plain is suddenly shaken by the report of forty pieces of cannon. At that clap of thunder, all arise and stretch forth their hands to heaven . . . O king! O people! pause . . . Heaven is listening, and the sun is bursting expressly through the cloud . . . Pay attention to your oaths!

Oh! how heartily the people swear! How credulous they still are! . . . But why does the king not grant them the happiness of seeing him swear at the altar? Why does he swear under cover, in the shade, and half concealed from the people? . . . For God's sake, sire, raise your hand so that everybody may see it!

And you, madam, do you feel no compassion for this simple, confiding, credulous people, who were dancing just now so cheerfully, between their melancholy past and their formidable future? Wherefore that doubtful expression in your handsome blue eyes? A royalist has noticed it: "Do you see the enchantress?" exclaimed Count de Virieu . . . Can you then, from this spot, behold your envoy who is even now receiving and congratulating, at Nice, the agent of the massacres in the South? Or else, do you imagine you perceive, in these crowds of people, the distant armies of Leopold?

Listen! This is peace; but a peace of an entirely warlike character. The three million armed men who have deputed these, have among them more soldiers than all the kings of Europe. They offer a brotherly peace, but they are nevertheless quite ready for the fight. Even now several departments, Seine, Charente, Gironde, and many others, are willing to give, arm, and equip, each six thousand men to march to the frontier. Presently, the Marseillais will also demand to march; and, renewing the oath of the Phocians, their ancestors, will fling a stone into the sea, and swear that, unless they be conquerors, they will not return till the day when that stone shall float upon the waters!

Index

Michelet's orthography with respect to family names was not always immaculate. In cases where his version differs from the commonly accepted spelling, the index lists the latter, with Michelet's variant in brackets.

[EDITOR'S NOTE]

467

Index

Index